The Greatest-Ever
BANK ROBBERY

from the library
of

The Greatest-Ever

BANK ROBBERY

THE COLLAPSE OF THE
SAVINGS AND LOAN INDUSTRY

Martin Mayer

COLLIER BOOKS
Macmillan Publishing Company
New York

Maxwell Macmillan Canada
Toronto
Maxwell Macmillan International
New York   Oxford   Singapore   Sydney

Collier Books

Macmillan Publishing Company

866 Third Avenue

New York, NY 10022

Maxwell Macmillan Canada, Inc.

1200 Eglinton Avenue East

Suite 200

Don Mills, Ontario M3C 3N1

Macmillan Publishing Company is part of the Maxwell Communication
Group of Companies.

Library of Congress Cataloging-in-Publication Data

Mayer, Martin, 1928–
    The greatest-ever bank robbery:the collapse of the savings and
loan industry/by Martin Mayer.—1st Collier Books ed.
        p.   cm.
    Includes bibliographical references and index.
    ISBN 0-02-012620-4
    1. Savings and loan associations—United States—Management.
    2. Savings and loan associations—United States—Deregulation.
    3. Savings and loan associations—United States—Corrupt practices.
    I. Title.
    HG2151.M39   1992
    332.3′2′0973—dc20   91–24526   CIP

Macmillan books are available at special discounts for bulk
purchases for sales promotions, premiums, fund-raising, or
educational use. For details, contact:

Special Sales Director
Macmillan Publishing Company
866 Third Avenue
New York, NY 10022

First Collier Books Edition 1992

10 9 8 7 6 5 4 3 2 1

Printed in the United States of America

For Louis and Elena

CONTENTS

GUIDE AND GLOSSARY

DEPOSITORIES, all of which may be chartered by either the federal government or a state and all of which make loans, include:

Banks. Get the money they lend in part through providing payments services (checking accounts), in part through "buying" it—paying interest to depositors and other lenders. Deposits are insured by the Federal Deposit Insurance Corporation (FDIC) "Bank Insurance Fund." Traditionally, banks make short-term loans to business, including builders, and invest in short-term government and commercial paper. Today they also make consumer loans and longer-term loans to business, as well as mortgage loans, and buy more varied paper. Larger banks also trade actively in the foreign-exchange and government bond markets.

Savings Banks. Virtually all state-chartered, mostly mortgage lenders, though they can also purchase and trade corporate bonds and in some states stocks and other financial instruments. FDIC insured. Until the 1980s, mostly "mutual" (legally owned by depositors), with self-perpetuating boards of trustees; now owned by stockholders.

Savings and Loan Associations (S&Ls). Also mostly mutual associations (except in California) until the 1980s; now mostly owned by stockholders (or the government). Deposits insured by the Federal Savings and Loan Insurance Corporation (FSLIC) until 1989; now insured by a "Savings Association Insurance Fund" in the FDIC. Essentially mortgage lenders, with power in some states to make "direct investments," do real estate development, and own other businesses. After 1982, federally chartered S&Ls also had wider latitude in investing depositors' money and trading the paper in which they invested.

Credit Unions. The last bastion of mutual ownership. Deposits are also shares, representing ownership interests in the credit union. Depositors must share a "common bond," usually the same employer. The biggest credit unions serve government employees. Deposits are insured by a Credit Union Insurance fund. Lending is usually restricted (by law) to consumer-related loans.

PRODUCTS AND INVESTMENTS

Deposits. All four categories listed above compete for public deposits, offering higher interest rates, free services, weekend banking hours, teller machines, etc. When interest rates were controlled, they offered "free gifts." As noted, deposits in all four are insured by government agencies to a maximum of $100,000 per account.

Investments. All four depositories use some of their depositors' money to make loans, some to buy investment paper. During the 1980s, Wall Street houses issued about $200 billion of "junk bonds" and packaged and repackaged housing-related investment paper (see below) in increasingly speculative ways. Government regulators permitted savings banks and S&Ls (but not commercial banks and credit unions) to buy and trade junk bonds and speculative mortgage paper.

OTHER SOURCES OF FUNDS

Loans. All four depositories can also increase their liabilities by borrowing from each other, from Wall Street, from insurance companies, and from Europe, usually by pledging existing assets as collateral for the loan.

GOVERNMENT AGENCIES

Chartering and Supervising Banks. The Comptroller of the Currency (part of the Treasury Department) for nationally chartered banks. Fifty state banking departments or commissions for state-chartered banks. The Federal Reserve Board for state-chartered banks that have chosen to become "members" of the Fed (nationally chartered banks must be members) and for bank holding companies (corporations that own banks). The FDIC for state-chartered banks that are not members of the Federal Reserve System. Each of these bodies employs its own "bank examiners."

Chartering and Supervising Savings Banks. State banking departments and FDIC. Federal charters are rare.

Chartering and Supervising S&Ls. Fifty state commissions, plus the Office of Thrift Supervision in the Treasury Department. Until 1989, the chartering and supervising agency was the independent three-member Federal Home Loan Bank Board. The Bank Board until 1989 also owned and operated the FSLIC, which examined state-chartered S&Ls.

Chartering and Supervising Credit Unions. Fifty state commissions, plus the National Credit Union administrator, who also operates the insurance fund.

A "temporary" *Resolution Trust Corporation* (RTC) managed by the FDIC under policy guidance from the Treasury Department, disposing of the assets of S&Ls that are insolvent or fail to meet the standards imposed by the Financial Institutions Reform, Recovery and Enforcement Act of 1989. The RTC is funded by the American taxpayer, who must carry the added debt burden of the bonds and bills sold by the Treasury for this agency. By summer 1990, the RTC, one year old, was the largest American financial institution, controlling assets with a face value of more than $200 billion, though their real value was much less. To the extent that the liabilities of the insured S&Ls under RTC direction exceed what the RTC gets for the assets, the taxpayer will be assessed for the losses. The law says that the RTC must close up shop on the last day of 1996.

QUASI-GOVERNMENTAL AGENCIES

The twelve geographically districted *Federal Reserve Banks*, ostensibly owned by the member banks in their district, which own stock in them and elect two-thirds of the directors. The Federal Reserve Banks issue the nation's currency and, through their "discount windows," lend money on short terms to depositories that can back their request for loans with the best collateral. The Federal Reserve Board in Washington appoints the presidents of the Banks and controls the interest rate they can charge at the discount window.

The twelve geographically districted *Federal Home Loan Banks*, owned by savings banks and S&Ls in their districts, which elect their boards of directors. They provide long-term credit to depositories that lend for housing purposes, financing themselves by the sale of bonds to the public. In 1990, more than $140 billion of such bonds was outstanding. Prior to 1989, the presidents of the Federal Home Loan Banks, ostensibly elected by the directors, were both the heads of this lending operation and the "principal supervisory agents" in charge of keeping the local S&Ls solvent and honest. Some control over the activities of an FHL Bank was exercised by the Federal Home Loan Bank Board. After 1989, the Federal Home Loan Banks lost their function as supervisors of S&Ls and became government-sponsored lenders subject to policy guidance by a Federal Housing Finance Board in the Department of Housing and Urban Development.

The *Federal National Mortgage Association* (FNMA, or "Fannie Mae"). Originally a government agency, now a private corporation with a line of credit at the Treasury, governed by a board on which a five-member minority is appointed by the president. Its function is to purchase mortgages, usually but not always insured by other government agencies (the Federal Housing Administration [FHA] and the Veterans Administration [VA]). The money needed to purchase these mortgages is raised by selling bonds to the public. The bonds are then paid off by householders' payments on their mortgages. In recent years, the FNMA has begun to package mortgages into "pass-through" certificates that entitle the holders to the payments made by householders as they are made.

The *Government National Mortgage Association* (GNMA, or "Ginnie Mae"). A government agency that insures and puts its name on privately assembled packages of what are already federally insured mortgages, to be sold to the public as pass-through certificates.

The *Federal Home Loan Mortgage Corporation* (FHMLC, or "Freddie Mac"). Originally a subsidiary of the Federal Home Loan Bank Board, now a private corporation structurally identical to the FNMA. Packages mortgages that typically are *not* government-insured into pass-through certificates. FNMA bonds and all these pass-through certificates, and all the various ways that Wall Street houses repackage this stuff, are legal investments for government-insured depositories, though no government agency significantly regulates the issuance or repackaging of this paper.

It is not surprising, perhaps, that this Rube Goldberg machinery malfunctioned under stress.

The Greatest-Ever

BANK ROBBERY

CHAPTER 1

The Dimensions of the Disaster

THE THEFT from the taxpayer by the community that fattened on the growth of the savings and loan (S&L) industry in the 1980s is the worst public scandal in American history. Teapot Dome in the Harding administration and Credit Mobilier in the times of Ulysses S. Grant have been taken as the ultimate horror stories of capitalist democracy gone to seed. Measuring by money, by the misallocation of national resources, or by the extent of the disgrace to prominent individuals and important professional groups, the S&L outrage makes Teapot Dome and Credit Mobilier seem minor episodes.

Almost from the moment the government admitted that taxpayers would have to pick up this burden, the S&L "bailout" has acquired a quasi-mythical aura. The primitive statement of what had happened became one of those incantations that pop up in American political discourse, like the manned moon expedition: "If we can put a man on the moon, why can't we . . . ?" When President George Bush declared his war on drugs and their dealers, New York governor Mario Cuomo derided the program by comparing the paltry hundreds of millions of dollars it was to cost with the hundreds of billions to be sunk into the S&Ls. When Washington mayor Marion Barry was arrested in a cocaine bust in January 1990, NAACP executive director Benjamin L. Hooks complained that Barry had been victimized. After all, "we haven't found all the people who've stolen all the money from the savings and loan associations and are driving Rolls-Royces and Jaguars."[1]

1

The monetary cost of the "bailout" will probably be more than $140 billion, counting only the government's out-of-pocket expenditures to "resolve" failed thrift institutions funded by government-insured deposits. Raising taxes to pay such a cost is of course politically impossible, so one must count also the interest that will be paid on the government's borrowings. On that basis, the cost by the year 2000 will be at least $300 billion; the cost by 2020, the top of our normal time horizon, will exceed $500 billion.

Trying to bring these numbers down to what ordinary people can comprehend, the press and politicians alike speak of $2,000 for every man, woman, and child—$8,000 for a family of four. And that doesn't count the couple of billion a year ($40 million a week, $8 million a day) the government will pay in additional interest on the rest of our $2 trillion-plus national debt: The more the government borrows, the higher the interest rate it must pay on all its borrowings.

Any occurrence of such dimensions can of course be studied in different perspectives:

Economic historians in the twenty-first century will doubtless concentrate on the irony of an administration that extolled the magic of the market while stimulating and then maintaining truly catastrophic overcapacity in an industry the government completely controlled. Players entered the game through a government charter and continued to play, however severe their losses, in violation of all capitalist principle—courtesy of a government that continued to insure their borrowings. This was not an accident: it was public policy. The splendidly named Competitive Equality Banking Act of 1987, passed by a Democratic Congress and signed by President Ronald Reagan long after everyone who was paying attention knew the dam had broken, specifically mandated "forbearance" for the benefit of insolvent thrift institutions that were losing more money every day.

Political analysts have already seen the S&L crisis as an illustration of the corruption that must ultimately infect any government where the costs of running for office are greater than those that can or will be borne by the relatively small community of the public-spirited. The years 1980–89 witnessed an irrepressibly powerful confluence of the interests of fast-growing S&Ls, Wall Street broker/dealers, gargantuan law firms, and elephantine accounting firms—all pressing to maintain and extend the incentives to waste and fraud implicit in what the government had done. Politics frustrated the cleansing action of the market, and those who profited from the market failure then prevented any change in policy. Aggressive entrepreneurs and cynical professional associations warped reputation in the study of economics, finance, and law by supporting—and supporting lavishly—only those academics who would toe their line. Then they used narrowly focused analyses by these pet academics to soothe the consciences of legislators and regulators who sincerely didn't want to believe they were doing what they did because they were being paid to do it. One notes in passing the triviality of dealing with this moral and intellectual disaster as an episode of "deregulation."

Future sociologists, like today's journalists, will study the irruption of criminality into what had been conservative, even beneficent, organizations. On one level they will tell of Texas cowboys, California sharpies, Beltway whores, and assorted mafiosi. More seriously, they will wonder at the loss of collective responsibility in the great law firms, accounting firms, and investment banks that permitted some of their partners and executives to conspire with criminals and even rewarded them for it, provided the income derived from the conspiracy was sufficiently great. On a more profound level, they will seek to learn why the fiduciary ties that had set the unspoken, self-dignifying rules of a competitive society had been so grievously weakened in the late years of the twentieth century.

Educational historians will look at the failure of our schools to teach citizens, politicians, or businessmen the most fundamental of economic rules—that rewards are necessarily, over time, correlated with risk. Lack of this rudimentary understanding lies behind the unwise legislation and perverse regulation, behind the dishonest accounting practices condoned by that profession, behind the ease, even eagerness, with which politicians, lawyers, and journalists repeatedly accepted each prosperous con man's pretensions to legitimacy.

The detritus of this disaster surrounds us in both tangible and intangible ways. Texas, Arizona, and Connecticut suffer a real estate collapse because lenders in the 1980s financed more building in these states—more shopping centers, office buildings, housing—than they could hope to absorb through the end of the century. (Apologists say the loss of value in real estate created the S&L crisis, but obviously it was the artificial inflation of such values by reckless lenders that produced the real estate collapse.) New York must live with the shrinkage and even collapse of giant investment firms built on the quicksand of excessive profits from exploitative dealings with insured S&Ls. Congressmen and regulators turn away in terror from what were once open and aboveboard relations with lobbyists for legitimate interest groups, driving the business of influencing legislation even deeper into the bowels of law firms that can claim attorney-client privilege. Accountants seek the safe haven of "consultancy," where there are no professional ethics and legal liability for bad work is unknown.

None of this helps much: We are learning the wrong lessons. Finding the right lessons to learn will require both a knowledge of what actually happened—names, dates, and places—and an understanding of how such incredible events and activities could have occurred. Only then can we address the more complicated questions of causation and validation that we must answer before we can truly say, as Treasury Secretary Nicholas Brady said when introducing the Bush administration's inadequate solution, "Never again!"

History repeats, said Karl Marx, discussing the rise of Louis Napoléon; the first time it's tragedy, and the second time it's farce. For all the damage done, this tale had a heavy leavening of farce from the beginning. Repetition—and it could happen—would be tragedy.

[1]

As the desert valley opens wide on the drive from San Bernardino to Palm Springs, the road enters a strange forest of tens of thousands of tapered white concrete poles about forty feet high, each topped with the three narrow steel sails of a modern windmill. Even on a fairly windy day, many of the sails are not turning, and many of those that do move are not being maintained. Nobody owns them—or, rather, they are owned by the unknown American taxpayer, a great, if reluctant, hero, through the agency of the now ghostly Federal Savings & Loan Insurance Corporation (FSLIC). The FSLIC got the wind farms in the liquidation of American Diversified Savings Bank of Lodi, California, which had provided the money to build them and had in fact owned most of them from the beginning. S&Ls can operate and take deposits only with a government charter, but that charter can be issued by either a state or federal government. When the state issued the charter, state law governed which assets an S&L could buy with those deposits, even though the federal government was insuring them. After January 1, 1983, California law allowed an S&L to use federally insured S&L deposits to do just about any damned thing its owners felt like doing.

American Diversified had been owned by Ranbir Sahni, an Air India pilot turned builder and banker (the last unlicensed professions). He acquired the bank in June 1983, when it was named Tokay Savings and Loan Association and reported total assets of $11.7 million. Having purchased it, he increased its apparent capitalization by "donating" some inner-city rehab projects he had built with government assistance; later appraisals would give these properties only a fraction of the value he had claimed. This transaction was approved by Larry Taggart, the stout, self-confident, mustachioed forty-year-old California S&L commissioner, a former branch manager for a San Diego S&L, whose father was the largest single contributor to the political campaign chest of Republican governor George Deukmejian. Regulators have never required owners of S&Ls to put their own capital into an S&L beyond what would be necessary to fund perhaps 6 percent of the institution's assets. (The rest is carried by depositors, who in effect lend their savings to the S&L.) By 1983 that capital requirement had been dropped to only 3 percent. With $3 million in "equity" from the asserted value of his properties, Sahni's S&L

could own $100 million in assets, and he could get the money to buy those assets very easily, simply by promising people that he would pay them more for their deposits than other S&Ls would pay. The depositors ran no risks; the federal government insured both principal and interest on every dollar deposited in American Diversified.

The former airline pilot was now airborne. His S&L did no consumer business and never wrote a home-mortgage loan. There were no teller windows, no street-level bank—just a single "savings office" nine flights up in a building in Irvine, California, that had a branch of another S&L on the ground floor. The money came in through "money brokers," who charged S&Ls a commission for finding them depositors. Some of these money brokers were Wall Street stockbrokers (who liked commissions two to ten times greater than they were paid when they bought stocks for their clients); some were mom-and-pop shops that advertised in newspapers and magazines for people who wanted the highest return they could get for insured deposits. American Diversified paid the highest return in the country. Most such deposits were just under the $100,000 that was the maximum the government insured: When the government finally closed American Diversified in June 1988, the *average* account was $80,807, about ten times the average account in the average S&L. Between June 1983 and December 1985, when Taggart's successor as California S&L commissioner issued a cease-and-desist order prohibiting Sahni from taking any more brokered deposits, American Diversified grew from $11.7 million to $1.1 *billion*. The FSLIC was on the hook for all of it.

With this money, American Diversified dabbled in the markets for financial futures and options and bought some stocks and bonds, but mostly Sahni "invested" in two wholly owned "service corporations," one called American Diversified Capital and the other called American Diversified Investment. These companies in turn organized tax-shelter partnerships, the kind that were very popular among the very rich in the mid-1980s. Among them, the S&L and the "service" subsidiaries had fifteen "development" offices nationwide. The assets they acquired were a remarkable collection. Sahni was big on energy technology. In addition to the windmill farms, he had arrays of solar cells out in sunny fields and a chicken farm planned to make money not through the sale of eggs or drumsticks but through the processing of chicken shit into methane to power a new generation of automobiles. He also used depositors' money to buy a nationwide wireless paging system that could summon people to their patients, clients, or offices. There were shopping centers and condo projects galore. And there was about $300 million face value of junk bonds, most of them from the bottom of the trash can. Not much of this stuff generated earnings to pay interest on the depositors' accounts; so much of the new money raised from the money brokers was used, as in any Ponzi scheme, to pay the interest owed on the last bunch of certificates of deposit.

American Diversified was the nation's fastest-growing S&L, and according to the services that rate such things, either the most profitable or the second most profitable in the country per dollar of assets. Of course—as nobody bothered to tell the press or the regulators (or, apparently, the accountants)—a lending institution that takes big fees for every loan it makes necessarily shows accelerating profits at times of accelerating growth. And in situations where the borrower pays the fees by taking a bigger loan, which means the S&L is paying itself, there aren't any real profits until the borrower begins to pay back what he borrowed, which in these situations never happens. Sahni was to some degree a partner in most of the 145 real estate developments to which American Diversified had lent money.

This is why honest accounting rules firmly distinguish between loans and investments, and permit banks or S&Ls to take profits from loan fees only gradually, over the life of the loan. Unfortunately, S&L accounting practice was far from honest. As long as everybody purported to be living within the very general "Guide" provided for such audits by the American Institute of Certified Public Accountants (AICPA), there was no objection from that source. Quite a lot of false reporting was actually mandated in the Regulatory Accounting Principles adopted by the Federal Home Loan Bank Board. And until the summer of 1989, the Bank Board was the federal government agency that chartered, regulated, and supervised S&Ls. The three members of the Bank Board were also the board of directors of the FSLIC, which insured people's deposits. So, in a sense, the government had only itself to blame when Touche Ross & Company and then Arthur Young & Company (called in as replacements after Touche had choked on some claimed profits) certified preposterous balance sheets for American Diversified.

To stop American Diversified from growing, the FSLIC put the S&L into a conservatorship in 1986, removing Sahni from authority and appointing its own agent as CEO. "What could you get them on?" says Joe Humphrey, chief economist until 1987 at the Federal Home Loan Bank of San Francisco, one of the twelve "district Banks" that were the operating end of the Washington-based Bank Board. "You said, 'You can't make that investment,' and they'd say, 'Hey, the state law says . . .'" The conservator hired Peat Marwick to do an audit as of mid-1986, and that audit showed American Diversified with a "negative net worth" of $417 million. The Bank Board couldn't shut it down because the insurance fund didn't have the money to pay off the depositors, and the losses just got worse and worse. Finally, in 1987, Congress agreed to "recapitalize" the FSLIC, and in 1988 the Bank Board formally declared American Diversified insolvent, paid off the depositors, and took possession of the assets. As far as anyone has been able to figure out, the losses by then totaled $800 million. "I remember we called American Diversified once and wanted a balance sheet figure," Humphrey says. "Sahni didn't know what we were talking about. None of these people was brilliant."

It should be noted that the three-quarters-of-a-billion-dollar loss in American Diversified occurred not in troubled Texas or Arizona but in booming California; also, that the cost to the taxpayer from this one S&L, which nobody ever heard of (its name doesn't appear in any of the first four books on the S&L disaster published in the fall of 1989), was roughly as much as the federal government had at risk in the much-debated bailouts of New York City, Lockheed, and Chrysler *put together*.

Though there are dozens of other similar stories, that of American Diversified remains totally implausible. "A company with $11 million in assets lost $800 million," wrote Jonathan Gray, a bushy-haired bank stock analyst for the investment banking house Sanford Bernstein, in a report to the FDIC. "With perhaps $500,000 in equity, it destroyed $800 million of insured deposits, a kill ratio of 1,600 to 1.... This anecdote is tantamount to a news report that a drunken motorist has wiped out the entire city of Pittsburgh."[2]

American Diversified's leading competitor for the title of most profitable in 1984–85 was Vernon Savings & Loan of Vernon, Texas, a Dallas suburb. Vernon was owned by Don Dixon, another builder, and had been chartered by the state of Texas, which also had permissive rules on what S&Ls could buy with depositors' money. Most of Vernon's asset portfolio was in the form of loans, but some were to Dixon's own Dondi Enterprises. Dixon was a bigger spender than Sahni. In 1983 he and his wife used depositors' money to tour Europe with friends in a rented Rolls-Royce and Learjet, dining every night in a different Michelin three-star restaurant. His S&L hired prostitutes to entertain customers and directors. (Vernon's president pleaded guilty to this one, though his lawyer argued at the sentencing that one of the most important recipients of said gift, a regulator, couldn't get it up, anyway, and therefore wasn't really bribed.) He bought a half-dozen Learjets and the sister ship to Franklin Roosevelt's presidential yacht, *Sequoia*. This he kept at anchor in the Potomac, to be used by congressmen for entertaining friends and raising money. Durward Curlee, a lobbyist for the Texas Savings & Loan League, made the boat his home away from home when he was in Washington, which, according to Dixon, legitimized its use for fund-raising parties for Jim Wright and Tony Coelho. In Texas, at least, a man's home is his castle.

Dixon redecorated a gorgeous house in Del Mar, next to La Jolla in the "big money" suburbs of San Diego, all at the expense of his S&L, because, after all, he entertained borrowers there. Many of his borrowers were his friends. He spent more than $5 million for art to hang in his office and in the house in Del Mar. There was also a ski chalet in Beaver Creek, "because, as you know," William Black, then deputy director of the FSLIC, told a House subcommittee, "the seasons change, and you want to be in appropriate places at different times of the year."[3] Just before things went bad on him, Don Dixon of Dondi Enterprises started building a new $5 million residence in Rancho Santa Fe.

One delicious link between Sahni and Dixon is Larry Taggart, who after departing the commissioner's job in California went to work as a consultant for Texas thrifts, including Vernon, fighting to prevent the Federal Home Loan Bank Board from closing down insolvent S&Ls. Dixon paid Taggart $10,000 a month, plus expenses, and seems also to have arranged a loan to him to acquire an S&L of his own in California.[4] (This plan fell through when the FSLIC refused to give his S&L deposit insurance.) As part of these services, Taggart wrote a letter in 1986 to Don Regan, then Ronald Reagan's chief of staff (whom he apparently didn't know—the letter is addressed to "Dear Honorable Regan"), warning him that "actions being done to the industry by the current chief regulator of the Federal Home Loan Bank Board are likely to have a very adverse impact on the ability of our Party to raise needed campaign funds in the upcoming elections. Many who have been very supportive of the Administration are involved with savings and loan associations which are either being closed by the FHLBB, or threatened with closure."[5]

Taggart also worked closely with the people around House majority leader (soon to be Speaker) Jim Wright to hold down the recapitalization of the FSLIC then pending in Congress. "Those dollars," Taggart later told a House Banking Committee hearing, "were only designated to seize and take over associations." That was certainly true enough: The Texas S&Ls were bleeding money from every orifice, and the taxpayers were one day going to have to transfuse every bit of that blood to pay back the depositors, because these S&Ls were never going to stop bleeding. But the Bank Board couldn't take them over and close them down because the insurance fund was itself insolvent. The obvious purpose of the bill was to give the government money to pay off depositors and stop the losses at the busted S&Ls. Taggart was proud of the efforts he made to keep the government off the

Texans' backs. "There were just too many of us that are true Americans," he told the House Committee, "to put up with that kind of stuff."[6] In April 1990, Vernon's chairman and CEO, Woody Lemons, Taggart's friend, was sentenced to thirty years in prison by a federal judge who described him as "a thief in every sense of the word."[7]

Most of Vernon's growth from $82 million to $1.8 billion was in the form of loans to developers, some of whom had banks of their own that could lend to Dixon to help his construction ventures. Rosemary Stewart, a lean, wiry lady with a fluff of gray-blond hair who has been in charge of enforcement activities at the Federal Home Loan Bank Board throughout the time of troubles (and, to hear her tell it, never made a mistake in all those years), says, "Vernon is the most written-about failure in the industry, but the only thing Vernon demonstrates is the lack of examiners—it seemed in fine shape in 1983, but we didn't have the manpower to get back to it until 1985. We moved on it fast then, but it was too late."

In point of fact, Vernon was deeply troubled in 1983, when a visiting examiner reported "significant regulatory violations, unsafe and unsound practices, lending deficiencies, inadequate books and records, and control problems."[8] It was not until midsummer of 1985 that the first "cease-and-desist order" against dishonest practice was given to Vernon by the Bank Board and not until November 1987 (after House Speaker Jim Wright had delayed the action by intimidating regulators for a full year) that Vernon was actually closed down, with a loss of $1.3 billion that had to be picked up by American taxpayers.

When the state of Texas seized Vernon, 96 percent of its loans—a *Guinness Book of World Records* number—were delinquent. Linton Bowman, a large and easygoing Texan in his sixties who had worked most of his life in Texas S&Ls, was then the Texas S&L commissioner. He notes that his office has been criticized for not moving sooner against Dixon but argues amiably that it was hard to close down an institution that the national rating services were calling one of the two most profitable in the country. It was especially difficult when Arthur Young, a Big Eight accounting firm, kept giving the place clean statements, the last of which was dated only five days before Vernon was seized.

Much of the alleged profitability of both American Diversified and Vernon arose from fictitious "sales" of property, often property they owned themselves from the foreclosure of previous loans. The sales, at grossly inflated prices, were financed by the S&Ls themselves with loans to the buyers, who were usually friends and relatives of the management. There was no risk to these friends and relatives, because the loan was "nonrecourse" to the borrower, who could always satisfy his liability merely by returning the property. And there was always something in the deal for them, because the loan would end up being larger than what the S&L charged them for the property. (These were called "drag" loans, because the borrowers dragged away some money for themselves.) The interest to be paid in the first year was part of the loan, and after that first year the "purchasers" could walk away. The S&Ls would foreclose and become the owners of this property, which they then would carry on their books for the amount of the loan that had been canceled by the foreclosure. The profit from the fake "sale" of the year before was never canceled and remained on the books of the S&L or in the pockets of its owners. There were no cash worries, of course; cash came from insured deposits. Big Eight accounting firms audited these transactions and gave them a seal of approval.

Here as elsewhere in the S&L industry, the instrument of choice was the ADC loan. The initials stood for acquisition, development, and construction of a building project, perhaps a residential subdivision, an office building, or a shopping center. Such loans carried extraordinarily heavy up-front fees that the rules of the Federal Home Loan Bank Board permitted S&Ls to take right down to the bottom line on the day they were booked. And because a developer was not likely to see any returns on his investment for several years, ADC loans frequently were "grossed up" to include the interest payments that would have to be paid during the first two to five *years*. The borrower never saw this money: The bank simply took down some of the "interest reserve" every month for twenty-four, forty-eight, or sixty months and credited itself with earnings.

With both the up-front fee and two or three years' worth of interest in the totals, an ADC loan could be written for a sum of money greater than the appraised value of the property. And that appraisal was already an inflated number. Vernon—it was standard Texas procedure—would ask the appraiser for an oral estimate. If the number was high enough, it would be put in writing; if it wasn't high enough, the appraiser was thanked for his time and trouble and paid in cash to leave no record. A new appraiser was then hired. "Everybody knew that if you couldn't get the loan from anybody else, you could get it from Dixon," says a Dallas builder who doesn't want to be identified because of a pending lawsuit with the FSLIC about a loan from Vernon on which he defaulted. A few accountants—first Price Waterhouse and Kenneth Leventhal, then Peat Marwick, and eventually a dribble of others—insisted that these were not really "loans" but equity investments and that the fees were therefore not income at all. This cost these firms a lot of business. The CPAs who took the big fees to certify the books for these S&Ls were really co-conspirators.

Another property owned by taxpayers at this writing is a 6,230-acre parcel forty miles north of Dallas, formerly the Flying M Ranch, now called Stonebridge. First Gibraltar Savings of Texas converted this property into a pair of golf courses surrounded by roads and subdivisions on which nobody has built. This was a venture put together, like the thrift itself, by J. Livingston Kosberg, a banker who had been a nursing-home operator. He was close to Robert Strauss, a small, smart, jovial (until crossed, when his eyes narrowed menacingly) older man with a manicured fringe of white hair. Strauss was a Washington-based Texas lawyer who was chairman of the Democratic party nationally when Richard Nixon was president and later ran Jimmy Carter's campaign against Ronald Reagan.

The formation of First Gibraltar in 1984 is worth a digression. I happened to be in Strauss's Washington office, questioning him about his expectations for the television coverage of the upcoming election, on the day the Federal Home Loan Bank Board permitted Kosberg's First Texas (a $2.8-billion S&L and the fourth largest in the state) to acquire First Gibraltar Savings (at $4 billion the state's biggest S&L). The deal had been pending for a year and should never have been approved at all. First Texas was a sinking ship, losing money on its lending operations. Even in 1984, when interest rates were well down from what they had been, First Texas was earning less on its loans than the interest it was paying its depositors. And First Gibraltar Savings was already undercapitalized. Nevertheless, the Bank Board at Strauss's urging permitted Gibraltar's owners to take out $268 million in cash. The largest single owner of Gibraltar at that time, incidentally, was New Yorker Saul Steinberg, a pioneer of the 1980s school of the-hand-is-quicker-than-the-eye finance and a beneficiary of the money-raising mastery of Mike Milken of Drexel Burnham. What with Strauss on one side of the deal and Milken on the other, the Bank Board was completely surrounded by political influence.

A reporter named Charlie McCoy, then twenty-three years old, was writing the story of this transaction for the *Wall Street Journal* and planned to include some information Strauss saw no reason for the public to learn. In my presence, he chewed McCoy out on the telephone for a quarter of an hour, informing him that he (Strauss) was close to Warren Phillips, CEO of Dow Jones, and thus McCoy's employer, and Strauss would have his ass if there was stuff in the story of which Strauss disapproved. In fact, the material Strauss wanted to hide did appear in the paper the next day. McCoy, a Texan who had been brought up to admire Strauss, "was shocked," he said the other day, "that the man would be so unprofessional in trying to get a story changed." But he wrote carefully, and you had to know what the numbers implied to know what the story said.[9] One notes as in a dream that this thrift and Vernon and a few others—all insolvent—were stitched into one $12 billion S&L by the FSLIC in late 1988 and sold to Milken's friend Ron Perelman of Revlon. To make the deal satisfactory to Perelman, the FSLIC had to provide a subsidy that has been estimated as high as $5 billion, some of it in the form of notes guaranteeing as much as ten years of high return on loans that were actually in default, some of it in the form of tax credits.

The Stonebridge property was not part of what the FSLIC turned over to Perelman, probably because of its close connection to First Gibraltar's star board member, Strauss's son Richard (who was further blessed in Dallas by his aunt, the mayor). It had been at young Strauss's behest that First Gibraltar had bought this land with $135 million from its hoard of federally insured deposits. Another $8 million went to Ross Perot, who thought *he* had bought Flying M. And maybe $150 million was spent to improve the property. Richard got a management contract worth $2.9 million a year; Robert's firm foreclosed First Gibraltar's mortgages. The FSLIC, of course, retained young Strauss as manager of Stonebridge—until March 1990, after House Banking Committee chairman Henry Gonzalez had denounced the "sweetheart deal." In June, FSLIC finally found a purchaser, a Japanese who paid $61 million.

We move north and find the roads out of Denver littered with unoccupied office buildings owned by Silverado Savings & Loan. This S&L was owned and operated by a very smooth, beautifully dressed, and thoroughly convincing young man named Michael R. Wise, still in his thirties when he took control in the early 1980s. He mouthed the shibboleths of banking being an information business rather than a lending business and became a factor in the leadership of the Federal Home Loan Bank of Topeka and even the Financial Accounting Standards Board.

Wise's game was to buy back from his friends the office buildings they had built with loans he made them, giving them a profit on the transaction. This profit they would then invest in Silverado stock, permitting Silverado to show an increase in "equity," which in turn permitted the S&L to increase its insured deposits and the volume of its ADC loans. Regardless of whether anyone ever rented the offices, accountants would permit the property Silverado acquired in these transactions to be carried on the S&L's books at the price Wise had paid for the building—*plus* something extra every year to cover the costs Silverado incurred by holding it. Thus, interest on the cost of the building, taxes, the maintenance expenses, and the costs of trying to rent it—all could be added to the "value" of the property for accounting purposes.

"They were just trading paper for paper," Nicholas Scheidt of Apex Realty Investments told *Business Week* after Silverado was first put into a conservatorship by the Bank Board. "They created equity on the balance sheet but no real value."[10] When the Bank Board accepted subordinated debt as part of the capital that could be leveraged thirty-three to one, Silverado created debt, too. Some $4.5 million of debt was issued to four senior officers, and booked as capital in a way that indicated that cash had been paid for the paper. But in fact nobody had put new money into the institution: "The debt had been issued in lieu of additional salary," President Kermit Mowbray of the Federal Home Loan Bank of Topeka wrote in his explanation of why Silverado had been seized, "and accounted for as prepaid compensation expense."[11] Another Silverado story surfaced in summer 1990, when the FDIC sold 141 fancy New York City co-op apartments. Silverado owned them because their previous owner had sued to rescind a deal in which the S&L lent him $22 million, of which $10 million was for the apartments—and another $12 million was to take Silverado out of a bum mortgage on wildly overpriced land in Denver. Fearful of publicity, the S&L canceled the debt and took the unsold apartments. Silverado grew from $250 million in 1982 to $2.7 billion in 1988; its collapse cost the taxpayers a billion dollars.

Wise was a prominent Republican; so was his stockholder Larry Mizel, CEO of M.D.C. Holdings, for which Milken raised $500 million in a junk bond offering. (A lunch for Ronald Reagan that Mizel chaired in Denver in 1984 raised more money for that campaign than any other single function.) M.D.C. did real estate transactions with Silverado; it also at one point controlled Imperial Savings of San Diego, another Milken customer. It had close relations with other questionable Milken followers, like San Jacinto of Texas, part of the now bankrupt Southmark Corporation, and Charles Keating's Lincoln Savings, which we shall encounter later. Among the services all these operations provided for Milken was the purchase of junk bonds he was finding it hard to sell elsewhere. When (as time went on, *if*) he found another purchaser, he would give them a tip. One reason for the collapse of the junk bond market and of Drexel Burnham itself, in February 1990, was the 1989 law that forbade S&Ls to purchase any more of this stuff.

The largest beneficiary of Wise's largesse was a builder named Bill Walters, whose office buildings were purchased for several times their economic worth, with Walters pumping back about a third of the proceeds in stock purchases. Among Wise's board members at Silverado was Neil Bush (son of then Vice-President George Bush), who came aboard in 1985, just as things were heating up, and resigned in the summer of 1988, just as they were heating up in a different way. Young Bush voted to approve the purchases from Walters even though Walters was an investor in his JNB Exploration Company—and there was a million-dollar loan to that venture from a little bank Walters himself owned elsewhere in Colorado.

In the fall of 1989 the Securities and Exchange Commission (SEC) settled a complaint against M.D.C. with a "consent decree" in which M.D.C. formally admitted nothing but agreed to reverse certain profits it had claimed from fake land sales and promised never to play such games again. In early 1990, Wise, Mizel, Walters, and others associated with Silverado agreed to orders by the FDIC and the agency that succeeded the Bank Board in the Bush S&L bailout program, prohibiting them from ever holding any position as officer or director of an insured bank or S&L. The month before, President Bush had attended a fund-raising lunch in Colorado co-chaired by Mizel and Walters; his son Neil sat on the dais. Neil has refused to accept even the mildest rebuke from the S&L regulators on the grounds that he doesn't think he did anything wrong, and at this writing, proceedings against him are pending.

California, Texas, and Colorado are by no means alone in the damage they suffered from reckless S&L lending. There are empty shopping centers in Hillsborough County, too far from Tampa consumers, empty office parks in Austin, busted hotels in Shreveport and Phoenix, unsold condos in New England, and grimly unfinished resorts in Oklahoma and Arkansas that represent the debris from the explosion of government-guaranteed thrift institutions in the first half of the 1980s. Much of this money was supplied from far away by institutions that had been conservative pillars of their communities before the U.S. government insanely invited them to take a flier. Broadview Savings in Cleveland had been run by one family for forty-two years, and before a family feud invited some gamblers into management was probably the most respected institution of its kind in Ohio. Its last annual report just before the government put it into receivership—and after new management had spent three years unloading junk and shrinking the establishment from $2.1 billion to $1.4 billion—showed properties financed by the association in New York (two high-rise condos); Lake Tahoe (a time-sharing resort); Boca Raton (a country club); Albert Lee, Minnesota (a shopping mall); Austin, Texas (469 acres of undeveloped land); Mesquite, Texas (a vacant medical office building); Tulsa (two office buildings); and Telluride, Colorado (a resort hotel).

But the worst damage lies hidden, in the torn moral fiber of American finance, law, accounting, and politics.

[2]

The S&L crisis became a scandal of these dimensions mostly because nobody wanted to hear about it—not regulators, academics, congressmen, or the White House, not accountants, lawyers, newspaper and magazine editors, or TV producers . . . and not the American public. Distinguished reportorial work in the *Dallas Morning News* as early as 1983 and in the *Orange County Register* in 1985 drew virtually no attention. I myself had a piece on the Op-Ed page of the *New York Times* in December 1982, six weeks after the passage of the Garn-St Germain bill that took all restrictions off the interest rates S&Ls could offer for insured deposits and most restrictions off what they could do with the money. The piece explained more or less soberly why the former Prudential National Bank had changed its name to Crazy Louie's, NA ("Our interest rates are insane"; see appendix B). This easygoing *reductio ad absurdum* was picked up by a few people, most notably Professor Edward J. Kane of Ohio State, whose book *The Gathering Crisis in Federal Deposit Insurance*,[12] published in 1985, was the most accurate prediction of the course of the hurricane.

But the swindles, like the industry itself, were a backwater, and, worse, the subject was inherently technical. As the Bush bailout bill moved through Congress in the summer of 1989, P. J.

O'Rourke wrote an article for *Rolling Stone* in which he argued that the story was "an awful example of what's replaced democracy in modern America—dictatorship by tedium. . . . This allows the boring government officials to do anything they want, because any time regular people try to figure out what gives, the regular people get hopelessly bored and confused, as though they'd fallen a month behind in their high-school algebra class."[13]

The books written on this subject to date have been rather like the famous story of the Indian blind man describing the elephant. One sees the Mafia; one sees Texas cowboys infecting the whole country with financial AIDS; one sees the regulators goofing off; one sees a malfunction from the continuation of inadequate laws into an era when they became destructive. All of this is true up to a point, and of course there is nothing wrong with telling the stories, which are great fun in themselves. Indeed, I have been doing nothing but that in this chapter. But the stories do not explain what happened. Moreover, the search for a community of villains leads away from the true enormity of this event.

Who got the money? The Wall Street investment houses got more than any other group, much more than the Mafia types or the Texas real estate developers. And depositors themselves, of course, got some of it, for they were paid higher interest rates than their money would otherwise have earned. Who could have stopped this atrocious theft from the government insurance funds and didn't? The accounting profession, which acquiesced in the most outrageous and dishonest "practice" that misstated both the balance sheets and the profit-and-loss accounts, year after year. Who protected the thieves? The nation's great law firms, dozens of them, in New York and Chicago as well as in Washington, Texas, and Los Angeles, which bullied regulators, threatened suit against them personally as well as against their agencies, created mazes the regulators would have to wander through before they could stop the looting by clients of these firms who could pay anybody's fees because deposit insurance gave them the key to the U.S. Treasury.

Emory Buckner, the great trial lawyer of the 1920s who founded one of the giant Wall Street law firms (now called Dewey,

Ballantine, Bushby, Palmer & Wood), would never enter an affirmative defense for anyone he believed to be guilty. "Clients," he told a meeting of the Association of the Bar of the City of New York in 1929, "are not entitled to have lawyers who disbelieve their stories."[14] By the 1980s, to quote the comment of a banker friend who used to be a lawyer, "for half a million dollars you could buy any legal opinion you wanted from any law firm in New York." And in the case of an S&L fighting off a regulator, you could buy that opinion, without spending a penny of your own money, just by promising higher interest rates on government-guaranteed deposits.

Deposit insurance has proved to be the crack cocaine of American finance. Its presence draws remarkably unattractive characters to the operation of banks and thrifts. Their activities, which have indeed included murder, stretch the justice system entirely out of shape. Deposit insurance generates endless money to bribe politicians, accountants, and lawyers and to feed the great maw of the Wall Street machinery. It enables the regulators to validate what Hyman Minsky of the University of Washington in St. Louis has long called "Ponzi finance," the taking on of a new set of liabilities to pay out the interest coming due on an old set. We shall see in chapter 11 the contributions technology and market forces can make to reducing the abuse of this abominable "drug" in the next half-dozen years. But for the time being we will have to live with this dangerous substance all about us, and cultivate our suspicions.

[3]

My personal involvement with these matters probably started with my book *The Bankers*, published in 1975, and was heightened in the financing chapters of *The Builders*, a book about housing published in 1978. Among those who read these books was a young congressional staffer and, later, congressman named David Stockman, who became Ronald Reagan's director of the Office of Management and Budget (OMB). I met Stockman one evening, when he was quite new in that job, at the home of a friend. We sat talking until after two in the morning about what the application of the new administration's philosophy would mean in cold cash. Despite what has been said in recent years by Sen. Daniel P. Moynihan, Stockman did believe in those early days that tax reductions and deregulation would, in fact, stimulate such growth that the lower tax rates would pay for the continuing expansion of government programs that ought to expand. I didn't believe this, but I agreed that the federal housing programs the administration had inherited were a disaster, spending too much government money for too little housing for the poor. A few weeks later, in early April, I got a call from a man named Edwin J. Gray, who identified himself as director of the Domestic Policy Staff at the White House. He asked me to be a commissioner on the new President's Commission on Housing.

When the commission was organized in Washington in July 1981, I was assigned to a finance committee chaired by Maurice Mann, a fifty-two-year-old Boston economist of vast capacity and humor who served in Nixon's OMB, worked for the Federal Reserve Bank of Cleveland, became president of the Federal Home Loan Bank of San Francisco (where he approved the nation's first legal adjustable rate mortgages [ARMs]), and then went to investment banking. In 1981 he was in San Francisco packaging mortgage-backed securities and brokering thrifts for A. G. Becker-Paribas, something he would later do for Merrill Lynch. Some years thereafter, he would become chairman of the Pacific Stock Exchange. Also on the committee were Ken Thygerson, a curly-haired blond academic turned thrift executive who would later build the Federal Home Loan Mortgage Corporation to its present eminence and then undertake (and fail at) the resurrection of San Diego's crippled Imperial S&L; Preston Martin, former chairman of the Bank Board and soon-to-be vice-chairman of Paul Volcker's Federal Reserve Board, then in the process of winding down the mortgage-packaging business he had started and sold to Sears Roebuck; and Pete Herder, a Tucson builder who became president of the National Association of Home Builders. Later in the twelve-month life of the commission, we would be joined by Sherman Lewis, vice-chairman of Shearson Lehman.

These were, in various ways, interesting meetings. Three times in the previous twelve years—in 1969–70, 1973–75, and 1979–81—the average interest rate depositors earned at savings institutions had fallen below the nation's inflation rate on its most stingy measurement. (The stingy measurement is the GNP implicit price deflator; the Consumer Price Index would have shown an even worse result.)[15] This was the government's fault. From 1966 to 1980, the government had controlled the interest rates S&Ls could pay, setting them to yield (most of the time) a little more than the rates the equally controlled commercial banks could pay. But when rates on the government's own Treasury bills rose above the government's maximum on insured deposits, marketing ingenuity in the mutual fund business devised an instrument that yielded depositors more than either banks or S&Ls could pay but still provided a safe return on their money. This was the "money market fund," supervised by the SEC rather than by the banking regulators. Such funds could own only paper that matured in less than nine months (at the beginning, most of them held only three- and six-month Treasury bills), and they were compelled to publish their portfolios so that investors and their advisers could make their own assessments about the safety of these investments. Such funds employed armies of telephone solicitors who sucked money out of the banks and thrifts, "disintermediating" institutions whose function was to take money from savers who wanted to earn interest and lend it out to the consumers of credit who were willing to pay interest.

In the 1970s, to keep their wards in business against such nonbank competition, the banking regulators kept raising the rates they allowed banks and thrifts to pay for new money. The system was jiggered to cheat the older generation that continued to keep money in the lowest-rate passbook accounts. And in 1980, in the Depository Institutions Deregulation and Monetary Control Act, Congress took the first steps toward eliminating interest-rate controls entirely. Among the early results of this action was a spanking increase in S&L costs, as the S&Ls had to pay depositors more for their money. In the first half of 1981, for the first time in history, the thrift industry as a whole lost money. S&Ls

were still the largest single source of funds for homebuilders and homebuyers. Housing construction fell to the lowest levels since World War II. No subject was more important to a Commission on Housing.

To our first meetings came Richard Pratt, the Reagan administration's new chairman of the Federal Home Loan Bank Board. A professor at the University of Utah, Pratt was young, black-haired and bull-shouldered, intensely aggressive, a motorcycle aficionado, a doctrinaire free-marketer, withal a nice fellow and (unfortunately) by far the most intelligent man ever to hold that job. The combination would make him, as we shall see in chapter 3, the angel of death for the thrift industry.

We heard from Treasury secretary Donald Regan, architect of the Merrill Lynch colossus. He was very funny about the industry's favorite cure for what ailed it—the idiotic All-Savers Certificate that had been proposed in Congress as part of the new tax code. This very special provision would create a very special certificate of deposit (CD) that would exempt $2,000 of interest payments from all federal taxation for each household. Two weeks later, Regan endorsed what he had ridiculed to us, as part of the bidding war in Congress that turned the defensible tax proposals of the new Regan administration (you might like them, you might not, but they were defensible) into the theft from the public purse that was the 1981 tax bill.

Though the All-Savers folly was expunged from the tax code a year later, it cast a long shadow forward. A provision in the bill that permitted thrifts to pay as much as 2 percent commission to brokers for arranging the purchase of the certificates brought Wall Street into the money-brokerage business. Sherman Lewis said that in the process of brokering such deposits into the Boston Company, a trust company Shearson had just bought as a subsidiary, the brokerage house pocketed in two months commissions that exceeded the entire cost of the acquisition. Merrill Lynch made a public agreement with California Federal Savings & Loan to put a billion dollars of its customers' accounts into tax-exempt All-Savers Certificates at Cal Fed at a 1 percent commission, which meant $10 million of found money for the brokerage house.

We heard from Roy Green, a compact, earnest man who was president of what was then called the U.S. League of Savings and Loan Associations, whom I had met not long before as CEO of a Jacksonville thrift called Fidelity Federal Savings. As I write, I have before me his "Statement of Condition" as of June 30, 1979, which popped out of an old file. It shows $224 million in total assets, with $216 million of it (96 percent) in safe stuff—first mortgages, loans against passbooks, cash and U.S. government paper, and Home Loan Bank stock. Green was not a swinger. Three years later, the Bank Board would appoint him president of the Federal Home Loan Bank of Dallas, not to be (as everyone now says) a "tough regulator" but to be a sympathetic, able, honest, experienced S&L man who could persuade the honest and able men in Texas to put up with the tough regulators he would hire. Alas, it wasn't the honest and able who controlled the Texas Savings & Loan League and had the ear of the state's congressmen. One of the few who supported Green was Rep. Henry Gonzalez of San Antonio, who took no money from political action committees and had a skeptical view of the cowboys who had taken over the S&L industry in his state.

What Green wanted from the Housing Commission that day in 1981 was an expansion of the limit on insured deposits from the $100,000 set in 1980 to $250,000, to make it easier to raise big chunks of money. I remember the scene vividly: the dark walls and dusty bookcases and antique lamps of the librarylike conference room at the Executive Office Building, Green boldly leading his delegation of hangdog S&L executives like Don Carlo bringing the Protestants of Flanders before Phillip II in Verdi's opera. I told him it was the name my father gave me that I would be signing to the commission report and that I couldn't do that to my father.

My longest and most obstructive argument at any of the meetings was with Preston Martin—former chairman of the Bank Board and later vice-chairman of the Federal Reserve—in one of the early sessions of the finance committee. The staff of the Housing Commission had recommended a statement approving direct investment in real estate by insured S&Ls. (Yes, we had a staff;

its offices were in one of those reconditioned federal houses on Lafayette Square opposite the White House, and perhaps as a symbol of what was wrong with the execution of federal housing policy, the building *after reconditioning* had no bathroom!) I thought permission for direct investment was not only an invitation to trouble but also a violation of the spirit of capitalist enterprise. A real estate developer who has to borrow money in the open market and pay market rates should not be subjected to competition from a rival who can raise his funds more cheaply through gathering federally insured deposits. Martin, cautiously supported by Thygerson, insisted that S&Ls could not survive unless they could capture at least some of the increases in the market value of real estate that were an inevitable result of inflation.

In the end I yielded, on the grounds that Martin knew more about the subject than I did, though I felt it was always bad public policy to reduce mankind's fear of inflation by protecting people against it. They did throw me a sop in the final text of the recommendation, which read: "Thrift institutions should be permitted to invest in real estate of various types (including joint ventures with developers) only through service corporations or holding companies. The separation of real estate activities from the deposit-taking entity is necessary for the protection of insured deposits in these institutions."[16] These wholly owned "service corporations," however, would never be allowed to go broke so long as the parent S&L could raise deposits and keep funding them, and holding companies, as we shall see in the tale of Charles Keating and Lincoln Savings, will always exploit rather than support the S&Ls they own. When California, Texas, and Florida permitted their state-chartered S&Ls to put much (and in California all) of their investment portfolio in the service corporations that did real estate development—and the federal government in the Garn-St Germain Act of 1982 greatly increased the asset powers of federally chartered associations—there was no protection at all for the insured deposits.

Because of where we sat and to some extent who we were, the members of the Housing Commission were kept informed about the new "regulatory accounting" rules Pratt and the Bank Board designed in 1981 and 1982 to conceal what had become the insolvency of the thrift industry. And in effect we all signed on to approve the new rules. But most of us were queasy about what Pratt was doing. In December 1981, I was in print in a magazine called *Financier* describing the regulators' various fiddles with accounting practice and commenting that "the vice with all these ideas is that they are ways to lie with numbers."[17] The piece still holds up pretty well, as you can judge for yourself in appendix A.

What I missed, because it was unimaginable, was the chance that the White House and Congress and their foolhardy academic advisers would rewrite the law less than a year later to permit insured banks and S&Ls to offer any interest rate they wished on short-term money market accounts. This provision of the Garn-St Germain Act of 1982 destroyed the immune system that had protected the insurance funds. Prior to 1983, when the act took effect, a bank or S&L that was in trouble would shrink, as depositors who had money there beyond the insured maximum withdrew their funds and even some insured depositors shunned contact with a failing institution. There would be no way for such a bank or S&L to lure new money, because the government put a ceiling on interest rates. Once that ceiling was gone, a failing institution, desperate for funds and willing to take any gamble that promised a hope of recovery, would simply offer more interest than could be paid by any bank or S&L that had to earn what it paid its depositors by making normal loans and investments. The new accounts authorized by Garn-St Germain would inevitably kill the insurance funds. This is not hindsight; it was obvious from the first day. Appendix B offers my *New York Times* Op-Ed piece from December 1982, which lays out the scenario. What I couldn't imagine in 1982, and still find it hard to imagine today, was that the U.S. government, having eaten the insane root, would remain forever a prisoner of its own lunacy.

I reprint what I wrote at the time not to brag but to refute the common defense by former Bank Board members like Donald Hovde, by academics like Emory's George Benston, and by thrift executives like Thomas Wageman of Sunbelt Savings that the S&L

disaster occurred because energy prices collapsed and took with them the value of real estate in the southwestern section of the United States. "Nobody could have foreseen." The fact is that anybody could have foreseen: The government was asking to be robbed, and it was robbed—all over the country. No doubt, the states that drew much of their income from energy produced much of the disaster, but some of the worst losses were in Arizona, California, and Illinois; in New England, where the real estate climate turned just awful; and in Florida, where that beast rising from the swamp was no ordinary alligator.

What makes this story so appalling and important, however, is not that bankers, politicians, officials, academics, and journalists were slow to realize what they had done. People make mistakes, and correct them only reluctantly, after the consequences become obvious. Market economies perform better than command economies because those who make mistakes lose their money and failure stops them from frittering away a nation's resources. If the state takes away the market discipline that compels the recognition of mistakes—which is what deposit insurance can do, especially if it is taken as insurance for the bank or S&L itself rather than for the depositors—capitalism can generate losses and misallocation of resources even faster than socialism.

What happened to create the disgusting and expensive spectacle of a diseased industry was that the government, confronted with a difficult problem, found a false solution that made the problem worse. This false solution then acquired a supportive constituency that remained vigorous and effective for almost five years after everybody with the slightest expertise in the subject knew that terrible things were happening *everywhere*. Some of the supporters were true believers, some were simply lazy, and most were making money—*lots* of money—from the government's mistake. The stain of dishonest argumentation paid for by crooks spread over appraisal and accounting, over investment banking, and over law, scholarship, and politics. (Journalism suffered, too, though this was a classic case of Clough's encomium from across the waters: "You know you cannot bribe or twist, / Thank God, the British journalist. / But seeing what the man will do / Unbribed, there's no occasion to.") The stain spread much wider than anyone has wished to admit, and the rot reached much deeper.

The S&L story is desperately important not for the reasons usually given but because its development, maturity, and crisis raise profound questions about American society. In the light of this bonfire, we must ask whether our great professions are still capable of self-regulation, of giving honest service, and of accepting fiduciary duties in an age when all costs and benefits are reduced to monetary measurements and all conduct that is not specifically prohibited has become permissible. Watching the obedient dance of our officials and politicians when their patrons pipe a tune, unrebuked by a public that attends this show as it might any other, we must ask whether this generation of Americans remains capable of self-government.

Here is how it happened, what's likely to happen next, and what has to be done about it.

CHAPTER 2

An Accident Waiting to Happen

T HE THRIFT INDUSTRY was a predictable point of entry for major corruption in American finance. Despite its lovely reputation—Jimmy Stewart convincing the townsfolk in the 1946 film *It's a Wonderful Life* that this is our bank and we must all cherish it—the old-fashioned S&L was a nest of conflicting interests that squawked for sustenance from the customers' deals. On its board were the builder, the appraiser, the real estate broker, the lawyer, the title insurance company, and the casualty insurance company. (Also the accountant: One mutual S&L in Ohio that lost virtually all of its depositors' money was audited by an accountant who sat on its board, and nobody thought there was anything wrong with that.) Plus there was somebody from the dominant political party and from one of the churches. Many little mouths to feed. It is not unfair to say that nobody controlled what this board did. These were mutual institutions with no stockholders, and the board was essentially self-perpetuating. "A mutual savings bank," said a report by the staff of the FDIC in the spring of 1981, "is not responsible to any ownership."[1]

These institutions were not subject to discipline from the market or from the government. The industry was largely self-contained, with few competitors. Insured commercial banks were not allowed to take "savings accounts" until after World War II, when an aggressive bank in a New York suburb insisted on the right to put that label on its customers' time deposits. (This was

29

Franklin National of Franklin Square, Long Island, which eventually became the biggest bank failure between the depression and 1983.) And commercial banks, as the name implies, were mostly interested in lending to businesses rather than to people—indeed, S&Ls had come into existence in large part because banks were not interested in financing one-family houses. Until the McFadden Act in 1927, nationally chartered banks were prohibited from lending on the security of real estate.

And government regulation was relaxed. Thrifts could be chartered by either state or federal governments, and their powers—the branches they could open, the assets they could acquire, the inducements for depositors they could advertise—were a function of the state or federal law under which the charter was issued. Until 1974 all federal charters had to be for "mutual" institutions, where the depositors owned the bank, and only a handful of states allowed stockholder-owned S&Ls (most importantly, Texas, California—and Ohio, which had what proved to be an accident-prone state deposit insurance system). Texas, peculiarly, had no change-of-control statute until 1983. Someone who wanted a charter for a new S&L had to demonstrate that he wasn't in jail at the time of his application, but anyone could buy an S&L just as he could buy a shoe store on the main street. When the legislature did create such a statute, it left the burden of proof with the commissioner—that is, an applicant was entitled to an S&L license unless the commissioner could prove he wasn't. In 1988, a Governor's Task Force on the S&L industry recommended to Texas governor William P. Clements, Jr., that the law "be amended to place the burden of proof of meeting the applicable statutory criteria upon the applicant." That's a good idea; but as of spring 1990 its time had not yet come.[2]

Even state-chartered institutions, however, could be subject to some federal control, because the FSLIC could make its own investigation of state-chartered S&Ls to determine if they were likely to become a danger to the insurance fund. A new S&L couldn't open for business, practically speaking, until the FSLIC gave it an insurance license, and, at least in theory, ownership of an existing S&L could not be changed without FSLIC approval. If action was required, however, the Bank Board's legal staff was constitutionally timid. "They always worried," said one of its alumni, "that if you litigated and lost—and you would be going up against the biggest law firms in the country—you'd lose authority everyone had always assumed you had."

In 1977, in an Arkansas case (an interesting venue, for the fraction of Arkansas thrifts that came unglued is the highest in the country), a federal court ruled that the regulators could not consider the likely economic viability of a new S&L in an area when determining whether to issue a deposit insurance "policy" for this thrift. The decision responded to a real problem, because banking regulators' ability to protect very profitable local monopolies had long been a major source of corruption in American politics. And there may indeed have been reason for the judge in this case to grant an insurance license to a thrift in the little town of St. Helena, Arkansas. But the rationale for the opinion was nutty: Congress certainly had not intended to subject the taxpayer to unlimited risk for the sake of increasing competition among thrift institutions. (The St. Helena lawsuit had been financed mostly by a young lawyer named Patrick Forte. Forte had been denied an FSLIC license for an S&L he had started in Virginia because another S&L in that same valley had protested; after the St. Helena case was won, Forte got his license. Some years later, he would become president of the Association of Thrift Holding Companies, still fighting the authorities, now for a membership ranging from Citicorp to Lincoln Savings.

In 1978, as part of the Financial Institutions Regulatory Act, Congress passed a Change of Control provision that gave thrift regulators sixty days to determine whether a new owner of a thrift was a suitable proprietor (and authorized FBI checks for the purpose). But it was not until 1986 that the Money Laundering Control Act "*required* the FSLIC to investigate the competency, experience and integrity of a person seeking to acquire control [and] provided supervisory agencies with authority to subpoena documents and records. . . . These amendments," to quote former president Norman Strunk of the U.S. League of Savings & Loans and UCLA professor Fred Case in their book *Where Deregulation*

Went Wrong, "came some years too late. It remains to be seen whether even they will do the trick. Clearly, however, inadequate use was made of the previous law."[3]

Through the 1970s, both the state S&L commissioners and the three-member Federal Home Loan Bank Board tended to be cheerleaders more than supervisors; indeed, the Home Owners Loan Act of 1933, which created the national chartering and supervising system, imposed a "duty" on the secretary of the Treasury to buy preferred stock in federally chartered S&Ls if "in the judgment of the Board the funds are necessary for the encouragement of local home financing in the community to be served and for the reasonable financing of homes in such community."[4] When there were disputes about how S&Ls should be supervised, the regulators and the trade associations tended to be on the same side. R. Dan Brumbaugh, Jr., formerly deputy chief economist of the Bank Board, noted in his book *Thrifts Under Siege* that the U.S. League of Savings & Loans was "involved in creating and staffing the Bank Board and in determining the shape of the legislation concerning federal insurance of accounts at savings and loan associations."[5] The first history of the Bank Board reported that in its early years "the United States Savings and Loan League wrote many FHLBB regulations."[6]

As late as 1983, Ed Gray reports, he learned that he was going to be nominated as head of the Bank Board from William B. O'Connell, then president of what had come to be called the U.S. League of Savings Institutions. The way the Reagan White House worked, this job was a gift the industry could give—which is, of course, not unrelated to what happened to the industry. Nor was it just the White House. "The fact is," Gray told a House Banking subcommittee in January 1989, "when it came to thrift matters in the Congress, the U.S. League and many of its affiliates were the de facto government. What the League wanted, it got. What it did not want from Congress, it had killed. . . . Every single day that I served as Chairman of the Federal Home Loan Bank Board, the U.S. League was in control of the Congress as an institution. And this is simply the truth of the matter. . . ."[7]

Except in California, where shareholder-owned thrifts bankrolled whole developments and found ways around the limits on loan-to-value ratios, S&Ls did little but write mortgage loans on one- to four-family housing, sometimes because their charters required it, sometimes because holding within those restrictions got them wonderful benefits under the Internal Revenue code. And until the 1970s, the housing market was a sitting duck. It was a local business: The S&L in town had a huge advantage over outsiders in judging the value of the property, the strength of the neighborhood, and even the qualifications of the borrower. For federally chartered S&Ls, the legislation initially permitted only loans on the collateral of residential property located within fifty miles of the home office. Though in fact S&Ls tended to spend more than banks the same size, this was at least potentially a low-cost, high-return business.

Especially after the New Deal designed the level-payment, self-amortizing mortgage in the 1930s, the highly standardized nature of the mortgage loan meant that lending officers were rarely called on to make judgment calls. Nor were the examiners sent by the state S&L commissioners and the Bank Board: Until the mid-1980s, these worthies had nothing like the bank examiners' standard schedule for "classifying" loans according to their likelihood of repayment. People paid their mortgages, and if they didn't, the house was usually good security for the loan.

Meanwhile, reliance on neighborhood deposits produced cheap funding, and if more money was needed because housing demand outstripped this locality's savings, there were any number of ways that savings from other areas of the country could be tapped. Scattered around the country, for example, were twelve quasi-public Federal Home Loan Banks created by the Hoover administration in 1932 on the model of the Federal Reserve Banks and owned by the S&Ls that borrowed from them, as the Reserve Banks are owned, in theory, by the commercial banks of their district. (In both cases, ownership does not mean "control"; administrators in Washington decide who will be the CEOs of these institutions and can remove them as well.) Slightly fewer than half the directors of the Federal Home Loan Banks were "public" appointees chosen from Washington; the majority were elected by the S&Ls of the district and were almost always officers of those S&Ls.

These district Federal Home Loan Banks sold bonds that had the look and feel of government securities. They then lent the money to the S&Ls (but only against the collateral of their best mortgages and marketable paper) at rates lower than those paid by any other private borrower. Even so, the operation of the Federal Home Loan Banks generated profits available for dividends to their member S&Ls; in 1988 dividends from the Home Loan Banks totaled $1.2 billion, which was about 30 percent of the total profits of that part of the industry that made money. In early 1989 total advances from the district Banks to their members exceeded $145 *billion*, more than 10 percent of the total liabilities of American S&Ls.

Thrifts that had uses for more money than their localities generated could also get it the old-fashioned way—by buying it. Until 1966, S&Ls were not controlled in the interest they could pay. The Bank Board did some jawboning and established rules prohibiting newly chartered federal S&Ls from "stealing" deposits by advertising rates of return higher than their neighbors paid the previous year. (Until 1966, for reasons we shall look at presently, no federally chartered mutual S&L was permitted to contract for a rate of return on the money a customer left in its care; federally chartered S&Ls could make such payments only from profits.) But state-chartered California S&Ls were permitted to take deposits at advertised interest rates even though they were federally insured. They were deluged with demand from the tidal wave of housing construction that started in the state in the 1940s, and they raised a great deal of money to meet that demand by bidding just a little more, advertising their bids in the East Coast newspapers, and employing money brokers, who were then mom-and-pop operators, taking as much as 2 percent commission. In the 1960s, when the invention of term certificates made it possible to pay more money for new deposits without touching the rates on the existing passbooks, the large California thrifts got in gear with nationwide advertising campaigns targeted at the moneyed class who read East Coast newspapers.

A handful of East Coast banks, notably Wachovia in North Carolina and Franklin National in New York, fought back by selling over-the-counter bonds (technically, uninsured subordinated debentures) in denominations suitable for savings accounts, at interest rates higher than they would have been permitted to offer on insured deposits. The conflict between the coasts, fed by rising interest rates as the Vietnam War heated up, led to a little trouble in 1966, when Franklin alone took $420 million out of the Pacific Coast S&Ls. And advertising for deposits by offering higher rates generated endless trouble in the 1980s, when the memory of 1966 had faded and both Wall Street houses and Mafia types bullied their way into money brokerage. One notes in passing that the newspapers loved this business and asked no questions. The *New York Times* Sunday business section was still carrying ads from Maryland's corrupt Old Court S&L in May 1985 (the week before it collapsed) when everybody who knew anything in Maryland was scrambling to get his money out of an institution that was insured only by the Maryland Savings Share Insurance Corporation, which had no reserves to pay off depositors.

In the early years, moreover, the government's liability for finagling by an S&L was nothing like what it later became. The numbers speak for themselves: Herbert Sandler told the Senate Banking Committee in the summer of 1988 that in its first forty-seven years, from 1934 to 1981, the FSLIC had suffered a total loss of only $630 million. Strictly speaking, S&Ls did not have deposits; their customers owned redeemable shares in the enterprise. Interest was not controlled because formally no interest was paid; shareholders received dividends, which the S&L could pay only out of earnings. The shares were not legally redeemable on demand; by law an S&L had a year to pay the money back, and the government was not obliged to pay out from the FSLIC until that year was up. In fact, though S&L accounts until the late 1970s could not be used to make payments (you could take the money out at the window, but you couldn't write a check), postdepression S&Ls always delivered cash on demand. The authorities had seen what runs on the banks did to the economy and wanted no more of that. But in 1966, when interest rates rose above the levels that a prudent S&L could pay, California thrifts that had counted on a steady inflow from the East were in trouble. The worst disaster involved State Savings of Stockton, later the nucleus of Financial Corporation of America, the elephant of the industry in 1983– 84 and its biggest carcass in 1986–88. Over the July 4 weekend in 1966, State Savings had to be rescued by a form of government trusteeship.

This changed all the rules. After the Financial Institutions Supervisory Act of 1966 (though the law remained a little ambiguous), people had "deposits" in S&Ls just as they did in banks, and the FSLIC was as committed to paying off depositors fast if anything happened to their institution as the Federal Deposit Insurance Corporation was. The trade-off was that the S&Ls lost their freedom to set their own rates: the Federal Reserve Board would set ceilings on the rates S&Ls could pay just as it did (in its infamous Regulation Q) on the rates commercial banks could pay. But because banks were considered stronger, tougher, meaner, and better established—and the federal government still wished to encourage home ownership on the yellow brick road of the S&L—the legislation guaranteed the thrifts a "differential." Set first at one-half and later at one-quarter of 1 percent over what the Fed's Regulation Q allowed the banks to pay, that differential was sufficient to keep the majority of the nation's household savings flowing to the S&Ls.

In 1973 the Board of Governors, as part of Fed chairman Arthur Burns's drive to move banking into the market economy, authorized "wild card" four-year consumer CDs at whatever rates banks wanted to pay. Some banks went crazy: In New Orleans they offered more than 9 percent interest at a time when the Reg Q controls on savings were 5¼ percent, and within two weeks they bled almost 4 percent of the deposit base from the local S&Ls. The S&L League went to Congress, which, without holding hearings, passed in three weeks a law requiring the Fed to keep ceiling rates on all consumer-oriented deposits and to make certain that these rates were never higher than what the S&Ls could pay. In the late 1970s, when inflation first shot out of control and the Treasury had to pay in double digits to sell six-month bills, the

Fed, in its role as protector of the banks, declared an end to the differential whenever rates rose over 9 percent. The S&Ls felt the loss of their advantage; their share of new savings deposits was 60 percent with the differential and 40 percent without it. S&Ls, said Norman Strunk, executive director of the U.S. League, "were dealing with the most avaricious sector of American society, the American consumer."[8]

Finally, an S&L (or a bank) that wanted more money to make more mortgage loans could sell off some of its existing loans. Customers were to be found from the 1930s through the 1950s at the life insurance companies, which had fixed liabilities (the $10,000 policy paid off at $10,000 whatever the intervening inflation rate) and an appetite for the higher yield of mortgages. In 1955 life insurance companies held more than 20 percent of the nation's mortgages, more than five times the proportion they would hold a quarter of a century later. The old established East Coast savings banks were also willing customers into the 1970s, having more money in their vaults than uses for it at home. And when interest rates went up, a number of S&Ls in states with usury ceilings that controlled what they could charge for the mortgages they wrote themselves became customers for Texas and California S&Ls, which wrote mortgages at whatever rate the traffic would bear. These sales were often done on a participating basis (the buyer took only half the loan), and even if the entire mortgage was sold, the seller usually offered some degree of recourse (e.g., he was obliged to buy the loan back should the borrower default). This practice, too, became a source of bad habits in later years.

The housing legislation of the early 1930s contemplated an institution, a specially chartered but privately operated Federal National Mortgage Association (FNMA), that would make it easy for real estate agents to become mortgage brokers or for S&Ls to sell mortgages. This corporation would fund itself from the sale of bonds and use the proceeds to purchase mortgages that would secure and eventually pay off the bonds. The result would allow these assets to be taken off the books of the S&Ls and provide them more money to write more mortgages. But the battered

Finanzkapital of the 1930s was not up to the exploitation of such novelties, and the FNMA ("Fannie Mae") was launched in 1938 as a government agency, with interest on its bonds exempt from state and local taxation. In 1968, because the Comptroller General ruled that this operation had to be put on the budget, which made the deficit look worse, Lyndon Johnson privatized the FNMA to a status the lawyer Thomas Stanton was the first to call "government-sponsored enterprise." Thereafter, the FNMA was owned by its stockholders, with a minority of its board appointed by the president. But its obligations were still implicitly, if not legally, guaranteed by the taxpayer.

Until the 1970s, Fannie Mae dealt only with mortgages that were themselves government insured, by the Federal Housing Administration (FHA) and the Veterans Administration (VA). As time went on, it functioned less as a source of liquidity for S&Ls (most of which could raise additional money by giving people toasters for opening accounts or by borrowing from the district Home Loan Bank—and which disliked the limits on fees and the extra paperwork associated with the FHA mortgages) and more as a point of entry for a new breed of "mortgage bankers." These people had relatively little money at their disposal and lived by taking the fees for originating such investments rather than by collecting interest payments.

Every week, to service these mortgage bankers, Fannie Mae held "auctions" in which mortgage originators could buy an option to sell paper to FNMA thirty or sixty days hence at the interest rate that won the auction. If rates went up before the mortgage banker closed his deals with homebuyers, he could exchange their mortgage for his FNMA commitment at the lower rates and take the profits; if they went down, he could drop the option and do business with the homebuyer at market rates. Or he could, without risk to himself, guarantee the homebuyer a rate before the transaction closed—a significant advantage in what became a cutthroat competition for the fees and service contracts that sweetened the origination of mortgage loans. Fannie Mae got a fee for these options, which over time more than paid out the occasions when the mortgage bankers won their bet. In periods of volatile mortgage interest rates, such fees rose considerably. But because Fannie Mae funded its own activities with the sale of paper that expired before the mortgages did, the agency remained at risk—like an S&L—that rates would rise dramatically, lifting its cost of funds without lifting the return from its portfolio of long-term mortgages.

The privatization of Fannie Mae spawned two other issuers of mortgage paper. To take over the subsidy functions FNMA had fulfilled while it was still a government agency, Congress created the Government National Mortgage Association (GNMA or "Ginnie Mae"), which tapped the money markets in a somewhat different way. Instead of issuing bonds for money that would be used to buy mortgages, the GNMA approved pools of insured mortgages. Just about anybody—banker, broker, thrift, mortgage banker, finance company—could put together a package of mortgages to make a pool. Because the mortgages were all FHA or VA insured, the GNMA could add its own guarantee to the package with only slight additional risk, and that risk was more than compensated by the fees the mortgage bankers paid for the right to put a government label on their package. Participations in each pool were sold on a "pass-through" basis; that is, the buyer of what soon became known as Ginniemaes (spoken as one word) received a proportionate share in the payments made by all the homeowners whose mortgages had been included in the pool. Different pools, even when formed from mortgages of similar duration and interest rate, might provide quite different yields to purchasers of the participations if homeowners in one pool and not the other sold (or refinanced) their homes before the mortgage came due.

The homeowners knew nothing of this; they simply made their payments to the mortgage banker or thrift that had lent them the money. That mortgage banker or thrift, having collected origination fees, normally retained the "service contract" on the mortgage and deducted a tiny fee every month before passing the money on to the pool. (Anybody with the right computing machinery can service mortgages. In 1990 Citicorp collected from $70 billion worth, the great bulk of them originated and held by

others; and the second- and third-largest mortgage servicers—
Fireman's Fund Insurance and GMAC, the automobile financer
—don't originate mortgages at all.) The GNMA as a product was
developed mostly by John Heimann, who had come to the Department of Housing and Urban Development (HUD) from the
Wall Street houses of Smith Barney and Warburg Pincus and who
was later to become Comptroller of the Currency for Jimmy
Carter and head of the Merrill Lynch operation in Europe. Heimann, a small, handsome man with very black hair and a side-
wise grin, was then a young assistant to Robert Weaver, the first
secretary of HUD (and the first black cabinet member). The operation was, from its beginnings, a paragon of government restraint. When I was working on my book *The Builders* in 1977, the
agency (part of the otherwise bloated HUD) employed all of thir-
teen people to keep in touch with tens of billions of dollars of
securities.

The development of these salable instruments for housing finance brought into what had once been a simple game a great
variety of sophisticated players, especially the aggressive Wall
Street bond traders at Salomon Brothers. Involving them and
their customers was, as we shall see, the social reason for the
development of the instruments, but there was no social reason,
except greed, for the proliferation of profitable bells and whistles
that the investment banking houses and the finance professors
were able to hang on Collateralized Mortgage Obligations (CMOs)
and Real Estate Mortgage Investment Conduits (REMICs). "What
Wall Street is doing out in the open," Donald Shackleford of State
Savings Bank in Columbus, Ohio, told a Senate Banking Committee hearing in the summer of 1988, "is almost indecipherable
to the typical guy sitting in Ohio or Illinois or Kansas, or some-
place, trying to get risk arbitrage, or mismatched libor-funded
hedges, and the only guy that's going to make money on that
thing in the long run is the salesman, because you can't figure out
what you're doing."[9] Do not slide over that "in the open," for it
was obvious to all sophisticated observers that much else was going
on behind the anonymity of the computer screens.

Barring leadership of greater ability and fiduciary commitment than this nation had in the 1980s, the S&Ls were destined to get into desperate trouble, and the government was destined to bail out their depositors. But without the trading market for bonds and certificates collateralized by individual mortgages—and the remarkable Bank Board regulations that encouraged S&Ls to buy the risks of that market—we would not have seen so deep a collapse or so immense a hole for the government to fill. The bailout bill Congress passed in the summer of 1989 prevents S&Ls from using insured deposits to buy corporate junk bonds (bonds that have not received an investment grade rating from one of the major ratings services) but does little to control their gambling propensities in the mortgage paper market, which probably means that the carousel will come round again and the taxpayer will have to buy many more brass rings.

I'll mention one more kind of housing paper that S&Ls could originate, buy, sell, or hold, and then we can go back to having fun. This last is produced by the Federal Home Loan Mortgage Corporation (FHLMC; "Freddie Mac"), which was launched in 1970 by the Federal Home Loan Bank Board itself to give the S&Ls an agency of their own to perform the functions the FNMA performed for the mortgage bankers. Until the Bush bailout bill of 1989, Freddie Mac was owned, but not necessarily controlled, by the Bank Board: the bureaucracy there usually called its own shots. In 1989, while the Bush bill was pending, the FHLMC hired the high-voltage lobbying firm of Charls Walker to manage Congress. I called Larry White, then one of the three members of the Bank Board, to inquire by what authority he and his colleagues were spending public monies to fight the president in Congress. He said, "We haven't done it." I said, "Sure you have." This was evening. He said, "I'll call our general counsel and get back to you." Presently he called back: "Yes, we did," he said, and the sound of the voice rose and fell as though he were still shaking his mustachioed head. "They never told the Board they were going to hire a lobbyist; they say it was an administrative matter."

Under the new regime, FHLMC is a stockholder-owned, government-sponsored enterprise like the FNMA. The FHLMC creates "pass-through" paper: purchasers buy an income stream and return of principal from the homeowner, not a bond with fixed terms for interest payments and redemption on an announced date. Because Freddie Mac paper lacked a full federal guarantee, it had to be "overcollateralized"—that is, the face value of the mortgages pledged to the payments had to be greater than the face value of the pass-through instrument. In the eighties, moreover, urged on by the Bank Board, the S&Ls wanted to write adjustable rate mortgages instead of the old self-amortizing level-payment, fixed-rate instruments, and such ARMs were hard to package as bonds and sell without sweeteners for the pension funds and insurance companies. These imperatives, combined with Wall Street's need for product differentiation, greatly speeded the development of the CMOs and REMICs, which could be divided into segments to be sold separately.

Some of these segments would collect only interest payments from the mortgages, while others collected only the repayments of principal. Interest Only (IO) "strips" got nearly all the money in the early years if rates went up and people clung to their old mortgages; Principal Only (PO) "strips" got the money if rates went down and people refinanced. Other packages of mortgages might be sold so that a top "tranche" got all the payments for the first years until its face value was paid off; while junior "tranches" began collecting only later; and a very, very junior tranche would get what was left if nobody ever defaulted and a larger-than-expected number of householders stayed put and kept making monthly payments. Such considerations hugely complicated the business of investing in mortgages, usually increasing the profits of the sharp operators who created and sold them. Usually, but not always. It was a flier on this sort of segmented mortgage paper by its chief trader Howard Rubin that cost Merrill Lynch $375 million in 1987.

All this paper, simple or complicated, could be used as the substance of "repurchase" transactions. An S&L, needing cash immediately to originate mortgages or to gamble in the paper market, could borrow through selling Ginniemaes, Fannie Maes, or Freddie Macs under an agreement to buy them back (at a price reflecting the market interest rate on the day of the "sale") in thirty, sixty, or ninety days.* Thus, the paper recycled through Wall Street, making money for its creators not only on the day of sale but *saeculae saeculorum*. "In 1985," says Ken Thygerson, who was then head of Freddie Mac, "FCA [the Financial Corporation of America, parent of State Savings and American Savings, by far the country's largest S&L and greatest money loser] was the best investment banking client in the country. Freddie Mac made a fortune in FCA repos at 75 points over cost"—that is, to borrow money from Freddie Mac on the security of Freddie Mac's own paper, the FCA was paying Freddie Mac three-quarters of a percentage point more than the agency could have got anywhere else for a safe loan.

Over time, the differences between Fannie and Freddie greatly diminished. The enormous success of Ginniemaes essentially absorbed the supply of fixed-interest FHA- and VA-insured mortgages to be "securitized" and sold on the market. By the mid-1980s, the FNMA, like the FHLMC, had to distribute paper that would be paid off by homeowners with "conventional" mortgages (i.e., mortgages not insured by the federal government). And the FNMA switched its modus operandi from selling bonds and buying mortgages with the proceeds to the Freddie Mac system of packaging mortgages into pools for sale as pass-through participations. This is why the violent shrinkage of the S&L industry under the biting rain of bad publicity in 1989 had so little effect on the availability or price of mortgages. By then, a large majority of the new mortgages written every year were being securitized and distributed, mostly through these alphabet agencies, with the help of Wall Street investment houses and big commercial banks. And a growing fraction of the housing-related paper the S&Ls held in their portfolios was not the mortgages themselves but

---

*Because the original use of the repurchase agreement or "repo" was by brokerage houses putting the value of their inventory to use, "repurchase" as a term of art means a sale by the broker or investment bank with a pledge to buy back at a price higher than today's interest rate. What the S&Ls did, because they were the customers raising cash on their inventory rather than the dealers, is known as a "reverse repurchase" ("reverse repo"). Life being hard enough as it is, we shall use "repurchase" for what the S&Ls did.

various tranches of this derivative paper, which was presumably resalable and thus a source of necessary flexibility for an industry that had been forced to cultivate financial athleticism.

[2]

Why did this industry fall so deeply into the hole? The conventional answer, that the S&Ls were trapped by rising interest rates, is true as far as it goes, but it doesn't go beyond 1981–82, when the losses were very much smaller. That conventional answer speaks to the penalties inflation imposes on a banker who gets his funds by borrowing for short periods of time, and lends them out via long-term instruments. This is usually profitable, because rates for long-term debt should be higher than rates for short-term debt: The longer the loan, the more opportunities for things to go wrong.

In a rational economy, the rule is that the greater the risk of getting hit by the bullets, the greater the reward if the bullets are dodged. In economists' lingo, the "yield curve"—the line on the chart that graphs interest rate (vertical axis) against length of loan (horizontal axis)—will usually be "positive." (It will slope upward.) But, by definition, short-term liabilities "reprice" before long-term assets do. If interest rates rise, the intermediary will have to pay more for its funding, while the return on its investments will remain the same. This rather elementary point was not understood at all within the industry until quite late in the game, though it was gospel to the entire community of economists.

George Mitchell, vice-chairman of the Federal Reserve through the 1970s, a grizzled, blunt, brilliant economics professor, was perhaps the only member of that Board in the past generation who really cared about the operation as against the theory of the banking system. In the late 1970s he stomped around to the big S&Ls, urging them to sell as much as they could of the thirty-month CDs they had just been authorized to issue at rates one-quarter of 1 percent over the rates on U.S. Treasury paper of the same duration. But the thirty-month CDs carried a higher interest rate than six-month CDs (and a *much* higher rate than passbook savings accounts), and as late as 1978, when the inflation rate rose to 7.3 percent, the S&Ls were making 0.84 percent on assets, very nearly the best the industry had ever done.[10] The S&Ls sold the six-month certificates in great quantities: within two years, these "money market certificates" made up more than a third of all deposits at the thrifts. But nobody felt pressured to lock in money for a longer term at what were, after all, historically high rates.

In fact, the industry was hooked on Reg Q, the government controls over what S&Ls would be permitted to pay for savings. Anthony M. Frank, who built San Francisco's Citizen Savings into the Ford Motor Company's First Nationwide and resigned in 1988 to become postmaster general, gave a talk to a conference at the Federal Home Loan Bank of San Francisco in 1976. A German refugee as a child, with a suitably Italianate appearance for San Francisco and a sunny, outgoing manner, Frank was one of the smartest and most straightforward men in the business. His was one of the first federal conversions from mutual to stock ownership, and it was, says Preston Martin, head of the Bank Board at the time, a model of the way the thing should have worked: "All the profits from the conversion went to the little old lady depositors." But he was absolutely committed to government controls over what he could pay his depositors. In 1976, listing what the government could do for housing finance and the S&Ls, he began with "number one, long-term extension of Regulation Q with a rate differential. There is no number two, because the space between Q and everything else is so great."[11]

But this war had really been lost in 1970, when the Federal Reserve, as a quid pro quo to the banks for rescuing Chrysler's commercial paper in the aftermath of the Penn Central failure, liberated banks from interest-rate controls on CDs of $100,000 or more. After 1970, the Fed, instead of controlling bank behavior through a "money crunch," would have to keep poking up the interest rates until borrowers no longer wanted to borrow. Within a year, mutual fund managers had created "money market funds" that sold people pieces of these CDs and high-yielding Treasury bills, and the knell had tolled for ceilings on consumer deposits at S&Ls and savings banks, though the regulators, the industry, and Congress clung to them for another decade.

In the end, fighting along the Maginot Line of Reg Q made

it impossible to plan intelligent defensive strategies for what was quickly becoming a beleaguered industry. Because government control of interest rates made consumer deposits by far the cheapest source of funds in inflationary times, S&Ls (and some California banks, most notably Bank of America) opened branches everywhere in the states where they had wide branching powers. Branches are normally too expensive to be profitable unless they generate "core deposits" that can be lent by the home office as well as loans to local borrowers.

Mark Taper founded American Savings & Loan and built it into the nation's biggest; he then took enough money out of it in the 1960s to give the Los Angeles Music Center its experimental theater (the Mark Taper Forum). Finally, in 1983, two years before American Savings went bust, he sold it for almost $300 million. He laid it down as a rule that S&Ls could be adequately profitable over time only if their operating costs, their "G 'n' A" (general and administrative expenses), were less than 1 percent of their assets. With market interest rates at 9 percent or more and passbook deposit interest rates controlled at 5¼ percent, S&Ls expanded the number of expensive offices as fast as they could, until by 1980, at precisely the worst time, their noninterest costs went to 1.7 percent of their assets. Without confusing correlations and causes, it's interesting to note that more than two-thirds of the losses of the S&Ls in that year can be accounted for in the difference between costs under Taper's rule and what the industry actually spent.

The S&Ls' position in 1980–81 was even worse than it looked, because the lower interest rates that had to come would not generate profits anywhere near large enough to compensate for the losses the thrifts had suffered while the rates were high. The industry's assets were overwhelmingly in the form of ordinary homeowners' mortgages, and those were one-way option contracts. If interest rates rose, the lender was stuck with a low-yielding mortgage. But when interest rates fell, the borrower could prepay the high-rate mortgage by refinancing with a low-rate mortgage. The break point appeared to be about 200 basis points, or two percentage points—that is, if interest rates on new mortgages fell by two percentage points from the number on the existing mortgage contract, the borrower would refinance. (The saving is indeed considerable: On a $100,000 twenty-five-year mortgage, a decline in interest rate from 10 percent to 8 percent reduces monthly payments from $908.70 to $771.82.) Jonathan Gray of the investment house of Sanford Bernstein wrote of "the asymmetry of the industry's profit history (lose money when rates are high, lose money when rates are low)."[12]

It should be noted that this option did not come free to the borrower, though he and his congressman both thought so. Interest rates on mortgages were higher than interest rates on bonds, and the up-front fees (usually "points," deductions from the money the mortgagor actually received) made them much higher —and those higher rates and fees were in reality payments for the option. The changing values of the option affected the behavior of substantial institutions. The New York mutual savings banks virtually stopped writing mortgages in the late 1970s, first because the state's usury ceilings would have required them to write local mortgages at rates below their cost of funds, and second, because the Connecticut mortgages they had written at the high rates of 1974 (taking advantage of the absence of a usury ceiling in that state) had all been paid back in the low-interest-rate environment of 1977 and they didn't want to go through that again. Instead, they bought long-term government and corporate bonds, which had a fixed "coupon" and wouldn't be paid back until the expiration date.

A further whammy for the thrift industry's asset portfolio was the spread of idiotic state legislation prohibiting the enforcement of "due-on-sale" clauses in conventional mortgages. Under customary mortgage terms, the loan was made to the individual using the home as security. Thus, it could not be transferred to another individual without the consent of the bank, which would, as normal procedure, even in a time of stable interest rates, cancel the old mortgage and issue a new one to gain an origination fee. When rates went up, obviously, the bank wanted to close down the low-yielding assets and replace them with something that paid better. Under pressure from homeowners who wanted to sell (in a market where the price of the house is a function of the purchaser's monthly payments and the size of those monthly payments is a function of interest rates), state legislatures began to declare that mortgages were loans to the property, not the individual owner, and that they could be transferred to a new owner.

This did not help purchasers at all; it merely meant that more of their monthly payments went to the seller of the property and less to the S&L. The laws were part of the great intergenerational transfer that characterized American government in the 1960s and 1970s, when the parents of the baby-boom generation got theirs before their children could vote. ("Never trust anybody over thirty" was a valid slogan, but the people who uttered it, alas, never knew what it meant.) The immediate effect of the legislation prohibiting enforcement of due-on-sale clauses was to devastate the S&Ls that needed desperately to reprice their assets as the price of their liabilities went up.

In 1980 the California Supreme Court ruled in the case of *Wallingkamp v. Bank of America* that the California state law prohibiting enforcement of due-on-sale clauses applied to nationally chartered as well as state-chartered banks; and presently the rule was extended to federally chartered S&Ls in the case of *Fidelity Federal v. de la Cuesta*. Fidelity, with the encouragement of the Federal Home Loan Bank Board (which in 1976 had ruled that its regulations preempted such state laws), carried the case to the U.S. Supreme Court, which in 1982 told the California court to keep its mitts off federally chartered institutions. There was still life in *McCulloch v. Maryland*, the great case in which Chief Justice Marshall forbade a state to tax the federally chartered Bank of the United States on the grounds that "the power to tax implies the power to destroy."

Arguably, this sequence of events cost the American taxpayer around $30 billion. First the California decisions weakened all California S&Ls, which were prevented from enforcing their contracts for two years. Then, taken together with some changes in regulations on the federal level, the hostility and ignorance of the California courts led to wholesale switches from state to federal charter, which crippled the state's S&L commissioner, whose office was funded by a tax on the deposits in state-chartered institutions. In 1978 the California S&L Commission had 178 employees; in 1983 it had only forty-four, and still falling.[13] "You had your board pass a resolution authorizing management to switch from state to federal charter," says a man who ran a California S&L in those days, "and whenever a state examiner said he didn't like something you took that resolution out of your desk drawer and showed it to him."

Finally, this wholesale switching from state to federal charter stimulated from the California state legislature almost universal acquiescence to the Nolan Act, which removed virtually all restrictions on what state-chartered California S&Ls could do with insured deposits. The reduction in the number and wealth of state-chartered S&Ls had led to a significant drop in the money available to the legislators themselves. Federal S&Ls were not allowed to contribute to state political campaigns. California-chartered S&Ls were. As the California thrifts moved from state to federal charters to get out from under the law against due-on-sale clauses, the California legislators lost cash money. This quickly created a bipartisan consensus, and there was only one dissent in each house in the vote on the Nolan Act, which promised to bring back the gravy by giving state-chartered S&Ls power to invest or to play with depositors' money any way they wished. Some six years later, state legislator Pat Nolan resigned as Republican leader after the FBI released information that money had been taken on his behalf from the bagman of a sting operation.

Donald Crocker, who was then head of the legislative committee of the California Savings & Loan League, recalls that "the S&L industry didn't know anything about the bill, wasn't interested in it. There were some people who said, 'That's too much —that's not the nature of our business.' " But it's not the sort of gift horse any business community is likely to study too carefully. Not long after the passage of the Nolan Act, Congress, in the Garn-St Germain Act, specifically and authoritatively preempted state laws that prohibited federally insured institutions from enforcing the due-on-sale clauses in their mortgages (a perfectly appropriate exercise of federal authority, given the fact that all the country's taxpayers stood behind the insurance fund). But the horse and all the pigs were out of the barn, and Larry Taggart was out there pouring the slop into the trough for them. As he puts it, "I was pro-business."

The obvious palliative for the problem of the mismatched portfolios and the one-way option was the creation of an ARM that would shift the risk of interest-rate changes from the lending bank to the borrower. The first such mortgages were authorized in 1974 for California, Arizona, and Nevada state-chartered S&Ls by the Federal Home Loan Bank of San Francisco. The rate the borrower paid would be changed every six months according to movements in the average cost of funds for thrifts in that district. This was a complicated index, because the large California thrifts were heavy users of "jumbo certificates" with uncontrolled interest rates, while the many smaller institutions were strong in passbook accounts where rates were under a low ceiling. In any event, the instrument the Bank approved limited increases to half a percentage point in one year, five percentage points over the life of the loan. But from the point of view of the state-chartered S&Ls (federally chartered S&Ls were not permitted to write such mortgages until 1981), the values were considerable. The two largest, most profitable, and most heavily capitalized S&Ls in the country as of 1989, Great Western and Home Savings, were institutions that had decided in the mid-1970s that while they would continue to write level-payment, fixed-rate mortgages for customers, they would keep for their own portfolio only adjustable-rate instruments, selling off the others as they were acquired. In 1980 only 23 percent of mortgages held by West Coast S&Ls (as against 64 percent of mortgages held by New York S&Ls) carried interest rates of less than 9 percent.

In fact, the Federal Home Loan Bank Board could have approved ARMs for federally chartered S&Ls at any time; the only rule against them was a Bank Board regulation that came with the move to controlled rates on deposits in 1966. But the relevant committees of Congress had let the Bank Board know they would be deeply disapproving of any such thing. The most the Bank Board could summon its courage to do before the 1980s was authorization of a five-year "Canadian rollover" mortgage, where lender and borrower would renegotiate the interest rate every five years. The introduction of Canadian rollovers had little effect, because neither the public nor the thrift industry wanted them.

According to *Newsweek*, a transition-team memo for the incoming Reagan administration warned that in the S&Ls "the new Administration may well face a financial crisis not of its own making.... Confidence in the entire financial system could evaporate."[14] As the Housing Commission assembled, however, our first worries were less about the S&Ls, which could be supported for some time with words (as we shall see in the next chapter), than about Fannie Mae, which had to sell uninsured bonds to a suspicious market and make payments on them from an income stream that was increasingly too small for the purpose. In 1981, Fannie Mae held $62 billion of home mortgages—more than the ten largest S&Ls put together—and if you valued those mortgages at the price they would bring in the market, Fannie Mae was insolvent by no less than $10.8 billion.[15] The Ginniemae, Fannie Mae, and Freddy Mac operations were clearly the wave of the future. S&Ls, which had held almost 75 percent of the nation's home mortgages in 1975, held only about 35 percent six years later. In its final report, the Housing Commission would call for "an orderly transition to a more broadly based and flexible private housing finance system."[16]

[3]

Through the eight Reagan years, the struggle to save the S&Ls was supported by the homebuilders, the realtors, and the contruction unions, all of which saw the threat to this source of funds as a threat to housing. In December 1988 I gave a talk to the annual meeting of the National Council of Savings Institutions and heard its incoming president proclaim that at the top of his agenda was going to be the revocation of the increase in the premium for deposit insurance that had been put on the thrifts. He was confident that the community power of the S&Ls and the Washington muscle of the housing lobby, working together, could prevent anything awful from happening to the industry despite the exponentiating losses to the insurance fund. But when the Bush administration arrived with a promise to clean up this rats' nest, the S&Ls found they were not in a position to demand anything. The reason was only partly the public outrage, which was whipped up by the administration (and a week of front-page stories in *USA Today* leading the pack); even more important, when push came to shove in the conference committees that reconciled the House and Senate versions of the bill, was that the housing people had abandoned the thrift industry.

The source of housing finance is, properly, household savings. For forty years after the invention of the New Deal, these savings were channeled primarily to depository institutions. But around 1975 the tide turned dramatically. Pension funds became the dominant intermediary for savings in the United States, and the "contract thrifts" in general—pensions, life insurance companies, mutual funds—grew much more rapidly than the S&Ls, even while the S&Ls grew too fast. The members of the finance committee of the Housing Commission, while concerned about the S&Ls, considered it much more important to perform midwife functions for new mortgage instruments that would catch the fancy of the contract thrifts.

As economists, more or less, we were not even entirely certain that a strong case could be made for continuing to devote to housing as high a share of our national savings as we do. Chairman John Reed of Citicorp made the point neatly in a hearing on competitiveness before the Senate Banking Committee at the end of the decade: "The gross accumulation of financial assets, which importantly is the amount available for capital formation, is actually higher as a percentage of GNP [in the United States] than in either Japan or Germany. In this country, however, the household sector borrows back, depending on the interest-rate environment, approximately 7% of GNP. This simply does not happen in Germany or Japan. . . . We have a very efficient home-lending industry that allows consumers to borrow against their future earnings potential in order to buy homes. That lowers our savings rate."[17]

To some extent, then, the S&L disaster happened because the damage done to the industry by the inflation pressures of 1981–

82 was seen not as a national problem or a housing problem but as an S&L problem. Thus, the remedies sought were mostly trivial (indeed, they still are), and nobody thought it important to protect the industry or the government from those who would exploit the new rules entirely for their own gain. The political leaders of the country were engaged in restructuring the American economy to give the pigs what had once been the lion's share. So the intrusion of greed onto the S&L turf, which had once been, at least in theory, a ground of mutuality, seemed to them fitting and proper. But it wasn't.

Much of what happened was simply the result of stupidity. "In any market, as in any poker game, there is a fool," Michael Lewis writes in *Liar's Poker*, a description of his experiences in the investment banking house of Salomon Brothers, about half of which is devoted to telling the story of how Wall Street robbed the thrifts. "The astute investor Warren Buffett is fond of saying that any player unaware of the fool in the market probably *is* the fool in the market. . . . Various Salomon mortgage traders estimate that between 50 and 90 percent of their profits derived from simply taking the other side of thrifts' trades. . . . What was happening —and is still happening—is that the guy who sponsored the float in the town parade, the 3-6-3 member and golfing man, had become America's biggest bond trader. He was also America's worst bond trader. He was the market's fool."[18]

Some of the losses—the prevailing estimate is about a fifth, but all guesses from a tenth to a third are reasonable—were thievery by people who either knew they were thieves or knew at least that their way of doing business would not be acceptable in any other line of work. The General Accounting Office (GAO) of Congress did a study of twenty-six large thrifts that had gone belly-up between January 1985 and September 1987 and found egregious conflicts of interest in twenty of them. In one, the president of the S&L "formed a separate corporation to receive loan referral fees for identifying borrowers" to his own thrift; in another, the president creamed off, for the benefit of a mortgage company he owned, half of the $2 million his thrift paid to purchase a real estate development company.[19]

Whether or not the U.S. Attorneys can get a conviction in the case (the first prosecution of big bandits ended with a hung jury, with one vote for not guilty), it cannot have been normal business practice for Dallas S&L owner Danny Faulkner and eight of his friends to fake land sales to boost the price of seventy-seven acres in suburban Dallas by $13 million in one afternoon. The land flips were done so Faulkner could buy himself a Learjet 55 (to replace a Learjet 25 he now found too small, which went to S&L owner Spencer Blain as part of his "finder's fee" on the deal). "As God is my witness," one of the participants told Dallas *Morning News* reporters Allen Pusey and Christi Harlan, "the only reason we cut that land deal was to help Danny Faulkner buy his damned jet."[20] Tom Gaubert, former finance chairman of the Texas Democratic party, has been suing to get his S&L back from the FSLIC, which seized it, he insists, while it was still solvent. (He was acquitted in Des Moines of charges that he ruined an S&L in that city by fraudulently valuing land on which the Iowans made a loan. But there is uncontradicted testimony of forged appraisals and postdated contracts in his operation. Even the most habituated viewers of *Dallas*, which all these people watched, cannot have believed that such behavior was common.)

Structural change itself made an unrecognized contribution to the disaster as the conversion from mutual to stockholder ownership loaded the proprietors with money that had to be employed somewhere—and had to be leveraged, taking on bundles of deposits, to maintain an appropriate return on equity. Paul Nadler of the Rutgers Graduate School of Management blamed conversion for the spreading of the fearful Texas disease to the long-established New England mutual savings banks in 1989: "With the vast amount of new funds burning a hole in their pockets, many newly converted thrifts pushed to make any loan available—often providing enough money to finance both the construction and the early interest payments."[21] With the industry in disgrace and eager to make itself invisible for a while, it's hard to remember how big the deals that took the S&Ls to joint-stock organization turned out to be. When California Federal converted from mutual to stock format in 1983, it was the second-largest "initial public offering" in the history of the SEC; only the flotation of the Ford Motor Company by the Ford Foundation had been larger.

The shift from mutual to stock organization brought in the "new people" the old-timers in the industry like to blame. "Most of us," said Roger Lindland, a former head of the FSLIC who became president of Great American Savings in San Diego, "had trained as tellers. We felt obligations to depositors. How people can take in an old lady's money and then play these games with it . . ." His chairman, Gordon Luce, an elegant, gracious man who was Ed Gray's employer before he went to the Bank Board and Larry Taggart's before he became California S&L Commissioner, nodded behind Lindland. "I had never thought this industry would have these people in it." A senior S&L examiner, bought away from the Office of the Comptroller of the Currency where she had been a bank examiner, gave a concise statement of what she considered the problems of the thrift industry: "You know what's wrong with this industry, Mr. Mayer? What's wrong with this industry is that the people who own these institutions are *slime.*"

The decision to let builders buy thrifts was obviously foolish. Rosemary Stewart, director of enforcement at the Bank Board, says there was no choice—builders had the money, and nobody else wanted to get into the business—but if this was the only open door, the Bank Board and the state commissioners should have assumed all doors were closed. Lin Bowman of Texas told Paul Zane Pilzer, "It is the nature of the developer to circumvent regulations. The builder who makes a lot of money makes it because he gets around the city council, because he gets around the planning and zoning commission."[22] J. W. G. Goodman (television's "Adam Smith") claims to have seen a piece of film in which a grizzled westerner explains to the camera, "Look, when you get a fox in a henhouse, you get a lot of dead chickens. That doesn't mean that's a bad fox. That's what a fox will do in a henhouse. You give a builder a chance to build with insured deposits he can raise with a phone call whenever he needs some money, and he'll cover the earth with housing."

But after all this is said, the crucial fact remains that the industry had no antibodies to protect itself against the eruption of fraud and abuse created by the government in the first two years of the Reagan administration. The industry's traditional mutual form of organization had kept away the greediest and most short-sighted; until the 1980s it was almost universally understood, as I told the annual conference of the Federal Home Loan Bank of San Francisco in 1987, that you weren't supposed to get rich in the S&L business. In this situation, society and the people in the transactions could easily tolerate the comfortable and assuredly profitable back scratching that characterized relations among the beneficiaries of a home purchase. When the situation changed, however, there was no code of conduct that would lead the honest men to ostracize and seek to thwart the crooks. The SEC and the Federal Reserve Board in the 1980s were as naively deregulatory as the Bank Board, but stock brokerage and commercial banking boast traditions of fair dealing and fiduciary obligation (sometimes, admittedly, honored in the breach) that have kept the stock market and the banks from accepting most of their government's invitations to cut corners. At the S&Ls, unfortunately, it was every man for himself.

CHAPTER 3

Mr. Pratt Puts the Pedal to the Metal

... fraudulent financial reporting usually does not begin with an overt intention to distort the financial statements. In many cases, fraudulent financial reporting is the culmination of a series of acts designed to respond to operational difficulties.

—Report of the National Commission on Fraudulent Financial Reporting (1987)

EVERYBODY likes Dick Pratt, cheerful bully, raconteur and motorbike racer, a man with a large head and broad shoulders who radiates health and strength. I like Dick Pratt, too. He has a cutting wit, a gift of phrase that can blow an antagonist completely out of the debate, and a certainty that he is right that would be totally intolerable in anyone else. ("My conclusions," he once said at a public meeting, "always turn out to be intuitively obvious, and, I think, rather commonplace.")[1] His information is not always accurate. In February 1989 he told me that his people at Merrill Lynch brokered customer funds only into "investment-grade" S&Ls, at a time when Merrill customers had $900 million in Gibraltar Savings of Beverly Hills and probably half that much in Lincoln Savings of Irvine and Imperial Savings of San Diego, institutions that shared two major characteristics: They were all insolvent, and they were all good customers for Merrill's mortgage-backed securities and junk bonds. (In the case of Lincoln, Merrill also had nice business as the lead underwriter of Euronotes, one of Lincoln's subsidiaries sold in London.) But the fact remains that everybody likes Dick Pratt, and so do I.

In September 1985 I gave a dinner speech at the annual work-and-play Pebble Beach conference of the Real Estate and Urban Economics Advisory Board of the University of California. Ed Gray, sitting chairman of the Bank Board, was in the audience with his mother, and after I finished, Maury Mann, chairman of the occasion, called upon Gray to deliver a few words. He did. In the back of the room, Pratt, Gray's predecessor and the author of the deregulations that had doomed the industry, rose to denounce Gray for his lack of faith in the free market as the proper correction to the distortions and dangers Gray was warning the world about. In every way that one man can be right in an argument and the other can be wrong, Gray was right and Pratt was wrong. In every way that one man can win an argument and the other lose it, Pratt won and Gray lost.

There were other occasions, too, when Pratt effectively beat up on Gray. A year after he left the Bank Board to become vice-chairman of what was then called Merrill Lynch Mortgage Trading, he held press conferences in Washington to denounce Gray's attempt to stop the activities of money brokers who took high fees to rustle up funds for S&Ls, often enough failing and crooked S&Ls, that were willing to pay depositors more than the going rate. (Merrill was big in this activity, pocketing commissions that ran from $40 million to $70 million a year; when Gray and his colleague William Isaac at the FDIC tried to end it, Merrill's PR people invented slogans about "the sledgehammer rule" and tried, not unsuccessfully, to portray the situation as one where the government was beating up on little guys.) But when I asked Gray in 1989 about his predecessor, he said earnestly, "I could call Pratt and ask his advice; I had good relations with him."

Oddly enough, that was almost true, especially in Gray's first months on the job, when he was accepting guidance from Pratt's general counsel Thomas Vartanian. The occasion on which Gray most required Pratt's help was the day in August 1984 when Financial Corporation of America (read American Savings & Loan, the nation's largest by a big margin) needed a fast billion dollars of new deposits to replace money that had flooded out for reasons we shall look at later in this chapter. It was probably the worst bank run of the postwar era, and in the end, $6 billion was required to stanch it. At Gray's request on the darkest day of this drain, when Paul Volcker's Federal Reserve was pondering whether their rules permitted them to help, Pratt set in motion the purchase of a billion dollars of American Savings CDs by the Merrill money market fund.

Then, suddenly—the tale is worth telling—Pratt had to back off. Don Regan, then secretary of the Treasury and very much in the loop of discussion about the prospects for American Savings, was in the early stages of what turned into a large feud with the new chairman of the Bank Board. Gray had already been given the most damning of labels: "not a team player." He remembers that the only conversation he ever had with Regan, just after he was appointed, consisted entirely of Regan saying to him, "You're a team player, aren't you?" and of his reply, "Of course." Regan had been chairman at Merrill and, though no one would have admitted it, still had a lot of influence on what the firm did. Pratt for some reason was in Washington and checked in with Regan. That afternoon, he backed away. The bottom line on this episode, incidentally, was that American Savings had to pay even more for its money and sell its CDs to the customers of Prudential-Bache, one of a few big Wall Street houses not already up to the gunwales in American Savings paper. Pru-Bache chairman George Ball had to be roused on a trip to Spain to give his okay.

Pratt's hearty manner takes the edge off his constant belligerence, but what really redeems him is a breathtaking honesty about the problems that he will admit he has not solved, after you agree he is right about all the things he insists he is right about. Forty-four years old in 1981, he was a professor of finance at the University of Utah when Ronald Reagan nominated him to be chairman of the Bank Board (as Sen. Jake Garn of Utah settled in to be the first Republican chairman of the Senate Banking Committee since 1954). Entirely conscious of the damage that was being done to the S&L industry by inflation—he had been an economist with the Savings and Loan League in the late 1960s, as a young Ph.D.—Pratt thought that the cost savings and competitive opportunities opened by deregulation would save that part of the industry that was worth saving. In the end, he believed, a small number of large S&Ls would swallow the inefficient and poorly managed two-thirds of the industry, and through increasing their size and diversifying their portfolios (reducing the residential mortgage component, adding commercial and consumer loans and direct investment in real estate and corporate securities), they could boost their earnings enough to keep the S&L charter valuable. As he admitted to Ned Eichler, however, he had come to the Bank Board "hardly thinking about deposit insurance."[2] And soon he saw that his planting was going to yield strange fruit as long as deposit insurance was the fertilizer.

In December 1982 Pratt, still chairman of the Bank Board, made a speech at the annual conference of the San Francisco Home Loan Bank. According to Eichler, "he advised his audience, mostly California Savings and Loan executives, how to run an association to beat the system: 'One approach [Pratt said] would be to start ten or fifteen thrift institutions or commercial banks and engage in the most risky activities legally allowed. If you believe that return is related to risks, the expected value of your returns would be higher than under any other approach, while at the same time, you could buy your funds on a risk-free basis through offering U.S. government obligations in the form of insured savings accounts. That is a scenario that we, as regulators, and that you, as management, are going to have to operate under, because that opportunity is a realistic one.' "[3] Five years later, as an emeritus, he gave the same audience a more technical scenario involving the use of two charters, one to bet on rising rates and one to bet on falling rates. After a few years, you cash in the winner and keep the winnings—and turn the other one over to the government, which pays out your losses.

"It seems to me," Pratt said, "we have an insane asylum run by the inmates."[4]

But it was Dick Pratt who had fired the guards and suspended the rules and introduced liquor with meals, and in general, put the lunatics in charge. Some of the Federal Home Loan Bank Board regulations that destroyed whatever immune system the industry had were written before Pratt's time, and some of the decisions that demonstrated the Bank Board's willingness to pander to adventurers and crooks and politicians were taken after he had returned to the private sector. But it was during Pratt's two years as chairman of the Bank Board that the road to hell was paved and polished. He wrote the worst of the regs, and more than any other single person he wrote the Garn-St Germain bill of 1982 that codified the perverse incentives the government gave the industry. (On its introduction in the fall of 1981, it was known as "the Pratt bill"; it went through Congress like a dose of salts, with virtually no hearings in either Senate or House Banking committees.) Everybody likes Dick Pratt; and I like Dick Pratt, too. But if you had to pick one individual to blame for what happened to the S&Ls and to some hundreds of billions of dollars of taxpayer money, Dick would get the honor without even campaigning.

[2]

Fair is fair. The first thing Pratt did on assuming the mantle in April 1981 was absolutely right: he authorized all federally insured S&Ls to write ARMs, with interest payments recalculated periodically according to some contractually specified independent index of market interest rates. His predecessor Jay Janis had been specifically warned not to try such a trick, but this was the juiciest segment of the Reagan honeymoon, when supply-side fiscal policy and deregulation were seen (and not only by true believers) as a sure way to unleash the magic of the marketplace. Lawrence Kudlow, then chief economist of the OMB, came to a meeting of the Housing Commission with a "favorite graph" that showed the price of oil and the price of gold moving in tandem.

I muttered that this item of evidence might be used to show that Arabs bought gold but wasn't of much value for any other purpose; and I soon found I was committing *lèse fonctionnaire* and must mend my ways. Even so, the liberation of mortgage rates was a courageous act—even Senator Garn asked for special assurances that the change would never impede the flow of money to housing—and no chairman before or, I think, after Pratt would have had the guts to do it without specific congressional authorization.

But the industry was already much too sick to be resuscitated simply by permission to write new mortgages that would yield more revenue for the lender-intermediary whenever he had to pay more for the funds he lent. In 1981, 85 percent of U.S. thrifts were losing money, and while only 2 percent were insolvent by Bank Board definitions that allowed S&Ls to value their assets unrealistically, there was a limit to how long the other 83 percent could keep losing money before somebody brought their bones to the knackers. By the end of 1982, 7 percent of the nation's S&Ls were insolvent; by the end of 1983, after interest rates had come down a good ways, the fraction was up to 9 percent. "By then," wrote Bank Board chief economist James R. Barth and his deputy Michael G. Bradley, in a presentation to a Federal Reserve Bank of Cleveland conference on regulation in the fall of 1988, "there was mounting evidence that what was once viewed as an unprofitability problem had become an insolvency problem."[5] Indeed, Pratt had seen the future—and the fact that it didn't work—as early as December 1982, when he told the San Francisco conference that "the Federal Savings and Loan Insurance Corporation . . . will be exposed to operating risks such as have never occurred in the past. . . ."[6]

The regulatory system as structured in the first two years of the Reagan administration, however, had left both the government and the industry very nearly defenseless. Pratt's Bank Board and (as we shall see in the next chapter) Congress had dismantled not just the regulatory structure but the accounting rules that had allowed the operators of these institutions, their boards, and their examiners to get some kind of fix on where they were and where they were going. The list of changes is very long and very scary.

[3]

Let us start with one that was entirely unnecessary and quite unrelated to the problems the industry faced in 1981. Prior to that year, a joint-stock S&L that wanted federal deposit insurance had to show at least 400 shareholders, with at least 125 of them from the local community the S&L would serve. No individual could own more than 10 percent of the stock, and no "control group" could own more than 25 percent. In those days, California S&L commissioner William Crawford argued, the board of directors "had oversight. . . . They knew the territory and they knew the borrowers, and they knew the savers." Then, almost immediately after taking office in the spring of 1981, Pratt reduced the required number of stockholders to one.

Why? "It seemed a bizarre requirement," Pratt said the other day. "You didn't have to have four hundred stockholders to get deposit insurance if you were a bank. Why should you need four hundred stockholders to get insurance if you're an S&L? Bank holding companies are one shareholder." But individually owned banks had been around since the very early nineteenth century, before anyone dreamed of such a thing as deposit insurance. They were necessarily grandfathered when the FDIC was formed, and relatively few had been formed since. (Experience with those that had been formed—e.g., Frank W. Sharp of Texas, Tennessee's Butcher family—was very bad.) When Pratt dropped the rule against letting individuals print U.S. government obligations (for an insured deposit is a U.S. government obligation), he invited into the business what Keith Russell, the youthful, bespectacled president of California's Glenfed, calls "the guys who want to hit home runs. But the cardinal rule of financial services is that there are no home runs." There are, of course, home runs in land development. "When you put a developer in there that is lending money to himself," Crawford said, "there is no one to say no.

"If you do not have a good board of directors, if you do not have a good internal auditor, if you do not have a system for people to blow the whistle, if you do not have some public interest directors, you are asking too much. Because at the Board meeting they say, those in favor say aye. Those who oppose, report to the cashier for severance pay. And that is what happens. And . . . if you do go along, you get raises and you get high salaries. And you would be surprised what high salaries and jet airplanes and helicopters and express limousine use will do for your personality. It really will change it."[7]

Though some of the worst hanky-panky occurred under the aegis of a holding company (see chapter 7), Pratt's decision to approve insurance charters for individually owned S&Ls was hugely expensive to the insurance fund. A report by the GAO to Congress, investigating the causes of some twenty-six large thrift failures, noted "the presence of a dominant figure" at nineteen of them. "[T]he dominant individual may . . . initiate a large number of poor-quality loans . . . before the board is aware of risks assumed, may commit the institution to unsound courses of action, or may undertake abusive practices. . . . Members of the board at another failed thrift said they did not question the business decisions of the former chairman because he owned the federally-insured thrift—they thought he could run his business as he pleased. However, when that thrift failed, it was FSLIC which incurred the loss, estimated to be $1.3 billion."[8] Concern that such would be the results of individual ownership had motivated the original Bank Board rule. As the man in France said two hundred years ago, its abrogation was worse than a crime; it was a blunder.

[4]

The "capital" in a bank is, at least in theory, the fraction of the money the bank uses that represents the investment of its owners. In mutual institutions, the capital was called "net worth"—when you took the value of all the assets and subtracted the total liabilities, how much was left? Before 1980 the law said that S&Ls had to have "net worth" equal to at least 5 percent of their insured deposits. Because mutual institutions could grow their net worth only from retained earnings, however, the Bank Board gave new S&Ls *twenty-five years* to reach that target. And in 1970, when inflation (as much as 4 percent) threatened the earnings of S&Ls—and the prescribed procedure for avoiding trouble was to grow, acquiring higher-yielding assets to increase the average return on the portfolio—the Bank Board permitted established S&Ls to maintain that 5 percent net worth ratio, not against their current deposits, but against their average deposits in a five-year period.

Significantly, until the Depository Institutions Deregulation Act of 1980, this "net worth" was called a "Federal Insurance Reserve" (FIR), for that was its function under the Bank Board system: The capital of the S&L was the cushion that kept the insurance fund from being hit by an institution's losses. In 1979 the U.S. League of Savings & Loans asked Congress to reduce the statutory FIR requirement from 5 percent to 4 percent. Jay Janis, chairman of the Bank Board, called for a reduction to 3 percent and got authority for the Board to do such dirty work itself. In the fall of 1980 the net worth requirement was reduced to 4 percent, and in January 1982 Pratt took it down to 3 percent.

All the rules that had been designed over the years to help mutual S&Ls build capital slowly through surplus were now extended into a world of shareholder-owned S&Ls where, presumably, capital requirements were met by the sale of stock and could be satisfied from day one. This new world, moreover, was one where the old requirement of 400 shareholders for a deposit insurance policy had been abandoned. And to make expansion even easier, the Bank Board in 1981 dropped the rule that had prohibited S&Ls from taking more than 5 percent of their total deposits from money brokers. Brokered funds in the old days had been considered supplementary, helping S&Ls take advantage of opportunities that came up when they were fully loaned. Such funds were not supposed to be part of the permanent deposit base: Either the S&L would carry out a growth plan that increased the amount of money available from its neighborhood (eliminating the need for more expensive brokered funds), or the loans financed from the brokers would be sold and the money used to pay off those depositors.

The All-Savers program of 1981, with its tax-exempt interest payments, clearly contemplated a greater inflow of brokered funds, and Pratt seized the chance to go whole hog, removing *all* limitations on deposits bought from money brokers. The Bank Board, general counsel Tom Vartanian wrote enthusiastically, had killed off "what must now be admitted to be an outdated bias that consumer deposits would always be the most stable, reliable and cheapest source of depository funds."[9]

The Federal Home Loan Bank of San Francisco did some calculations in the mid-1980s and demonstrated that with a $2 million investment, a man with an S&L charter could grow his institution to $1.3 billion in deposits over five years without violating the capital requirements. Any self-proclaimed venture capitalist who got his hands on a state S&L charter with wide investment powers (and California's Taggart gave out 210 of them in a year and a half) could get the use of $99.85 of other people's money for every 15 cents he put in himself. And he could get it cheaply, because government insurance guaranteed his depositors that every penny they put in would be repaid, with the advertised interest. This was quite an attractive offer; enterprising law firms held seminars up and down the state of California, drumming up business for Taggart's office. Because state-chartered S&Ls were permitted to contribute to political candidates, the legislature was deeply enthusiastic. "Lowering the capital standards," Pratt says, nodding briskly, "did allow the problems to increase. No question about it."

Three other deceptions relating to the measurement of net worth multiplied the industry's losses. The most prominent was the intrusion of supervisory goodwill as a balance-sheet asset, to enable the Bank Board to organize mergers so that two sick thrifts would look healthy when joined together. On the theory that businessmen are rational, accountants setting up the books after one company purchases another assume that if the price paid is greater than the value of the net tangible assets acquired (in this case, the portfolio of loans and investments, the headquarters building, branch offices and telephones and safe deposit vaults, etc.), there must also be "intangible assets" that justify the deal. There is a brand name, a franchise, or a customer list—*something* that explains the buyer's willingness to pay a premium over what the visible assets of the thing are worth. The brand name or franchise will yield earnings in the future, just like a tangible asset, and is therefore a reasonable entry in the ledger. Like any other asset, it depreciates, which cuts down future taxes.

In California, William Crawford told the House Banking Committee, "the old law said that good will had very doubtful value and should not be reflected on the books of an association without the approval of the Commissioner. And with that approval, it should be written off over a relatively short period of time, no longer than five years."[10] The Federal Home Loan Bank Board had never been that tough, but to the extent that S&Ls were permitted to book goodwill following their acquisition of another S&L, the longest write-off period ever permitted before 1981 had been ten years. For commercial companies that aren't banks or S&Ls, the usual write-off period for goodwill is forty years.

Pratt again saw no reason why S&Ls should be discriminated against: in July 1982 the Bank Board ruled that S&Ls, too, could write off acquired goodwill over forty years. All by itself, this improved the chances that a merger would produce reported profits. Prior to July 1982, an acquiring S&L that booked $100 million in goodwill would have had to take a hit of $10 million a year; after July 1982, until the rules were changed, that cost would be only $2.5 million a year. Pratt says that the heavy hitters in California, the Great Westerns and Worlds and Home Federals that are now so conservative, wanted even more generous provisions for goodwill if they were to acquire some of the garbage the Bank Board wanted them to buy: "They wanted goodwill on the public utility model, with all the write-offs falling in the later part of the forty years."

In double-entry bookkeeping, every asset must be matched with a liability. Goodwill on the asset side became "supervisory goodwill," counted as part of capital on the liability side. If the required capital ratio is 3 percent, each dollar of supervisory goodwill permits the S&L that has it to carry thirty-three dollars in assets (which are funded with the deposits the government insures). Thus the spectacle, quite common in 1983, of the merger of two insolvent S&Ls that show enough "capital" after the merger to support a great burst of growth.

Some of this goodwill was undoubtedly legitimate. At a time when brokered deposits cost 14 percent and CDs were going at 12 percent, access to money from passbook accounts that paid only 5¼ percent had cash value. "If you remember back to '79, '80, '81," says Walter Schuetze, an older man with thin gray hair and almost rimless glasses who is the accounting theoretician for KMG Peat Marwick, "the folks in California were acquiring S&Ls in Illinois and Florida, leapfrogging state lines, which they hadn't previously been able to do. That was a good, bona fide asset. It was a cheap way to get deposits, instantaneously. Back in '79, the premium on core deposits got to 6 percent [i.e., access to a million dollars' worth of passbook accounts paying 5¼ percent was selling for $60,000]. I thought those were good assets."

The problem was that many of these mergers were not economically rational. Despite its access to cheap passbook account deposits, the S&L that was being acquired was losing, not making, money on its franchise and brand name and branches. The more money the institution was losing, the greater the gap between the book value of its assets and the market value that was the true measure of what the purchaser had bought—and thus the larger the goodwill item on both sides of the ledger. This was intuitively crazy: not even Dick Pratt could argue seriously that the franchise value of an S&L that was losing more money and was farther under water should be greater than the franchise value of an S&L that was just a little worse than breaking even and was within reaching distance of positive net worth. But that's what the books showed. Not surprisingly, the mergers that produced the greatest quantity of supervisory goodwill also produced the biggest failures and the greatest cost to the insurance fund, a few years down the road.

Guided by the Financial Accounting Standards Board (FASB), an independent body we shall visit later, the SEC refused to permit publicly traded S&Ls to write down goodwill on the forty-year schedule Pratt and the Bank Board had approved. The compromise Pratt was able to work out with SEC chairman John Shad gave the purchaser a maximum of twenty-five years in which to pay out any such item through the profits the goodwill was supposed to generate. The FASB was still unhappy—"though I'm not sure there's any theoretical justification for what we did," says board member James Leisenring—and eventually issued an opinion requiring purchasers of S&Ls to write down their goodwill over a period of time matching the duration of the assets acquired by the purchase. (Home mortgages, for example, are estimated to last on the average twelve years; if the goodwill on the books was derived from the low market value of low-rate mortgages in a high-rate year, the acquirer would have to write it off over twelve years.) The argument was that what gave the goodwill validity was that good assets—and something more than 98 percent of home mortgages are good assets—will in fact pay their principal in full. So whatever losses may appear in the books, because the purchaser must write the assets he is buying down to their market value, will be recovered automatically over time if the loans are held to maturity.

Keeping the books on a forty-year goodwill basis legitimates fraud, because after twelve years, when the mortgages have been paid in full, 70 percent of the goodwill survives on the asset side of the ledger. Even on a twelve-year basis, amortizing goodwill can produce misleading reports of a thrift's financial condition. If interest rates fall, which means the mortgages in the portfolio rise in market value, the purchasing S&L can sell the paper and pay out the profits as dividends to its owners, rather than using this money (as it should) to wipe out the goodwill created by the fact that on the day they were acquired the market value of the paper was below its face value. Then when the interest rates turn up again—as they did in 1984–85, 1987, and 1988–89—the S&L goes right back into the tank, at the expense of the U.S. taxpayer. The fact is that Pratt structured a situation, which his successors at the Bank Board mostly maintained, where the purchaser of a sick S&L was virtually guaranteed a profit he could pocket and was protected against any loss. The insurance fund could never climb out of the hole. Every time the interest-rate cycle went into its climbing phase the hole automatically got deeper. And the profits that were reported, even by large and reputable companies like Great Western, First Nationwide, Home Savings, and Citicorp, were in part fictitious.

Worse yet was a regulation adopted in November 1982 permitting S&Ls to credit themselves with "appraised equity capital." An S&L that owned commercial property, as increasing fractions did, either through foreclosure or because some important states permitted direct investment of S&L deposits, could credit itself with any increase in the appraised value of that property and take that credit into capital. Given the low professional and moral state of real estate appraisal, this rule was a direct invitation to cheating. In "daisy-chain" situations, where a number of S&Ls worked together (Empire, Alamo, Vernon, Sunbelt in Texas; Lincoln, Centrust, Imperial, Western of Dallas, and San Jacinto in Milkenland), it was child's play to trade land parcels and securities back and forth (incurring no tax liability, for the trade of like assets did not create taxable gain) at prices that apparently grew and grew. Such trades generated their own fake profits and gave appraisers whose main tool was the recent sales prices of comparable property an excuse to rocket up appraised values of all the land in that neighborhood. Then the S&Ls could peddle new deposits through money brokers or on the phone without violating capital restrictions. It should be remembered that each dollar of new capital created by reappraising owned property permitted an S&L to raise thirty-three dollars from the public in deposits the government insured.

As time went on, increasing numbers of thrift owners, especially in Texas, credited themselves with the increased value of the property they owned and took the supposed "profits" out in dividends, bonuses or perks. (There was never any problem about getting cash dividends for noncash profits; all you had to do was sell more certificates of deposit.) Later, after the bubble had burst, similar procedures could be followed, and were, to avoid recognizing losses in owned property. In Texas these procedures, developed originally to protect the value of bad loans, were called "trading the dead horse for the dead cow."

[5]

The most dishonest and in the end devastating of all the ways the S&Ls were encouraged to lie about their condition was "loss deferral," which the Bank Board approved in September 1981 and expanded in May 1982. Under the terms of the Board's "Memorandum R-49," S&Ls were permitted—nay, encouraged —to sell loans on which they showed a loss. Having done so, they could take the loss for tax purposes, writing down previous years' profits and claiming credit for overpayment of taxes (such raids on the public purse having been approved in the Reagan tax law passed in August). But for purposes of regulatory accounting, they would not have to take the hit against this year's profits. Instead, they could write off the loss over the life of the loan.

In the beginning, the most common tactic was to exchange mortgages for Fannie Mae or Freddie Mac pass-through paper with a comparable market value. Prior to the exchange, the mortgages were valued at their cost; after the exchange, by generally accepted accounting principles (GAAP), the FNMA paper should have been valued at market. In presenting its condition to the public, however, the Bank Board permitted the seller to present the acquired asset as though its cost had been the same as the asset for which it was swapped, less a straight-line depreciation over the life of the original loan. The IRS rebelled against this deception and denied some $1.5 billion of tax credits; and the question went to court, where, in late 1989, the S&Ls won. "The admitted objective of Memorandum R-49," federal appeals court judge Jerre S. Williams wrote, "was to allow S&Ls to engage in transactions which would allow them to realize their losses on mortgage loans for federal income-tax purposes, but which would not be treated as giving rise to losses for regulatory accounting purposes."[11] Still, Judge Williams ruled (not finally, of course; the case will doubtless be on appeal somewhere well into the 1990s), the losses were real, and the Bank Board's accounting fantasies did not alter that fact, so the S&Ls were entitled to their tax credits.

At most S&Ls the opportunities presented by the new regulation were seized in a straightforward way: Mortgages were packaged into mortgage-based securities and sold into the market at a loss, which the Bank Board permitted the thrifts to amortize over the life of the loan. And the new accounting rule cast an immense and ever-darkening shadow forward, because it was the instrument by which the investment bankers and the traders wedged their way into the thrift industry.

Herbert Sandler, a balding, eggheaded, tall, athletic transplanted New Yorker who, with his wife, Marion, runs the $13 billion World Savings in Oakland, California, vividly remembers what happened. "The tin men," he says, affecting the accents of a movie con man while making reference to the movie about aluminum-siding salesmen, "came out of Wall Street. They said, 'Pssst. You dere, you with da S&L. Yer in trouble, yer board's upset, because yer showin' a loss, you got too many low-yield mortgages. But we can package doze mortgages for you into mortgage-backed securities, and we can sell doze securities, and you won't even have to show a loss onna sale. Then we can take all da money you get from da sale and put it into some high-yield paper we're underwriting, and yer gonna be a hero—yer gonna show a profit.' And," Sandler adds in his own voice, "everybody took those deals." Under the new rules, the ambitious S&L operator could buy loans other than mortgages, and junk bonds were loans. Among those who took the invitation offered by the Bank Board's approval of loss deferral was "the candy man" (to use the label pinned on him by Robert Monks of Institutional Shareholders Services): Michael Milken of Drexel Burnham Lambert.

Though he managed to get a green light for loss deferral from a "task force" of accountants put together by the Federal Home Loan Bank of Little Rock (Peat Marwick's Schuetze was part of the task force), Pratt was afraid that the accounting profession would sabotage his new rule, and he made a pilgrimage to Stamford, Connecticut, where the FASB had a parklike monastery. There the seven senior philosophers of accounting and some dozens of "practice fellows" in their twenties and thirties (accounting's equivalent of the Supreme Court clerks) labored over dilemmas brought to their attention by the AICPA or the SEC. The chairman of the board then was Donald Kirk, a handsome, soft-spoken, rather patriarchal figure with a neatly trimmed beard who has since moved on to be a professor at the Columbia University Business School. The first request Pratt presented to Kirk was whether the FASB, which was supposed to do its work in the light of day, could meet secretly with anyone. The decision came down that if a government agency asked for a private meeting, the charter of the board would permit it. Typically, Pratt came alone. Jim Leisenring, then new at the FASB and the chairman of its Auditing Standards Board, remembers his presentation of the desperate condition of the industry and his insistence on the need for loss deferral. "Do you," Pratt said in peroration, looking around at the directors, "want the demise of this industry on your conscience?"

Kirk sighed at the recollection: "You have to have sympathy —at least tolerance—for the pleas of federal regulators when they call for public policy. But the greater danger is that the auditing committee will become sympathetic to the industry. Main, Herdman wrote a pamphlet that was a rationalization for the loss-deferral approach. I remember talking to the senior man and saying, 'How can you justify this?' People have criticized 'historic cost accounting' [carrying a loan on the books as worth whatever the borrower owes, regardless of the current market value of that loan if it had to be sold]. Taking that custom the next step forward, and carrying a loan at face value even *after* you sell it—you've destroyed the rationale [which was that these loans held to maturity would be paid back at par]."

In the end, Kirk says, "FASB took the position, 'You can be tolerant, but stop monkeying with the balance sheet.' If you want to set capital requirements at one percent, or minus one percent, do it. You have the legal right to do it, but stop concealing the condition of the institution." Pratt went ahead, anyway, and it turned out that if a client paid an auditor enough money, the auditor was quite willing to do lots of things the FASB condemned. As of spring 1990, the FDIC had suits in the millions of dollars filed and pending against Ernst & Young, Touche Ross, Deloitte Haskins & Sells, Grant Thornton, and Coopers & Lybrand, claiming damages to the government insurance funds from fraudulent accounting practice. The suit against Ernst & Young, for its audits of Western Savings of Dallas by the then separate Arthur Young & Company, alleges that the S&L was insolvent in 1984 by $100 million and in 1985 by $200 million. But it was permitted to keep growing to a total size of $2 billion in assets, $1 billion of which turned out to be worthless, because Young "grossly overstated and inflated estimates of the thrift's financial condition and operations."[12]

Even insiders in the S&L disaster have little sense of how much damage was done by the consequent eruption of Wall Street into the little world of the S&Ls. The debilitation of the industry is in large part the result of its contact with a more intelligent, more sophisticated, more amnesiac, more mechanical, more predatory form of life. It was like the Indian tribes when the white settler brought them measles. A real estate developer in Dallas describes the scene: "When the salesmen from Wall Street worked over the S&Ls here, it was like rocket scientists selling to drivers of Conestoga wagons. And all around the encampment were the regulators, scratching their heads and wondering how the wagon drivers had managed to get those blocks of wood so they could roll." I myself gave a talk in 1987 to a convention of the Florida League of Financial Institutions in one of the Disney World convention hotels in Orlando. Immediately before me was a kid from Salomon, touting the liquidity, yield, and inherent safety of the collateralized mortgage obligations his firm packaged. I noted apologetically as I began—he was polite enough to stay to hear me, and the grin on his face never changed—that the chief trader of this stuff for Merrill Lynch, an alumnus of the Salomon shop, had just lost his employer $375 million dealing in these pieces of paper, so they couldn't really be entirely safe.

There was a lot of prestige on the other side; almost without exception the professors of finance acclaimed these instruments and their hedging capacity—the protection they offered against interest-rate swings. A friend of mine on Wall Street was at a social occasion with a director of Gibraltar of Texas who bragged all night about what wonderful advice Salomon was giving them. But

Salomon was selling the S&Ls these bonds and segmented pieces of the bonds from its own inventory; there was no way the price Gibraltar was paying could be below the market price. And since this market has no ticker tape, no public record of trades (indeed, no workable clearing system, so that every trade is hermetically sealed between the parties), there was plenty of opportunity for Salomon or its fellows to remain heroes to their customers even as they charged considerably more than the market price, or paid considerably less.

Still, the way Pratt had structured the regulatory accounting system for S&Ls, the amateurs had reason to be happy. Banks had always made some of their money trading bonds or foreign exchange, and it was an understood, gentlemen's agreement, which could have the force of law if an intelligent examiner caught you violating it, that these trading accounts would be kept separate from the bank's investment accounts. This required a certain amount of intestinal fortitude and idealism when the trading account showed a loss, because there was, after all, no visible difference between the ten-year Treasury bond carried at par in the bank's investment portfolio and the ten-year Treasury bond that had to be carried at market in the trading account. But the bank examiners looked for evidence of switching between the portfolio and the account, and different people were involved in handling the two.

At the S&Ls, it was all one. Alfred Politz once observed of political polling that if you have the intelligence of a dime you will get it right half the time. Even the worst traders will once in a while buy something that goes up. As S&L accounting was done, such winners could be sold at a profit that the owners could take home as dividends, while the losers could be buried in the portfolio "at historic cost," the price that had been paid for them, even though they were now worth less, and sometimes much less. Charles Knapp of Financial Corporation of America (FCA) used this accounting freedom to report remarkable profits while building up hundreds of millions of dollars of unrecognized losses in the investment portfolio. It was the first rumblings from the SEC about the invention of profits at FCA that triggered the run Ed

Gray tried to stanch with brokered funds from Merrill, as noted previously.

The irrepressible Taggart, who later went to work for Knapp, said the run came because the regulators were picking on him. Among the holdings the examiners had insisted on valuing at market instead of historic cost were millions of shares of American Express, Merrill Lynch, and Disney. "They are sizable chunks that you put around when you are that large," Taggart told the House Banking Committee, complaining that if the regulators had not forced Knapp to value those stocks at market price, he could have held on to them long enough to make a whopping profit. He did not give any explanation of why he thought that S&Ls alone in all the world should be allowed to carry such inventories of securities at cost rather than at what is, after all, a daily price in a liquid market.

But these things were normal in the mid-eighties. "From 1983 to 1986," Pratt says without passing judgment, "more than one hundred percent of the earnings of thrifts came from nonrecurring items"—i.e., sales of paper or property that showed a profit. All the junk bond customers were in this game. Some did it on a larger scale; some did it on a smaller scale.

"[Lewis] Ranieri's sales force," Michael Lewis wrote about the Salomon Brothers mortgage bond operation, "persuaded the thrift managers to trade their bonds actively. A good salesman could transform a shy, nervous thrift president into a maniacal gambler. Formerly sleepy thrifts became some of the biggest swingers in the bond markets. . . . Salomon trader Mark Freed recalls a visit he paid on a large California thrift manager who had been overexposed to Wall Street influence. Freed actually tried to convince the thrift manager to calm down, to take fewer outright gambles on the market, to reduce the size of his positions, and instead hedge his bets in the bond market. 'You know what he told me,' says Freed, 'he said hedging was for sissies.' "[13] Lewis, who saw the story only from the Wall Street side, does not realize that this was perfectly rational behavior by a thrift president. He didn't have to worry about his losses, because by Pratt's regulatory accounting principles he didn't have to show them (and he couldn't run out of liquidity so long as he had a deposit insurance franchise); in the meantime, he could pocket his winnings.

Half a dozen years later, this game was still being played. Early in 1990 the government seized Florida's $12 billion Centrust, one of the nation's biggest purchasers of junk bonds from Mike Milken and Drexel Burnham. Its CEO, David Paul, was a homebuilder who had originally capitalized this thrift in part with properties he would have been hard put to sell for the price at which they were appraised, and in part with his yacht, which he continued to use. Paul was among the highest of high lifers, with a gold-leaf-inlay ceiling in his Miami office, an apartment in New York's Hotel Carlyle (President Kennedy's favorite) paid for by Centrust, and an art collection also paid for by Centrust, though the best pieces were kept in his home. (After all, he entertained customers there.) The art included a $13.2 million Rubens, *Portrait of a Man as Mars*, which Centrust purchased through Sotheby's. The Rubens provoked scorn and laughter from some *Wall Street Journal* reporters, who had been told by art dealer David Tunick that "with the Rubens he got absolutely taken to the cleaners."[14] In fact, according to art historian and appraiser Charles Scribner III, who looked at the canvas for the state of Florida, Paul's was a "luminous Rubens," one of the master's greatest paintings, and probably the best investment Centrust ever made.

Though Centrust had bad assets of all kinds, it was the junk bonds that drew the most attention. Paul complained bitterly that the government had no right to make him take losses on Centrust's junk bonds, even though their market value was less than half what he had paid for them. For years, Deloitte Haskins & Sells had certified that he could keep valuing this paper on Centrust's books at its original price. In 1990, after the bailout bill had ordered that S&Ls dispose of their junk, Deloitte lost its appetite for such practices, but Price Waterhouse, which had decided to open a thrift-auditing section at just the wrong time, came jauntily in to give Paul his clean statement. He was truly furious at the government: How dare these low-paid bank examiners question the judgment of world-ranging, high-priced accountants?

When the FASB first issued its rule against forty-year depreciation periods for goodwill, somebody at the Bank Board complained to Floyd Norris of *Barron's*, "Of course, exaggerated profits are bad, but the resultant negative effects could be far worse. Failed banks cause more damage than inflated earnings."[15] Pratt himself wrote, just before leaving office in April 1983, that the "problems [at the S&Ls] "could have been handled with minimum losses to the insurance fund had FSLIC closed S&Ls when their net worth approached zero. However, such a policy would have resulted in the closing of every S&L in the country."[16] The builder/academic Ned Eichler commented, "The last sentence was patently false. Hundreds of associations had net worths of over 3 percent under GAAP accounting, and far more were at zero percent to 3 percent."[17]

Pratt's case may be a little stronger than Eichler admits, because stripped to their tangible net worth by the removal of some famous GAAP fig leaves, very nearly all the industry might have looked moribund. But half the S&Ls Pratt's agency insured were doomed to go under in the next decade despite one of the longest runs of apparent prosperity the nation has ever known and interest rates that were from one-third to one-half lower than those of the previous two years. And they were doomed *by the accounting procedures Pratt instituted.* They were going to lose money every year, almost no matter what happened around them, because an ever-increasing portion of their asset portfolio, valued according to the new regulatory accounting principles, did not and could not yield a return. Securities that have already been sold pay no interest, and revalued property pays no more rent than it did before the appraisers said it was worth more. Losses would continue to accumulate and be hidden until the industry imploded. "Unless current accounting rules are drastically revamped," Jonathan Gray wrote in his report to the FDIC in early 1989, "the safety of insured deposits can never be secured. If it is possible to show a profit when you have a loss, the illusory profit can be paid out as a dividend, and the cash flow obtained from deposit growth."[18]

Unfortunately, Pratt by temperament, political conviction, and political convenience believed that the thrifts could—indeed, had to, because there was no other way—grow out of their dilemma.

He pushed them toward endless growth. Edward J. Kane of Ohio State has pointed out that the stock market liked this strategy: "[M]anagers and stockholders in zombie and near-zombie thrifts benefit from the placing of funds into risky loans and investments . . . because taking on these risks increases the aggregate market value of FSLIC's guarantees. . . . Typically, the price of a zombie firm's stock jumps in the months immediately after . . . adopting an investment strategy of doubling up and going for broke."[19]

And that was, of course, the criterion the Reagan administration valued most highly: An increase in the price of the stock meant that the market had blessed the strategy. It never occurred to Pratt to look back or to think like Kane that what the market rewarded was not the increased economic value of the firm but the increased value of the taxpayers' guarantee of the deposits, which allowed an S&L to undertake, at a relatively low cost of funds, risky ventures that would be very expensive to fund on any other basis.

Federal judge Jack B. Weinstein, chief judge of the Eastern District of New York (from the East River out to the end of Long Island), let himself go commenting on the habits Pratt instilled in the people who worked at the Bank Board. He was conducting a nonjury criminal trial of Carl Cardascia, president of Flushing Federal Savings & Loan, which failed in 1986 after blowing a lot of money in loans to someone who was trying to refurbish the Gotham Hotel on New York's Fifth Avenue. There was good evidence that Cardascia's relations with the refurbisher were something closer than arm's length, but Judge Weinstein released the defendant, anyway, because, he said, the Bank Board itself had encouraged Flushing Federal to take extravagant risks with its depositors' money as the only way to stop its losses. "That doesn't condone criminal and incompetent activity," Judge Weinstein said. "But Congress and the Home Loan Bank Board are directly responsible for what happened here. The government, in removing adequate controls over this bank, led to the activities now complained of. . . ."[20] Cardascia was then tried again, for another piece of crookedness, and convicted, and this time Weinstein let the conviction stand.

General counsel Tom Vartanian of the Bank Board had seen it all in such a different way. Writing an introduction to a book in 1983 about the new Garn-St Germain Act, Vartanian acclaimed "a well-designed system of regulatory changes" that assured that "this industry will have the regulatory tools to once again go with the flow of the trend in financial delivery systems and attain profitability. Whether they realize it or utilize the tools they have is up to each institution, but each and every federal savings and loan association clearly has the opportunity to become 'a lean, mean financial machine.' "[21]

[6]

To this day, Pratt insists that there was no choice. The nation was in deep recession in 1981 and 1982, the worst since World War II. Closing down scads of S&Ls, paying their depositors, and selling their assets would have reduced the supply of funds for housing, scared the pants off Main Street, and made the recession much worse. And in this case, honest market-to-market accounting might be misleading. When interest rates fell—and they had to fall someday, or the industrial economy would be as broke as the S&Ls—the market would automatically lift the value accorded to fixed-yield assets now punished in their pricing by the plunging value of money. "There was," Pratt says today, "clearly a strategy of believing the cycle would turn, and when the prime rate came down they'd be all right." Finally, Pratt had been hired to do what elected officials wanted him to do. Neither the president nor Congress wanted him to lay waste the S&L industry.

If you couldn't slay the dragon, Pratt decided, you had to feed him. But that was false, and demonstrably so. There is what the scientists call an existence theorem in the story of the mutual savings banks (MSBs, as distinct from S&Ls), which for historical reasons were insured not by the FSLIC but by the FDIC. They were in worse condition than the S&Ls coming into the eighties. The FDIC successfully shrank them, consolidated them, and for the most part put them on their feet to walk by themselves. The cost of this rescue and recapitalization was about $2 billion. In

1980, S&Ls as a group had something like four times as much money as the grouping of MSBs. Following the procedures adopted by the FDIC in dealing with the savings-bank crisis rather than the procedures actually followed by the FSLIC would have saved the taxpayer several hundred billion dollars.

The credit for the effective management of the MSB crises of 1981–83 must go mostly to FDIC chairman William Isaac, physically not very different from Pratt, though on a smaller scale, also a small-town boy (from Bryan, Ohio) and just as ideological (he made a speech during his tenure at the FDIC calling for an end to *all* bank legislation), but not quite so opinionated. His industry was different and his organization was different, but the important thing was that his principles were different, and for the most part he lived by them. He was under pressure from the administration and from most academic economists to endorse Pratt's growth policy, and he wouldn't. He gives credit first to his director of supervision, James Sexton, who put a memo on his desk early on, arguing that one bank might grow out of it, two banks might grow out of it, four banks might grow out of it—but the industry as a whole could not possibly grow out of it. "There's only so much good business out there," Sexton said. Requiring that they do grow and grow, Sexton wrote—eight years before Judge Weinstein's comments—would lead them into ever-riskier investments and eventually down the sinkhole at much greater cost to the insurance fund and everybody else.

MSBs were state-chartered institutions, mostly in the New England and Middle Atlantic states. They had been around a long time; many had charters dating back to the nineteenth century. They were conservatively run, with less concentration in the mortgages that had proved so dangerous in the debt deflation of 1930–31. Though they paid "dividends" rather than interest in deference to their mutual status, money in an MSB was legally a "deposit," and when Congress decided to insure bank deposits, it made the state-chartered mutuals eligible for coverage by the FDIC. There wasn't much risk: Before 1981 the FDIC had handled failures at only two MSBs.

They enjoyed powers that varied from state to state. In New

York, MSBs could underwrite life insurance, and in the state of Washington they could operate a brokerage house. Most of them could hold corporate as well as U.S. government debt securities, and Massachusetts permitted some equity investment. Massachusetts had its own insurance fund that was in fact better capitalized than the FDIC itself, and the existence of this separate fund had played a role in the deregulation of banking in the 1970s. Because the law that prohibited the payment of interest on demand deposits was in the Federal Deposit Insurance Act and the Massachusetts MSBs had no relations with the FDIC, a Worcester, Massachusetts, savings bank run by a refugee from Citibank was able to offer the first interest-bearing checking account, later imitated across the country (including the name negotiable order of withdrawal, or NOW) and approved by Congress for all banks and S&Ls in 1980. If MSBs were "qualified thrift lenders," meaning that they had at least 60% of their assets in U.S. Treasury paper and in mortgages on one- to four-family homes, MSBs could be members of their district Federal Home Loan Bank and get inexpensive funds by borrowing there.

Partly because of their heavy holdings of government bonds, MSBs were less profitable than S&Ls. Their peak-earnings year in the period 1960–80 was 1978, when the Carter administration was driving down interest rates. That peak came at fifty-eight "basis points" (0.58 percent of assets; a "basis point" is one one-hundredth of a percentage point). S&Ls that year earned eighty-four basis points. In 1980, while the S&Ls as a group were still marginally profitable, MSBs were losing money, and things were getting worse by the minute.[22] In both 1981 and 1982, both groups lost, but the MSBs were much worse off in proportion to their assets. By 1986, after the FDIC had done its work—and despite the more honest accounting standards the FDIC had imposed on them—mutuals were much more profitable. That year, mutuals averaged earnings of 107 basis points on assets as against a derisory 1 basis-point return at the S&Ls.[23]

New York City was the worst off in 1981, for New York State had a "usury ceiling" limiting the interest that could be paid on home mortgages. This meant that the New York savings banks had pretty much stopped writing home mortgages (a source of reduced earnings, because mortgages paid interest rates more than two percentage points greater than the rates paid on Treasury bonds). And *this* meant that MSBs had a desperate problem that S&Ls in 1981 did not have: liquidity. Mortgages, on the average, return a cash flow of 1 percent a month from the repayment of principal, money that is available for reinvestment or, if necessary, the repayment of deposits. Should even a fairly small fraction of the depositors in an MSB come round for their money— and with money market mutual fund rates a good deal higher than what the average MSB depositor was earning, that was a reasonable prospect—the bank would not be able to repay them without selling parts of its investment portfolio. And those sales would be at a horrendous loss. The banks had mostly bought bonds that would not mature for many years, because those were the bonds that paid the highest interest. They forgot or ignored the fact that when interest rates rise, the long bonds drop farthest in price. "The average maturity on the portfolio at the New York Bank for Savings," Isaac recalls with a shudder, "was twenty-five years."

I myself got an epiphanous moment from these problems in the fall of 1979, when I was working on a study of banking for the Twentieth Century Fund. John Heimann, then Comptroller of the Currency (the chief regulator of nationally chartered banks), was a friend of almost thirty years' standing, and we talked about the liquidity menace at the New York MSBs, which he knew well from his two years as New York State Commissioner of Banking. Later that day I spent an hour with Sen. Daniel Patrick Moynihan, also an old friend, and he asked me in a senatorial way what I thought he and his colleagues should be doing that they weren't doing. I told him that the New York City savings banks were in bad trouble and something would have to be done.

Such as?

Well, one step might be to see if some other bank would buy into the problem. In those days, banks were not allowed to go across state lines to buy other banks or start branches, and some strong institutions elsewhere in the country might take the worst-afflicted savings banks off the regulators' hands to get access to New York, if Congress would give them a go-ahead.

How would one do that?

Well, talk to Heimann. He has a draft of legislation in his desk drawer, waiting for someone to introduce it.

Good idea, Martin.

(More discussion.)

Good idea. Could you do me a favor?

Sure.

When you get back to New York, could you ask around and find out who'd be *against* it?

And that, of course, is the real world of politics. No criticism of Senator Moynihan intended, but the truth is that when push comes to shove, the question of whether an idea is sound and useful matters less than the question of whether it would rouse truly dedicated opposition. This is not the least of the reasons why the S&L losses exponentiated to their monstrous size.

About six months later, in April 1980, Moynihan, as the head of a group of ten senators from states that chartered MSBs, did make a suggestion to the Federal Financial Institutions Examination Council (FFIEC). The suggestion, alas, was not an end to geographically segregated banking but the adoption of accounting rules that could permit mutuals to sell assets at a loss and amortize the losses over many years. Heimann, as chairman of the FFIEC, sent back a more or less courteous rejection: "The deferral of realized losses would result in an artificial inflation of reported earnings and overstate the amount of capital available to absorb future losses and prevent insolvency."[24] Eighteen months after that letter, with Heimann gone and the FFIEC looking the other way, Pratt put such a rule into effect for the S&Ls. More than any other single action by the Bank Board, this approval of accounting rules that Isaac and Heimann had sensibly rejected made the collapse of the industry inevitable.

Bill Isaac was a Carter appointee to the FDIC, the obligatory Republican on the three-man board. (Heimann, incidentally, was one of the other board members: by statute, the comptroller sits on the board of the FDIC.) Isaac had been a bank lawyer in

Kentucky, which then had a Republican senator on good terms with the president, and he had been of some help to regulators picking their way through the smoking and dangerous ruins of a drug-related bank in Miami with unnecessarily close relations to Kentucky. In mid-1980, Isaac went to Acting Chairman Irvine H. Sprague with his concerns about the MSBs, especially those in New York, and Sprague set up a task force with Isaac at its head. The task force worked from December 1980 to September 1981, by which time President Reagan had appointed Isaac chairman of the FDIC. The basic report, never published, was about 50 pages long, buttressed with more than 100 supporting documents. It established both the factual background and the policy guidelines for what the FDIC would do with the MSBs in the next two years.

Isaac described these guidelines and their development in a speech to the Annual Conference of the National Association of Mutual Savings Banks in Atlanta in May 1982: "We have had two principal goals," he said. "The first has been to resolve the problems of the failing institution at a reasonable cost to the insurance fund without raising public concern about a large bank failure. Our second goal has been to insure that the resulting institution is financially sound and has the ability to compete effectively in its market and . . . serve the credit needs of its community free of excessive government control. . . . Early on we considered various accounting and other techniques which might have allowed us to defer facing up to the problem. We rejected these approaches. We concluded that the problems in the savings bank industry were real and could only be corrected through real solutions. Paper solutions could only leave behind a debilitated industry for perhaps decades to come."[25]

Isaac told his examiners to apply GAAP and to count only tangible assets. The rule was that no institution with less than 5 percent net worth on that measurement would be allowed to grow beyond the normal accretion of interest on customer accounts, no institution with less than 1 percent net worth would be allowed to grow at all, and any institution with less than zero net worth would be shut down or sold off. And a corollary held that when an institution was sold with FDIC help, *all* its senior officers and directors were to be out on the street. "Controversial in the industry," said a *Wall Street Journal* story, "is Mr. Isaac's 'throw the bums out' policy."[26]

The National Association of Mutual Savings Banks commissioned a study by Wharton Econometrics that blasted the FDIC approach and recommended instead a collection of "cost-free accounting solutions" not unlike what the Bank Board was doing, plus a "mortgage warehouse" program under which the FDIC itself would buy from the savings banks, at par, enough of their low-rate mortgages to fill their cash needs and relieve them of liquidity concerns. If the FDIC continued on its present path, Wharton warned, the cost of the rescues would reach $20.3 billion in three years, and the insurance fund had total resources of only a little more than $12 billion. Isaac savaged the study in his speech for stressing "underlying macroeconomic assumptions and methodology" while ignoring "projected asset yields, funding costs, deposit growth and portfolio structure."

The first savings bank to be rescued was New York's Greenwich, in November 1981. This was costly—a cash infusion of 17 percent of the bank's deposits was necessary to make it salable—and messy. Laura Gross, a reporter for *American Banker*, had got wind of something about to happen and called Isaac for information. His secretary said he was out of town, and Ms. Gross decided that meant New York. She called around to various hotels and found a "Mr. Isaac" and other people from the FDIC registered at the new Vista Hotel in the World Trade Center. She got herself a clipboard and a pad and went up to the floor where the hotel told her the FDIC was holding a closed meeting. As people got out of the elevator, she asked them whether they were there for the FDIC meeting, and when they said they were, she asked which bank they represented, noted the name on her pad, and then told them the room to which they should go. The next day, *American Banker* had a story with the names of all the banks that were being solicited to bid for the Greenwich. The bank lost half a billion dollars in deposits in a matter of days, and the rescue had to be expedited.

All told, Isaac's FDIC did ten savings-bank rescues between November 1981 and the spring of 1984, at costs that ran fairly steadily down. The sale of what had once been the largest in New York, the Bowery Savings Bank, was to a syndicate of investors headed by the former builder and later mayoral candidate Richard Ravitch; Larry Tisch, of Loew's Hotels and later CBS; and the Millstein Brothers, who had created the conglomerate that owned Standard Brands. Bowery's basic problem was a portfolio of very-long-term U.S. Treasuries and mortgage bonds. ("A pile of shit Salomon had sold them," says a man who was in a position to know.) By the terms of Ravitch's deal, the FDIC had to guarantee the new owners of Bowery against any further losses on that portfolio but would receive a piece of any improvement in its value. The cash infusion was $100 million from Ravitch and friends and $300 million from the FDIC.

Three years later, after Ravitch had cut the bank's employment roster and expenses by about one-third, Bowery was sold to the Los Angeles–based Home Savings of America, the second-largest S&L in the country, for $200 million, which Ravitch and his partners kept. The consultant Bert Ely says that the organization of the thrift bailout under the 1989 FIRREA Act has been impeded by "the bureaucratic fear of doing another deal akin to the Bowery Savings transaction. . . ."[27] But Isaac feels no regrets whatever. Ravitch and his colleagues managed the portfolio cleverly, selling whenever interest rates fell enough to boost the price of fixed-rate bonds; the rising tide floated not only the boats but much of Salomon's shit. The FDIC's share of the proceeds paid back half its initial investment in the deal. Bowery is not only back on a sound footing but safeguarded against future troubles by the deepest pockets and arguably the best management in the S&L industry. The advertising for the bank, still featuring Joe Di-Maggio, does not mention that this grand old New York institution is now owned by Californians.

The FDIC under Isaac missed a few and did some of its business with Jacks who thought they could grow financial beanstalks. Buffalo Savings, with FDIC assistance, absorbed New York City's Union Dime and New York Bank for Savings as well as Buffalo's own Western New York Savings, changed its name to Goldome, and went into various businesses its top management (who were Merrill Lynch alumni) did not understand, including direct investment in real estate. Lawyers for the other New York City MSBs protested an FDIC assistance deal that protected Goldome against *additional* losses in its downstate division. "Buffalo," said a Rogers & Wells letter of opinion, "has been given an unfair competitive advantage [by an] operations subsidy that makes the FDIC a business partner of Buffalo for 15 years."[28] Another mistake was made in Philadelphia, where the Philadelphia Savings Fund Society (PSFS) moved to a phase of aggressive expansion and ultimate decline after absorbing the Western Savings Fund Society. But New York State law in those days prohibited the placement of more than 5 percent of assets in direct investment, which kept Goldome's losses to size, and the PSFS, among the strongest of mutual savings banks, had moved to joint-stock ownership in a way that protected the insurance corporation from serious loss. And the FDIC purchases were done without much accounting gimmickry.

Things got a little hairy later, after New York State changed its law in 1986 to broaden considerably the direct investment powers of both commercial banks and savings banks. Governor Cuomo was desperate to hang on to the banking business, and the banks were big contributors to legislators' campaign committees. (People pick on California and Texas, but the New York State legislature is almost as bad in terms of the favors it will do for the financial-services industry, and it always has been; in the nineteenth century, Elihu Root, a state senator, complained of the "black horse brigade" of lobbyists who came riding up to Albany every spring.) Seaman's Bank for Savings under FDIC auspices was permitted to run a shop that used insured deposits to take speculative positions in exotic mortgage-backed securities and had to be rescued in 1989 under unfavorable conditions. (In 1990, the rescued Seaman's was sold to Chase Manhattan Bank at a cost of about half a billion dollars to the FDIC.) And Goldome, under the new "liberalized" New York State banking law, dug itself deep in a pit with consequences that are still uncertain. By 1986 the FDIC was busy elsewhere and more permissive in general than it had been in Isaac's time. His successor, William Seidman, for example, has allowed what are in effect FDIC-owned banks to adopt high-growth strategies that will give *his* successor worse headaches than Isaac left him.

"I would fault the FSLIC for saying they didn't have enough money," Isaac said the other day, looking back on the difference between what he did with the savings banks and what Pratt and his successors did with the S&Ls. "We took the position that we would do deals the way they ought to be done. If that meant the FDIC went broke, we would go to the Congress and say, 'We're broke.' In the end, we didn't have to do that, but the Bank Board did. When you pretend that insolvent banks are not insolvent, you make the insurance fund insolvent, too."

CHAPTER 4

Congress Disconnects the Brakes

Only once in a lifetime do historic events occur that shape the future of an industry. In my opinion, in the thrift industry, that event occurred on October 15, 1982, when President Reagan signed into law the Garn-St Germain Depository Institutions Act of 1982.... The Act is a resounding testimonial to the deregulatory efforts of the Reagan Administration and to the progressive and enlightened philosophies of the Senate and House Banking Committees.... [It] attempt[s] to remove artificial regulatory constraints that have prevented thrift institutions from serving the public and profiting from that service to the greatest degree possible.... The possible contribution to thrift earnings that will be made by the new investment powers in Title III can be illustrated by examining the experience of state-chartered associations in Texas....

> —Thomas P. Vartanian, then general counsel to the Bank Board, now head of the banking group at the large law firm of Fried, Frank, Harris, Shriver & Jacobson (1983)

B ETWEEN the first housing legislation of the early depression days and, say, 1980, when campaigning for office became so abominably expensive, the banking committees of Congress were always by their own choice housing committees first of all. They had jurisdiction over both topics (the Senate Banking Committee also has jurisdiction over the securities business and the SEC), but what they wanted to do was housing. Housing was an area where a member of Congress could give goodies to voters as well as to builders. Banking was where the goodies went to lobbyists for big-city banks or country banks, to big or little S&Ls, to credit unions, or, in the Senate, to Wall Street investment firms. No voters. As these institutions had conflicting interests and didn't like each other, votes on banking issues were almost sure to get you in trouble with somebody. Voters were more important than contributors in Congress as late as the 1970s, though by then it was becoming a close call. What the S&Ls always wanted was to be identified with housing, not to get in the middle of the banking wars.

Moreover, what banks do touches closely one of the vital functions of government, for it is the lending activities of private bankers that create the money supply. The Constitution gives Congress "power to coin money [and] regulate the value thereof," and in the modern world money is mostly demand deposits in banks. It is not a function legislators wish to undertake, because they know in their hearts, as a German central banker once put it, that "every politician needs a central banker to hide behind once in a while." Wright Patman from Patman's Switch, Texas, who served forty-six years in the House of Representatives and was chairman of the House Banking Committee longer than anyone in history, liked to say that Congress had "farmed" its monetary powers to the Open Market Committee of the Federal Reserve Board. "It's a sham and a shame and a disgrace," he said in 1974, anticipating by fourteen years the complaints of journalist William Greider, "the way the Fed has secretly operated this country."[1]

Patman was a cherubic and cynical populist demagogue who winked at his country banker friends when he went out to rouse the animals on the campaign trail. And he was a lazy man, totally illiterate in economics, who thought that rolling back the interest rate savings banks and S&Ls could pay would help Americans buy homes. But in his deliberately primitive way he was much smarter than big-city bankers realized. He liked S&Ls more than he liked banks, and as long as he was chairman of the Banking Committee (until 1975), the S&Ls had a protector.

The 1960s were the era of S&L legislation. In 1964, S&Ls received authorization to invest some of their depositors' funds in their own "service corporations," which could conduct business operations prohibited to the S&L itself. In 1966 the Financial Institutions Supervisory Act imposed interest-rate ceilings on what federally insured S&Ls could pay for deposits but ordered the Federal Reserve, which set the ceilings, to let S&Ls pay a little more than banks. The same law gave the Federal Home Loan Bank Board, as the regulator of S&Ls, power to issue cease-and-desist orders to thrifts that had just flunked their exam. This was power the Bank Board of the 1980s was extremely reluctant to exercise, largely because the administrative procedures associated with it were intensely time-consuming and the varmint could sue, using insured deposits to pay for more and better lawyers than the Bank Board had.

In 1967 the S&L Holding Company Act permitted the ownership of S&Ls by nonfinancial commercial and industrial companies like Ford Motor, Sears Roebuck, and Berkshire Hathaway. In 1968 the Housing and Urban Development Act empowered S&Ls to accept "deposits" at contractual rates of interest rather than sell "shares" that projected interest earnings in the form of dividends but could not legally promise them. The same law authorized S&Ls to issue subordinated debt, borrowing for the first time by means other than savings accounts or advances from the home loan banks. A dozen years passed—the entire Nixon era and the first three years of the Carter presidency—before there was another law that significantly affected the S&Ls. Lots of studies but no law. Then the industry's sorrows came, not single spies but in battalions.

The genius of the Depository Institutions Deregulation and Monetary Control Act of 1980 (a Carter administration initiative) was its elimination of many of the old distinctions between institutions where people leave their money. Once there had been "banks," "savings banks," "savings and loans," and "credit unions." They were separately chartered, regulated, and empowered to perform different, though sometimes overlapping, functions. From now on, for many purposes, the law would treat all these organizations as a single set of "depository institutions." They would all have the right to offer interest-bearing checking accounts, and would have to keep reserves against them at a Federal Reserve Bank. They could all write residential mortgages and make consumer loans. The S&Ls got several things they badly wanted from the new legislation: State usury ceilings on mortgage loans were outlawed, federally chartered S&Ls were given statewide branching powers no matter what individual state laws might say, all geographic limits on S&L lending or service-company operations were dropped, and associations were given the power to put up to 20 percent of their assets in commercial loans and corporate-debt instruments.

But Congress, pressured by consumer advocates and a misguided housing lobby, continued its traditional refusal to approve variable-rate mortgages, and the S&Ls were losing one thing they cared about enormously: the interest-rate ceilings of the Fed's Reg Q, with the differential that let them pay a little more than banks. Some interest-rate controls would be kept under the new law, but only for a while. Congress instructed the bank, thrift, and credit-union regulators to work together to phase out all interest-rate ceilings over a maximum of six years.

The House and Senate bills were quite different, and the conference to reconcile them was quite contentious. Inflation had become a national preoccupation, and Federal Reserve Board chairman Paul Volcker was clearly willing to see interest rates go to historic highs. Rising interest rates meant big losses in the S&L portfolio if anybody ever looked at the market value of the paper, and it meant a shrinkage in home starts, the lifeblood of S&L lending operations. No bill had emerged from a similar conference the previous September, and it seemed at least possible that this conference, too, would be fruitless. Finally, the big California

S&Ls agreed to withdraw their objections to the bill, on one condition: The limit on insured deposits had to be raised from $40,000 to at least $100,000 per account. Sen. Alan Cranston carried their water to the table. Although an increase in the maximum savings account that could qualify for insurance was not in the draft bills that had gone to conference and no words of instruction on the subject were in the briefings by the staffs to the negotiators, the deal was cut late at night, and the bill passed.

By raising to $100,000 insurance coverage that had originally topped out at $2,500 (and only four years earlier had stood at $25,000), Congress inadvertently crossed a Rubicon. The average depositor, after all, had only about $6,000 in the savings bank. Insurance that went to $100,000 looked like a way to save not the depositor but the institution. Two years later, the FDIC and the FSLIC got permission to give "open bank [or thrift] assistance" whenever they thought in their wisdom—inevitably, a very political wisdom—that this would be "the least cost solution" to the insolvency of a depository.

We were on our way to the great scandal of the bailout of Continental Illinois, where in effect *all* the money expended by the FDIC went to giant foreign depositors and anonymous holders of Euronotes issued in tax-shelter locales like the Netherlands Antilles. Next came the hugely expensive nationalization of the banking system in Texas, and then the Bank Board's "Management Consignment Program," which kept zombie thrifts walking the earth year after year at an ultimate cost that must be counted in the tens of billions of dollars. Meanwhile, the decision to deregulate by cooperation of the five separate bank, thrift, and credit-union regulatory agencies produced an incredible mass of new regulations expressing the need to compromise the views of separate bureaucratic empires. And while the big money-center banks seemed to do well under the new regime—they were making out like crazy in Latin America, or so they told their stockholders—the S&Ls sank rapidly into the sinkhole.

The stage was now set for a financial-institutions bill aimed at taking care of the S&L problems, and in October 1982, the Garn-St Germain Depository Institutions Act, named for the chairmen of the two banking committees at that time, was signed into law. At the signing ceremony, President Reagan said, "I think we hit a home run." Pratt and his general counsel, Vartanian, had supervised its preparation. The three key titles, Vartanian wrote for a Practising Law Institute pamphlet, "were developed by the FHLBB in close consultation with the Reagan Administration, which enthusiastically endorsed and supported their passage."[2] Senate Banking Committee staff director Danny Wall said modestly that he had been a "lab assistant" in the preparation of the bill; Richard Hohlt, a former assistant to Sen. Richard Lugar who had become Senate lobbyist for the U.S. League of Savings Institutions, claimed somewhat greater credit.[3]

Mostly the bill validated what Pratt had already done to gun the engine and accelerate the S&Ls out of their morass. Its purpose, said the Senate conference report, was to enable the S&Ls to "improve their ability to generate current earnings to sustain the growth capital needed for future operations."[4] But there were also novelties. Any one of these novelties would have been a disaster for the future of the S&Ls. Taken together, they were the financial equivalent of a nuclear attack on the deposit insurance fund. The Bank Board was eager to see the provisions put into effect at once. Instead of writing new regulations to implement the new law, Pratt and Vartanian announced omnibus memoranda, telling the S&Ls and their lawyers that they could make their own readings of the law and get going and the Bank Board would trail along later to okay what they did.

Before proceeding to an examination of how the provisions of the law imploded on the industry, let us take a minute to look at the legislators whose names it bears. Fernand St Germain had a safe seat in Rhode Island and had come to the chair of the banking committee by seniority. He was a tubby man with a mustache, vain of his appearance, a poor boy who had made himself rich in Congress by borrowing money in sweetheart deals and investing it in condominium projects that benefited from government tax help. (The condos were built by old friends who were also contracted to build subsidized housing.) In addition, he had his hand in a chain of International House of Pancakes restaurants for which his entire investment was carried by banks whose regulators he oversaw. He loved being entertained by bankers. Having been elected before 1980, he was the beneficiary of House rules that allowed congressmen to keep for their own use money raised for their campaigns, and he had squirreled away one of the largest war chests in the country. After an investigation of his petty swindles had produced a slap on the wrist from the House Ethics Committee and a series of nasty articles in the *Wall Street Journal*, he lost his seat in 1988. Believing the public opinion polls that said he was a goner, he pulled all his political advertising off the air in the last days of the campaign and kept the money. After his defeat, he opened a consulting office in Washington that reportedly does good business.

Jake Garn is an entirely different story. A wraith of a man with a long bald head and a rather spacey manner (he was the senator who went up in the space shuttle, and some staffers like to say he never came down), he is a former mayor of Salt Lake City and a Mormon of high principles. Dick Pratt was a trusted protégé, and Garn reposed even greater trust in M. Danny Wall, an architect who had served him on the Salt Lake City Planning Commission and had stayed with him through his career. Wall became Senate Banking Committee staff director when Garn became chairman, and Garn later had him made chairman of the Bank Board, two jobs for which Wall was neither prepared nor equipped. Wall's wife was Garn's personal secretary. The Garn Institute of Finance at the University of Utah (chaired by Pratt, with Vartanian as its president) is his monument, and its two annual conferences (a late-winter Downhill Conference on the Utah ski slopes—Pratt is irrepressible—and an early-winter session in Key Largo) are his pleasure. I was a paid speaker at the 1988 Key Largo conference myself and had a lot of fun. Garn said my presence showed how open-minded the institute was.

Garn thought he would go down in history as the author of the 1982 act, and indeed he does, in ways that are very disturbing to him. In August 1988 the Senate Banking Committee, now returned to Democratic hands, held hearings, despite his objections, into the state of the S&L industry, and he blew his stack at three

S&L CEOs who placed the blame on his law. "As one of the most ardent supporters of state's rights," he said, "I am sick and tired of sitting and listening to people try and blame this problem on deregulation at the federal level. . . . You may have some problems with federal law, but relatively speaking, compared to mushroom farms and all of the things allowed by states, the federal law is very tight, relatively speaking."[5] He looked back to 1986, when one of the witnesses before him, representing the U.S. League, had opposed the recapitalization of the FSLIC (which would have permitted the Bank Board to close down the institutions that had the worst money hemorrhages). The witness, Gerald Levy, of Milwaukee's Guaranty Savings, had delivered a statement saying, "We believe that media attention to the condition of the insurance fund in our industry has been out of all proportion to the magnitude of any realistic assessment of our problems." Garn sarcastically repeated those words, then screamed at Levy: "And this senator was here saying that was bullshit, and that there was a huge problem, and trying to get some FSLIC passed, and the industry was opposing it. . . . I'm just trying to get some balance. . . . [R]egulatory mistakes have been made, and mistakes have been made by this Congress—boy, I'll testify to that! But I can't sit here and look at charts that dump it all on this side of the coin. . . ."[6]

Alas, a lot of what happened must be blamed on Jake Garn's law. When I said so at Key Largo, one of my audience, who is now out of a job and can't be quoted, came up and said, "I was at the Bank Board in those years, and you're right. It wasn't the specifics of the law, it was the spirit that gave all these guys the notion that anything goes." And that's true. But it was the specifics, too.

[1]

Probably the single most damaging provision in the law was the elimination of all regulation of the ratio between what an S&L could lend to a developer and the appraised value of the project for which the loan was made. The 1980 Deregulation Act had set limits of 66⅔ percent of appraised value for loans on unimproved land, 75 percent for loans on land with water and sewer systems or with frames beginning to rise, and 90 percent for low-income housing or in situations where insurance covered the risk of loss. The last was already a considerable loosening, because the Bank Board had asserted for years that no more than 80 percent of value should be lent on construction projects. Given the moral status of real estate appraisal as a profession, that was dangerous enough. Now, as we shall see, Garn-St Germain was increasing greatly the proportion of their assets that S&Ls could have in commercial real estate—and at the same time eliminating all control over how much could be lent to build and carry commercial properties. And the Bank Board was permitting developers to buy S&Ls.

To understand how significant this change was, one must consider what normal procedure was at a well-run S&L. William Ford, economist turned Federal Reserve Bank president turned S&L executive, was Tony Frank's sidekick in the glory days of First Nationwide. First Nationwide had recently emerged from its cocoon as a medium-sized San Francisco S&L by winning two exquisitely beneficial deals from Dick Pratt's Bank Board to take over failing franchises in New York and Florida and become the first such institution with branches touching both oceans. Frank had sold his S&L to National Steel, then seeking to diversify into financial services, in another deal that was better for his stockholders than for anybody else, and as National Steel sank into the Monongahela, Tony negotiated the sale of his little but ambitious bank to Ford Motor Company for about $250 million more than National Steel had paid. But the strength of the operation was the California bank, and a major strength of that bank was its lending to developers.

"Most of this," Ford recalls, "was in the Bay Area and in Los Angeles, where we had depth of knowledge of local markets. A guy we know comes in and says, 'I've got a piece of land south of Walnut Creek. We'd send out guys to look at the land, make sure it was actually zoned for apartments, make sure there were no ecological problems. Then we sent out appraisers, *our* appraisers, and they'd come back and say, "It should be worth ten million.'

Then we might lend eight million—if he can demonstrate that his costs won't go above eight million. We make no payments to the developer except his overhead, usually two, two and a half percent for his trailer, his computer, his secretary. If he can save something out of that, he keeps it; if it doesn't cover his costs, he pays them himself.

"All payments to his contractors and his subs go through our people. We go out and see that the work was done, see that it was done right, and then we pay the subs directly. That's on his loan. We charge him anywhere from one-half percent to two and one-half percent over prime, depending on how well we know him. It's the hardest thing, getting the track records on these guys. And then we get back principal and interest and half of a decent, hard-earned profit."

This sort of lending for acquisition, development, and construction was a legitimate business. First Nationwide's fees were no more than their costs in setting up the loan; their payoff would come at the end, when the properties were sold. And they split the profits on the sale with the developer. In short, First Nationwide made money by choosing good borrowers, a condition somewhat easier to fulfill in the 1970s and 1980s in the Bay Area than elsewhere, though a lot of guys lost money in San Francisco, too. The operation rested—absolutely properly—on the builder's ability to make money. And a builder's full dedication to that purpose could be assured only if he had his own capital in the deal.

Contrast these procedures with what was going on in Texas and elsewhere in California—and, Ford found when he took over Cleveland's Broadview Savings, in Ohio. The Ranbir Sahnis and Don Dixons and Danny Faulkners and Charlie Knapps lent money from their S&Ls in lump sums up front. The contractors might pay their subcontractors, or they might not; the work might be done well or badly—the lender had made his loan and was out of the picture. His profits came out of the initial fees and the interest that was built into the loan and could be taken down to the bottom line every month or every quarter. "They had a loan production office in Florida," Ford says of the Broadview he inherited. "They took rides around the area in jet helicopters and dropped parcels of as much as fifty million dollars on developers with high-risk projects." An S&L's reported profit for several years—maybe for many years, if you could keep trading dead horses for dead cows—would have nothing to do with its judgment in choosing borrowers. The more borrowers you funded, whether they would repay or not, the more profits you could report. Under Garn-St Germain, this way of doing business was made legal beyond question. Ludicrous, but legal.

Moreover, the law and its implementation made the expansion of such activities a certainty. Immediately upon the passage of Garn-St Germain, the Bank Board raised the limit on commercial loans to 40 percent of total assets in an S&L. Commercial banks in those days were not permitted to lend more than 10 percent of their capital (usually about one-half of 1 percent of their assets) to any one borrower. (Now the rule is 15 percent.) But S&Ls were permitted to lend 100 percent of capital to an individual borrower. Under that rule, the failure of one project could bust the bank, and failures are by no means unknown in real estate development. Here we have a suburban subdivision where the dowser couldn't find water; there we have the site of the former town dump, with methane plumes in the cellars. Such things can be a total loss. If the S&L had lent 100 percent of its capital to finance 100 percent of a project that couldn't be sold, its owners no longer had their own money at risk.

Even before Garn-St Germain, the Bank Board had designed a program that permitted decapitalized thrifts to pretend they still had some of their own money in the game. Working with teams of lawyers and outside accountants, Vartanian explained, the Bank Board had developed a "net worth certificate" program permitting S&Ls to print their own capital. The way the scam worked was that the FSLIC and the busted S&Ls exchanged notes. The notes from the S&L became an asset of the insurance fund (which could be carried on its books at par); the notes from the FSLIC were a government obligation that the S&L could consider part of its net worth. This program was specifically enacted into law by Garn-St Germain. The Financial Accounting Standards Board the next year said, Your father's mustache. Accountants who cared about their professional reputation, and there were some, refused to consider this transaction an addition to capital, or even "net worth."

Some years later, in 1987, William B. O'Connell, still president of the U.S. League, wrote a furious Op-Ed piece about the FASB in the *New York Times*: "Although this group has a profound influence on the economic life of the country, the members are not publicly elected, nor appointed by or answerable to any elected official body. Nevertheless, the board has issued rules that sometimes go against the expressed will of Congress. . . . In 1982, Congress passed the Net Worth Certificate program whereby the Federal deposit insurance agencies . . . were authorized to purchase capital certificates from affected institutions. This program was designed to buy time for such institutions to return to health when interest rates declined to more traditional levels. The wisdom of Congress was borne out by the fact that most of the institutions that were allowed to use the Net Worth Certificate program have returned to health, saving the Federal insurance agencies billions of dollars."

One notes before proceeding that this last statement is simply untrue. The majority of the institutions that used these certificates were unhealthy when O'Connell wrote and have since gone under, with exaggerated losses to the fund. Almost two years before O'Connell wrote, a Bank Board study by James Barth, R. Dan Brumbaugh, Jr., and D. Sauerhaft had shown conclusively that "the costs of resolving an S&L's insolvency rises on average with the length of time during which regulatory response is delayed."[7] But in 1987 the cockamamy accounting that Congress and Pratt's Bank Board had mandated was still accepted as the real world by the U.S. League (if not by the GAO), and under those rules these guys still seemed to be breathing.

Donald Kirk, retired from the FASB, replied on the same page: "For financial information to be useful, it must possess certain characteristics, the most noteworthy of which are comparability, credibility and neutrality. . . . The challenge to neutrality is never-ending. It is ironic that while tax reform was being contemplated by those frustrated with the social engineering in our tax code, others in comparable Government positions were devising rules to call losses 'assets' and liabilities 'equity.' ... The Bank Board ... encouraged transactions designed to create equity out of thin air. ... The intention was to mask the weakness of ailing financial institutions, with the hope that it would become somebody else's problem. The 'somebody else' is, ultimately, you and me—the taxpayers." History has judged between O'Connell and Kirk, but O'Connell's friends have not yet paid the political price.[8]

Meanwhile, Garn-St Germain in effect had removed the last controls on the interest rates banks and S&Ls could pay (see appendix B). From January 1, 1983, money market accounts with checking privileges could be offered to anyone at whatever interest rate was necessary to draw the funds. Given their deposit insurance license, the removal of interest-rate controls, the availability of net worth certificates, and the five-year averaging method of calculating required capital, the owners of what had just become a decapitalized S&L could raise endless money and take it to whatever gambling tables were most convenient. If they won, they kept it (deducting a little for their dues to the U.S. League and its political action committee); if they lost, the government would pay. Worse yet, if they gambled in the mortgage-backed securities, collateralized mortgage obligations, and junk bonds the Wall Street salesmen tried to sell them every day (often with an unspoken offer that the Wall Street house would also raise the brokered deposits they could use to buy the stuff), they could divide their bets into winners and losers, cash their winners immediately, and bury their losers in the investment portfolio at "historic cost." This, too, was legal under Garn-St Germain and the regulations to implement it written by the Bank Board.

Garn-St Germain also validated the reckless trading of hedges, including the writing as well as the purchasing of puts and calls that Pratt's Bank Board had approved in May 1982. And the sale of mortgages "with recourse"—that is, under an arrangement whereby the buyer can return the loan and get his money back if the mortgage goes sour. In effect, the S&L kept the risk of the loan—but the Bank Board permitted it to book the transaction as a completed sale and take the profits. Further leveraging of the portfolio was made possible by approval of large-scale repurchase agreements with the Wall Street houses. This game was played by using brokered deposits to buy marketable instruments (usually mortgage-backed securities) that could then be pledged against a loan (often enough from the firm that had supplied both the brokered deposits and the securities) to buy more securities with the same money, thus doubling the bet. The Wall Street houses made a commission or a markup on each and every one of these transactions.

Testifying before a sympathetic Henry Gonzalez in San Francisco in January 1989, the president and one of the directors of the first Hispanic S&L in the United States insisted that the regulators who closed them down were prejudiced against the Spanish-speaking and gave as his proof an FSLIC statement that their losses had totaled $417 million. Impossible; they'd never had more than $277 million in deposits.[9] But if you're doubling up through repos and playing in futures and options, you can easily lose more than you brought to the table. And if you're a Bank Board that relies on Wall Street houses to broker funds into busted S&Ls and do repurchase business with them to keep them liquid, you pay off the gambling losses and keep the gambling winners happy even though your legal obligation runs only to the depositors. (Presidio had other problems, too. Sherman Maisel, University of California professor and former Federal Reserve governor, who served on the board of the FSLIC-sponsored S&L that acted as receiver after the boom was lowered, remembers one officer telling him that Presidio had "a five-plus-five policy. If anybody offered them five points and five percentage points over prime, they made the loan.") All this was—most of it still is—legal. As the man said in Dickens, the law is a ass.

One grants Senator Garn his point that the Texas, California, Florida, Louisiana, Arkansas, and Oklahoma legislatures behaved even worse than he and his colleagues did. But what Congress did in 1982, and what his protégé Dick Pratt's Bank Board did from 1981 to 1983, would have been more than enough to sink the industry and rob the taxpayer even if there had been no state charters or state laws. Senator Garn's law goes, Hee Haw.

[2]

Probably the best case history, because it involved so much fiddle-faddle and so much money, is FCA, a Delaware corporation doing business with a California charter as American Savings and Loan. This was a Standard & Poors 500 stock; with $34 billion in assets on the day it had to be rescued ($36 billion four years later, when it had to be sold to Robert M. Bass), it was one of the ten largest depository institutions in the United States. This place was the lengthened shadow of one rather small man, Charles Knapp, an owl with thick glasses and a not-quite-convincing smile, a San Franciscan with some experience on Wall Street who had come back to the West Coast to work with Nate Shapell, a Hungarian-American builder who taught him how to go into the revolving door behind someone and come out of it ahead of him. In 1975, Knapp took over Budget Industries, a miniconglomerate that owned State Savings of Stockton, California—the same State Savings that nine years earlier had precipitated the crisis in California thrifts and led to the imposition of Reg Q interest-rate ceilings on the industry. He immediately changed the name from Budget Industries to FCA. Total assets at year end 1975 were $433 million.

Knapp came into his own with inflation. Primarily a mortgage lender to the single-family-home buyer, FCA expanded with the mid-California market in the late 1970s, growing 15 percent a year, then 20 percent, then 25 percent (not far off the rise in housing prices in his markets at that time). Then, in 1980, FCA took off, growing by 60 percent. The 1980 report explained that

> the Company's progress has been due to an early recognition and complete acceptance of the premise that fundamental change in real estate lending is necessary for its survival and prosperity in today's hostile and unpredictable business climate. . . . Innovation, flexibility and a recognition of harsh economic reality have caused FCA to evolve into what may now be described as a sophisticated asset management company. . . . The profit growth of State Savings and Loan Association last year was unmatched by any other company in the industry. . . . State never closed its window to the home buyer, the owner/builder or the developer and in most of its geographical areas

of concentration, State was one of the very few institutions with lendable funds. . . . To fund its accelerated loan volume, State increased its savings deposits to $1.3 billion at year end, a 74% increase. This growth in the deposit base has been accomplished by the development of an intricate and well balanced plan utilizing sales executives and institutional money desks, together with production incentives. The traditional source of lendable mortgage funds, the small saver, no longer exists. . . . Our production oriented account executive network places major emphasis on the merchandising of various types of certificates of deposit, directly to the rate conscious corporate, pension fund or other large investor. . . .[10]

By the next year, when growth soared to 111 percent, the song had changed a little. The 1981 report noted that State now got 29 percent of its revenue

from sources other than interest on real estate loans. Therefore, FCA believes that a comparison of the yield on all State's earning assets (investments, loans and real estate held for sale) including interest, loan origination fees, loan commitment fees and profit from sale of real estate, with the average rate for all funds (deposits and borrowings) is more meaningful in measuring the performance of State's business than the traditional comparison of average yield on loans with average rate on savings accounts.[11]

Indeed, the chairman's report shows an average cost of deposits in 1981 at 15.4 percent, and an average cost of funds (brought down by the bargains in borrowings from the Federal Home Loan Bank of San Francisco) at 14.6 percent. The average yield on the loan portfolio was only 14.9 percent. Gross profits claimed for the year, before taxes, were less than $29 million. Income from sources other than interest on loans was about $110 million, or four times the year's earnings. A 1980 reference to a maximum of 3 percent of assets in direct investments rather than loans disappeared in 1981. FCA had moved into uncharted waters.

More than two-fifths of all FCA deposits at year-end 1981 paid an interest rate higher than 16 percent, and almost 82 percent of them were from institutional sources. "State believes that these market rate deposits are a stable source of funds," the annual report said, "as long as it continues to pay competitive interest rates." That's where the money would come from in the future, too: State had agreed to sell ten of its thirty-nine branches. Though there was much talk about originating mortgages for sale into a secondary market, the fact was that in 1981, State sold only $61 million of loans (rates went up all year, making the inventory worth progressively less on the market as time passed), while it bought $586 million worth from mortgage brokers and originated $1.616 billion—more than its total assets the year before. Dick Pratt says Knapp was "the pure case of irrational behavior: He was originating mortgage loans at twenty-five basis points below what he could have got in government securities." Charitably, Knapp was making an immense interest-rate bet—and he was right. In the summer of 1982, just in time, Mexico went broke, told Federal Reserve chairman Paul Volcker about it, and the chairman (already under pressure from some of his fellow board members) began to ease the Fed's grip on the money supply. Assuming that State's mortgages were sound and its projects (where State had made loans to builders or taken an equity interest) were well thought out, the FCA was going to make a lot of money.

And I must admit in passing that I thought so myself. While unhappy with the accounting gimmickry the Bank Board had promoted (again, note appendix A), I couldn't see much point in the industry simply lying there and waiting for the death that advanced inexorably from the foot of the bed, month after month, as the interest that had to be paid on deposits remained greater than the interest that was being earned on the portfolio. In 1982 everybody who ran an S&L had a little card in the breast pocket of his shirt that he pulled out for conversational purposes at conventions. It showed the calculation of the number of months to go before his depository was insolvent. Very rapid growth to raise the average yield on mortgages seemed one of the few plausible ways for the industry to stay afloat. I had not thought of James Sexton's point that there wasn't that much good business out there—and I had forgotten the lesson taught me in 1974 by no less than Serge Semenenko, the éminence grise of the old First National Bank of Boston, that the number of borrowers who can survive while paying those interest rates is a lot smaller than the number who think they can.

What happened to Knapp was predictable and was correctly predicted by the old-timers in the California S&Ls, who hated his guts, anyway, if only because he was a flamboyant and arrogant joker with a movie-star wife who flew racing aircraft. He would become the sucker-lender to the people with the bad paper and the bad projects. What was not predictable was how resourceful Knapp would be when his world started caving in around him. Jaye Scholl of *Barron's* pointed out some years later that this was not the first time Knapp had wriggled out of a deep hole. In 1976, soon after he took control of Budget Industries, he was confronted with a $9 million loss on loans to a failed developer, Padre Island Investment Company. He exchanged the loans for preferred stock in the company, which he could carry at par, there being no market for it. And as he made loans to other developers, he required them, as part of the price for the loan, to buy some of this preferred stock. This did not get him the best borrowers, of course, but for the time being it avoided the recognition of past losses.[12] Then, when the new loans to the friends who helped carry the old ones went bad, the game could be played again.

The extremely rapid growth of State in the early 1980s and its willingness to pay monstrous rates for new funds were dictated by the need to make vast quantities of new loans to keep this process going. The preferred-stock gimmick was rare; usually it would be the old loan, or the property State owned through foreclosure of an old loan, that would be assumed by the new borrower. Often the sales would be conditional in some way or made "with recourse." (State agreed to take back the property and refund the purchase price later.) Not all of this was hidden from the prying eyes of the examiners. As early as May 1982, a joint examination of State Savings by the California Department of Savings and Loan and the Federal Home Loan Bank Board produced a rating of four on a scale of one to five, and a meeting where the "topics discussed included the risks involved with State's current philosophy of sustained growth, high level of certificates of deposit of $100,000 or more, major underwriting deficiencies, noted increase in scheduled items [i.e., loans the examiner considered doubtful or worse], accounting for loan fees, low level of net worth, transactions with affiliates, etc." Despite the optimism of its annual statement, "State's management indicated that it was aware of the noted weaknesses and had taken actions . . . to eliminate the noted deficiencies."[13]

Then, at the end of 1982, the passage of Garn-St Germain and the Nolan Act in California opened up new fields to conquer, new chances to grow. And the arrival of Larry Taggart as state commissioner gave Knapp a most useful friend at court. Further opportunities descended from heaven with the arrival of Wall Street, especially Salomon Brothers, as a counterparty in mortgage trading. And an opportunity arose for State Savings to make a quantum leap: Mark Taper, founder and chairman of American Savings & Loan, wanted to sell his holding company, First Charter. Buying First Charter, FCA would become by some margin the largest S&L operator in the country.

When Edwin J. Gray took over from Dick Pratt as chairman of the Bank Board in May 1983, the sale of First Charter to FCA was about to come to the Board for approval. Pratt says, "It never came to my desk; the staff was still looking at it." (In fact, he had assigned the problem to someone from Salt Lake City, then working for First Federal of Rochester, New York, who had not yet reported back.) Gray says it was all ready to go when he arrived. Both may be telling the truth. The formal submission of FCA's application to acquire First Charter had been made to the Federal Home Loan Bank of San Francisco on March 3, and the bank did not forward it to Washington officially (with its recommendation for approval) until June 9. The theory behind the deal was that giving Knapp a traditional and established S&L would calm him down, enable him to back away from his aggressiveness at State Savings. And State Savings, at least on the surface, was for all its razzle-dazzle still basically a housing lender. "My colleagues," Gray recalls, "were saying that this is a marriage made in heaven. There was going to be great synergy. State Savings would close down its money desk and use the American Savings branches as its source of funds. They said, over and over, 'We can assure you that Charlie says once he has this he'll join the group of civilized S&L operators and run this as an S&L should be run.' "

Gray's instincts told him something was wrong with this deal, and he insisted on a meeting where his directors and outside accountants would both be represented. They all voted to go ahead. (Gray thought the deal they had approved gave the Bank Board power to move quickly if Knapp violated his business plan and was furious later when he learned that the only handle the regulators had on Knapp was his need to borrow from the Home Loan Bank.) In August 1983 the marriage was consummated. Mark Taper took $298 million cash money out of the deal; the other First Charter stockholders got stock in the FCA. State and American were merged, with the American name as survivor. Because the purchase price of First Charter's assets was a lot more than their tangible value, FCA took onto its books no less than $1,108,443,000 of goodwill.

And, of course, Knapp did not reform. FCA's annual report for 1983 boasted that deposit growth had been $6.4 billion quite apart from the First Charter acquisition. Total assets had climbed from $1.8 billion in 1980 to $6.6 billion in 1982, and now to $22.7 billion in 1983. And in 1984, FCA grew more than a billion dollars a month. Bill Ford recalls a planning session with Tony Frank in connection with the hundredth anniversary of the founding of the association that had turned into First Nationwide, then at $10 billion. Frank commented with amazement that Knapp had grown $10 billion in one year. Some of that, Frank knew, had been done by making loans that First Nationwide had turned down—not infrequently, for sums larger than the money for which the borrower had applied when seeking help from First Nationwide. (This was the "trash for cash" program in action.) Everyone in the industry knew Knapp was having just awful trouble blending the corporate cultures of State and American, which had been among the more solid and stolid of the California thrifts. People who had quit or been fired littered the California landscape. At best, there was no way anyone could grow a depository by $10 billion a year and keep control of it.

Larry Taggart, in his testimony to the House Banking Committee in January 1989, remembered that just before the July 4 weekend of 1984, a number of S&L executives met with officers of the Federal Home Loan Bank of San Francisco, and all agreed that somehow Knapp had to be stopped. They thought Taggart as California state commissioner might do something helpful. Taggart, who later went to work for Knapp in the not very successful investment company Knapp launched with the $2 million severance fee he won from FCA as his price for leaving quietly, said he wasn't having any part of that. Then it developed that the banking regulators had been outflanked. Knapp had filed registration statements with the SEC in connection with new debt issues. The SEC had already forced him to reverse some alleged asset sales in 1981 and 1982 on the grounds that the money credited to FCA by the "sale" had been lent by FCA to the borrower. Now the agency's securities division landed on the company for a whole range of deceptive practices and forced the reversal of an alleged $75.3 million profit in the second quarter of 1984 to a $79.9 million loss. Suddenly the institutional "market rate deposits"—which still accounted for half of FCA's funds even though American Savings now had 122 branches—were no longer "a stable source of funds."

Knapp printed a special report by his chief economist, Dr. Jerry E. Pohlman, stressing that *"managing* rate risk, rather than attempting to *eliminate* it, is the key to . . . profitability. . . . Liability management . . . involves developing multiple sources of funds to reduce liquidity exposure should any individual source of funds dry up. [Because FCA raised funds] throughout the interest rate cycle, we have been able to remain in the lending markets at times when others have retreated. An unfortunate but well-recognized result of this is a higher-than-average ratio of scheduled items [i.e., loans classified by examiners as doubtful or worse] to assets. This is not surprising in light of the fact that American originated comparatively large volumes of loans during tough economic times. The real question is, what was the total impact of this lending policy? The answer is that our lending philosophy has also resulted in a significantly higher yield on the company's loan portfolio. . . ."[14] No sale: Some $6 billion fled the association.

The Bank Board demanded that Knapp go and replaced him with William Popejoy, formerly head of the Federal Home Loan Mortgage Corporation. Popejoy, a handsome, sociable banker, had been president of American for Taper and had turned around Financial Federation, a holding company of eleven S&Ls, some of them in not very good shape. He couldn't fund the association through his own or the institution's contacts, and as noted before, the Bank Board in Washington had to scramble, first to Merrill Lynch, then to Pru-Bache, for brokered deposits in ten figures. Ed Gray flew back to Washington from a vacation in France. He and his assistant, Shannon Fairbanks, spent Labor Day weekend in touch with the Federal Reserve, trying to figure out how enough collateral could be qualified fast enough for the Fed to supply funds to stanch the run. Taggart was off camping in the Sierra, unreachable by phone. Gray never forgave him. The situation stabilized when the Home Loan Bank of San Francisco found in FCA's vaults $4 billion worth of mortgages and mortgage-backed securities that could be used as collateral for the loans American Savings needed to pay off the big depositors.

Popejoy found a terrible mess. A quarter of a billion dollars' worth of mortgage-backed securities supposedly held by FCA at New York's Chase Manhattan Bank could not be found and may never have existed. Included in American Savings' assets were billions of dollars in Lizbos ("Loans serviced by others"), and nobody knew which of them were performing and which were delinquent and how large the losses would be. Because Knapp would buy anything, he had been victimized all over the Southwest by mortgage brokers unloading their garbage. Then he had sold chunks of the garbage to third parties, lending them the money to buy and not holding them to repayment schedules. "The problem everywhere was the absence of paperwork," Popejoy remembers. "We had seven billion dollars of loans on which we had inadequate documentation. Payments came in and we didn't know where to credit them. We went out to people's homes to try to reconstruct the files. You can imagine how helpful people are when you come around and say you've lost the information about their mortgage." For one $5 million loan, the only documentation in the files was a note to lend the borrower that amount written on the business card of J. Foster Fleutsch, a large, bearded, gregarious young friend of Knapp's who was chairman and CEO of the savings bank.

An auditor who now works for an asset disposition firm that is a subsidiary of a major insurance company was hired to look at files on FCA loans made to some hotels. One, which he didn't identify (Popejoy said wearily that it was Monterrey Plaza), was a situation where FCA had lent money—we are talking in the vicinity of $20 million—to a man building a hotel on land owned by someone else. Looking in the files, the auditor found a letter from the lender that held the mortgage on the land. The landowner hadn't been paying his mortgage and the lender was threatening to foreclose. If he did, FCA's loan on the hotel would have gone up in smoke. The deadline mentioned in the letter was two days from the date the auditor found it. He took it up to management and asked: "Do you guys know about this?" They thanked him.

FCA had among its assets property for sale carried at about a billion dollars, knowing that if it were actually sold it would bring much less. And there was something like $6 billion in mortgage-backed securities, carried at what FCA had paid for them, regardless of their current market value. Many of these were losers, because Knapp (like Popejoy, two years later: "Look," he says, "I didn't write the accounting rules") had taken advantage of the opportunity to sell the paper that had gone up in price and take the profit, while burying in the portfolio the paper on which he showed a loss. These embedded losses would reach $1.8 billion in the summer of 1987, before the stock market crash bailed out the fixed-income market and saved FCA from its second liquidity crunch. Finally, Knapp had a common-stock portfolio, including ten million shares of American Express—and American Express stock had had a bad summer in 1984.

"When I came in, our future strategy was pretty obvious," Popejoy said five years later. "We had to shrink the company, sell branches to build net worth, take the losses, and go to adjustable rate mortgages. By the first part of 1985 it was obvious our losses were going to be several hundred million. Our net worth was going to be much reduced. Then it turned out that when they merged in 1983, they did it by a pooling of assets, and the billion dollars of goodwill was assessed to the branches. That meant we couldn't sell the branches, because any funds we got for them would have to be used to write down the goodwill. We had huge amounts of nonaccruing and phony assets. Our liabilities were $34 billion, and we had only $30 billion of earning assets. So we had to work through the synthetic markets, do a lot of hedging, to get the spread we needed. We played war with Dr. Mark Powers, a mathematician who knew more about options than anybody else in the country. We had gone from $34 billion to $29 billion, and it was clear we couldn't live. They did a study of what it would cost to liquidate us, and they came back with a number, $5.5 billion. I was asked by the Bank Board and my board, 'What could we do?' And the only answer was growth, take interest-rate risk —no underwriting risk, no credit risk. We had to follow a strategy of desperation to carry the bad assets. They kept saying in Washington 'How are you going to get out of this?' And we kept saying, 'We're trying. . . .' "

This was not, on full consideration, a plausible solution. Futures and options are zero-sum games, and the odds are strongly against even a big savings association when it plays them against the Wall Street houses that own and operate the markets. Larry Connell is a lawyer who was banking commissioner for the state of Connecticut and then head of the National Credit Union Administration before he became an S&L CEO, mostly on arrangement by government regulators who needed skilled help to hold down the losses on beat-up thrifts. (In 1990 he was struggling, not very optimistically, to hold down the damage at San Jacinto of Texas.) "It's idiocy," Connell said, "to have a country bumpkin—and anybody who hasn't spent his life on a Wall Street trading desk is a country bumpkin—playing against the guys who live in the market."

Popejoy doesn't quarrel: "The field is littered with people who thought they knew what they were doing in the futures markets." But he argued that Knapp and the government had left him in a condition where no other course was possible. American Savings' credit standards, while Popejoy ran it, were tight as could be: only 10 of 48,000 loans went sour. His strategies were approved, and to some degree mandated, by Washington: After March 1986, when Bank Board chairman Edwin Gray sent Popejoy a letter promising that the board would take no action against American Savings simply because it had no net worth (a letter Popejoy printed in FCA's annual report), all significant asset or liability decisions were run through Gray's office. Gray also gave Wall Street houses "comfort letters," promising that the FSLIC would stand behind all of FCA's borrowings. It was the Bank Board that decided in early 1987 that FCA should be sold and hired Salomon Brothers to locate a purchaser.

Nothing worked. Popejoy bet interest rates would fall, and they soared. If the stock market hadn't crashed on October 19, 1987, it would surely have gone the next day, because the Bank Board after a frantic weekend of negotiations was prepared to announce that Monday that FCA had failed and the FSLIC couldn't pay off the depositors in American Savings. Instead, the "flight to quality" from the collapsing stock market raised the prices of all government and government-insured debt paper. FCA's losses receded, and the Wall Street houses, which had no desire to add negatives to the market, agreed to continue doing repurchases for American Savings. Even so, FCA came into 1988 more than $3 billion in the hole.

"If FCA were anything but an S&L," I wrote in a column for the *Los Angeles Times*, "the shutters would have been put up years ago and the postal service would have been told to refer the mail to the dead letter office. . . . Right now, FCA is what the British call a 'quango,' for Quasi-Autonomous National Governmental Organization, and Popejoy is a quangocrat playing chicken."[15] Popejoy told me the other day that his people put up a sign in the executive dining room proclaiming themselves quangocrats. Nobody blames him for the end result, which was the sale of FCA in 1988 to Robert M. Bass and his associates, at immense cost to the taxpayers, a subject to which we shall return. Almost uniquely in the history of such government-subsidized deals, Popejoy was allowed to remain as CEO of one-half the shrunk operation.

All this hopelessness clearly originated before 1984. But on January 31, 1984, the Big Eight accounting firm of Arthur Andersen reported

> [T]o the Board of Directors and the Stockholders of Financial Corporation of America [that] we have examined the consolidated balance sheets of Financial Corporation of America. . . . Our examinations were made in accordance with generally accepted auditing standards and, accordingly, included such tests of the accounting records and such other auditing procedures as we considered necessary in the circumstances. In our opinion, the financial statements referred to above present fairly the financial position of Financial Corporation of America and subsidiaries . . . in conformity with generally accepted accounting principles applied on a consistent basis.

CHAPTER 5

Mr. Gray Throws Himself Beneath the Wheels . . .

Mr. Kanjorski: You were in the White House at one time. You did know a fellow by the name of Ed Meese, did you not?

Mr. Gray: Yes.

Mr. Kanjorski: Did they deregulate his department, too?

Mr. Gray: Department of Justice.

Mr. Kanjorski: Yes. Is there not a telephone there that you could say, Mr. Attorney General, we have got problems? What are we going to do about them? Did you do?

Mr. Gray: Yes.

Mr. Kanjorski: And what were Mr. Meese's comments?

Mr. Gray: I was never there as a regulator. You see, you have to understand. The White House—

Mr. Kanjorski: Did you call to the attention of the highest law enforcement officer in this land and under the Ronald Reagan Administration the conditions that we are hearing testified today?

Mr. Gray: Absolutely.

Mr. Kanjorski: And what was his response to you, sir?

Mr. Gray: Keep up the good work.

> —from the San Francisco
> hearings of the House
> Banking Committee
> (January 13, 1989)

WHAT finally stuck in Ed Gray's craw, one suspects, was the realization that he had been made chairman of the Federal Home Loan Bank Board because he was supposed to be a dope and a patsy who would go along with whatever the U.S. League and the Reagan administration wanted. "I was brought up in this Reaganesque philosophy," he said when it was all over. "When I was in Sacramento, I wrote ninety percent of all Ronald Reagan's policy statements. And when you do that, you exaggerate. Later, they would say to me, 'What you're doing is not the policy of this administration,' as though that answered all the questions. I said, 'I was a policy director for this administration, I think I know what the policies are supposed to mean.' " On his way out, he told Jim McTague of *American Banker*, "I often asked myself, What would Ronald Reagan do if he had all the facts? Then I tried to act accordingly."[1] But the people pounding on him were the people who gave Ronald Reagan his facts.

Gray is well named; there are no bright colors to Edwin J. Gray. A slow-spoken, conventionally handsome man in his fifties, a little tubby, with a round face and thinning hair, he came out of jobs as a writer for a radio station and for United Press International to public relations for Ronald Reagan in the California statehouse. When Reagan was out of office, a job was found for Gray in corporate communications at Gordon Luce's San Diego Federal S&L (later, Great American). His *Who's Who* listing showed a single affiliation: member of the executive committee of the California Taxpayers Association. Having been press secretary for the Reagan-Bush campaign, he slipped naturally into the White House after the inauguration. With his S&L background, he was the formal liaison with HUD, the Housing Commission, and the Federal Home Loan Bank Board (though the person who carried the water for the White House was Ann Shannon O'Connor Fairbanks, a smart, wily, wiry Irish blonde who had written a Ph.D. thesis on the S&L industry and whose husband, a Washington lawyer with good Republican connections, was about to be made Reagan's negotiator in the Middle East).

Doubtless because he had known the president way back when, Gray was the first choice of the U.S. League to be chairman of the Bank Board when Pratt let people know he would leave in the spring of 1983. Gray had gone back to San Diego in the summer of 1982 (his wife hated Washington and stayed at their home in La Jolla), but the call was irresistible. He was working again for Gordon Luce, a gracious, slender gentleman. Luce says today that when Ed asked his advice, he said the job offer was a compliment and it would be okay if the government could afford to give him on-the-job training, but Luce wasn't sure it could. Gray wanted to take Ann Fairbanks with him as one of the other two board members, but the White House personnel department had other ideas, so she went over as Gray's personal assistant and chief of staff.

If one had to rank the chairmen of the Bank Board by ability, Gray would probably stand somewhere in the middle (Pratt was a hard act to follow), and it's fair to say that much of the staff looked down on this flack pretending to be an administrator. Four years later, one of them told Jim McTague of *American Banker* that they began warning Gray early of trouble ahead, but he didn't understand what they were saying: "He knew a lot of buzzwords."[2] At the beginning, certainly, Gray saw no evil. He went to the annual convention of the Texas League of Savings & Loans to urge them to take full advantage of the new powers given them by Garn-St Germain and their own state law. (The title of the talk was "A Sure Cure for What Ails You."[3]) Interest rates were still declining, and on the books of the established California associations, which was, after all, Gray's home base, the mortgages and the GNMA pass-through certificates were returning to profitability. The S&L industry was one where the Reagan revolution had already occurred, and Gray's job was to preserve it and help the private sector garner the fruits.

By midsummer of 1983, however, Gray's attention had been caught by a clearly unwholesome pattern of growth in Texas and an immense rash of applications for insurance charters in California from people who had been attending seminars on "How to Use the New Legislation to Get Rich Quick." Members of the staff at the FSLIC and some of his old friends from California told him horror stories about newcomers to the business who were bidding up deposit rates, making dumb loans and dumber investments, and growing at an unbelievable pace. Ed Gray was a Reaganite; the Reaganite solution to such problems was to "defund" the miscreants—cut the tax revenues to keep the Democrats from introducing new social programs, cut the appropriations to starve the activist groups that were sucking at the federal teat—by taking away their government sources of money.

The supergrowers were all—necessarily—big customers for the money brokers, Wall Street firms, and (this is not necessarily redundant) unsavory operators who had sprung up around the country to ply this riskless and essentially dishonest trade based on nothing more substantial than the stupidity of a government that had separated reward from risk. *Most* of the deposits in the Penn Square National Bank in Oklahoma that had failed so noisily the previous July had come in from money brokers. The business was drawing some very disreputable characters, like Mario Renda, a former tap-dance teacher whose First United shop on New York's Long Island had close ties to the Teamsters Union pension fund and various Mafiosi and who often arranged the loans that the banks and S&Ls would make with the money he brokered in. Like other crooks who came into the S&L business, Renda acquired a complement of Rolls-Royces, mansions, furs, and houses in the Caribbean; but unlike most, he went to jail. Wall Street was becoming more involved. Even after the Penn Square failure presumably had sounded the tocsin, Merrill Lynch put $248 million of its customers' money into government-insured deposits at the collapsing First National Bank of Midland, Texas, which had to pay the nation's highest rates because it was collapsing.[4] Gray went to have a talk with Bill Isaac at the FDIC. "There were people who never forgave me for it," he says. "I was consorting with the enemy." They agreed to work together to control what Gray liked to call, quite correctly, the sale of federal insurance by unlicensed brokers. On October 25, 1983, the two of them issued a joint "Advance Notice of Rulemaking."

Gray had another forty-three months as Bank Board chairman. From that first proposal to put the kibosh on money brokerage to his departure in something not far from disgrace in

June 1987, Gray never stopped warning the other members of the Bank Board, the industry, the Congress, the policymakers in the executive branch, that unless something was done to prevent abuse of the new rules for regulating thrifts, the S&Ls were going to be in terrible trouble. The speeches hold up quite well years later. For example: "Deposit and asset growth," Gray told a U.S. League convention in October 1984, "are spiraling upward at a dizzying pace which . . . is unrelated to real or even regulatory net worth, and which is not even faintly related to the level of reserves on hand at the FSLIC. . . . This is a problem you must come to grips with honestly, forthrightly and expeditiously if you expect your separate thrift system to be around for very long."[5] But he paid a price for these warnings: From the first publication of the "Advance Notice," he never had another happy day at the Bank Board.

When Nathaniel Nash of the *New York Times* went to see Gray in Miami in December 1989 to prepare a profile for his paper, he told Gray that the piece might more properly be run at the Easter season, for Gray had been crucified and resurrected. As 1990 opened, Gray was in a condition approaching apotheosis, and I for one was delighted to see it. We had a minor personal relationship that grew out of my telling the industry, at a second anniversary meeting celebrating the 1982 publication of the "Report of the Housing Commission," that the people who were complaining about Ed were crazy. He was the real friend of the industry, while the people who wanted no limits on growth were its enemies. Nobody else was backing him that week; he came up to the platform after my talk with a heartfelt word of thanks. Something not very different in what was an even harder time for him came in September 1985, when I said nice things about him at the dinner in Pebble Beach before people whose good opinion meant a lot to him. This book owes much to Ed Gray, who ran the world's best clipping service on several of the topics covered here and supplied me with material that would not have been easy to find.

One must also report that when the *Wall Street Journal* noted that I was writing a book on the S&Ls, I had several telephone calls from people who had worked at the Bank Board during Gray's tenure, asking me not to let Ed rewrite history. Several very bad decisions were made during Gray's watch: the sale of American Savings & Loan to Financial Corporation of America, permitting Mark Taper to take out $289 million cash from an enterprise that would be a burden on the insurance fund less than a year later; the sale of Gibraltar of Texas to First Texas, allowing Saul Steinberg to pocket a whopping profit on a failed institution; and the sale of Lincoln Savings & Loan to Charles Keating, who only five years earlier had signed an SEC consent decree (which means he entered no defense) in a case where he had been charged with arranging fraudulent loans to himself and his business associates from a bank owned by his friend and employer Carl Lindner.[6] He also helped an FSLIC cover-up of jiggery-pokery at the Lake Placid Club in New York, which had become FSLIC property after the failure of the fraudulent North Mississippi (!) S&L. And it was on Gray's watch (also, in fairness, on Larry Taggart's, who as state commissioner refused to issue the necessary cease-and-desist orders) that a busted Beverly Hills S&L was allowed to grow, to sell stock to the public, and to fiddle with Werner Rey, a Swiss businessman who had Robert Vesco connections.

Though friends propped Gray up as a hero opposing House Speaker Jim Wright's scandalous interventions on behalf of crooked Texas S&Ls, the fact is that he caved in and essentially gave Wright what he wanted in every case but two—he wouldn't fire Texas enforcement director Joe Selby or prop up Don Dixon's Vernon S&L—and in the Vernon case, Texas State Commissioner Lin Bowman had already decided that Dixon had to be removed. In fairness to Gray, one should also note that when he wanted to close Lamar Savings of Austin, the financier of endless unoccupied office buildings, Bowman said it would have to wait until the legislature went out of session; Stanley Adams, the outsize, bearded nut who owned Lamar—he once filed an application for a branch on the moon—had too many friends there.

Tom Gaubert was a big fund-raiser for Jim Wright and had been finance chairman of the National Democratic Congressional Campaign Committee. Gray's Bank Board permitted Gaubert to sell a parcel of land owned by his Independent American S&L at a big profit in a deal financed by Independent American itself, in order to build up the thrift's capital to a point where the Bank Board could okay its acquisition of two other thrifts. Enforcement Director Rosemary Stewart (who got in big trouble in 1989 for her collaboration with Gray's successor, Danny Wall, in permitting Lincoln Savings & Loan to escape the conservatorship the field regulators had recommended) wickedly but not unfairly told the House Banking Committee that she was furious with Gray because he had yielded to Wright and appointed an "independent counsel" to examine whether the Bank Board had been unfair to the Speaker's friend Gaubert.

Friends of Dick Pratt point out that most of what Pratt did was Bank Board regulation, which Gray could have undone. This is a little disingenuous, because every time Gray poked his head out of that trench, Pratt or someone else at Merrill Lynch shot at him. In fact, Gray did pull back a number of Pratt's more egregious regs. But many of his new regulations were watered down in the process of adoption just enough to give the unprincipled lawyers who worked for the S&Ls—members of great national firms but thoroughly unprincipled for all that—enough room to wriggle out. Or, rather—and this was very common—opportunity to advise that if you broke the rules, the odds were that nothing would happen to you.

Justice Oliver Wendell Holmes, Jr., advised students of law in the nineteenth century, "If you want to know the law and nothing else, you must look at it as a bad man, who cares only for the material consequences which such knowledge enables him to predict, not as a good one, who finds reasons for his conduct, whether inside the law or outside of it, in the vaguer sanctions of conscience."[7] A very high proportion of our richest and most famous lawyers today do look at the law from the perspective of a bad man, either because they are themselves bad men (not impossible) or because they have abdicated all judgment in their choice of clients. Disreputable clients, after all, pay better. The failure of Gray's Bank Board to control the egregious crookedness of so many S&Ls must be laid in large part at the doorsteps of the great Washington, New York, Chicago, Dallas, and Los Angeles law firms. More than eighty firms, for example, represented Charles Keating and American Continental Corporation (the parent of Lincoln Savings) in his five years of tussles with the Bank Board. Among them were Akin, Gump, Strauss, Hauer & Feld of Dallas; Arnold and Porter of Washington, D.C.; Baker & Botts of Houston; Hogan & Hartson of Washington, D.C.; Jones, Day, Reavis & Pogue of Cleveland; Kaye Scholer Fierman Hays of New York; Sidley & Austin of Chicago; Stroock Stroock & Lavan of New York; Vinson & Elkins of Houston; Weil, Gotshal & Manges of New York. All these firms have more than two hundred lawyers to feed; and Keating has estimated his legal fees as high as $70 million.

A study by the GAO of forty-seven "Near-Failing Thrifts" found that between January 1986 and December 1988 the Bank Board had taken 17 formal actions to stop their practices, of which 10 were effective and 7 were not, plus 185 informal actions, of which 77 were effective, 77 were not effective, and 31 were indeterminate.[8] And many of the tighter regulations Gray put through in his last year—"the serious efforts to get rid of the Dick Pratt bullshit," as chief accountant Tom Bloom put it—were "postponed" by Danny Wall when he became chairman, on representations from the lawyers that the restrictions they imposed would be too great.

Meanwhile, the Wall Street houses quickly learned that they would be paid off no matter what happened to their customers. Some S&Ls lost more money playing the market than the total of their deposit liabilities, which was easy enough to do when you were playing with futures and options on government bonds and other financial instruments—and you could stay in the game by selling anything you owned on a repurchase basis and get more money to buy again. "Doubling down" became a popular strategy. "You've got a loss on what we sold you last month," the city slicker said to the country bumpkin, "but we'll buy that back from you on your agreement to repurchase from us, and then you'll have money to buy some more of it. Then the price has to go back only half as far for you to break even, and when it goes up, you'll have bigger profits." Sure you will.

The Federal Savings & Loan Insurance Corporation repeatedly paid off and guaranteed the Wall Street firms that counseled, facilitated, and profited by this irresponsible behavior. In effect, the Bank Board on its own motion gave investment houses that lent money to S&Ls the same guarantees against loss that the law gave to depositors on their deposits, enabling S&Ls to borrow more money and lose more money. This was done through "repurchase agreements": The S&L "sold" the Wall Street house a million dollars' worth of government bonds or government-insured mortgage certificates under an agreement to buy them back in two weeks, a month, or three months at a higher price, reflecting the difference between the interest on the paper during that period and the interest the Wall Street firm was charging the S&L for the loan.

These repurchase agreements were very profitable business for the Wall Street houses, which could in turn pledge this paper to the banks and get the money they lent the S&Ls at rates considerably lower than what they charged the S&Ls. Because the FSLIC was guaranteeing the transaction, the Wall Street house did not have to worry that its collateral would lose value in a market collapse. If for any reason the S&L couldn't buy back these bonds and certificates, the FSLIC would put up the cash. Under Gray's administration, the insolvent S&Ls had grown so dependent on brokered deposits and on such agreements that the regulators could not afford to antagonize even the worst vampires of the money market. And repurchase agreements, after all, brought money without brokers' commissions, and at lower interest rates than the S&Ls had to pay for brokered deposits. Every penny the S&Ls could save on their cost of funds, the Bank Board argued, was a penny less they lost, which thus protected the insurance fund. "We were desperate," says NYU professor Larry White, who was a member of the Bank Board while Gray was chairman, "to find lower-cost money for the S&Ls." But if they used the new money to place more losing bets, which is what happened, the only gainers were the Wall Street firms that took the other side of the bet.

In short, Gray, like his successor Danny Wall, was always being bullied or, worse, ignored by S&L owners and trade associations, senators and congressmen, lawyers and accountants, Wall Street prestidigitators, professors, and consultants, all the scoundrels who had found ways to make money out of the government's mistakes and were willing to fight to the death to prevent the government from correcting them. But Wall was willing to be bullied; he looked for guidance to the people who were bullying him. By contrast, Gray sat late at night in the office the Bank Board had reconditioned for him at a cost of $47,000—with a kitchen and a couch where he sometimes crashed because it was too late to go home, and with a security guard on the fifth floor to supplement a system with electronic controls because Washington is dangerous late at night—agonizing with members of his inner circle about what he ought to do next.

He incessantly warned the world what was happening, and time and again he tried to stop the abuse of the peculiar rules that defined legality in the operation of an S&L. He found ways around the shortage of examiners and put on track (though it went off the rails, for reasons we shall examine later) a system for disposing of assets that might have broken the FSLIC out of its bureaucratic shell. If he couldn't stop the spread of what Edward Kane of Ohio State brightly called "zombie thrifts," he at least slowed their growth. With absolutely no help from Congress and with a legal staff never confident of the Board's authority, living constantly with the fear that the truth might spark an unmanageable run on the bank with incalculable consequences, Gray kept riding the tiger. Someone else might have done better; many others, as was demonstrated after his departure, might have done worse. "I never professed to have anything more than good judgment and honest instincts," Gray says. That doesn't, of course, get you far in Washington; but the readers of a book like this one are presumably a higher court.

One must also note the extreme loyalty of the people who formed Ed Gray's inner circle: Ann Fairbanks, now making more money than she knew existed as part of the Robert Bass circle at American Savings, who returned to work at the Bank Board in a wheelchair after a brain tumor operation because Ed needed her; Robert Sahadi, a young economist who has moved on to be the man in charge of securitization activities at the FNMA; Thomas Bloom, the Bank Board's bright young chief accountant who unsuccessfully tried to get his elders and betters at the AICPA to study what they looked like in the mirror; Norman Raiden, who had helped Beverly Hills S&L in its shenanigans with the Bank Board and was thus less easily foxed by lawyers for other frauds after he became Gray's general counsel; and William Black, a red-bearded young lawyer who served as counsel to the FSLIC and to his great credit became persona non grata with both Jim Wright and Charles Keating to the extent that neither would attend a meeting if he was there. All these people feel a strong affection for Ed Gray, and a man wins loyalty like that from people like these only by earning it.

[1]

Gray's initial assault on money brokerage in January 1984 was a rather abstract idea. What he had brought back from his meeting with Isaac was a proposal for what they called a "zero-based" rule. Deposit insurance would adhere to the individual who placed the money, with a $100,000 ceiling. Thus, each broker could have for all of his customers together no more than $100,000 insurance. Gray never denied that this would kill the money brokerage business. Isaac, who cared about the ideology of the thing, argued that he was seeking a free-market solution. Let the deposit brokers themselves become the insurers of the deposits they moved around the country. Or let them buy private insurance with some fraction of the fees they were paid for the money.

Accepting the argument of the brokers and some of the banks and S&Ls that money brokerage served a function by moving funds from regions where housing or auto sales were slow to regions where they were brisk, Isaac insisted that the system needed incentives for the brokers to investigate the institutions where they put the money. "Deposit brokers," he said in testimony to a House committee, "are wonderful people. Some of my best friends are deposit brokers. But I would like them to operate without a federal guarantee. I would like them to select banks based upon the soundness of the banks. . . . We can't have brokers out drumming up business all over the country to hand money to problem banks so they can make lousy loans. . . ."

Congressman Doug Barnard, a small, courteous Georgia Democrat with manicured white hair who had been a banker in private life, didn't like the rule at all and felt it would deprive banks in his district (suburban Atlanta) of funds they needed. Big banks might still get money under Isaac's system, but little banks without a national name would be out in the cold. He insisted that there had to be another way. So did Sen. Alan Cranston, brutal as always in defense of those in the financial services industry who contributed to his campaigns, who denounced "the steadfastness of the regulators in their public comments of their intent to proceed to a final rule despite an overwhelming number of comments to the rule calling for a more moderate approach."[9] Later he would accuse Gray of violating the Administrative Procedures Act by "putting pressure on people where your regulatory authority is involved," because Gray had told a U.S. League conference that if he couldn't control money brokerage, he might have to increase insurance premiums.[10] Donald Regan's Treasury Department was bitterly opposed; on the day before the "zero-base" proposal was published, Deputy Secretary Tim McNamar kept Gray on the phone seven hours, alternately cajoling and threatening, to try to make him back off. But Isaac and Gray, pointing out that smaller banks had other ways to raise money through correspondent relations, said they had a first responsibility to their insurance funds, as indeed they did.

Two spectacular failures of institutions funded with brokered deposits put a fire in Gray's belly on this issue in the first quarter of 1984. One of them was San Marino S&L in California, which had engaged in collusive sales of land and condos in partnership with two San Diego real estate developers while growing from $23.9 million in 1980 to $841 million in 1984. While the Bank Board and the California Department of S&Ls were moving to close it down, San Marino raised a quick additional $40 million from brokers for one last (unsuccessful) fling. This was Gray's home territory, and the shock was personal, made especially personal because these people had been big Republican contributors, and both the White House and the Treasury let Gray know of their displeasure at his action. The other, involving an institution with more than 83 percent of its deposits imported from brokers, was Empire of Mesquite, Texas, which arrived before the Bank Board on March 14, 1984, with a staff recommendation to close it down. Accompanying the paperwork was a twenty-one-minute, homemade videotape entitled "Report on Empire S&L of Mesquite, TX," the evidence of what used to be called a horseback survey by real estate consultant Frank Augustine, who rode a small plane and a chauffeured car to take pictures of projects funded and controlled by Empire and a nest of con men inside and outside the S&L industry. On the Interstate 30 corridor leading west from Dallas to Lake Roy Hubbard, there were thousands upon thousands of unoccupied and unsold condominiums.

"A project called Snug Harbor," said Augustine's flat, funereal voice "—vacant. On Faulkner Point North, numerous projects, numerous buildings, totally vacant. No sales effort, no leasing effort, and across the street, more slabs and active construction. Notice the incredible waste, the total lack of contractor control. . . . Angel Cove, a large project, high density, no occupancy, building after building, 24-to-30 plexes, still unoccupied, still building . . . Faulkner Gardens, Faulkner Corners . . . In those buildings where some occupancy is found, it is believed the occupants are contractor employees. . . . In the distance, numerous projects, virtually 100 percent complete, no occupancy, and the land between the camera and the buildings is being prepared for more development. . . ."[11] Gray would see that tape dozens of times and make it available for friends to view. I showed it in early 1989 to a businesswoman from Dallas who had been puzzled about why her city had suffered so severe a depression; she cried at the end, conscious of the extent to which this sort of swindle had damaged the city's legitimate enterprises and those who work in them.

How all this had come about had been detailed several months before Augustine made his tape, in a splendid series in the *Dallas Morning News* by Allen Pusey and Christi Harlan. They described the astonishing exploits of a gang formed by Paul Arlin Jensen, a thirty-three-year-old Mormon con man with connections to television's wholesome Osmond family; Clifford Ray Sinclair, an indicted phony loan broker who had cheated people in Alabama and Arkansas and was loose in Texas only because that state had refused to extradite him; Danny Faulkner, an illiterate ("dyslexic" was the way he put it) painting contractor who bought an S&L with the proceeds of the paint job on the Dallas Cowboys' stadium; W. L. ("Bubba") Keetch, a mortgage banker with a mail-fraud conviction on his record; and Spencer H. Blain, Jr., an experienced S&L executive from Austin who, when the scam began, was vice-chairman of the board of the Federal Home Loan Bank of Little Rock (later moved to Dallas), which was the authority figure for Texas S&Ls. Among others involved were state senator Ted Lyon, whose law firm put together the deals by which greedy "investors" were paid to "lend their net worth" to the borrowings that supported the construction projects, and Texas attorney general Jim Mattox, who wheeled and dealed for his own account with the authors of the fraud.

The scheme was to inflate the price of land parcels in the Dallas area, enabling participants to trade them back and forth and eventually dispose of them at immense profits. Though Faulkner would later plead that he couldn't have had *mens rea* (guilty intent) in these matters because he couldn't read what he was signing, it was a genuinely ingenious plan, with many pieces that fit together perfectly. The conspirators' first requirement was a lender. Jensen entered into agreements to buy two small-town S&Ls but did not actually buy them (thereby avoiding conflict-of-interest rules). Keetch secretly controlled another S&L. So did Faulkner. The next step was to find some apparently legitimate investors who would sign contracts committing themselves for hundreds of thousands of dollars on notes to banks and S&Ls that would put up the money to build on the land parcels. The deal offered to them by Senator Lyon's law firm—and snapped up by doctors, lawyers, and businessmen—was one where the corporations to which they were "lending their net worth" paid them a fee up front (from $21,000 to $43,000 in each transaction). In one project, the investors received a prospectus claiming, "This will show you a return of $200,000 in the two-year period, with no cash output on your part"—in addition to the fee.[12] And since the fee was borrowed money—just some of their own note returned to them—it meant it wasn't taxable. Whoop-de-do, fellas! Whaddaya know about that?

Some investors were recruited at fancy breakfasts held at a diner out by the sites to be developed. Attorney General Mattox and Democratic gubernatorial candidate Mark White came to some of them, lending legitimacy and collecting contributions. The deals were closed at the offices of the Dallas Title Company, which supplied appraisers with false documents of comparable sales and made fortunes from the new title insurance policies that had to be written for each sale of land. (Its employees also benefited, according to the sworn testimony of its manager, by taking their own participations in the land to be sold at inflated prices.) One investor told the *Dallas Morning News* reporters, "I was dumbfounded. There were dozens of people signing dozens of documents. It seemed like it went on forever." Another said, "[The closing] was the only place you'd see all these people you were investing with. If you looked at them, they looked like people qualified to make good business decisions. . . . I wanted to ask questions, but I didn't want to be a jerk."[13] Few of the investors understood that each of their notes underwrote the entire borrowings of the corporation that would develop the land, not just some finite share. When this was called to Senator Lyon's attention, he said, "Anybody who would go down there and sign a note for that much money and not read the papers is pretty stupid if you ask me."[14]

Money was made here in lots of ways. The land speculators flipped the property, selling it back and forth to each other at prices that might multiply by ten in a single day. One transaction detailed by Pusey and Harlan involved 24.6 acres for which two of the inner circle paid $806,000. They divided it into 16 parcels, had them appraised for $16.4 million (by an appraiser who later pleaded guilty to fraudulent appraisal), and sold them to investors who signed notes for $8,075,240, of which they got back $270,000 cash in fees for signing. Appraisers charged five times their normal fees for these deals and sometimes were permitted to take a piece of the deal for themselves. Three appraisers, whose letterheads bore the Master Appraiser certification of the American Institute of Real Estate Appraisers, did virtually all the work on the half-billion dollars or so that was processed through this system, and they were all partners in some of the projects. So were the S&Ls, through their service corporations, and the owners of the S&Ls.

The notes signed by the investors were then sold by the S&Ls that had put up the money, sometimes to other S&Ls in the loop, sometimes far afield. Tom Gaubert was prosecuted in Des Moines because an Iowa S&L wound up with the final, ludicrously undercollateralized note on Texas property Gaubert had flipped. He was acquitted, former S&L commissioner Lin Bowman thinks correctly, not because there was no wrongdoing but because the jury thought Gaubert was merely doing what his buddies had told him to do and didn't understand it was wrong. If a note was sold, the originators could book their fees (which often ran four or five "points"—$20,000 or $25,000 on a $500,000 loan) as immediate profit, payable to the owners. Of course, the way Arthur Young and Coopers & Lybrand did accounting in the Texas market in the early 1980s (and those were the dominant firms), originators could take the points as current income even if they didn't sell the loan. The contractors (owned by the developers) then got theirs through inflated prices, and the suppliers to the contractors took a piece, with kickbacks all round.

By March 14, 1984, when Gray saw the videotape, this horse was long out of the barn. David Cates of Cates Consulting told the House Committee on Government Operations that if the Bank Board had been on the ball, there were grounds to intervene in Empire "in mid-1982, certainly by early 1983."[15] Many of the land flips and other horrors already were known to the Texas Savings & Loan Department, and as early as May 19, 1983, Commissioner Lin Bowman had imposed a rather toothless "supervisory agreement" on Empire. For once even the accountants were worried: Coopers & Lybrand kept asking for an extension on the date for filing Empire's audited reports for the fiscal year ended September

30, 1982. "Coopers & Lybrand," Bowman told the committee, ". . . assured us they were unhappy with the situation." But after thinking about it a while and after taking Empire's money, Coopers & Lybrand decided to sign Empire's statement, after all. In August 1983 the Bank Board began a "Special Limited Examination" that immediately turned up big, big problems, leading to criminal referrals to the Justice Department. But between August 1983 and March 1984, when Gray saw the videotape, Empire's deposits, the money it took from the public that the FSLIC would have to pay off, rose from $180.3 million to $308.9 million.[16]

These are entertaining stories, and they account for a fair piece of the losses at the S&Ls. They were hard to catch at the beginning, because land flips are by no means always criminal. Texas land was often contracted for on long options, and there could be valid reason for exercising the option and selling the land rather than selling the option. Moreover, a developer like David Fox of Fox & Jacobs, a builder of huge tracts of genuinely affordable, decent housing (Fox was the hero of my book *The Builders* in 1978), often bought land adjacent to the land on which he was going to install a large residential community. It was known that Fox did not inventory land. On the day he announced a project, adjacencies became much more valuable to builders of shopping centers. No small part of Fox's initial financing on his projects came from what could be considered flips of the property next door to his building sites.

And, of course, the S&Ls that indulged in this activity seemed hugely profitable. The year before Empire was taken into custody by the sheriffs, *National Thrift News* had rated it the most profitable S&L in the country. (The next year, the gold medal would go to American Diversified, then Vernon.) "Do you want to go into court," Texas S&L commissioner Lin Bowman said defensively, "and tell the judge why you're seizing what the industry's trade magazine just called the most profitable S&L in the country?" One notes in passing how much must be wrong with the law, accounting practice, and journalistic measuring standards when year after year fraudulent enterprises earn the rank of "most profitable."

Obviously, loans with fees and several years' reserve to pay interest built into the loan were really investments and should have been accounted for as investments. But until 1986, the S&L Guide of the AICPA was mum on the subject, and like the appraisers, the accountants were paid more than their usual fees to hide the truth about what these guys were doing. Sandra Johnirgan, who later moved on to head the Pritzkers' S&L empire, was then supervising thrift work at the Arthur Young office in Dallas, which *never* questioned whether S&Ls could claim immediate profits from self-funded fees and interest payments on an ADC loan. She was also chairperson of the S&L section of the AICPA. Except to the extent that the S&Ls were making direct investments in the land and the projects—and that was, as Jake Garn screamed at Gerald Levy, mostly a matter of state law—the sort of scam perpetrated by these several dozen Texas S&Ls was not a product of federal deregulation and probably could not have been prevented by better regulation, unless the Bank Board could carry the AICPA with it, which under the circumstances was pretty unlikely. (As late as August 1989, in fact, when the AICPA circulated a draft of a new "Proposed Audit and Accounting Guide" for S&Ls, the S&L section was still insisting that an ADC loan did not become an investment unless the S&L was to receive more than half the residual profits on the project.)[17] What deregulation had done was make possible the easy accumulation of all the money these conspirators needed through the combination of Pratt's relaxation of rules and Congress's elimination of control on interest rates.

By March 14, when Gray saw the Augustine tape, Texas S&L commissioner Lin Bowman had already seized Empire, and the Bank Board's action merely transferred control from the Texas authorities to the Federal Savings & Loan Insurance Corporation, for liquidation purposes. But the monstrosity of what was portrayed on the tape (Gray called it "fiduciary pornography") gave him unstinting support from the other members of his board. The support came not only for his brokered deposits rule, which was formally adopted on March 25, but also for firing the president of the Federal Home Loan Bank of Dallas.

This was hard for Board member Mary Grigsby, who had come to the Bank Board from a job with a Texas S&L, less hard for

Donald Hovde, a Wisconsin developer and real estate broker. Hovde was a big man with heavy shoulders and a large rectangular head under a mop of gray hair. (He usually wore a golf club blazer, because what he really cared about was golf.) A man of considerable ability, Hovde had chaired Realtors for Reagan in 1980 and had come over from HUD—where he was under secretary—because he was tired of doing the work of Secretary Samuel Pierce without getting the status or the credit. He had not opposed Gray. "I felt we had to get our arms around brokered deposits," he says. "When that developer community moved in on the S&Ls in Texas, I said, 'My goodness!' because I knew that cast of characters. But I wasn't sure Ed was following the right approach."

In fact, Gray was not following the right approach if his goal was to limit the use of brokered deposits by S&Ls. He had a tool at hand that was unquestionably legal: He could simply restore the regulation Pratt had removed, limiting brokered deposits at an S&L to 5 percent of total deposits. That was Hovde's recommendation, and Gray consulted with William McKenna, a veteran S&L lawyer with a sweet smile and knobs of white hair like a character in a Dickens movie, who had been chairman of the Housing Commission. The problem was that the FDIC had no comparable authority, and the end result of imposing the 5 percent rule on S&Ls might well be the drain of brokered deposits to the country banks that were historically the great enemy of the thrifts. "Ed didn't want to win," McKenna remembers, "unless Isaac could win, too." So they went for the redefinition of depositor, which was valid for both or neither. And presently Judge Gerhard Gesell ruled that the deposit insurers did not have the authority to discriminate between deposits placed directly and deposits placed through brokers. Gray and Isaac went to Congress for legislation, and Gray dragged the U.S. League with him (for the League knew perfectly well that Gray could, if he wished, impose the 5 percent limit on its members), but recourse to Congress was hopeless. "In 1984," Hovde recalls with a shudder, "we had some forty institutions that grew by more than *one thousand percent*. And we had no way to stop them."

Dick Pratt argues that the whole struggle over money brokerage was a waste of time: "A crusade to stop brokered deposits was
looking for the keys where the lights are brightest." Lin Bowman
feels it's unfair or worse to pick on Texas regulators for the over-
optimistic view of the state's growth potential: "I went to a chamber
of commerce dinner in Houston in 1986, and the dinner speaker
was this fellow Naisbitt whose book was on top of the best-seller
list. He said that by the end of the century Houston was going to
be the biggest city in North America and Austin was going to be
the fastest growing. The governor got up and put his arm around
Naisbitt's shoulder, and said, 'That's my boy.' We may have been
stupid down here, but we weren't alone." But Gray was right to
target what he targeted in early 1984. Without brokered deposits,
the little guys, who in aggregate blew most of the money, could
not have grown large enough to make much nevermind. And
S&Ls like Empire and Alamo and Vernon and Gunbelt (officially
Sunbelt) took their gigantic losses before the energy industry collapsed, when the oil price was still around thirty dollars a barrel
and the high-tech companies were flowing to Austin and Texas
was apparently flourishing.

[2]

In the spring of 1984, shortly before the Bank Board and the
FDIC imposed their brokered deposits rule, Gray went before
Congress asking for additional powers for the FSLIC. He wanted
the deposit insurer to have discretion "to limit the asset and liability
powers of state-chartered thrift institutions." He wanted authority
to impose a surcharge on the insurance premiums paid by S&Ls
"undertaking highly risky activities." And he wanted power "to
halt an unsafe and unsound practice" by the issuance of a cease-
and-desist order to the owners of the institution, even though he
still lacked final proof that continuation of present practice would
create insolvency or dissipation of assets. He also asked Congress
to make his agency, like the FDIC and the Federal Reserve, independent of the OMB and the executive budget review process.
Like the bank regulators, the thrift agency paid its own way with

assessments on the regulated and should have the power to use that income to strengthen the enforcement of its regulations. Instead, David Stockman's OMB was interposing itself between the Bank Board and Congress, insisting that neither the number of examiners (down to 700 for 4,000 thrifts) nor their salary (in 1984 the Bank Board was still starting examiners at $13,500) could be increased.

None of what he asked for did Gray get from Congress in 1984 or later. So toward the end of the year, he began to move by regulation—reregulation, as the Reagan White House called it with fear and loathing. The first proposal was an effort to restrict growth and require greater net worth from institutions that wished to grow. Growth greater than 25 percent a year was prohibited without special waiver from the Bank Board acting as the board of directors for the FSLIC. Five-year averaging was eliminated on a phased-in schedule as a method of calculating net worth. A week later, Gray dropped the other shoe by proposing a rule that restricted direct investments, limiting them to the greater of 10 percent of a thrift's asset portfolio or 200 percent of its net worth. Anything over that limit would have to be reserved against by a capital infusion of at least 10 percent of the price of what was being acquired. This was more permissive than the rule Garn-St Germain had imposed on federally chartered thrifts, which at least in theory permitted only 3 percent of assets to be in the form of direct investment, but it was much tougher than the law in California, Arizona, Texas, or Florida. Gray was using his authority as the insurer to impose federal controls on state-chartered thrifts, too, regardless of what the state laws and the state S&L supervisors might say.

Both these proposals provoked fury from the U.S. League, which was still pushing limitless growth as the salvation of the industry, and especially from Texas, where a high fraction of the S&Ls were playing Ponzi games that could appear profitable only if they could mask the collapse of the old loans with phony income in the form of fees. Gray ducked that year's convention of the Texas League of Savings & Loans, sending down instead board member Mary Grigsby and his assistant, Ann Fairbanks, on the theory that chivalry would protect them. Grigsby, nevertheless, came to the convention wearing a Groucho Marx mask. Fairbanks remembers being grabbed at the shoulders by Durward Curlee, the Texans' political lobbyist, who shook her and yelled, "Nobody is going to deprive us of our God-given right to make a profit."

Though William O'Connell of the U.S. League had told Gray that the growth rules were a bad idea—the essence of the Pratt deregulation and the Garn-St Germain Act had been the promotion of growth to get out of the trap of low-yielding assets—there was a generally acceptable commonsense validity to what the Bank Board had done. Not many thrift managers would be able to cope with the strains and stresses of a growth rate exceeding 25 percent per year. There was a general exemption for institutions with less than $100 million in assets and an exemption also for S&Ls with enough tangible net worth to keep a cushion between their liabilities and the insurance fund if some of the newly acquired assets went sour. And specific exemptions could be given on application if the S&L had a case to make.

But the rules limiting direct investment were another story. It was while urging him not to proceed with this one that O'Connell held out to Gray the prospect that if he kept his nose clean and did what the League wanted him to do, he could be O'Connell's successor, at a salary that was then $275,000 a year. The opportunity to use insured deposits for direct investment was what brought new money to the industry: Charles Knapp had made a merchant bank out of the FCA, with huge investments in the common stock of American Express, Disney, and Merrill Lynch; Gary Driggs in Phoenix had used the deposits of Western Savings to buy an airline (Air West); Charles Keating, formerly a lawyer for the Cincinnati billionaire Carl Lindner, had just purchased Lincoln Savings & Loan of California and transformed it from a home mortgage lender to an Arizona land developer and player in the takeover market. Mike Milken and Drexel Burnham were interested; so was Salomon Brothers. S&Ls could protect themselves against the return of inflation only if they got a piece of the action, which meant an equity stake in the projects they financed.

Gray was presiding over a shrinking insurance fund that was supposed to be protecting a rapidly rising mountain of deposits. He had lived through the phenomenal losses of San Marino and Empire, both largely caused by activities that should have been defined as direct investments, and he had been terrified by the brush with illiquidity at Charles Knapp's Financial Corporation of America, which could have wiped out the entire insurance fund. He had noted the tale of a promoter and money broker named J. William Oldenburg, who had originally appeared in the newspapers as the owner of the Los Angeles Express in the new U.S. Football League and the man who paid $34 million, the biggest price ever for a quarterback, to sign Steve Young to a ten-year contract. Oldenburg had bought 363 acres of land in Richmond, California, for $874,000 ($80,000 down), then bought State Savings and Loan of Salt Lake City for $10.5 million, and then sold the former to the latter for $55 million. Not until December 1989 was he convicted of anything related to this, and then the jury could agree only on one count of fraud, for "making a false entry in the minutes of a meeting of State Savings' board of directors."[18] (And then the trial judge threw out that conviction on the ground that the prosecutor hadn't addressed that issue; the case is to be retried.) In his commonsense way, Gray reached the sound (and correct) conclusion that projects to which S&Ls contributed the equity as well as the loans generated greater losses.

There were some interesting numbers. The December 1984 issue of *Savings Institutions*, the magazine of the U.S. League, showed that S&Ls growing at a rate of more than 50 percent a year had by far the highest proportion of real estate development activities as a percentage of assets, also the highest reported return on assets, the highest reported net worth—and, by four and five to one over the industry average, the greatest use of brokered deposits. "Supervisors," Norman Strunk and Fred Case wrote in their U.S. League–sponsored history of the thrift debacle, "should have suspected that something was wrong; they should have instinctively known that such rapid growth and large profits could not have been sound."[19] But decision making was not in the hands of supervisors; politicians and academics were in the saddle. Robert Sahadi, a recent University of Cincinnati economics Ph.D. who had come on board early in 1984 to be the Bank Board's director of policy development, remembers that "we didn't have convincing knock-'em-dead evidence" to back the rule. Indeed, the Bank Board's chief economist, James Barth, was bullish on direct investment. Like most academics, he believed the "modern portfolio theory" that said diversification itself gave protection against disaster. He had not considered the possibility that deposit insurance and the perverse incentives it provided made modern portfolio theory quite irrelevant to the analysis of this industry.

Many of the S&Ls that were heavily engaged in direct investment were owned by Republicans who had made significant contributions to the Reagan campaign in the election that had just ended. Don Regan, moving over to be White House chief of staff, believed in helping contributors to the party and also believed in modern portfolio theory. He was outraged by Gray's "reregulation" of the industry and began plotting his removal. Keating of Lincoln Savings hired economists, including George Benston of the University of Rochester, to do studies on direct investment for thrifts. Benston, a free-market Democrat (which means he thinks the world is naturally nice and thus excludes the possibility of fraud from his calculations), thought direct investment was the cat's meow: "[R]eturns before taxes on assets other than direct investments are negative . . . before tax returns from direct investments are positive and quite high."[20]

Benston's formal study, which had been submitted the previous October, included a list of thirty-four S&Ls with more than 10 percent of their assets in direct investments. The list was headed by North America S&L, a Southern California venture by a dentist and his beautician girlfriend, where unbeknownst to Benston, many of the assets claimed were bank CDs the owners had forged; second came Ranbir Sahni's American Diversified, described in the first chapter of this book; fourth was the crooked Centennial S&L that forms the centerpiece of the book *Inside Job*; later came Beverly Hills, Oldenburg's State Savings, San Marino—a roster of thieves. These thirty-four were cited as evidence for Professor Benston's insistence that Gray's proposed direct investment rule would cripple the entrepreneurs the industry needed; it was "unsound conceptually, unsupported by meaningful evidence, and likely to be damaging to both the savings and loan industry and the Federal Savings and Loan Insurance Corporation." Of the thirty-four, at least thirty-two were insolvent by 1989.[21]

More weight was wanted. Keating hired lawyers, including four of the largest firms in New York. Arthur Liman of Paul, Weiss, later to achieve notoriety as the Senate counsel in the Iran-Contra hearings, recommended that Keating reinforce Benston with Alan Greenspan, former chairman of the Council of Economic Advisers for Gerald Ford, at the height of his reputation because he had been chairman of the committee that crafted the compromise on Social Security taxation. Greenspan was then a private consultant heading a not very successful firm that dissolved in 1987 on his departure to become chairman of the Federal Reserve Board. His specialty was what he once called "statistical espionage,"[22] and the book on him in that capacity was that you could order the opinion you needed. The PBS public affairs show *Frontline* reported in May 1990 that Greenspan was paid $40,000 for writing a couple of letters and testifying for Keating.

Greenspan endorsed Benston's study, and went much further. Accepting Keating's figures on his own company as the truth, he hailed his client as representative of the group of new S&L venturers who were going to save the industry. Later, in a fawning and false letter to the Federal Home Loan Bank of San Francisco supporting Keating's application for an exemption from the rule on direct investments, Greenspan expressed confidence that Keating's operation of his S&L could not pose a risk of loss to the FSLIC "for the foreseeable future." (See complete text of Greenspan's letter, appendix C.)

Neither Greenspan nor Benston referred to—or, perhaps, understood—the peculiar accounting conventions that permitted S&Ls to book a stream of profits on unsold land and construction projects. Under the rules of the AICPA—rules continued in the 1989 draft of the AICPA's guide *Audits of Savings and Loan Institutions*[23]—owners of unimproved real estate and construction projects can increase the reported value of these assets by their expenditures for holding and development costs, including interest. Builders of course must find someone to finance such expenditures, but S&L owners who are also developers can simply pay them out of insured deposits. Most S&Ls booked a further increase in the value of their properties based on the salaries of the people involved with the projects. Several are known to have calculated these increased valuations by applying the interest rates they paid for their highest-cost brokered deposits (including the fees to the brokers) rather than an interest rate reflecting their average cost of funds. Such things were approved by the Big Eight accounting firms, at least six of which were quite willing to go along with what they called "aggressive accounting" if the fees were high enough. Not infrequently, as noted in chapter 3, the most inexcusable accounting practice was quite acceptable to the Bank Board.

Greenspan and Benston did not consider the objection to direct investment by S&Ls that came from Kent Colson, executive director of the National Association of Home Builders, who argued that his members who had to borrow their funding in the market should not have to compete directly against S&L owners who simply converted insured deposits to the working capital of construction companies. Nor did it enter their theorizing that the sort of builder most likely to acquire an S&L was the undercapitalized gambler. One such person said to Michael Patriarca of the San Francisco Home Loan Bank, who had questioned the capital adequacy of his thrift, "Look, if I had enough capital I wouldn't need to be in this kind of business."

Direct investment was also a states'-rights issue. If the FSLIC refused deposit insurance to institutions exploiting the enlarged investment authority awarded to them by state law, then deregulation of asset powers by the states would become meaningless. Rep. Frank Annunzio of Illinois, a Democrat who was a major beneficiary of campaign largess from the S&Ls, introduced a resolution ordering the Bank Board to delay the imposition of the new rule for at least six months. Its ostensible proponent was the National Association of State Savings and Loan Supervisors. ("Is it true that the State Savings and Loan commissioners wanted to postpone the regulation for six months?" Annunzio said to Gray in the fall of 1989, when Gray was testifying before the House Banking Committee on Keating matters and Annunzio was trying to insulate himself from that political disaster. "Nah," Gray replied, shaking his head. "They wanted to kill it."[24] More than half the members of the House signed on as sponsors.

Gray testified strongly at the hearings on Annunzio's bill: "With all due respect to you ladies and gentlemen on the subcommittee, the responsibility for the mounting losses to the FSLIC—losses that we are now seeing from bad assets resulting from what have turned out to be bad direct investments—would fall squarely on the shoulders of the Congress itself, to the extent that such a delay would impair our ability to deal with such problems."[25] He did get support from one S&L commissioner, William Crawford of California, who was looking at the same horrors Gray saw. And the pressure from the other state commissioners diminished sensibly when Keating told a public meeting that he had never in his life met a regulator whose intelligence he respected. Despite its immense initial sponsorship, the Annunzio resolution never emerged from the committee.

As adopted in January 1985, Gray's new regulation grandfathered all investments made prior to his public proposal on December 10, 1984. And it was, of course, much less restrictive than the limits the banking laws imposed on commercial banks. It did not interfere with investment in junk bonds (which were loans, not ownership pieces) or seek to restrict gambling in the futures and options markets. And it sunset automatically in two years: If the Bank Board did not adopt another resolution controlling direct investment before the end of 1986, state-chartered S&Ls would again be free to do whatever the state law let them do.

CHAPTER 6

...Which Roll over Him

HAIRMAN EDWIN GRAY gave Congress his first budget for the Bank Board on May 5, 1983, seven days after assuming office. It was, necessarily, Pratt's budget. It called for thirty-eight fewer examiners than the Board was employing in the current fiscal year, to save $300,000. There were going to be fewer S&Ls, and they were going to be healthier—and besides, more of the necessary information was on computers and could be retrieved more quickly. The Reagan administration was gung ho for paperwork reduction, and from January 1, 1984, S&Ls were no longer going to submit detailed monthly reports to their immediate supervisors at the district Federal Home Loan Banks. Instead, a sketchy quarterly report would be substituted, so there would be less work for supervisors to do.

In the 1984 budget, the entry-level salary for an examiner was to be $14,390, as against $17,000–$17,900 in the bank regulatory agencies. The average salary for an S&L examiner was $24,775, as against $30,750–$37,900 for bank examiners. There were fewer than 700 examiners in the system for about 3,500 thrifts, and the turnover rate was about 14 percent. (Up to 23 percent in key districts like Dallas and San Francisco; Dallas would presently, at precisely the wrong time, become a supervisory desert, when the Home Loan Bank headquarters was moved there from Little Rock. Most supervisors elected to remain in Arkansas, where there was lots of work for people with S&L experience because the local S&Ls were growing wildly.) Examining an S&L, of course, was relatively simple work; like Tolstoy's happy families, home mortgages routinely paid each month are all alike. S&L examiners in 1983 still did not have the bank examiner's power to "classify" loans according to the degree of risk that they wouldn't be repaid. Unlike the bank examination report, which has a secret section in the back containing the examiners' views of what should be done in this institution (normally for the use of its board of directors), the S&L examination report was a neutral document. Just the facts, please.

Within six months Gray knew this system was on all counts insufficient for his needs: There weren't enough examiners, and they weren't adequately trained. Many S&Ls, including some of the most venturesome and crooked, were not being examined at all: FirstSouth of Pine Bluff, Arkansas, went from December 1982 to February 1985 without an examination and during that period grew from $500 million to $1.3 billion, much of it by purchasing other thrifts (with Bank Board approval) and lots of it through bad loans, especially to officers and directors. Its counsel, E. Harley Cox, a former president of the Arkansas Bar Association, protected some of the bad loans from prying eyes by purchasing them himself—with money lent to him by FirstSouth in an arrangement whereby he could sell the loan back at face value for whatever reason whenever he pleased. (Cox's firm later paid $12 million to the FSLIC to avoid suit over its dealings with First-South.)[1] One of the largest loans had gone to the construction of Clint Murchison's busted Sundance condominium project in Palm Springs, California. I gave a talk to the annual conference of the Arkansas Savings & Loan League in Fayetteville in the summer of 1984, and before flying out asked its executive director what he thought I should talk about. "Oh," he said, "they're very gloomy." I'll cheer them up, I said. "Don't try that," he said. "You'll lose credibility." How come? I asked. "Well," he said, "they've just learned that when a man comes to Arkansas for money to build condos in Palm Springs it means he can't raise it in California and there may be a reason for that."

Today it is a cliché among deregulators that if deregulation is to work, there must be increased supervision; but when Gray suggested such a principle to the OMB and the Office of Personnel

Management, he was sent to Coventry. This was in late 1984, during the first cut at the making of the federal budget. Gray's insistence that he needed more lines for examiners plus upgrades for examiners and supervisors never got past Constance Horner, one of David Stockman's deputies, who explained to him that deregulation meant fewer, not more, examiners. Why didn't he take the problem to Ronald Reagan? someone once asked Gray. After all, he held a presidential appointment and knew the president. You don't understand the White House, Gray replied, and then added that it had never crossed his mind to take his problems to the president; Reagan didn't like to hear about such things.

Instead, Gray went to William McKenna, Los Angeles S&L lawyer, former counsel to the Bank Board, and chairman of the Reagan Housing Commission. With board member Donald Hovde, who may have been the original source of the proposal, they worked out a plan whereby the budget for the examining and supervisory staff would be transferred out of Washington to the part-private and very profitable district Banks. They were not accountable to the OMB and could hire as many examiners as they thought they needed and pay them as much as was necessary to get first-rate people. In November 1984, at a Kansas City meeting of the three-member Bank Board and the presidents of the twelve district Home Loan Banks, flesh was put on the bones of the transfer idea. "Then we took it to [Senator] Proxmire and [Senator] Garn, and to [Representative] Eddie Boland," said Hovde, "and we got authorization to go ahead."

This proposal highlighted a weakness in the Bank Board's supervisory structure. The Home Loan Banks were essentially sources of liquidity for their member S&Ls, passing on the proceeds of bonds they sold to the national money markets (on a "consolidated" basis, as a joint venture of all the Home Loan Banks together, regardless of which was actually lending the money). Perhaps because they were jointly liable on the bonds, the Banks were very conservatively run, requiring the best collateral on their loans—no Federal Home Loan Bank has ever taken a loss, though Dallas in 1987–88 ran some risks that made its sisters shudder. The presidents of the Banks reported to their own boards as much as they did to Washington, and they were the principal supervisory agents for their districts. Examiners housed at the district Banks visited and examined the S&Ls and passed on their findings to the local supervisory staff.

Prior to the Pratt days, all the locals could do was refer suggestions to Washington, but in 1982 the Bank Board gave them "power" to negotiate voluntary supervisory agreements with their wards. "Pratt," said Ken Thygersen, thinking back to the days of the Housing Commission, "didn't understand the inherent weakness of an examination staff who liked to get along with the people they regulated and considered themselves partners. And didn't understand risk." In any event, anything requiring any degree of compulsion had to go to higher authority. Only Washington could issue cease-and-desist orders, and only the chartering agent (the Bank Board or a state commissioner) could declare an S&L insolvent and turn it over to the FSLIC. Prior to the Gray days, it was generally true that Washington didn't want to hear about trouble and encouraged cozy relations between the industry and the district Banks. But Washington, if it got the information, could also be tougher. Gray in 1984 began to demand that the districts negotiate supervisory agreements, and the number of such voluntary submissions to regulatory authority rose from 0 in 1981 and 5 in 1982 to 233 in 1985. In a pinch, as Gray demonstrated in Dallas early in 1984, the Bank Board could remove the president of a local Home Loan Bank and require the appointment of its own man.

Still, there was something uncomfortable about turning over the staffing of supervision to the Home Loan Banks: It had the look of making the fox the policeman of the chicken coop. The board of each Bank was populated mostly by the CEOs of the S&Ls of the district; there was reason to believe that an "establishment" in the industry controlled who got criticized for what. Charles Knapp was not entirely wrong when he said his rivals were behind the supervisors' drive to cut him down to size (though it was a good idea, whoever had it), and even the inexcusable Charles Keating, rightly or wrongly, argued that Gary Driggs of Western Savings and Gene Rice of Merabank, his competitors in

Phoenix, sat on the board of the Federal Home Loan Bank of San Francisco and went unchallenged for years on activities not entirely different from his own.

On the other hand, the Home Loan Banks were independent entities and profit centers beyond the reach of the OMB. They could expand the examination staff to whatever size they wanted and raid other agencies for experienced examiners and supervisors, paying whatever wages were necessary. And if the OMB wished to challenge the legality of this move, which initially it did, the Justice Department was now in the hands of Gray's friend Ed Meese. The transfer was scheduled for July; in May, Ms. Horner told Gray that the OMB had relented and would give him an additional forty-five examiner slots if he would back off the transfer proposal. Gray laughed at her: With Congress and Justice on his side, he didn't need the OMB.

Moving the selection of examiners to the district Banks doubled the size of the police force in thirty months: from 747 on July 6, 1985, to 1,524 on December 31, 1986. It also brought in a cadre of experienced and sophisticated people. Two men who had served as Deputy Comptroller of the Currency—and had bravely ordered Bank of America, then the nation's largest, to pass its 1986 dividend—became enforcement directors in Dallas and San Francisco, respectively. Senior examiners from the FDIC, the OCC, and the Federal Reserve abandoned their own ships to swim over to the district Banks for salaries typically 35 percent (and often 50 percent) over what they had been earning. This made for major politico-bureaucratic problems at the Bank Board, because it meant that people making more than $100,000 a year were reporting to people who made $50,000 a year. Gray closed down the old Office of Examination and Supervision and substituted an Office of Regulatory Policy, Oversight, and Supervision (ORPOS) that was organized under the aegis of the Federal Home Loan Bank system; this meant it could be funded by assessing the district Banks rather than on the agency budget and could thus pay salaries competitive to those in the field. The total costs incurred rose dramatically, probably to more than $150 million a year. As none of this was directly charged to the government or to the S&Ls themselves, the program had a high order of support both on Capitol Hill and in the industry.

Though everyone claims more than he achieves, there's no question that the people who came in from the bank regulatory agencies in the 1985–87 period vastly improved the supervision of the wounded industry. In December 1985, over some dead bodies at the U.S. League, Gray put a major tool in their hands with the passage of regulations that for the first time authorized S&L examiners to classify loans and compel the examined to put aside reserves against potential losses. This brought onto the books in visible form the evidence that a management was "dissipating the resources" and was risking insolvency, which were grounds for a cease-and-desist order from the Bank Board.[2] And it gave examiners something they could do when they found, as they often did, inadequate or nonexistent documentation for loans. The power to examine state-chartered thrifts in this way was inherent in other powers awarded the Bank Board by the Garn-St Germain Act, but the power to put a state S&L into conservatorship or receivership had to be renewed by Congress after four years, or it lapsed. Congress didn't move, and in October 1986, at what was perhaps the worst possible time, the examiners lost their statutory authority to take over state-chartered S&Ls that were not visibly insolvent. This authority was not restored until the fall of 1987.

Joe Selby in Dallas, a former acting Comptroller of the Currency who earned the nickname "The Hammer," was surely the most effective of the transplants from the bank regulatory agencies, followed by his former sidekick Michael Patriarca in San Francisco. But except perhaps for Topeka (an important exception because its jurisdiction included Oklahoma and Denver), all the districts became much better regulators in the 1985–87 period. It was hard work, and they were bitter about the publicity the Bank Board received in the spring of 1989, after the Bush administration decided it was time to recognize the problems of the S&Ls. "To be held up to public ridicule after doing the job we were told to do is a little disappointing," said Patriarca, a tall, courteous young man with a large face and an impressive head of dark red hair. This was a few weeks after the FDIC, the banks' insurer, had been told to seize 220-odd insolvent thrifts, excluding the FSLIC and the district Banks from what had been their supervisory duties. "FDIC said their mission was to stop the fraud and stop the risky activity. We had already changed the management and the board in all these institutions, and they had the Maytag repairman role."

Unfortunately, the movement of examiners to the district Banks did nothing for the FSLIC, which was still under the thumb of the OMB. The FSLIC was immensely overloaded with the detritus of exploded thrifts and was seriously understaffed. In 1980 it had only 34 employees; even in 1985 its roster was only 159, mostly inexperienced. Historically, the FSLIC had disposed of busted thrifts rather than of their assets—that is, it had arranged for failed S&Ls to be merged into successful S&Ls, with some cash assistance from the insurance fund to compensate the acquirer for the poor quality of the portfolio he was acquiring. The FSLIC was a very sleepy outfit, rule-bound (one of its officers never went anywhere without a copy of the Home Loan Act, which he waved in the air as authority for whatever he wanted to say or do), and exceedingly political, working with a narrow group of lawyers, asset managers, and purchasers. In 1989, after I published an article in the *Wall Street Journal* touching on the work of the FDIC and the FSLIC, I received a letter from a small corporate real estate investor on the West Coast, who wrote that he would rather live again his three years in Vietnam than negotiate another deal with the FSLIC. The time consumed was endless. John M. Berry of the *Washington Post* reported in August 1987 that as of that date, "FSLIC has never closed the books on an S&L liquidation."[3]

By 1985 the FSLIC's books showed assets with a face value of $2.5 billion, most of them in Texas, and the agency lacked talent to manage or sell them. It wasn't easy for outsiders to find out what the FSLIC had for sale, and buying property from the FSLIC was a lot easier if your own lawyer was part of the club. Lawyers' fees ran from large to "excessive," as the Bank Board's own counsel once labeled them. Over the course of the next year and a half, the book value (i.e., acquisition cost) of the FSLIC portfolio would triple, and much of that was foreseeable.

Late in 1985 Gray, Hovde, and McKenna tried to build on the

precedent of moving the examiners to the district Banks by forming a Federal Asset Disposition Association (FADA). This organization, of which McKenna became chairman, would use "private sector management and marketing techniques to manage problem assets in the FSLIC at the lowest cost consistent with sound operations and to sell these assets as fast as is consistent with obtaining the best possible return for the FSLIC and its receiverships." The FADA would have a charter as an S&L, and the FSLIC would own all its stock. As a private instrumentality, it would be able to pay top dollar for its personnel and to hire them on the basis of ability alone. A headhunter was engaged, and he came up with Roslyn Payne, a very intense, pale, slim woman with deep black eyes and jet-black hair, who had been running two offices of Genstar, a publicly owned diversified realty company in Los Angeles. Her appointment was a measure of how nonpolitical the FADA was to be, for she was known to be a registered Democrat. Her salary was $235,000 a year.

"I think what Bill [McKenna] and Hovde had in the back of their minds was the Home Owners Loan Corporation from the depression," Payne says. "That agency bought bad mortgages from S&Ls and others and held them until economic conditions improved, and in the end returned a profit to the government." But that was never in the cards. The FADA was not to own anything: The FSLIC would always have title, and thus the FSLIC would not only make the decisions about what assets should be put into the FADA pot, but would always have to approve any sales the FADA might wish to make. Business that went to the FADA was business that did not go to the friends and often former or future colleagues of the FSLIC staff, who were being paid less than a third of what Ros Payne was being paid. It is fair to say that they did not put a high priority on making the FADA look good. "We asked for power of attorney to close deals," Payne recalls. "We asked them to respond to proposed deals in a timely manner so we could proceed. Guess how many times they changed the forms. We would submit a deal, and it would come back: 'Information is incomplete.' "

At best there wasn't much property in the FSLIC portfolio.

As Ann Fairbanks, Ed Gray's assistant, put it, "This was a savings and *loan* business. What these people had were bad *loans.*" Payne explained her problem to the U.S. League convention in November 1987: "In states like Florida and California, which combined hold nearly a third of the value of all FADA-managed loans and properties, the judicial foreclosure process may mean a wait of two or three years before gaining clear title to a property."[4] And that's when the path to a clear title was straight. Many of these were bad loans with several lenders, all of whom had to agree before the property could be sold or even managed. Many other loans were so poorly documented that getting title to the mortgaged property was the sort of job that sends all of a lawyer's daughters through college. In a number of cases, most or all the lenders were the FSLIC's wards.

Thurman Connell was acting director of the FSLIC. The previous director had left the place a hate-filled shambles, and Gray was looking for someone with an independent reputation to take over on a permanent basis. Connell worked hard to get his district offices onto the same wavelength and attempted to establish a rule that S&Ls under FSLIC supervision would not sue each other, but the mess was unimaginable. Many loans, of course, had been put through a daisy chain of fake sales and resales to conceal from accountants and examiners the fact that they were delinquent, illegal, the work of insiders, etc. And the messier it was, the more likely it was to wind up on Ros Payne's plate. In the total package at FADA, four-fifths of the alleged value was in "problem loans" rather than real property.

Though a large data base was assembled and a number of distressed properties were repackaged and sold at better than appraised value, the FADA quickly became what Rudolf Bing, when he ran the Metropolitan Opera, liked to call "an outstanding disaster." Part of the problem was political: The FADA was caught in a larger war between those, like Gray and McKenna, who wanted to decentralize both the Bank Board and the FSLIC, placing greater authority in the field, and a permanent bureaucracy that wished to maintain centralized control. (The bureaucracy won.) And part was simply personality. Payne was by general

agreement a shrewd manager, careful planner, and clever re-
cruiter of both in-house staff and outside contractors; she was also
self-righteous and arrogant, though I would myself prefer the
adjectives straightforward and confident. What she wasn't was a
politician, in an intensely political post, where the outfits that had
historically worked with the FSLIC's assets had all the contacts
she didn't have.

Nor did Payne have much sense of public relations. The FSLIC
leaked a flood of negative stories about her and the FADA to the
press. A lot of this mud has stuck: In January 1990 the *Wall Street
Journal* ran an article about the need for the new Resolution Trust
Company (RTC) to avoid the sweetheart deals at the FADA, none
of which was in fact anything near as sweet as what the FDIC,
RTC's parent, had done for the commercial banks of Texas.[5] CBS
News came to meet and film the overpaid dragon lady. She heard
a few essentially insulting questions and then, muttering something about not having to put up with this, rose to her feet behind
her desk and walked out of the camera's eye, leaving the TV
cameras, cameramen, and interlocutors to find their own way out
of the office. This was *lèse majesté*, the ultimate social offense in
modern America, though there were those whose hearts went out
to her. We peasants in the print media found the whole episode
pretty funny, but it wasn't funny to Ros Payne; she returned to
California and even more money than she had made at the FADA
as a partner with her husband in the asset reorganization firm of
Jackson Street Partners in San Francisco, which doesn't get business from the FSLIC.

[1]

But the real problem with the FSLIC was that the insurance
fund was broke. Unlike the FDIC, which looks capable of handling
bank insolvencies because it keeps its books on a mom-and-pop
cash basis (and permits problem banks to overvalue the real estate
on which they have foreclosed), the FSLIC put its contingent
liabilities on its books. So the members of the Bank Board, which
owned and operated the FSLIC, knew that they could not pay off

the insured depositors in any number of small busted S&Ls (or any *one* of a number of larger busted S&Ls), simply because the cash wasn't there.

Though Pratt's holding actions had centered on encouraging his wards and their accountants to fudge the numbers, there had also been three instances where he put together groups of insolvent thrifts into one "phoenix" S&L, named for the bird that rose from the ashes of the fire that had consumed it. The newly assembled thrift would be just as insolvent as its parts had been, but that fact could be masked by crediting the phoenix with goodwill to compensate for the loss of market value in its portfolio of fixed-rate mortgage loans. Two of these (Talman Home in Chicago and First Rochester) worked out fairly well when interest rates came down, though neither had recovered sufficiently to be out of the fishermen's net when the Bush bailout bill passed in 1989. The First Rochester phoenix contributed its successful leader, James Cirona, to the presidency of the Federal Home Loan Bank of San Francisco in 1983. But Pratt's problem was S&Ls that had bet on interest rates and lost. Gray had to keep alive S&Ls that had for whatever reason shown loathsome credit judgment. No change in interest rates, no improvement in the external economy was likely to help them. They could keep themselves going, with ever-greater losses, simply because they had a deposit insurance license and access to a telephone, through which the money brokers would pour money in their direction if they paid enough for it. But their losses were going to keep increasing, *saeculae saeculorum*.

And Garn-St Germain multiplied the losses that had to result by approving a cockamamy plan of Net Worth Certificates. At the discretion of the Bank Board, the FSLIC would issue notes to S&Ls that could be counted as part of their capital. To pay for these government-agency notes, the S&Ls would issue notes of their own. Pratt's board had begun such a program without legislative authorization; general counsel Thomas Vartanian, who had admired the profitability of Texas thrifts in his preamble to the Practising Law Institute handbook on Garn-St Germain, bragged about his and his advisers' cleverness in devising the instruments. Gray's Board extended the damage with an interpretation that once the Bank Board had started issuing such net worth certificates to an institution, it was obliged to continue issuing them to make sure the beneficiary retained an apparently positive capital position. In the meantime, of course, worthless notes from busted S&Ls piled up on the FSLIC's books as presumed assets of the insurance fund, contributing to the insolvency of the FSLIC itself.

The premium S&Ls paid the FSLIC for deposit insurance was one-twelfth of 1 percent of the deposit base, yielding in 1985 about $700 million, substantially less than was required even by the limited cash outlays the Bank Board had to make in connection with transferring the assets of S&Ls that state regulators had closed. In February 1985, Gray called the condition of the FSLIC to the attention of the industry by imposing a special assessment of one-eighth of 1 percent on deposits, more than doubling the existing insurance premiums. Initially "temporary," the assessment was renewed every year and legislatively continued in the 1989 bailout bill.

But these sums were peanuts next to what it would cost to resolve even the fifty or so worst insolvencies. Even among the Bank Board's economists, believers to a man in the magic of the marketplace, it was unthinkable to leave these institutions in the hands of their existing management. Instead, Gray and his staff developed the Management Consignment Program (MCP), under which the management of an insolvent S&L was dismissed and the institution was placed in the hands of a team seconded for the purpose from a successful S&L. More than seventy-five such deals were negotiated. The S&Ls that were put into conservatorship or receivership in this program were those that had taken full advantage of the new powers they received from state charters or Garn-St Germain: As a group, Dennis Jacobe of the U.S. League wrote in an internal memo, they had gone from a portfolio invested 66.9 percent in mortgages and 17.7 percent in "nontraditional assets" in June 1982 to a portfolio invested 35.2 percent in mortgages and 42.3 percent in "nontraditional assets" in 1986.[6] They were the people Alan Greenspan and George Benston had praised only eighteen months earlier. The losses were much worse than anyone realized, because the examiners (like Greenspan and Benston) had accepted the S&Ls' own evaluation of their owned property and highly leveraged real estate loans. When the program began in June 1985, the MCPs had an alleged net worth of 0.4 percent of their assets; by June 1987 the books showed a negative net worth, − 26.4 percent of assets.[7]

The typical MCP contract paid the S&L that accepted the job 135 percent of the salary and benefits of the people assigned, plus a flat fee of $30,000 a month. The real incentive for most of those who undertook the work was the chance to eliminate harmful competition. Insolvent S&Ls could keep themselves alive only by paying higher rates for deposits and by supporting high-risk projects. They sowed dragon's teeth all around the country—remote land developments or yet another shopping center, commercial building, or golf course–condo community in an area already saturated with such things (financed by more prudent lenders at a time when the demand had not yet been satisfied). One of the things that was killing decently managed S&Ls was the steady loss of value of the projects they had financed in the past. The new projects that drove down prices and rents in the area were built by developers who didn't give a hoot whether what they built sold or not so long as somebody paid them to build. And the S&Ls that financed them did so because their balance sheet needed the up-front fees and interest payments they could take as income even though the money was really part of what they were lending. The new outside manager would put a stop to all that—and if the institution could in fact be made viable, his employer would have the inside track in the race to acquire it.

Because the MCP was conceived as treatment for a dead limb rather than as surgery, the results were sickeningly bad. The universal experience of the S&Ls that contributed management was · that their previously sensible executives immediately raised interest rates at the institutions they were sent to manage. It was the only way to keep the funds rolling in. This produced screams of rage from branch managers who found their customers running across the street to do business with the busted S&Ls their own people were managing. R. Dan Brumbaugh, formerly deputy chief economist at the Bank Board and one of the devisers of the strategy, writes somewhat superciliously, "This criticism misses the point. MCP institutions' deposit rates generally reflect the failed strategies of the previous owners and managers who attempted to grow their way out of their problems, leaving assets whose market value is below book value. A sudden reduction in deposit rates would lead to withdrawals that would drain liquidity and exert pressure to sell the assets."[8] But the purpose of seizing these S&Ls should have been to sell assets and shrink the institutions.

In fairness, the MCP thrifts, having grown on the average by 127 percent in the two years before they were taken into the program, did shrink a little when they got new management, but not nearly enough. Instead of selling the good assets, the new managers pledged them at their local Home Loan Bank as collateral for advances that maintained the size of their bloated S&L. Nearly all of them took on new business, much of it related to the siren calls of the Wall Street houses that sold their merchandise to S&Ls they financed by brokering in deposits and arranging repurchase agreements. After all, profits made on new business would cut the eventual cost to the FSLIC, wouldn't they? The sad fact is that Gray's Bank Board still had a vestigial hope that many of the dead S&Ls, sustained with a slight color of life through the infusion of "capital certificates" by the FSLIC, would rise from the grave by reasserting profitability. What congressmen wanted, after all, was not honest accounting, a stable financial system, or the preservation of an insurance fund; they wanted what they called "forbearance" for their constituents and especially for their contributors. They got it—reluctantly from Ed Gray, then enthusiastically from his successor Danny Wall, who was, after all, a creature of the Senate.

Forbearance could scarcely be avoided if the FSLIC didn't have the money to guarantee a purchaser against losses from the portfolio he purchased, let alone to pay off the depositors and close the place down. Nobody could be an effective Bank Board chairman without an armamentarium of spikes to put through the heart of Ed Kane's "zombie thrifts." The need to stop these walking dead had to be the first priority, because while they wandered about gathering high-rate deposits and making bad loans, they bled the life out of the healthy sectors of the industry. And they would ultimately bleed the taxpayer. Gray, as early as October 1985, went public in Congress with a proposal to "recapitalize" the FSLIC so that he would have the cash to pay out the depositors in the most bloodthirsty S&Ls. The plan was to add an immediate $3.5 billion to the insurance fund. The money would be raised by the sale of bonds that would later be repaid by the industry from insurance premiums. Like the special assessment he had instituted in the spring, this was enormously unpopular in the industry, and Don Regan, whose finger was now measuring the political winds from a desk in the White House, decided the time had come to strike.

In June, Regan had begun spreading rumors that Gray was on his way out. Donald Hovde, previously an unambitious member of the Bank Board, apparently decided around that time that he would like to be chairman, and in June delivered to a happy Texas Savings and Loan League convention a remarkable speech complaining, "If the perception is that the [FSLIC] fund is weak or insolvent, then I'm concerned about that—because it simply isn't the truth."[9] By October, when Gray proposed his recapitalization, all the newspapers knew he was resigning; the *Wall Street Journal* carried a story saying that Regan felt only Gray's departure could resolve "the turmoil in the industry." A successor was known: James Needham, former president of the New York Stock Exchange and an old friend of the White House chief of staff. This was the first year of Ronald Reagan's second term; it was still presumed that his chief of staff spoke for, not just in lieu of, the president.

Gray had not in fact expected to stay much more than two years, but now his back was up. He went over to the White House to talk to Ed Rollins, one of Reagan's and his companions back in the California days, a normally cheerful, roly-poly professional pol who was leaving mostly because he didn't want to work for Don Regan. Gray recalls that Rollins said, "Regan's determined to get you, and he probably will, but if you want to stay, just hold on." One should note, because Gray himself now tends to forget it, that the industry rallied round to call for his continuance in office. Regan was the man from Merrill Lynch; Gray was not alone in his suspicion that Regan had a hidden agenda, a plan to destroy the S&Ls as privileged providers of housing finance. Sure as shooting, Needham would not stand in the way of such an agenda.

So Gray hung on, fighting for an agenda that had not changed. By January 1986 he had convinced the Teasury Department of the need to pump money into the FSLIC, and Deputy Secretary George Gould endorsed a program of bond sales to be repaid through insurance premiums. A sober second look had convinced both Gray and Gould that $3.5 billion was nowhere enough, and the proposal that went to Congress in April called for a bond issue of $15 billion, capitalizing the proceeds of the special assessment Gray had imposed the year before. As a permanent cost, the extra one-eighth of 1 percent premium would be a substantial burden, much weight in the saddlebags in the race for consumers' funds. It would mean that S&Ls had to pay an insurance premium of 21 cents for every $100 of deposits, while banks paid only 8.33 cents, and money market funds (not to mention the mortgage packagers, Freddie Mac and Fannie Mae, which sold paper that carried an implied government guarantee) paid nothing at all. Even so, the numbers could be made to work only on the assumption that the total deposit base of the nation's S&Ls would grow at an annual rate of 7 percent.

It was not an extravagant assumption: After all, most accounts at S&Ls grew 7 percent a year through simple crediting of interest. But if in fact there were many too many S&Ls for the work this sort of institution would be doing in the future, then the $15 billion wouldn't clean up the problem, and the survivors, with lower total deposits, couldn't pay off the debt incurred to raise the $15 billion. The long-established leaders of the industry, who felt strongly that they should not have to pay for the malfeasance of the Pratt-Vartanian generation of S&L owners, saw clearly that Gray and Gould were underestimating the amounts that would be needed as the industry shrank. Gray reports that one of the most able of them said to him, "We don't want to do anything now. In another year or two it will be obvious that the government has to pay for it. Wait." When he persisted, the staff director of a congressman much beholden to the U.S. League told him that he'd never hold another job in the industry and he'd wind up sleeping on the grates outside the State Department with the rest of the homeless. A leadership cadre that knew the losses were worse than the government believed acquired a mass following who couldn't believe it was as bad as the government was saying —and, of course, the enthusiastic support of the thieves whose thievery would prosper so long as the FSLIC lacked the funds to put them out of business. With the help of the accountants, the lawyers, and the Wall Street types who were bleeding the industry, they put an all-but-irresistible squeeze on a Congress that looked to all of them for campaign contributions.

[2]

The fight over the FSLIC recapitalization deepened the cost of this disaster to the taxpayer by some tens of billions of dollars. During the course of the battle, in October 1986 the FSLIC lost some of its authority over state-chartered thrifts that had been awarded it in the Garn-St Germain Act. Actions were taken by Jim Wright, the incoming Speaker of the House of Representatives, to assure and maintain the FSLIC's disabilities for the benefit of friends in Texas whose S&Ls were among the worst offenders in the industry. These actions were, as we shall see, the true (though not the stated) cause of his departure from politics in 1989. Under the eye of history, these events are the story of the transition years at the Bank Board, the isolation of Gray, and his replacement by Danny Wall; we shall tell that story in chapter 9.

For now note only—but note well—that the shortage of money in the FSLIC was in itself a determinant of the Bank Board's attitudes toward the Godzilla rising from its own swamp. Riches build assertiveness, and poverty compels timidity. Arthur Burns, as chairman of the Federal Reserve, could take actions that would cause a flight of funds from Franklin National Bank, because the Fed and the FDIC could easily pay off any depositors who wanted out. William Isaac, as chairman of the FDIC, could close down the Butcher brothers' chain of banks in Tennessee and Kentucky, brushing off both the fact that Jake Butcher had been a Democratic candidate for governor and the insistence of what was then the accounting firm of Ernst & Whinney that these crooks (now in jail) were legitimate businessmen and the regulators were just too unsophisticated to understand. If need be, the FDIC fund could pay back every penny in every bank: not to worry.

At about the time Ed Gray was scheming to find funds to keep FCA from going under, the FDIC announced that it had suspended repayment of deposits that had been brokered into Strong's Bank of Dodgeville, Wisconsin, because the deposit broker, High Yield Management, Inc., of Clifton, New Jersey, had put too much money recently in too many banks that had failed. The FDIC suspected that High Yield had also brought these banks the bad loans that killed them. "The FDIC is investigating High Yield . . ." the announcement said, "to see if the $1.1 million in deposits it placed are 'linked to fraudulent transactions.' "[10] (Eventually, the FDIC did pay. Even in the interim, High Yield kept going, shifting its daily ad in the *New York Times* from the boast that all deposits it placed were insured by the FDIC to a boast that they were insured by the FSLIC; but the event cost them business.) As the collapse of the state-insured Ohio S&Ls demonstrated in the spring of 1985, confidence in promises of deposit insurance was not limitless: If people doubted the solvency of the fund, there could still be runs on the bank—indeed, on many banks. The FSLIC had to be nervous, and it was.

Obviously people are selected to fit jobs: Pratt was installed at the Bank Board to strip regulation from the industry; Gray and Wall were appointed as men who would not rock the boat. Gray was a public relations man, and PR men are not assertive. Years in the Senate as a manservant had made Wall timid and subservient: "You can't imagine unless you've worked there," he said of Congress a week after his resignation, while under fire from Congress, "what little kings all these people become." Moreover, as they insist (Wall a little more than is seemly), their formal powers were closely circumscribed. In 1966, mostly on demand from the lobbyists of the U.S. League, Congress had written into law a collection of time-consuming "due process" restrictions on moves by the Bank Board to penalize, compel, or seize ill-managed S&Ls. Gray had won at least formal agreement from the League to support new legislation that would codify the Board's power to take action against S&Ls that were operating in an unsound and unsafe manner, dissipating the assets, or failing to keep their books and records in order—but Congress wouldn't move.

Within the system, one school, headed by William K. Black, the Bank Board's litigation director, held that you should assume you have the power to stop something that clearly ought to be stopped. Judges don't want to look like fools. "Most of the work we do," said Michael Patriarca in San Francisco, "is on apparent authority." But the Bank Board legal department, Black said, "had an incredibly passive risk-averse attitude. They always thought of the bad precedent you would set by losing the case. And because you never brought a litigated case you never got a precedent at all." Both Gray and Wall lament that their lawyers said they couldn't take over control of an S&L until it was demonstrably insolvent. And by the time an S&L reached zero net worth on a regulatory accounting principles standard, its real losses were typically ten percent of its total assets. If the taxpayer is to be protected, the insurance fund must take control of what the institution is doing with the insured deposits some months before the situation disintegrates.

But regulatory government—and every regulator who is both smart and dedicated knows this—really works not by law but by announcement effect. The SEC wins almost all of its cases without trying them, simply by judicious use of publicity, and the Federal Reserve put a stop to the shenanigans of Michele Sindona at Franklin National Bank by publicly denying his request to add a factoring business to his holding company. The House Committee on Government Operations suggested in 1984 "that merely bringing an action, merely going to court—whether for a permanent or a temporary injunction—will often have a salutary effect in remedying the problems giving rise to the action."[11]

In the closet at the Bank Board was a shillelagh that could

have been used to beat to death any S&L that was recklessly endangering the industry's insurance fund. An announcement that the FSLIC was investigating an institution with an eye toward the possible withdrawal of its insurance franchise would have brought any S&L to its knees in a matter of days. Depositors would have taken out their money, and the Wall Street brokers would have headed for the hills. If the S&L sought an injunction against such action, it would merely publicize the risk now suddenly attached to its deposits and borrowings. An important fraction of the industry would have supported the withdrawal of insurance from any of at least fifty S&Ls widely known to be run in an unsafe and unsound manner.

Threats could also have influenced the behavior of the accounting firms—and did so, once. After the Vernon fiasco, Gray and Dallas Home Loan Bank president Roy Green were mad enough to start proceedings to bar Arthur Young from serving as accountant for insured S&Ls. Word that this was afoot got to New York, and Young's managing partner called Tom Bloom, the Bank Board's accounting theoretician, to ask what the firm could do to avoid what would be at best a painful and costly labeling. A treaty of sorts was negotiated, which involved the movement of some Young personnel and a new discipline in the Texas partnerships to make them no worse than everybody else in Texas. Soon thereafter, at Bloom's urging, the American Institute of Certified Public Accountants established a subcommittee chaired by Arthur Young partner Donald Ellwood to plan revision of the inexcusable rules that permitted S&Ls to take profits on securities holdings that rose in price while burying in the inventory, at cost, securities holdings that declined in price. When this subcommittee seemed likely to bring in a new and more sensible rule, the full committee disbanded it. By then, Danny Wall was chairman of the Bank Board, and Bloom was powerless even to complain.

Every so often, the Bank Board or one of the Home Loan Banks would privately drop a neutron bomb on an S&L that needed Wall Street funding. Merrill Lynch, for example, brokered deposits into several large S&Ls that were clearly candidates for government seizure. Typically these CDs cost the S&L issuing them about two percentage points or so more than market interest rates. (Merrill kept 30 percent of that for itself and gave its customers the benefit of the other 70 percent; Merrill also made a market in these CDs, enabling customers to evade the "penalty for premature withdrawal" that was part of the legal structure of these financial instruments.) The government had the right, on taking over a busted bank or S&L, to cancel such contracts and offer the depositors a choice of their money back with previously accumulated interest or a new account at lower rates. Before rolling over funds in a busted but not yet seized S&L, Wall Street houses (not only Merrill) began to demand "comfort letters" from the Home Loan Bank system, promising that these high-rate certificates would be honored—at the expense of the taxpayer—for their full duration. By delaying their approval of such comfort letters (though approval was eventually given in virtually every case), the regulators could force the proprietors of the S&Ls who needed that money to do what they were told.

But such incidents were rare. Starting in early 1987, when the GAO declared in a published report that the FSLIC was insolvent, the normal situation was that an embattled S&L would bully its regulator with threats to go broke and start a run the FSLIC could not pay off. Both Gray and Wall urged the district Banks to give the comfort letters. Shortly after his retirement, Wall said that the one issue on which he completely changed his attitude and his vote after the passage of the Bush bailout bill was the question of maintaining the high rates promised by an S&L's brokered CD after the S&L was seized by the government. Previously he had always voted not to inconvenience the brokers (in the case of Merrill Lynch, not to penalize them: Merrill traded CDs for its own account, maintained an inventory, and might be stuck with losses). Once the bailout bill was law, he voted to reduce the cost of funds to the S&L. "I turned one hundred and eighty degrees," he said. "Now we had the money to pay off the CDs. It makes a big difference to have money."

When Charles Keating told the Bank Board that they had

better let him do what he wanted with Lincoln Savings & Loan, because they couldn't afford the costs of his bankruptcy and the insolvency of his S&L, he was not so original a thinker as he and some of the regulators thought. He was simply the worst of a bad lot.

CHAPTER 7

Lincoln Savings Kills the Women and Children . . .

> Financial accounting emphasizes the economic substance of events even though the legal form may differ from the economic substance and suggest different treatment.
>
> —Accounting Principles
> Board Statement #4,
> Section 1022.17(12)

I F Charles H. Keating, Jr., had not existed, it would have been impossible to invent him. Sixty-six in 1989, a champion swimmer when a boy, very tall, lean, with a fixed and rather ghastly grin of big teeth, he was both unique and paradigmatic. Everything about him was lifelike but larger than life. He was a dictatorial man, scattering lavish rewards and severe punishments at whim. When he wished to convince someone not subject to his will, he would lean forward, put his face in the other person's face, and shout things like "What this industry needs is *leadership*."

Keating controlled Lincoln Savings & Loan but refused to be an officer or director. Asked why by a representative of the Federal Home Loan Bank of Seattle, he said he "did not want to go to jail."[1]

Others in the S&L business made contributions to political campaigns to win access and influence in government; Keating bought senators and got someone who was quite literally deeply indebted to him appointed to the Federal Home Loan Bank Board by President Ronald Reagan.

On the local scene, Keating's American Continental Corporation (ACC) never had a request for a zoning alteration turned down or even delayed. A litigious man in regulated businesses, Keating gave $50,000 to the campaign of an Arizona state attorney general who was unopposed for reelection.

Others used government-insured deposits to dabble in the markets; Keating put $100 million of such deposits into a risk-arbitrage fund owned and operated by Ivan Boesky. When the regulators objected that $100 million might be a little much to put into one avowedly risky investment, Keating's people said it wasn't really one investment, because, after all, Boesky dabbled in lots of things.

Nepotism has never been unknown in American banking, but nowhere except ACC could one find a large (at its peak $6 billion) financial enterprise where five of the top eight officers were the chairman's son, daughter, and sons-in-law. Some received top positions, paying half a million dollars or more in salary, at ages twenty-four or twenty-eight.

Others accumulated raw land for speculation and capitalized the interest on the purchase price (i.e., assumed that the financial costs of continuing to hold the land added to its value as an asset) even as the land got less salable. Keating treated his land expenses as income year after year after year, though not a spade was turned on the property.

Just about every crook in the S&L business complained to politicians that honest regulators were conducting a vendetta against them; Keating got the Bank Board to take the knowledgeable Federal Home Loan Bank of San Francisco supervisors off his case and substitute ignorant but friendly guidance from Washington.

Not long after Keating had "persuaded" the accounting firm of Touche Ross to okay his booking a $56 million profit from a fake transaction that even Arthur Young had refused to permit, I suggested to Tom Bloom, who had been the accounting theoretician at the Bank Board in the Gray days, that when you considered all the things Keating had got away with, you sort of had to admire the guy. "Admiring Charlie Keating," said Bloom, "is like admiring the Joker in *Batman*."

Keating did his country one immense service: He sold directly to the public, at the offices of Lincoln Savings, about $235 million of unsecured subordinated notes in his American Continental Corporation (ACC), the holding company that owned Lincoln Savings & Loan of California. In 1986, regulators, worried about the exposure of the deposit insurance fund, were beginning to limit the money Keating could take out of Lincoln to finance his own speculations. By then no underwriter, not even Drexel Burnham, with which Keating had done a lot of business, would touch his notes with a pole, so he could not hope to sell them to institutions, the usual purchasers of such paper. James Grant, publisher of *Grant's Interest Rate Observer*, nominated these unsecured ACC notes for the title of "the worst securities available."[2]

The notes were structured for direct public sale by the 300-plus-lawyer New York firm of Kaye Scholer Fierman Hays & Handler and the Cleveland firm of Jones Day Reavis & Pogue, the second largest in the country. Federal regulators noted that these notes protected the FSLIC, because ACC's failure to pay them off would not create a claim on the insurance fund. California securities regulators came from (and returned to) law firms Keating feed. So both gave their approval to the sale of this garbage out of Lincoln Savings branches, where ACC said it would "rent offices."[3] (One notes in passing that this raises the issue of responsibility for protecting the investor in bank or thrift paper: "[B]ank and thrift regulation," two Connecticut lawyers wrote angrily in early 1990, "has become little more than a frantic search to limit deposit insurance exposure."[4] The sales were made by employees of Lincoln Savings (though both state and federal regulators had been assured that couldn't and didn't happen). ACC and Lincoln used the same A-shaped logo and print styles in their advertising.

The ACC notes, sold in $1,000 denominations, paid higher interest than insured deposits. Their purchasers were mostly elderly, because special efforts were directed at the retirement colonies and because the old folks really loved the idea of the higher interest. The selling technique was often bait-and-switch. Customers would answer ads offering high-rate insured CDs in the S&L, and their interlocutor would switch them to the note from the holding company, which paid even higher interest. And it had to be better, didn't it, because it was the *owner* of the S&L who stood behind it—a Fortune 500 company. Employees at the branches got bonuses for selling the notes.[5]

Some 23,000 Californians got stuck with this paper, which became worthless in the spring of 1989 when ACC sought the protection of the court in bankruptcy. Chairman Henry Gonzalez (D-Tex.) called some of Keating's victims as witnesses in his investigation of why the Bank Board had let Keating proceed for so long about his lousy business without regulatory restraint. Prior to the testimony by these old people, who talked of their impoverishment and their loss of medical treatments, the S&L outrage had been merely an impersonal matter of businessmen who had stolen from the taxpayer; and the average voter, while superficially annoyed, could sense nothing new in the scenario: Washington made its living by stealing from the taxpayer. Now there were individuals, dignified, suffering old people who had lost money they desperately needed. Their poverty could be compared to the life-style of a thrift owner and the members of his family who, from 1985 to 1988, had taken out of this enterprise no less than $34 million in salary and in the sales of their ACC stock back to ACC or its employee stock ownership plan (ESOP).

Because the disaster could be personalized, television began to pay attention. Politicians who had taken money from Keating and done favors for him were suddenly in deep trouble. For the first time, the examination reports of a corruptly operated S&L were put on the record. Though the odds were still strong that Washington lawyers would be able to lobby indefensible banking legislation through Congress in the early 1990s, the uproar over Keating opened up a possibility that for the first time since the 1950s the unbribed fraction of Congress would be in control—as indeed they had been, oh, so briefly, when the House Banking Committee finished its markup of the Bush bailout bill in the spring of 1989. The nation would then owe a great debt to Charlie

Keating—who, if still on the loose, would doubtless find a way to collect it.

[1]

Charles Keating, as even he would probably agree, should never have been allowed to own an S&L. It was not just a question of temperamental incompatibility, though Keating was the kind of American lawyer (not as uncommon as the profession pretends) who should never be allowed a license in any regulated business, because he regards regulations as challenges to his cleverness rather than as expressions of public policy. One can argue that such people shouldn't be licensed as lawyers, either, but we seem to have lost that war.

Apart from temperament, there was a specific reason to deny Keating access to an S&L. As an officer of Carl Lindner's spreading conglomerate American Financial Corporation (AFC), he had been involved with Lindner's Provident Bank in Cincinnati. The SEC had brought charges against him and his law firm in 1979, alleging improper loans to insiders and friends, plus failure to report a pattern of loans to purchasers of assets Lindner wished to sell. On a small scale, Keating as executive vice-president of AFC had done what he would later do at Lincoln. Lindner paid $1.4 million from his own funds back to his company, and Keating consented to a permanent injunction barring him from violation of several SEC regulations.[6] Such a consent decree should have barred Keating forever from the ownership of an insured depository.

"But Keating," Steven Pizzo and Mary Fricker wrote in an article for the *Arizona Republic*, expressing what has become majority opinion on how this man got started in this business, "was just the kind of visionary entrepreneur the S&L industry was convinced would be its salvation, and he won easy approval for his purchase of Lincoln Savings."[7] In fact, by the time Keating got around to making the deal for ACC to acquire Lincoln, in October 1983, the Federal Home Loan Bank of San Francisco was growing wary of builders as proprietors of S&Ls. The California Department of Savings & Loan was then in the hands of Larry Taggart, and of course approved the transaction immediately; but James Cirona, president of the San Francisco Bank, was reluctant to proceed. Five years later, Darrel Dochow, director of the ORPOS at the Bank Board, summarized the reasons for Cirona's reluctance:

> First, there was no evidence of any thrift industry experience among the senior officers of ACC. Second, being an out-of-state entity raised concerns of funds flowing out of California to support activities that would not benefit the association's local community. Finally, supervisory problems had already become apparent with firms associated with real estate development firms owning savings and loans. ACC addressed those concerns through submitting a new application that (1) offered a continuity of management by naming the then current Lincoln officers as officers of the association subsequent to acquisition, (2) stated that there would be no interruption of the association's then current program of community lending, and (3) gave assurance that no regulations pertaining to affiliated transactions would be violated.[8]

Keating promised that a majority of the members of the board of Lincoln Savings would not be on salary from Lincoln Savings, and he kept that promise in his fashion: All the members of the Lincoln board were on the payroll of the parent company, ACC.

Despite later statements by Alan Greenspan and Jack Atchison of Arthur Young & Co. to the effect that Keating had "rescued" a dying thrift and returned it to profitability, Lincoln Savings & Loan was in no way a distressed or even a problem institution. It was essentially a family business, with more than 40 percent of the shares in the hands of Donald Crocker, his brother, and his two sisters, whose father had founded it. Crocker was a lawyer, a Stanford graduate, who had dropped his practice to come back and help his father in the mid-1970s, when the S&Ls had their first timber-shivering crash with inflation. Like most S&Ls, Lincoln had lost money in 1981 and 1982 and had made its 1982 losses manageable only by selling off one of its most heavily trafficked branches. But with the decline in interest rates in 1983, the S&L had returned to profitability. Having seen Lincoln through the awful years, Crocker wanted to move on to something else. Keating came up with a bid of $51 million for Lincoln, about one and a half times book value (two and a half times what the stock was selling for in the over-the-counter market). Some $19 million went to the four Crocker siblings. It was enough. Crocker first started an investment company to buy and mend sick thrifts, then became West Coast director of the FSLIC. At this writing, he is president of J. E. Robert, Inc., one of the nation's largest asset management and disposition firms.

The Lincoln Savings Keating acquired had the lowest ratio of delinquent mortgages of any large thrift in the state of California. Many of its Orange County branches were in black and Hispanic neighborhoods, and it was among the state's most committed lenders to "mortgage-deprived areas." Keating, in his business plan, announced that he would continue with the current management in place and follow Lincoln's previous policies of concentrating on home mortgages in its primary market areas of Southern California. In February 1984 the Federal Home Loan Bank of San Francisco gave its approval to the change of control, and ACC took over. Almost immediately, despite the promises in his application, Keating fired virtually all of Lincoln's senior management. Lincoln thereupon stopped writing home mortgages, began soliciting deposits from money brokers, and began investing the cash in speculative securities and land development activities. Darrel Dochow told a conference-call meeting of regulators in February 1988 that Keating had said one of his mistakes was "not realizing that he would be held to live by the things he said in the business plan."[9]

Some years later, Keating told a meeting of his group and regulators from the Federal Home Loan Bank Board that he'd had to dismiss the Lincoln executives and change the course of the institution because its condition was much worse than he had thought when he bought it. They were incompetent—indeed, Crocker had told him he was right to get rid of them.[10] Crocker says both of these statements are lies. ("One of the reasons I sold Lincoln to Keating was that he said his business was a family and my people would become part of his family.") Keating's immediate violation of the promises he made to gain control of Lincoln had two long-standing effects: One was that he could argue at every turn that the San Francisco Home Loan Bank, in trying to control what a government lawsuit later called his "racketeering," was really carrying on a vendetta against him because of his little mistake of "not realizing" he was supposed to live by his promises; the other was that the San Francisco Bank took a somewhat more careful look at all aspects of Keating's business and knew him to be what California Savings & Loan Commissioner William Crawford later called "a con man."[11] This was five years and many swindles before Bank Board chairman Danny Wall referred to Keating as "someone who has in the course of his career been very successful, in financial transactions of one kind or another."[12]

[2]

ACC was a company built on the chassis of Continental Homes of Phoenix, Arizona, a subsidiary of Carl Lindner's Cincinnati-based American Financial Corporation (AFC). Keating had been executive vice-president of AFC, and his move to Phoenix in 1976 was considered exile by people in Cincinnati. In 1978, Keating bought the homebuilding company from Lindner, who did not retain a stake in it though he has other interests in Phoenix. That was a great year for housing, and Keating expanded rapidly on borrowed money to Chicago, Salt Lake City, Seattle, and Denver. In SEC filings associated with an underwriting of ACC stock by Drexel Burnham in 1983, Keating's company described itself as the largest homebuilder in Colorado and in Phoenix, and the seventh largest in the country, all told. Among its major sources of income was a mortgage-banking subsidiary that wrote mortgages on these homes and sold them into the secondary market. Either because the stock was hard to sell or because Drexel considered it a good investment, more than 1,400,000 shares of ACC remained in Drexel's hands. This represented more than 10 percent ownership of ACC and by law should have been reported to the SEC, the California Department of Savings & Loan, and the Bank Board when ACC applied for permission to buy Lincoln. It was not.[13]

The Chicago operation failed in 1980; Salt Lake City and Seattle, in 1982. As each local company went under, it took with it the local mortgage sub. There is every reason to believe that Keating went after an S&L because he had lost access to other sources of funds and needed government-insured deposits to finance his operations. In 1985 the Colorado subsidiary collapsed with substantial losses—admittedly $9.4 million, and almost certainly more. Eighteen months later, ACC abandoned homebuilding in Phoenix, leaving the actual production of houses to friends it bankrolled, and began concentrating entirely on hotel operations, Wall Street shenanigans, and the development of planned communities where friends would do the actual building. All of this was to be funded by Lincoln Savings, for ACC had quickly spent the proceeds of its Drexel Burnham underwriting and had no money of its own. (As early as 1985, it carried $99.40 of debt for every dollar of tangible net worth.) To support Keating's varied speculations, Lincoln grew from about $1 billion in 1983 to almost $6 billion at the time of its seizure by the government in 1989. Losses to be picked up by the taxpayer were estimated in early 1990 at $2.5 billion, and because Keating's involvement with Wall Street was such that he was always risking more than his deposit base, the estimate may be low.

Lincoln Savings, as a part of ACC, necessarily started off like gangbusters. As was normal in purchase accounting in the S&L business, Keating wrote down, as far as he permissibly could, the value of the tangible assets he was acquiring. He then took the difference between written-down value and previous book value as goodwill, which could be added to capital and used as a base for expansion. Goodwill in 1984, despite the objections of the FASB, could still be written off on a forty-year basis if you had an accountant as friendly as Arthur Andersen was to Lincoln. Meanwhile, as interest rates declined and the mortgages matured, the paper Keating had bought in the "old Lincoln" portfolio rose in market value and could be sold at a large bookkeeping profit. Much of the profitability ACC declared for Lincoln Savings in the first two years derived from sales of Lincoln's "seasoned" mortgages, which purchase accounting had put on the books at low valuations. Another big chunk of the reported profits derived from the familiar and dishonest Empire of Mesquite–Vernon Savings–American Diversified business of loans for acquisition, development, and construction, where the fees and the first two to three years' interest payments were included in the loan.

Keating's operations were fancier than those of the Texas thrifts, but they were in fact equally doomed to failure. Because he was in a hurry, he paid more for his funds than anyone else, and because he needed yield, he reached for bigger gambles— lower-rated junk bonds, takeover stocks, land that was farther away from the city. Much of what he bought would pay off, if at all, only over a long period of time, and he had to pay interest daily to his depositors, quarterly to other lenders. Some of that interest could be paid by getting the Wall Street houses to broker in expensive deposits, as in the Texas Ponzi scheme. Some of the investments could be funded by using the surviving good assets in Lincoln for repurchase agreement or by pledging them to note issues in the London market, à la Charlie Knapp. But the SEC and the examiners would also demand *profits*. Somehow, Keating had to make sales—of property, investments, loans—at prices that permitted him to book profits. This could not be done on a third-party, arm's-length basis, because the values weren't there: Keating was one of Buffet's fools in the market. A Bank Board that had been deceived and deceived and deceived by Keating (alas, because it wanted to be deceived) wrote to his board of directors in December 1988, when it was much too late,[13] "All of the income reported has been self generated either through capitalized interests on large development projects, or sale of assets financed by the association."[14]

Actually, this was a little strong: Several of Lincoln's early ventures were winners. Lincoln's first big investment after Keating acquired it was in the common stock of Gulf Broadcasting—$132 million, or almost twice the S&L's net worth (a violation of California regulations). Carl Lindner's American Financial had started the Gulf play as an effort to extort greenmail from a takeover candidate, and Keating took over Lindner's 19 percent ownership of Gulf at a price almost 30 percent above that day's market price. There seems to be no question that Keating saw his S&L as a future operator of a chain of TV stations. (The subsidiary that bought the stock was then named Lincoln Communications; subsequently, the name was changed to Phoenician Financial.) Two months later, ACC sent the Gulf file to Michael Milken at Drexel Burnham, and soon after, Drexel was hired to "explore opportunities to maximize" the value of Lincoln's shares.[15]

Gulf, however, had other plans and presently announced the sale of the company to Taft Broadcasting, at which point Lincoln sued. So did Gulf, alleging that Keating had bought the stock on insider information from Cincinnati sources. The suit said Keating had sought to bribe the chairman of Gulf Broadcasting by offering him a five-year, $500,000-a-year contract as a consultant and had made extravagant demands for payoffs to go along with the sale to Taft.[16] The settlement of the cross-suits brought Lincoln a $50 million profit. As part of the settlement agreement, Gulf agreed to pay ACC, not Lincoln, $10 million on top of the price of the shares. It is by no means clear that Lincoln ever received any of this money, though it was Lincoln's insured deposits that had paid for the stock and the FSLIC that had borne a considerable risk. A January 4, 1985, *Value Line* report on Gulf said, "If Gulf is not sold, the share price will probably tumble," and set a likely resting place at a level that would have produced a loss of more than $25 million on Lincoln's holdings.

Several of Lincoln's early contacts with Drexel Burnham were highly profitable—to somebody. Drexel put the S&L into debt securities of Playtex and Memorex, and the bonds came with virtually free warrants to buy stock. Both companies became outstanding turnarounds. Lincoln bought the Playtex stock for $420,000 and sold it to its parent, ACC, for $2.1 million, booking a profit of almost $1.7 million. ACC then sold these shares (mostly to Centrust Savings in Florida, another Drexel baby) for $12.47 million and a profit of $10.37 million, which went to Keating rather than Lincoln.

The Memorex story is somewhat shadier. Lincoln first asked permission, on May 19, 1987, to sell the shares to ACC at $35.32 per share. It then withdrew the request. Then it sold to E. C. Garcia, "a troubled borrower of Lincoln," to quote the examiners (we shall meet Garcia again), for $12.61 a share, in the amount of $1 million. In October, ACC bought the shares from Garcia for $2 million. In March and April 1988, the shares were sold for $13.3 million. Lincoln made $800,000; Garcia made $1 million; ACC made $11.3 million. When the regulators complained, ACC officers confessed themselves puzzled: Lincoln had made money on the deal; why should the government inquire any further than that?[17] Testifying before Judge Stanley Sporkin in the case to overthrow the government's seizure of his S&L, Keating added a perfectly lovely Keatingesque postscript explanation: Lincoln had sold the Memorex stock early at a low price, permitting ACC to reap the profits, because regulators had pressured the S&L not to engage in risky equity holdings.[18]

Once he had his hands on real money through Lincoln's insured deposits, Keating could also play a role of sorts with the Englishman James Goldsmith, one of the busiest of the 1980s breed of corporate raiders. Keating (or, rather, Lincoln S&L) was among Goldsmith's backers in his assault on Crown Zellerbach, and Lincoln pocketed some immediate and prospective profit when Goldsmith made his deal. Later, Lincoln funded Garcia and Centrust (again) to buy it out of the residuals of the Crown Zellerbach deal, at a very substantial profit that could be booked whether real or not. (The SEC decided it wasn't, which was a precipitating cause of ACC's bankruptcy.) Lincoln Savings subsidiaries thereupon put no less than $75 million into Goldsmith's General Oriental Investment, Ltd., and Keating, in several public forums, proclaimed his belief that Goldsmith was the financial genius of the age.

But there are no other success stories. (Indeed, both the Bank Board and the SEC believe that the Goldsmith ventures are structured to help Goldsmith rather than ACC and will ultimately prove unsuccessful.) The rest is a litany of losses papered over to look like profits. And the losses in sum overwhelm the profits.

Very early on, thanks in part to Keating's long acquaintance with former Texas governor John Connally, Lincoln, under its new management, became part of the daisy chain that traded bad loans and bad properties in Texas to generate fake income.

Among Lincoln's first investments after Keating took it over in the spring of 1984 was The Uplands, 3,280 acres in Austin, acquired for about $47 million from Barnes-Connally, the former governor and Treasury secretary's partnership with Ben F. Barnes, a former lieutenant-governor of Texas. Barnes-Connally undertook to continue managing and developing the property at a guaranteed return to the purchaser of 13 percent the first year and 18 percent the second. Lincoln's AMCOR subsidiary booked $8,756,000 of revenue on this property in 1985, though not a penny was paid and no development was done, except the drilling of two wells for water.

In April 1986, Lincoln let Barnes-Connally out of the contract without pressing for the payments. In 1986, Lincoln's then president told examiners that the decision not to try to collect those management fees was motivated by fear that "Connally or Barnes [would] use their 'political clout' in Texas to undermine the project."[19] Nevertheless, Lincoln continued to carry some $14 million on its books as payments on The Uplands, income now regarded as legitimate "capitalization of interest" for an ongoing project. And Arthur Andersen, Lincoln's accountant at that time, approved. By June 30, 1988, though the value of property in Austin was at best half what it had been three years earlier, Lincoln was carrying The Uplands at $98,100,000. Arthur Young was now the accountant, and they approved that figure.

Most of the Texas involvement came through Southmark, another beneficiary of fund-raising by Michael Milken of Drexel Burnham. Southmark was the nation's worst disaster in the limited-partnership-cum-real-estate-development-cum-S&L-ownership scam, with total losses almost certainly exceeding $4 billion. Some of Lincoln's Southmark relations were the simple trading of dead horses for dead cows with Southmark subs, including San Jacinto Savings, but one piece rather stands out: a $20 million loan to something called Dulles Partners, a creature of "Fast" Eddie McBirney of Gunbelt Savings in Dallas.

Keating was a crusader for morality and had first come to public prominence when President Nixon appointed him to a national commission on pornography; he owned and operated a crusade he called Citizens for Decency Through Law. McBirney was the symbol of gutter life in the S&L business, the man who held the famous party at his S&L's hospitality suite in Las Vegas where prostitutes stripped, then unzipped the flies of the big customers and proceeded as directed.[20] The crusader against pornography was not too straitlaced to do business with Eddie McBirney.

Most of Lincoln's real estate loans were of the acquisition-development-construction variety, with the borrower putting up virtually nothing and Lincoln paying itself the fees and the first year's interest on the loans. Some were joint ventures from the beginning, especially where the building was to be done on Lincoln's land. Keating was a believer in large "planned communities," most of them rather remote from a central city, because land was cheaper farther out from the center and would thus show greater appreciation if all went well. After the failure of his first planned community in the Denver area (it turned out the soil was unstable . . . what price expertise?), Keating concentrated these ventures in the Phoenix area. Immense amounts of money were involved: Between the loans to R. A. Homes, a family venture of Senator De Concini's campaign chairman, and the loans to a friend with the splendid name of Conley Wolfswinkel, Keating committed nearly $200 million of Lincoln's insured deposits.

The largest single piece of the Wolfswinkel investment was for something called Rancho Vistoso outside Tucson, 7,430 acres on which Keating and Wolfswinkel planned to build almost 11,000 homes. The procedure by which the first $50.9 million loan was made to this project was described with some wonderment by the examiners who looked at Lincoln in 1986. The loan was approved by the board of directors on January 21, 1985, though the written application for it did not arrive until January 31. Lincoln's appraisal of the value of the land also arrived January 31. In 1986, when the amount advanced to Wolfswinkel rose to $73 million, Lincoln had a new appraisal made, indicating a value of $95.0 million, assuming that all the homes would be built and sold within six or seven years. But Keating and Wolfswinkel had paid too much for the land. They would have to build at high densities and high prices in a town where both density and price are usually low. Moreover, there were almost 100,000 other homes platted for planned developments near Tucson (plus countless more in small developments and as infill pieces on just plain property). A marketability study performed by outside consultants for the Federal Home Loan Bank of San Francisco indicated that it would take thirty to thirty-three years for demand in Tucson to absorb the houses to be built in the planned developments—and forty-five years for the Wolfswinkel properties to be bought. That was while Tucson was booming.

Lincoln's single largest land-development project was a planned community called Estrella, west of Phoenix near Goodyear, Arizona. In 1987, Lincoln booked a $15.3 million gain from the sale of land in Estrella. As it happens, we know how that alleged profit was procured. On September 9, 1989, M.D.C. Holdings, another Milken-financed operation with varied relations to Lincoln, consented to an SEC order requiring it to reverse a $2,178,000 profit M.D.C. had booked on the sale of land in Rancho Acacias in Riverside County, California. That sale for cash, the SEC said, had been matched the same day by M.D.C.'s purchase of land parcels in Estrella for $16,862,000. According to the SEC report:

> In a memorandum prepared by a former senior M.D.C. official, it was contemplated that M.D.C. would purchase Estrella property in connection with a sale of the Rancho Acacias property. Further, M.D.C. determined that the buyer of the Rancho Acacias tracts was completely financed (including closing costs) by [an] affiliated savings and loan association. M.D.C. also determined during its internal review that the buyer of the Rancho Acacias tracts subsequently sold the properties to other entities that were financed by the same savings and loan association. . . .[21]

Between January 1, 1987, and June 30, 1988, Lincoln also claimed almost $55 million of profit on its Hidden Valley property. Virtually all of this, the government's racketeering suit against Keating says, was produced by sales financed by Lincoln itself. M.D.C. was involved here, too, as the recipient of a $75 million line of credit from Lincoln and the seller of some of its underwater properties for $16 million to the Lincoln sub that owned Hidden Valley. On its sale of Hidden Valley land to M.D.C., the government's suit alleges, Lincoln booked a profit of $8,587,000.[22]

One of Lincoln's bad loans would become politically important. This was a loan to Ocean Club Partners, Ltd., a Georgia limited partnership that included among its assets something called Sands Investment, Inc. Sands had lent $12.55 million to the Sands Ocean Club Hotel in Myrtle Beach, South Carolina, and had foreclosed on the property when the loan went into default. Lincoln then lent Ocean Club Partners $8.6 million to buy "units" in the hotel for resale as condos. The general partner was an Atlanta lawyer named Lee Henkel, Jr., who was also a limited partner in another Myrtle Beach venture called Ocean Dunes, also funded by Lincoln. Total Lincoln loans to these Henkel-related partnerships were $31 million. Henkel was a guarantor of the Ocean Club loan, on which payments were chronically delinquent through 1986. Both the Ocean Club and the Ocean Dune properties were appraised for less than the loans Lincoln had outstanding in 1986. Examiners that year recommended that Lincoln establish a reserve for losses on these Henkel loans—and those recommendations were among the very few with which Lincoln did not quarrel.[23] Until April 1987 at least, Henkel was personally on the hook for the Ocean Club loan if there was a default.

Keating's hotel properties included the worst of run-down: New York's Times Square Hotel on Forty-third Street and Eighth Avenue, a dormitory for Father Bruce Ritter's later-infamous Covenant House, a welfare dump and a source of crime throughout the neighborhood. And also the most elegant of jet set: The Phoenician, a $300 million bet on the future of excess, where rooms were priced from $300 to $400 a night when the joint opened in 1989 (the place is, at this writing, the property of the Resolution Trust Corporation [RTC] and is being operated as a branch of government). All of these were losers. The Federal Home Loan Bank of San Francisco noted drily in response to Alan Greenspan and George Benston and indeed some of the economists in the home office that the claims of expertise for

Keating were not a good defense of his massive hotel investments, for he'd never owned a hotel in his life before he bought Lincoln. Also among Keating's hotel failures was the Hotel Ponchartrain in Detroit. A once-elegant 475-room hostelry fallen on hard times, it was targeted as part of the city's downtown renewal program and became a sort of meaninglessly elegant place, with lots of marble and gold leaf, across from a convention center. I stayed there, in Detroit while visiting the Michigan Opera Theatre, one Sunday night the year after Keating acquired it. I remember being puzzled at the expenditure on the small handful of us in the establishment. I also remember that nobody at the main desk or the bell captain's niche knew where the opera house was.

A subsidiary of Lincoln acquired this hotel at the end of 1984, with $19.5 million of Lincoln's insured deposits. About $8.6 million of Lincoln's money was spent on refurbishments, and then Hotel Ponchartrain Limited Partnership (HPLP), formed in large part by officers of ACC and Lincoln and borrowers from ACC, bought the place for $36.7 million, allowing the Lincoln sub to book a $9.5 million profit. The partners put up notes rather than cash; another Lincoln loan funded the deal. Under the terms of the 1981 tax act, the losses on the operation of the Ponchartrain, which were considerable ($10.6 million in 1986, $11.7 million in 1987), were deductible from other taxable income by the limited partners. Keating and his family among them took $5.5 million of tax loss in the first three years. The tax law changed at the end of 1986, and they may not have got all the money they had hoped to get. Indeed, the defense of the transaction by ACC was that "the partners have not received tax benefits as contemplated in the offering circular due to the retroactive change in the tax law."[24] But, of course, Lincoln had been put at risk to gain them those tax benefits.

In January 1986, HPLP laid off the first mortgage loan of $35 million onto San Jacinto Savings (a Southmark subsidiary), at a time when Keating was making lots of loans to other Southmark subsidiaries; ACC continued to guarantee $9 million of it. Then, in the late fall, without the vote of any board of directors of ACC, Lincoln, or the sub that made the loan, Lincoln lent another $20 million to the limited partnership, unsecured. An ACC lawyer admitted to reporters for the *Arizona Republic* that the purpose of this loan was "to forestall bankruptcy procedings while the partnership negotiated the sale of the hotel."[25] But the Ponchartrain situation was so bad that even a fake sale proved impossible. This loan was precisely the action Keating had sworn never ever to do again in the SEC consent decree of 1979. As of March 31, 1988, the appraised assets of the partnership were $20.3 million less than its liabilities. Clearly, Lincoln's $20 million loan was a dead loss—but it was being carried at full value on Lincoln's books.[26] Since the summer of 1989, the hotel has been the property of San Jacinto Savings, which foreclosed on the mortgage, and it isn't doing any better.

Because it was growing so fast and because everyone who did business with Keating knew they had a fish on the line, Lincoln paid more for its money than almost any other S&L in the country. Just before Keating acquired Lincoln, in February 1984, its average interest rate on deposits was sixty-five basis points *below* the average in the San Francisco Home Loan Bank district. (A basis point is one one-hundredth of a percentage point; the real numbers are 9.52 percent for the pre-Keating Lincoln, 10.17 percent for the eleventh district as a whole.) By December 1986 Keating's Lincoln was paying 117 basis points *more* than the eleventh district average—9.54 percent against 8.37 percent. And, in fact, its cost of funds was much higher, because 47 percent of all its money came from Wall Street money brokers, and they were robbing Lincoln blind. As of June 30, 1986, Prudential Bache was charging Lincoln a fee of 3.98 percent for the $238 million of clients' funds it had put into Lincoln CDs; Dean Witter was charging 2.86 percent for the $671 million its customers supplied.[27] These are hugely above the normal fees, and they say something about these brokers' attitude toward their customers. The lionlike brokers took more than half of what Lincoln paid for its money over the average cost of funds and left their lamblike customers with the remains. *Without* the brokerage fees, Lincoln's average cost of brokered deposits was 11.98 percent; with them, it was almost 15 percent.

To pay for the money, Keating had only a huge pile of overvalued assets that didn't return cash. Raw land has to be fenced and insured, taxes have to be paid, and it yields nothing. Construction loans don't pay cash interest until the building is finished and sold to its ultimate owner. The Phoenician, the Ponchartrain, and the Times Square hotels were all losing money wildly, and much of the junk-bond inventory was in zero-coupon bonds, which don't pay out until they mature.

Keating needed very sympathetic accountants who would permit him to capitalize the interest on the raw land, that is, assume that its value increased by the amount it cost him to carry it. (In one of the little bits of cheating the examiners found, Keating assumed that the value of his land inventory rose each year not just by the average interest he paid for Lincoln funds, but by the full cost of his superexpensive brokered deposits.) He needed friendly auditors who would agree that the fees and interest Lincoln paid itself on those ADC loans were really income. He needed kindly appraisers who would keep increasing the value of the hotels by the amount of their loss, year after year. And he needed very foolish examiners who would let him keep crediting to himself, year after year, the interest his unrated zero-coupon bonds would be paying if they paid interest annually instead of in a lump sum at the end. As the final Bank Board letter put it, "An indication of the worrisome condition of Lincoln's balance sheet [is] that it must rely on favorable accounting rulings on noncash transactions in order to offset the negative cash flow from operations."[28]

By and large, Keating got all these kindnesses—and they weren't enough. He had to sell some of his land to show a profit on the sale, and the only way he could do that was to rig collusive transactions for which, directly or indirectly, Lincoln provided the funds. The M.D.C. transactions noted above were standard procedure. When Keating sued the Bank Board for taking his S&L away from him, the government lawyers produced as a witness one Fernando R. Acosta, who testified under oath to a transaction in which, to quote reporter Jim McTague, he "bought $14 million worth of land he had never seen from sellers he didn't know with money he didn't have."[29] The money had been lent him by Phoenix developer E. C. Garcia, who was, as noted above, deep in the hole to Lincoln and who guaranteed to buy the land back in ninety days. Lincoln had supplied the funds to Garcia. Lincoln booked the sale as a $4.2 million gain.

Keating's lawyers said Lincoln had no idea Acosta was a straw man. As the charge against Lincoln was unsafe and unsound banking, the defense that they didn't know anything about their borrower was not really very helpful; but when a man is Charlie Keating's lawyer, it's any port in a storm. Later, Keating took the stand himself and said, Well, yes, he had known the buyer was a straw man, but Arthur Young had approved the bookkeeping, and such stuff was standard operating procedure in land syndication: "Land syndication is a separate discipline, and the savings-and-loan regulators never understood it and never liked it."[30]

Similar tactics on a grander scale were employed to prevent regulators from assessing a loss on the immense investment of insured deposits in the Phoenician Country Club. Keating went to Crédit Suisse, which worked out a deal by which the Kuwait Investment Office would announce that it had bought 45 percent of the hotel project at a price that would have permitted a profit to be booked. The problem was that Crédit Suisse took a $17 million fee for the service. Crédit Suisse got paid cash and also made a deal for $5 million a year to arrange advice to Lincoln on currency trading.[31] (Keating in 1988 felt a need to do currency trading, partly because everybody else was doing it and partly because it was supposed to yield high returns.) Lincoln lost $14 million in the foreign exchange markets in the first eight months of 1988, and then another $11 million in January 1989, presumably by following advice from Crédit Suisse. "We could never understand," John Meek of the Federal Home Loan Bank of Chicago told the House Banking Committee, "why ACC continued to trade so heavily in these markets when it was incurring such huge losses."[32]

With the passage of time, as Keating reached further and further in search of high yields, Lincoln's junk bond portfolio got increasingly rancid. By the time of the 1988 examination, no less than 77 percent of it was in bonds that not only were not rated as "investment grade" securities by Moody's or Standard & Poor's—they were not rated at all! Lincoln's junk bond holdings have become a litany of bankrupt or troubled companies: Integrated Resources, Revco, LTV, Western Union, Southmark, Pacific Asset Holdings, Gearhart, Lear Petroleum, Hyponex, Buyer's Club, First Texas Savings, E. C. Garcia, Busse Broadcasting (which has never made a penny), and many others. Lincoln bought Eastern Airline bonds at a little more than par shortly before Eastern was put into bankruptcy court. Now Drexel's Milken became a harsh master, urging that Lincoln help prop the price of fading junk.

In its final supervisory letter, the Bank Board specifically forbade Keating from buying "additional debt of Revco after the company had already defaulted on its bonds, trying to buy out the common shareholders of the Buyers' Club to save the association's preferred shareholdings, or purchasing more M.D.C. junk bonds while the company itself is purchasing its own debt for sixty cents on the dollar . . . for the purpose of trying to 'spend its way out' of a troubled investment. Since the source of funds for such activities is FSLIC insured deposits, this office cannot allow such a strategy to continue."[33] But Keating's board, which Keating controlled, insisted it did not have to follow the orders of a mere supervisory agent and kept gambling with the taxpayers' money.

Keating played the stock-options market with insured deposits. When the price of the underlying stock went up, he sold the option at a profit and took the profits. When the price of the underlying stock went down, he exercised the option, put the shares into Lincoln's portfolio, and carried them at what he'd paid for them, including the option price and commissions. The accountants and examiners okayed this remarkable procedure on the grounds that Lincoln had a stated and board-approved corporate policy that said it would use the purchase of options as a way to acquire the underlying stocks.

Perhaps the most revealing of Keating's purchases of paper is his participation in the Salomon Utility Model, which a Lincoln sub bought in April 1987. This was a fund of utility stocks chosen by Salomon with the help of a computer. The fund bought utility stocks the computer said were 8 percent "undervalued" and sold utility stocks the computer said were 8 percent "overvalued." That way, the Salomon salesman proclaimed, you had to make money. If the market went up, the undervalued stocks in the fund would go up more than the market; if the market went down, the over-valued stocks would go down more than the market; and either way the lucky investor would walk off with a profit. In July 1988, when the examiners made their examination, this totally hedged fund Salomon had sold to Lincoln as an absolutely safe investment had lost $5,667,651 of the $40,033,026 Lincoln had paid for it.[34] There is no record of how much Salomon made in managing fees or brokerage commissions on its utility model, but you can bet the farm that Salomon didn't show a loss.

CHAPTER 8

... And Some Bureaucrats and Five Senators

[T]he summation of the testimony as I see it is basically that Keating used a federally insured S&L to operate a carefully planned looting, and he had the umbrella of political protection to keep you at bay. Does that pretty well summarize it?

—Rep. Toby Roth (R-Wis.) to a group of regulators and bank examiners at a House Banking Committee hearing (October 31, 1989)

The assumption of responsibility by an agency is always a gamble that may well make more enemies than friends. The easiest course is frequently that of inaction. A legalistic approach that reads a governing statute with the hope of finding limitations upon authority rather than grants of power with which to act decisively is thus common. . . . [T]here is an enormous difference between the legalistic form of approach that from the negative vantage of statutory limitations looks to see what it must do, and the approach that considers a problem from the standpoint of finding out what it can do.

—James M. Landis, *The Administrative Process* (1938)

C HARLES KEATING acquired Lincoln Savings a few days before Ed Gray put in place his new regulations affecting brokered deposits and capital requirements for rapidly growing institutions. In his first effort to shake loose from them, three months after the acquisition, Keating asked the Federal Home Loan Bank of San Francisco to approve a $50 million issue of subordinated debentures (bonds that could be paid off only after all obligations to insured depositors were met) that would boost Lincoln's capital and permit its expansion. San Francisco, somewhat shaken by Keating's quick dismissal of the Lincoln executives his application for acquisition had said he would keep in place, pointed out that such expansion had not been contemplated in his business plans as originally filed. Would he explain what he wanted to do with the money?

So in August 1984, Keating filed a new business plan that contemplated $500,000 in equity securities investments and $7 million in corporate debt investments by the fourth quarter of 1986. Time passed, and by early 1985, Lincoln's equity securities investments were $190 million (more than half of it in Gulf Broadcasting), and its junk bond holdings were $170 million. Some $11 million of this was in bonds of the Las Vegas enterprise Circus Circus, a Milken client—a remarkable place for a crusader against pornography to put his money. This purchase also violated the California Department of Savings & Loan limit on loans to one borrower. The August plan was soon superseded by a November plan, equally fictional. This one indicated a desire to limit ADC lending and reduce the fraction of Lincoln's assets that would be in the form of direct investment. Almost immediately, Lincoln entered into a vast expansion of ADC lending and sought approval from the California Department of S&Ls for hundreds upon hundreds of millions of dollars of direct investment. This money would be stashed for future use in Lincoln's own "service corporations," waiting for Keating to find things he wanted to buy.

There was a rush about this in November 1984: Ed Gray was about to carry his Board with him in a regulation limiting direct investment to no more than 10 percent of an S&L's assets or 200 percent of its net worth. The new reg would apply to all investments made or contracted after December 10, 1984; anything to which an S&L had been committed on December 9 would be grandfathered. Keating had somehow learned these dates. Larry Taggart was about to resign as commissioner. He would join a San Diego investment advisory house called TCS (for Thomas C. Stickel). TCS needed capital; Keating generously had Lincoln put $2.98 million of insured deposits into stock that immediately thereafter had a book value about $700,000 less than what the S&L had paid. Though Taggart's name had begun to appear on TCS letterheads and SEC filings as early as November 3, he was still in office and could, for example, approve, on December 7, Lincoln's applications to purchase $300 million of stock in its own service corporation to give it some walking-around money.[1] Amusingly, Lincoln later claimed that its investment in TCS had been grandfathered, too—that Taggart had given approval for the thrift to buy stock in Taggart's own company. After all, why not?

The story of Keating's lobbying against the direct-investment rule has been told in chapter 5. While these efforts were pending, he applied to the Federal Home Loan Bank of San Francisco for an exemption from the regulation, permitting Lincoln to make about $1.2 billion of direct investments. It was as part of this application that Alan Greenspan wrote the letter presented in appendix C. Keating himself met with the senior officers of the San Francisco Home Loan Bank and represented that he expected to stop buying junk bonds. To some extent on the basis of that representation, the San Franciscans finally approved his nine-month-old request for authorization to sell $50 million in Lincoln debentures. Ignoring Keating's statement to the regulators, Lincoln continued to buy whatever Drexel offered for sale—and Keating had another reason why San Francisco would be prejudiced against him. When the examiners came in the spring of 1986, they found in Lincoln some $600 million more direct investments than the rules allowed.

In the fall of 1985, Keating played a typical card: He had a lawyer who was working for Lincoln tell Bank Board member Mary Grigsby that a big Southern California S&L wanted to hire Ed Gray to head the association. Gray referred Grigsby to Ann

Fairbanks, who found out it was Keating. After consulting with general counsel Norman Raiden, who agreed that Keating was simply trying to get Gray off the Bank Board, Gray sent Fairbanks off to meet with Keating. As instructed, Fairbanks listened, then told Keating, as Gray put it in a statement dated September 19, 1986, "I would have no interest at all in working for Lincoln because, among other things, my philosophy and that of Mr. Keating couldn't be more different. . . . [And] I was not available for employment in any event. I already had a job."[2] Treasury Under Secretary George Gould later told reporters that Keating had bragged about offering Gray a job for $300,000 a year. Keating's publicists finally admitted that Keating had made Gray an offer and insisted that Gray was prepared to accept. The reason Keating did not hire Gray, Keating's spokesmen said, was that Gray wanted to be CEO of Lincoln and Keating didn't think he was competent for the job.

Balked in Congress when Annunzio's resolution to postpone the direct investment regulation failed to make it out of committee despite sponsorship by more than half the House, Keating turned to more intense political action. In 1986 the beneficiaries of his significant largess were Sens. John McCain and Dennis De Concini of Arizona, Sens. Timothy Wirth and William Armstrong of Colorado, Sen. Mack Mattingly of Georgia, Sen. John Glenn of Ohio, Sen. Alan Cranston of California, Sen. Chic Hecht of Nevada, Sen. Donald Riegle of Michigan, and congressmen too numerous to mention, with special emphasis on the Arizona delegation, Chip Pashayan of California, and Doug Barnard of Georgia. Even more important, of course, was the access to the White House that is the invariable reward of large political contributors. The terms of both Mary Grigsby and Donald Hovde were up in the fall of 1986. Hovde had indicated that he was prepared to stay only if he became chairman; Grigsby was definitely leaving. And for Keating there was now great urgency to getting the "right" people on the Bank Board: the Federal Home Loan Bank of San Francisco had begun its regular examination of Lincoln Savings and its service corporations in March 1986 and was turning up some highly damaging material.

"Preliminary reports on the examination," San Francisco's director of supervision, Michael Patriarca, told the House Banking Committee in 1989, "disclosed substantial concerns in such areas as real estate underwriting. The reports also convinced us of the need to hire outside experts to help us evaluate investments for which we felt we lacked sufficient in-house expertise—particularly in junk bonds. In addition, evidence of substantial appraisal inadequacies convinced us to hire outside appraisers, primarily in Arizona, to evaluate selected properties as well as Lincoln's aggregate Arizona landholdings—which concerned our real estate specialists because of Lincoln's heavy concentration in speculative raw land investments.

"The Supervisory Agent and our examiners attempted to meet with Lincoln's officers on July 3, 1986, to discuss their preliminary findings. I say 'attempted' because Mr. Keating, though not an officer or director of Lincoln, did much of the talking, alternatively quizzing our examiners about who they reported to and attacking their performance of their duties. . . . [H]is remarks to our staff . . . included verbal abuse and threats to sue the Supervisory Agent in his personal capacity."[3]

Perhaps the most serious problem of all from a regulatory point of view was evidence that loans, investments in real estate, and purchases of junk bonds had been made on no analysis whatever and that ACC employees and employees of Arthur Andersen had collaborated in later "stuffing" the files with supposed justifications for the loans: An Andersen employee said in a sworn statement that he had prepared "quite a few" loan summaries long after the loans were made.[4] A Lincoln officer testified under oath that a summary of loans to Continental Southern, Inc. (another venture in which Atlanta lawyer Lee Henkel was a partner), had been put together for the first time almost two years after the first loans were made. He "testified that Lincoln's motivation for preparing the summaries in March 1986 was 'to get information in the file that clarified and improved it,' because without summaries in the files he felt that something 'was missing.' Under oath, [he] affirmed that the examiners' imminent arrival at Lincoln . . . was an important factor in Lincoln's decision to prepare the summaries."[5]

The investigation of file stuffing led to a criminal referral by the San Francisco Bank to the Justice Department, which decided it had bigger fish to fry. Andersen resigned the ACC account not long after. Arthur Young took it on—it was a big account, about 30 percent of the business done in Young's Phoenix office. Subsequent statements by Young said that the firm made inquiries of Andersen about why it had departed and was given the answer that the attitude of the San Francisco Bank was "adversarial," a splendid euphemism.

The San Francisco Bank proceeded to hire experts to look at the unusual things Lincoln was doing: Kenneth Leventhal & Co., a leading firm in real estate accounting, to examine the real estate loans and investments; and Professors Alan C. Shapiro and Mark I. Weinstein of the University of Southern California (in conjunction with the valuation consulting firm of Houlihan, Lokey, Howard & Zukin, Inc.) to look at the junk bonds and the equity holdings. Both found big unreported losses and inadequate (or no) policy statements to govern where Lincoln's money was invested. During the course of the summer of 1986, examiners found information about Lincoln's activities progressively more difficult to secure. At one point, ACC demanded through its mouthpiece, Peter Fishbein of the law firm Kaye Scholer Fierman Hays & Handler, that all requests for information about the operations of the S&L be sent to litigation counsel in New York, an absolutely unprecedented request by an institution that had a charter to offer deposits insured by the government, which merely wished to examine what it was doing with them. The regulators did allow lawyers from Kaye Scholer to sit with the examiners to see what they were looking at, in itself a remarkable concession.

Later, Keating would complain, and the complaints would be echoed by the congressmen who had taken his money, that the examination of Lincoln was unduly prolonged. And Jack Atchison of Arthur Young, whose expertise in the matters questioned by the examination was much less than that of Leventhal or Shapiro and Weinstein, would write a letter requested by Senator Donald W. Riegle, Jr.: "Because the experience of most of the FHLBB's more senior examiners is with traditional single family lenders, Lincoln Savings is different from their prior experience. Also, the more junior examiners generally lack the business acumen to understand complex real estate development projects or complex investment strategies. Hence, while the examiners' decision to focus on real estate, commercial and construction lending, and equity and debt investments may have been proper, they appear to have had neither sufficient experience nor knowledge to deal with Lincoln's transactions effectively. . . .

"Moreover," Atchison continued, "because Lincoln does not concentrate on single family residential lending, it does not fit the pattern for member institutions that the present FHLBB leadership has espoused. . . . This fact has, based on my observations, led to unusually antagonistic positions and actions by the FHLBB towards Lincoln. This is difficult to fully understand, because Lincoln's strategies have thus far proved successful and have turned an association headed for failure into a strong and viable financial entity."[6] The government's racketeering claim on Keating says that the "representations contained in the AY [Arthur Young] letter were false. Jack D. Atchison made these representations to forestall the regulatory authorities' intervention into the affairs of Old Lincoln and their wresting control of Old Lincoln from the Racketeering Defendants."[7] A little more than a year after writing this letter, but only a few days after giving Lincoln a clean statement for 1987, Atchison resigned from Arthur Young and went to work for Keating as executive vice-president of ACC, at a salary of more than $900,000 a year. Subpoenaed to testify about the letter (which may well have ended the political careers of the five senators who had been paid to want to believe in its contents and who acted as if they did), Atchison took the Fifth Amendment.

All this lay hidden in the mists of time in the summer of 1986, when Keating reached Don Regan in the White House with suggestions of new board members to replace Hovde and Grigsby. The replacements had to be done quickly, because Hovde's departure would leave Gray alone on a Board that could take formal actions only by a two-member quorum. One of Keating's recommendations was George Benston, the University of Rochester economics professor who on commission from Keating in had written the academic paper supporting direct investment by insured depositories. The other was Lee Henkel, the Atlanta lawyer who was deeply indebted to Lincoln on South Carolina and Georgia properties that were now appraised to be worth less than the loans Lincoln had made to his group. Keating and Henkel had been friends since their days together in the "Connally for President" campaign. Regan took both suggestions, and stories began to appear in the press. Benston, an alleged Democrat, was an abrasive character and had done studies that disapproved of laws designed to pressure banks and S&Ls to make loans in black and Hispanic neighborhoods; the U.S. League wanted none of him, and he failed to make it through the White House personnel process. Asked if he had a candidate with Democratic credentials who shared his views, Benston recommended Lawrence J. White, an NYU professor who was available for quick appointment because he had been proposed and vetted for a post on the International Trade Commission.

The Henkel problem was more serious, because it was admitted that he had been a lawyer for Keating, had once taken a personal, unsecured loan from Lincoln, and had certain undefined "business dealings" with Lincoln service corporations. It is unbelievable but probably true that the FBI did not find out from the Bank Board that its recent examination of Lincoln had turned up loans from Lincoln on which Henkel was guarantor and could be punished or let off lightly according to the whim of Charles Keating. In any event, on November 5, 1986, the White House cleared Henkel for nomination. November 6 was election day, and the election returned the Senate to Democratic control for the first time in Ronald Reagan's administration. On November 7, Henkel and White were given interim appointments to the Bank Board. Both were sworn in about ten days later and honored at a White House briefing for members of the Association of Thrift Holding Companies, an organization that had Lincoln among its members. Henkel told a happy crowd that he expected to be a "cheerleader" for the industry.

Gray's original direct investment regulation would lapse at the end of the year without some action to renew it. The election had strengthened his position somewhat, in that Sen. William Proxmire had returned to the chair of the Banking Committee and was an advocate of tight controls on direct investment. (So, by now, in fairness, was Jake Garn—but Garn would not have been vigorous about it.) And by the fall of 1986 the evidence was very strong that direct investment caused failure and imposed burdens on the insurance fund: Of the thirty-seven S&Ls Benston had surveyed and praised in his original study for Keating, twenty-one were either insolvent or projected to become insolvent within a year. But Gray needed two votes on the Bank Board, and it was by no means clear he had them. He had planned to offer a two-year extension of the regulation at a meeting December 18, but backed away when he saw he would lose.

Then Henkel, amazingly and surely unintentionally, came to Gray's rescue, offering a one-year extension with several modifications. One of them would have directed approval of all "inadvertent" violations of the limits on direct investment "through the misconstruing of the proper application of the grandfathering provisions." Such investments "shall be deemed grandfathered and [regulators] will allow the continuation and/or completion of such . . . investments." He said that while drafting his proposal he had spoken privately to eighty-six people in the industry who were concerned about the vagueness of the current grandfathering rules, then added with a laugh, "It was only thirty-six. I lied."[8] Those who had seen the Lincoln file knew immediately that Henkel's amendment would let Lincoln off a big hook. But it was by no means clear that anyone else would benefit.

The episode is extremely peculiar, because the night before the public meeting, the three members of the Bank Board had gathered privately in Gray's office to decide what would happen the next day, planning to present a united front. As Gray could not convince White to go along with a full-scale extension and Henkel could not convince White to accept significant modifications in the rule, the three men agreed on a seventy-five-day extension to permit hearings, information gathering, and further discussion. White was astonished at Henkel's behavior the next morning and still cannot explain what happened. We do know, of course, from his later denunciation of Senator McCain, that Keating "hates wimps."

Gray authorized acting FSLIC director William K. Black to tell the story of Henkel's amendment to Ken McLean, who would be the incoming staff director of Proxmire's Banking Committee and who was nosing about looking for evidence to support Proxmire's gut instinct that Henkel was a wrongo. McLean leaked to the press the number that was in dispute between Lincoln and the Bank Board: $615 million. When the *Wall Street Journal* called to confirm the number, Gray authorized Black to confirm it. At Henkel's request, Robert Sahadi of the Bank Board's policy group tried to determine whether any S&Ls other than Lincoln would benefit from Henkel's rule.

Sahadi, oddly, was the one person at the Bank Board who had reason for strong feelings about Keating. He had been a graduate student in economics, and his wife had been supporting the family by teaching English literature in a Cincinnati suburb when Keating and his pornography brigade landed on her for teaching a book (a Caldecott prize–winning novel) that had a masturbation scene in it. The matter got to the level of a school board meeting, at which there was a motion to fire Mrs. Sahadi; but in the discussion, a nun from the Cincinnati parochial system told the school board that all the Catholic schools in Cincinnati used the book and considered it an excellent, sensitive portrait of adolescence, and the Keating crowd slunk away. It is a measure of the decency of the people with whom Gray had surrounded himself that Sahadi bent over backward to help Henkel and came up with a statement that there might be as many as 109 S&Ls with some reason to be concerned about grandfathering. The general counsel's office looked further and found there were only two: One was Lincoln and the other, suitably, was Southmark's San Jacinto.

Most of the industry was on Gray's side—if only because everyone feared Congress would write something even more restrictive should the Bank Board fail to act—and so were Federal Reserve Board chairman Paul Volcker and FDIC chairman William Isaac, who sent letters of support. Eventually, White, with an economist's eye, would craft a new rule, relating the amount of direct investment a thrift could make to the tangible net worth of the institution—the amount of money its owner had at risk himself. This worked out to be tighter than Gray's former rule, and it passed 2–0, with Henkel recusing himself to avoid any appearance of impropriety.

By then Henkel was a dead duck. His insistence that his honor was unstained and unstainable had run into image problems. The *Washington Post*, which is where it counts, had run a balanced piece about Henkel and the issues involved, ending, however, with a little story about Henkel's description of himself as a man "who 'likes to get things done.' That trait was evident during an interview Sunday when Henkel and a reporter were told that, without a reservation, no one could be seated for brunch at the popular Willard Hotel dining room. When charm didn't budge the maître d', Henkel still got a table. 'I waved cash under his nose like a fan,' he said. 'If I can handle the Willard, don't you think I can handle this bank board business?' "9

The Justice Department had announced that the newspaper stories its people had examined seemed not to be substantive enough to order an investigation. Then, one suspects, someone let Ken McLean know that Henkel not only had loans from Keating but had *bad* loans from Keating. Proxmire called for a criminal investigation, and Henkel resigned. In one of those lovely explanations that are uniquely common in the Keating story, he said the reason he had to leave was that he had put all his properties in a blind trust and therefore he couldn't defend himself properly against charges. In May 1990, the PBS program *Frontline* reported that Keating had made a $3 million investment in a holding company Henkel had put into the trust.

Keating said he'd learned his lesson: "After the Henkel experience," he told Michael Binstein of *Regardie's* and the Jack Anderson shop, "I've given up trying to be responsible for who runs anything in this country."10 On March 27, 1987, he sued the Bank Board on the grounds that it had no authority to regulate state-chartered thrifts. And then he jerked the chains on Senators Riegle, Cranston, De Concini, Glenn, and McCain. Riegle had recently been given a helicopter tour of Keating's Phoenician Hotel and had been the beneficiary of $66,000 of Keating largess at a fund-raising dinner on March 23.[11] Less than a week later, Riegle asked Gray, with whom he had been friendly, to come to a meeting in De Concini's office, without anyone from his staff.

April 1987 was a parlous time at the Bank Board. The attempt to raise new resources for the FSLIC had been stalled in the House by the opposition of Majority Leader Jim Wright, though Gray had done just about everything Wright asked him to do. The regulators' only hope to get enough money to pay off the brokered deposits and close down the worst disasters in Texas and California was a Senate that would vote a major recapitalization plan and demand in conference that the House go along. The antagonism of these senators could be fatal to the regulators' plans. So Gray, who remained throughout a modest man with no great confidence in himself and never went anywhere without his staff, went alone to De Concini's office, where four senators (Riegle did not attend this meeting) told him they had reason to believe the regulators were picking on Keating. They also said they had doubts about the direct-investment regulation, which might not be legal. Why didn't Gray suspend the regulation until the courts ruled? In return, Keating would promise to redirect his thrift and make lots of home mortgages.

Several senators have denied that this is what was said, but this is what Gray told his staff when he returned from the meeting. Cranston, after publicly calling Gray a liar, later admitted to reporters that maybe something a little like what Gray said happened did happen. De Concini's denial is especially suspect, because reporters for the *Arizona Republic* dug up a memo that a member of his staff had given him for the meeting. The memo is broken into two parts: "What American Continental Wants from Gray for Concessions" and "What American Continental Is Willing to Do," which is in part the litany Keating had been promising since he acquired Lincoln three years before and in part another splendid piece of audacity: Keating was prepared to agree *as a concession* that he wouldn't increase his holdings of junk bonds alone beyond 15 percent of assets if Gray suspended the rule that prohibited him from direct investments—equities, land, properties—of more than 10 percent.[12] The memo also tells De Concini, in passing, that "Henkel sought to clarify the direct investment regulation so as to benefit AC." De Concini has admitted he took this document into the meeting and had it on his lap, but never really referred to it because Gray said he didn't know any specifics about the San Francisco Bank's examination of Lincoln. And the senator is outraged, of course, that such a document, clearly labeled CONFIDENTIAL, would become public property.

Gray said that if they really wanted to find out about Lincoln Savings, they would have to talk to the people in San Francisco, and he offered to set up a meeting in Washington. The meeting was held on April 9, with Cirona, Patriarca, Black, and Richard Sanchez of the San Francisco Bank and the five senators—Riegle came to this one. Bill Black kept notes for Gray, and these notes have been published by Pizzo, Fricker, and Muolo in their book *Inside Job*.[13] At the meeting, De Concini told the Californians that Lincoln was willing to go to a home loan program for 55 percent of its assets. This is not quite what his staffer had told him: She had said Keating offered "55 percent of new deposits (about $75 million)," which was about 2 percent of assets, and even that amount was "to be resold on the secondary market"—but De Concini seems to have felt he had his own expertise. He told the regulators, "I know something about the appraisal values of the Federal Home Loan Bank Board. They appear to be grossly unfair. I know the particular property here. [The reference was to the Phoenician Hotel.] My family is in real estate. Lincoln is prepared to reach a compromise value with you." Poor McCain agreed: "Land values are skyrocketing," he said, just as they were beginning to collapse. "That has to be taken account of in appraisals."

Glenn, whose former assistant Jim Grogan had become a senior officer at ACC and had raised the money for him from Keating, came on even stronger: "I've known [ACC] for a long time, but it wouldn't matter if I didn't. Ordinary exams take maybe up to six months. Even the accounting firms say you've taken an unusually adversary view toward Lincoln. . . . Lincoln has been told numerous times that the exam is being directed to continue by Washington." Riegle said, "The appearance from a distance is that this thing is out of control and has become a struggle between Keating and Gray, two people I gather who have never even met. The appearance is that it's a fight to the death. This discredits everyone. . . ." Cranston popped his head in the door to say he shared the concerns of the other senators.

The senators were nonplussed toward the end of the two-hour meeting by the obvious professionalism of what was the best staff in the bank supervision business, bar none, and especially by the San Franciscans' grim comment that they were making criminal referrals in the case. Patriarca at one point gave a typical example of Lincoln's procedures: a loan sale with recourse (i.e., the buyer could sell it back at the same price at any time) that Lincoln treated as a final sale, booking a $12 million profit. The buyer exercised his rights, and Lincoln bought the loan back for the same price —but never expunged the profit. Arthur Young as outside accountants found nothing wrong.

De Concini pulled out Atchison's letter: "Why would Arthur Young say these things . . . ?"

"They have a client," Patriarca said.

"You believe they'd prostitute themselves for a client?"

"Absolutely," said Mike Patriarca from the well of experience. "It happens all the time."

A moment's silence for the senators may be permitted. Mostly, they were parroting what Keating and his people had told them and their staffs. (The examination was being prolonged because Gray had a thing about Keating, the appraisals were being done by people who didn't know Arizona, etc.) It's easy to say they should have known better. Keating was awfully rich—Learjets with gold fixtures, and such—and if he hadn't been plausible, he'd never have gotten so rich. He had bought himself the very best references—Alan Greenspan and Arthur Young and Arthur Liman, of whom the Democratic senators thought so well that they made him counsel for the Iran-Contra investigation. More-over, government clothes with brief authority many people un-suited to its exercise. Congressmen fairly often find that when constituents complain about bad treatment by bureaucrats, they have a case.

To understand in this instance is not, of course, to pardon. De Concini, who had made a fortune in real estate with help from people who were borrowers from Keating (and defaulted borrowers, at that), kept coming back to the attack in ways that discredit him. One of those borrowers had been his campaign manager; when the news came out, he said he couldn't keep track of the business interests of all his supporters. The *Arizona Republic* ran a cartoon of a brothel labeled "Charlie Keating's Pleasure Palace," with girls going upstairs with two figures identified as De Concini's friends. De Concini himself was seated at an upright piano, a cigarette hanging from his lips, the gross madam of the establishment hanging over him. "I don't know what goes on upstairs," he was saying. "I just play the piano." That afternoon, De Concini gave back the $48,000 Keating had contributed to his reelection campaign.

Cranston's discredit came later, for he kept taking Keating's money—almost $900,000 of it for institutions helpful to his political career—and kept soliciting the Bank Board to do favors for "his constituent." Keating had stopped making mortgages to the homeowners of California, had closed his branches in moderate-income communities, and was shipping the money of Californians out of state to his own speculative ventures. Surely that was not the sort of constituent Alan Cranston would have approved and sought to help if he had not been paid to do so. Glenn should have been conscious of the fact that his desperate need for money (because he was driven to repay the debts he had incurred as a candidate for the presidency) might give him an overly rosy view of his contributors. He had, after all, lived through the scandal of Marvin Warner's Home State S&L on his own grounds, Ohio.

Others have been at least as shameless as the Keating Five. In 1985 and 1986, Rep. Larry Smith (D-Fla.) wrote to Gray on official stationery to complain that the Federal Home Loan Bank of Atlanta had limited the salary an S&L of which he was a board member could pay a dentist friend of his who was being hired as its managing officer.[14] Early in 1990, Sen. Orrin Hatch (R-Utah) made a phone call and wrote two letters to FDIC chairman L. William Seidman seeking to stop a lawsuit against officers of a busted bank. (Seidman replied, assuring him that there could be no legal action without the approval of "top management"—and five months after Hatch's letter, the FDIC had not sued.)[15]

Rep. Carroll Hubbard went to bat in 1986 for an S&L in his hometown of Mayfield, Kentucky: "To be completely open and candid with my friend Ed Gray, I want you to know that prior to being elected to Congress for the first time in 1974, I did substantial legal work for First Federal Savings and Loan Association in Mayfield. First Federal, to survive, must have financial assistance. . . ."[16]

Gray never saw the letter, because his staff thought it improper, and they didn't give Hubbard what he wanted. Three years later, Gray appeared before the House Banking Committee in the Keating hearings. Hubbard, identifying himself as a friend of Dennis De Concini, John Glenn, and Danny Wall—but not as a spurned solicitor of favors for a former client—went after Gray from the bench, accusing him of abusing his expense accounts to go to Hawaii, Australia, and Dublin, spending government money to dress up his office, and lying about his meeting with the senators: "Your testimony may be flawed." Chairman Henry Gonzalez had to cut Hubbard off with a statement that he would not permit "the badgering, the abuse, or the maltreatment of any witness."[17]

The true disgrace of the senators' intervention was their reaction in 1989 when Gray revealed it. Riegle concealed his contacts with Keating and his initiation of the meetings. And Cranston wrote Gray: "I did not participate in any discussion with you which even remotely resembles what you describe."[18] DeConcini repeatedly told untruths about his relations with Keating. McCain concealed for months the fact that he had accepted free rides on Keating's jets for himself, his family, their baby-sitter—and had taken vacations at Keating's Bahamian paradise. Glenn denied that substantive matters had been discussed at either of the meetings. What is ultimately disturbing about the five senators is not what they did for Keating, though in the case of Cranston and De Concini that's bad enough, but what they thought they could get away with after the story broke. The truth is not in many of these people in our Congress these days, and that's a terrible thing for the United States.

[2]

By 1986, Keating's corporate empire was beginning to unravel, pulled apart by the high interest he had to pay for funds and the low returns on the investments he made with those funds. By the end of 1987, his 10-K report to the SEC admitted, Lincoln's interest-bearing liabilities exceeded its interest-bearing assets by $1,086,000,000. Every year, he had a "negative spread," that is, his income from his investments was not enough to pay the interest he had to pay for his money, and he could survive only by selling property or by borrowing. In a style Texas had already made classic, he organized sales of loans and of properties he owned to people Lincoln would finance, permitting him to book fake profits. (Defending Lincoln before Judge Sporkin in January 1990, one of the senior executives maintained proudly that such behavior was not improper because 90 percent of those loans to purchasers paid off—but of course most of them were "paid off" only by refinancings, simply switching the name of the debtor.) Keating also, however, found three rather original cows to milk, and in the end it was his abuse of these sources of cash that brought him down completely.

One of these devices was an ESOP, a tax-advantaged way to raise money to give the people who work for a company a stake in it. Under the sort of ESOP American Continental adopted in 1984, ACC's employees were credited with shares in the company every year after their first two years of employment. In 1985 the ACC ESOP borrowed $23 million to buy stock for employees, $3 million of it from Valley National Bank in Phoenix, the other $20 million on an issue of ten-year notes backed by the very best collateral (Mitsubishi commercial paper, Freddie Mac pass-throughs) in the Lincoln Savings portfolio. Legal and other fees associated with the note issue ran $909,626. Of the $23 million, $12.2 million was paid to Drexel Burnham to bail it out of the

ACC stock it had held since the first public offering in 1983, and $8 million was paid to the Keating family and a few unrelated officers of ACC.

At the same time as the ESOP was running full blast, ACC was buying back its own stock, supposedly because the directors (all ACC employees) considered the shares undervalued. Much of this, too—$9.5 million worth—was bought from the Keating family. Some of the rest was purchased from the public in a rather thin over-the-counter market. Large purchases in such a market will move the price. As both the ESOP and the ACC treasury were buying so heavily from the Keating family at "market" prices, Alex Barabolak, the Federal Home Loan Bank of Chicago examiner who led the examination of ACC in the fall of 1988, expressed concern about "public stock price manipulation by ACC. The lack of policies and procedures and consistency in amounts of stock purchased and prices paid only reinforces our concerns." The report noted two occasions on which ACC treasury purchases in the market immediately preceding purchases from Keating had lifted the price that was paid to Keating.[19]

Some of the money necessary to buy the stock seems to have come from a "tax-sharing plan" first submitted to the San Francisco Bank in January 1986. Under this plan, Lincoln, instead of paying its taxes to the Internal Revenue Service, would forward them to ACC, which would handle all payments to the government. "This Agreement is straightforward and to the FHLBB should be a nonevent," the letter of transmittal said. "It merely contemplates Lincoln's payment to ACC of the portion of ACC's tax burden attributed to Lincoln." The San Francisco Bank looked at this thing backwards and upside down and saw a problem. One of the tightest strictures in the Thrift Holding Company Act forbade S&Ls to lend money to their corporate parents or to upstream dividends that came from capital or (worse) deposits. Keating knew the act well, having been Carl Lindner's lawyer in Washington in 1967, lobbying the Congress for favors when the bill was pending. Tax sharing could be a way around the restrictions on ACC's access to Lincoln's cash. If Lincoln sent ACC its predicted tax payments before they were due to the government or paid deferred taxes that Lincoln as a "stand-alone" entity would not have had to pay for some time, it would in effect lend money to ACC. Interest-free, too.

In several telephone calls and a letter dated March 7, 1986, the San Francisco Bank informed Lincoln and ACC that such a tax-sharing agreement could be approved only on five conditions: that Lincoln's tax liability was calculated on a stand-alone basis; that there would never be prepayment of estimated taxes; that ACC would reimburse any tax losses; that there would be no transfer of Lincoln's deferred tax liability to ACC; and that some pro rata share of any tax benefits ACC received by filing on a consolidated basis would go back to Lincoln. On March 14, ACC responded with a revised agreement, accompanied by a letter stating that the new agreement "addresses the five points raised in the March 7 letter . . . deletes the provisions cited as being objectionable and adds the language requested." The revised agreement was not carefully read in San Francisco, where a busy man assumed that the covering letter accurately described it. In fact, however, there were clauses embedded in the agreement that had been drawn to permit precisely what San Francisco had insisted would not be permitted.

Between April 1986 and September 1988, when the Bank Board was forced to face what had happened and issued a prohibition on further payments, $94.8 million of insured deposits were transferred from Lincoln to ACC for taxes that were not owed and were never paid. The tax-sharing agreement, moreover, acted as a stimulus to the fake sales that created fake profits for Lincoln, because some piece of every dollar of those fake profits could be declared taxable and forwarded to Keating & Co. Some of this money covered ACC's operating losses; some of it was used to buy the Keating family's stock.[20] In one of the grandest examples of Keating gall, ACC and Keating admitted that not a penny of the $94.8 million upstreamed by Lincoln was used to pay taxes and that there was no money in ACC to pay back the S&L—but then insisted that the government had no standing to complain because the Bank Board okayed the agreement.

It was also in 1986 that ACC began selling its unsecured notes in Lincoln S&L offices. This was indeed approved by the Bank Board, the SEC, the California Department of Savings & Loan, and the California Department of Corporations, all of which should be—and are—ashamed of themselves. (As early as 1987, Alvin Smuzynski of the Bank Board staff sent a memo to Kevin O'Connell that began, "In 1984 or 1985, at a time when we all must have been smoking dope, we gave American Continental Corp. 'blanket' debt authority. . . .")[21] Indeed, the ACC business plan for 1989, submitted to the Bank Board in November 1988, called for selling these notes at a rate of $10 million a month. By the fall of 1988 there was no other way to keep ACC out of bankruptcy: Virtually all of its assets that could be sold at their book price or better had been sold or pledged to loans from banks or Wall Street houses or the Euromarkets; $1.76 billion of Lincoln's $1.85 billion of U.S. Treasury and mortgage-backed securities had been pledged.[22] The company was losing money every day. Keating delightfully admitted to the chief examiner of the holding company that cash flow was negative—but only because of the costs of examination: If they'd get off his back, he'd make money. It was only by making quite incredible claims for the value of its Goldsmith partnership, its luxury hotels, and the land for its planned developments that ACC could pretend to have its nose above water. So Keating and his cohorts made the claims—and even in 1988, there were those in Washington who listened and wanted to believe.

[3]

San Francisco's recommendation that the Bank Board take control of Lincoln was sent out May 1, 1987. It arrived on Gray's desk when he had less than two months left to serve. Only the Bank Board could take such an action, and in this case, of course, there would be repercussions that might last for years. Normal procedure was to send this potato over to the ORPOS, headed by William L. Robertson, a senior bank examiner who had come from the Comptroller of the Currency to the S&L business not long after Gray arranged to boost the salaries in 1985. Gray put the papers on Robertson's desk and gave his successor, M. Danny Wall, a warning that this was going to be on his plate when he took over.

What was on Wall's Keating plate as an immediate matter, however, was a highly revealing article about Keating by Michael Binstein, one of Jack Anderson's reporters, in *Regardie's*. San Francisco has argued that the secret information in Binstein's article came from a report Washington had given the Senate Banking Committee and two dozen people who worked for the Bank Board. But some sentences are closely congruent with paragraphs in the report of the 1986 examination conducted by the supervisory arm in the San Francisco Bank. It is hard for someone not in government to get too angry with whoever it was that leaked the material, for there was great public interest in getting this information out. Certainly the poor devils in the California retirement colonies who bought Keating's unsecured notes would have been better off if the material Binstein quoted had been broadcast or published in a more widely circulated magazine. In his last days as chairman of the FDIC, William Isaac had argued that all examination reports should be made available to the public. As the law stands today, however, bank examinations are very secret, and those who see them are supposed to keep their mouths shut.

Like most presumably respectable people who are engaging in shady activities, Keating had a fear and hatred of leaks. He had already raised hell with a claim that some examiner had tipped off Salomon Brothers to a loss the examiners were making Lincoln take on Louisiana timberland. In fact, as San Francisco's Cirona replied when queried about this brouhaha, the land in question was involved in a lawsuit that had received a good deal of attention in the legal press, and nobody needed any leaks to know Lincoln had a loss there. In point of fact, the information that had been "leaked" was all in a public SEC filing, and it is hard to believe that Keating's lawyers, working for firms that routinely monitor such filings, did not know it. But now Keating had a case. Though he had cooperated with Binstein and may even have contributed to Binstein's knowledge of what was in the reports (for Keating and his senior people were loose cannons), he now threatened to sue the Bank Board for releasing information harmful to him that they had gained in a confidential examination. It was the first real weapon Keating had held in his hand.

Nevertheless, life went on. On July 23, three weeks after Wall had become chairman, ORPOS director Robertson submitted a document to the board members asking for a two-hour meeting on August 12 at which he would brief them on the Lincoln Savings situation. His recommendation was that the board go ahead with San Francisco's proposal. "Given the litigious nature of the association," Robertson wrote, "ORPOS believes that no Cease and Desist Order will be honored. Further, there will be some time before any such C&D will take effect, as we fully expect the association to seek a Temporary Restraining Order against any Temporary C&D, and go through the entirety of the administrative process. We therefore believe the only way to stop the association from speculating with the FSLIC's funds is through a receivership."[23]

A week later, Robertson was made subordinate to a new *executive* director of the ORPOS, Darrel Dochow, a bland young man with curly hair and a soft, high voice, a former bank examiner whom Wall had brought in from the Federal Home Loan Bank of Seattle to take charge of all supervisory functions. In the new rationalized organization—"Gray's problem," Wall said censoriously, "was that he had too many people reporting to him"—Robertson would not report directly to the chairman. And there would be no meeting of the Bank Board to consider his recommendation (which was not, Wall later argued with fine bureaucratic dignity, a *real* recommendation, because a *real* recommendation had three signatures; Committee Chairman Henry Gonzalez shook his leonine head impatiently and pointed out that the document *said* "RECOMMENDATION"). Some people saw a message here, and they were right.

Danny Wall is a fussy little man from North Dakota with a neatly trimmed gray-black beard who always wears a vest and talks very fast. He had not been trained in economics, accounting, or law (neither, of course, had Gray), and his qualification for the chairman's job was simply that he had been Jake Garn's staff director and then staff director of the Senate Banking Committee when Garn was chairman. Now that Garn was no longer chairman, amour propre led Wall away from the Senate. He had very limited analytic skills and demanded optimism from his subordinates so that he could communicate optimism to others. Tom Bloom's term as the Bank Board's accounting theoretician overlapped with Wall's time, and he remembers Wall saying to him once, after he had said he thought the shortfall in the FSLIC was somewhere north of $50 billion, "Why are you always so negative?" Bloom replied, "Well, you know, accountants are conservative," and Wall snapped back, "No. *I'm* conservative. You're a pessimist." Once Wall took over, Bloom recalls, people who came to him for advice on accounting problems never followed what he told them if the result would be to make an institution or the FSLIC look bad.

Wall's was a disastrous attitude for anyone who had to deal with Keating, for like any con man, Keating was optimism incarnate. L. William Seidman, chairman of the Federal Deposit Insurance Corporation, recalls that he ran into Wall one day in the summer of 1987 at the Executive Office Building (across the street from his and Wall's offices) and asked him how he was coming on his Keating problem. "That's all cleaned up," Wall said. "It's not a problem at all." Wall wanted desperately to believe in Keating, whom he met for a pleasant chat on September 24, 1987. (From that day on, San Francisco was not allowed to have any significant role in the examination or supervision of Lincoln.) For a year and a half, Wall found ways to duck taking any action that might disturb Charlie Keating's optimism. Even when it was all over and the staff had told Wall that Keating's last sham sale (of Lincoln itself) could not possibly be approved, he offered a ray of light: "I have no knowledge of anything other than my understanding and perspective as to this man's success over the years. And it is clear to me he may well pull a rabbit out of the hat. . . ."[24]

I think that anyone who reads the full record of the Bank Board's relations with Keating from Wall's accession to the end will feel that Wall was alternately terrified and conned by Keating, and led his people to a suspension of disbelief that was damaging to them individually, to the governance of the financial services industry, and to all taxpayers. Toward the end of the summer of 1987, the Kenneth Leventhal report that San Francisco had commissioned on ACC and Lincoln indicated monstrous problems, fake sales, dishonestly claimed profits, and possible abuse of the tax-sharing agreement. San Francisco asked for subpoena power to go in and get the facts. Wall refused and ordered the ORPOS to do a full-scale restudy of the 1986 examination. Michael Patriarca told *Frontline* cameras that Wall's assistant, James Boland, had told him the San Francisco staff should be grateful, not resistant: Keating was politically so powerful he would crush anyone in his way.

When the conclusion of the ORPOS study confirmed that San Francisco had it pretty much right and a cease-and-desist order should be entered against Lincoln, Wall again refused to bring the matter to the board. A memo that the House Banking Committee staff found in the Bank Board files—carrying the initials of general counsel Jordan Luke, who denies he wrote it—reports a comment by Kevin O'Connell, son of U.S. League president William B. O'Connell and one of Wall's favorites, that "anything to do with Lincoln is 'politically dangerous.' Mr. O'Connell said that the chairman told Darrel Dochow to 'take care of this,' because the chairman doesn't want anything to do with this association to go to the board." On February 2, O'Connell told Sanchez of the San Francisco Bank that Dochow was meeting with Keating at Wall's request and that Wall had "recommended that a 'peaceful resolution' be agreed upon."[25] Keating hired a new CEO for Lincoln, William Hinz, who had a good reputation in the industry. This won two months' further delay while San Francisco, still nominally in charge, waited for the new man to deliver an acceptable (and enforceable) business plan. Finally, Hinz had to tell Jim Cirona that he was not in control of the institution. Hinz resigned and accepted a "consulting" contract with Lincoln.

By then Wall had established a new "Enforcement Review Committee" to evaluate all recommendations for enforcement action against S&Ls. The voting members were Dochow, general counsel Luke, and George Barclay, president of the Federal Home

Loan Bank of Dallas, a career bureaucrat who would soon distinguish himself by dismissing Joe Selby, the stern director of supervision who had alienated Jim Wright's friends. (Two years later, Wall was furious at a newspaper story that said the decision had been 70 percent his and 30 percent Barclay's; really, Wall insisted, it had been 70 percent Barclay's and 30 percent his.) There were also two nonvoting members who in fact voted: Director of Enforcement Rosemary Stewart and Congressional Relations and Communications Director Karl Hoyle. He "brought to the deliberations," Wall told the House Banking Committee, "seventeen years of public policy perspective."[26] Dochow had now seen the light and had become personally friendly with Keating. He knew that whatever the examiners had found, Keating was really okay. As Dochow said at the Bank Board meeting of May 5, 1988, that gave away the store to Lincoln, "Staring across the table at him, watching his response to questions that he didn't know were coming, it looked to me as very sincere surprise; some of the things that had been represented were novel to him."[27]

Presenting the Enforcement Review Committee's conclusions in a draft for its members, Dochow wrote: "First, Lincoln is not insolvent now and will not necessarily be insolvent in the future. Second, there are many significant disagreements among experienced, competent and thoughtful individuals about the soundness and risks involved in Lincoln's operations. Third, Lincoln and the Agency Functions Group at the FHL Bank of San Francisco presently have a seriously adversarial relationship that prevents normal supervisory communications. And fourth, there *have* been repeated leaks of confidential Bank Board information that have damaged Lincoln's reputation." What was being recommended, in effect, was acceptance of the basic points of a "Memorandum of Understanding" Keating had personally delivered to Dochow.

In that "MOU," Keating had generously agreed to drop his lawsuit against the Bank Board for leaking information from the 1986 examination; to cooperate in another examination of Lincoln, provided San Francisco had nothing to do with it; "to take into account any advice or recommendations offered to the

ORPOS about the business plan"; and to accept a supervisory agreement that would grandfather his direct investments but prohibit new real estate developments for seven months. In return the Bank Board would agree not to "rehash" the contents of the 1986 examination; to let Lincoln modify its business plan so long as the modifications were reported two weeks in advance; and to permit Lincoln to acquire an S&L in another district, to transfer its headquarters to that district, and to be supervised through the Federal Home Loan Bank of that district rather than through San Francisco. Dallas Bank president George Barclay went along mostly on the grounds that, after all, the 1986 examination was now almost two years old.

Dochow arranged a meeting between the Seattle Bank and Keating, at which Keating offered to write a check for anything they had available, said he wouldn't *really* move Lincoln's headquarters away from Phoenix, and also said that he wouldn't serve on the board of Lincoln because he didn't want to go to jail. The Seattle Bank said, "No way." Specifically, "The Federal Home Loan Bank of Seattle opposes the proposed transfer of the supervisory and examination function of Lincoln Savings to the Twelfth District. . . . From our perspective, allowing the transfer of supervisory and examination efforts only buys the association time and may unnecessarily be increasing the risk to the FSLIC."[28] At the March 5, 1988, meeting of the Bank Board, Dochow presented this statement as "They do not wish to have Lincoln within their supervisory jurisdiction."[29] Presenting the matter to the House Banking Committee, Dochow said, Seattle "had decided to make a recommendation that would show support for a fellow district."[30]

As the discussions went on, Keating delivered to Roger Martin, Henkel's replacement on the Bank Board, a folder containing what he said was damaging information about Cirona, Patriarca, and Black of the San Francisco Home Loan Bank. Martin showed it to Dochow, who says there was nothing damaging to anyone in it but made two copies to show to others. Cirona heard about the file and requested a chance to see what was in it. Once Keating learned that Martin was distributing the file, he demanded its return, and Martin in turn demanded the surrender of the copies. The issue dissolved in the minds of all but those Keating had sought to discredit.

At the May 5 meeting of the Bank Board, most of the discussion centered on whether or not Lincoln should be promised the right to change supervisors. There was general agreement with the position of Rosemary Stewart, director of the Office of Enforcement, that because Keating would sue if any effort were made to impose anything on him, the quickest way to get control of the situation was to make a deal he would accept. Stewart fought for the rebuke to the San Francisco regulators—who had gone there from Washington jobs and were now making twice as much as she was—that would be implicit in an authorization for Lincoln to change supervisors. In an effort to get board member Larry White to go along, Wall agreed to modify the recommendations of his Enforcement Review Committee so that Lincoln would be promised only consideration of such a request and only after an examination was completed. Stewart objected: "That would be a very significant change in Option 1. . . . We, literally, spent hours on this very fine point, because we believe Lincoln has to be assured . . . that they could go."[31] In the end, White voted against, on the grounds that "forum shopping" by an S&L ought never to be approved, and the resolution carried, 2–1. Dochow personally would supervise the new examination, from Washington.

All that remained now was to put the deal into final language. The meeting for that purpose was scheduled for May 11. The day before, Margery Waxman of Sidley & Austin sent Keating a "Dear Charlie" letter, which the House Banking Committee made part of the public record in March 1990. "You have the Board right where you want them," Ms. Waxman wrote, "and you should be able to reach an agreement tomorrow which will completely satisfy you. As you know, I have put pressure on Wall to work toward meeting your demands, and he has so instructed his staff. They all know the Wednesday meeting is crucial to their future. . . . The points that you should come out with tomorrow are (1) San Francisco is finished. There is no going back to San Francisco, and nothing can be done to follow up their exam. . . . Nothing will be done in the exam that you are not aware of in advance. . . . The staff will not be able to enforce any violation of the agreement without going to the Board first and seeking approval. . . ."

The resulting "Memorandum of Understanding" was signed May 20. In Phoenix, Keating greeted the news with a lalapalooza of a party. "The window shattered as a squarish object was hurled from the second-floor office at the posh Phoenix headquarters of Charles H. Keating Jr.'s American Continental Corp.," the *Arizona Republic* reported. "It was May 20, 1988. Decorum—and a computer—had just gone out the window. A victory celebration had begun. There was Keating, a trim, 6-foot-5 former champion swimmer, striking a *Superman* pose, unbuttoning his shirt in front of his employees to expose a T-shirt with a hand-drawn skull and crossbones over the letters 'FHLBB'—Federal Home Loan Bank Board.

"A secretary climbed atop a desk to photograph the revelers. Robert Kielty, an American Continental executive, joined her on the desk—close enough for Keating to lash their legs together with a roll of transparent tape. Employees tossed beer bottles over expensive, carved wood desks and knocked over potted plants. Kielty grabbed a bottle of champagne and poured it down the front of another secretary's blouse. 'Get this champagne colder!' Keating yelled."[32]

At a press conference, spokesmen acclaimed the Bank Board's agreement that the 1986 examination had been malicious, and added some grace notes. In Washington Kevin O'Connell put a memo in the file "FOR THE RECORD: Given the astonishing statements reportedly made by representatives of Lincoln Savings in the wake of the signing of the Agreement, I feel compelled to make a permanent record of the following. . . . There appears to be an outright lie in today's *New York Times* article, in which the association asserts that the agreement means that there is no need for a restatement of earnings back to 1985. That issue was never addressed in the Agreement, and in fact, as we had discussed on Friday with their attorneys, we are assuming that the association set up the required reverses and income reversals required in the supervisory letter, as had been represented to us by Mr. Atchison on February 5th. If they did not, then we were lied to. If they did, then the comment in the article is blatantly false. . . . The SEC . . . have affirmed the findings of the SF exam. . . . The Agreement as signed, is a fiasco. . . ."[33]

On June 20, before the new examination even began, Keating made personal contact with George Barclay of the Dallas Home Loan Bank inquiring as to whether he could participate in the new "Southwest Plan" Danny Wall was promoting, by acquiring a Texas thrift. "The Memorandum of Understanding . . . between Lincoln Savings and the Federal Home Loan Bank Board," he wrote, "suggests that we will submit an application 'to move its headquarters to a district in which it proposes to acquire a savings and loan association.' "[34] When Dochow inquired about this letter, Keating responded, "The Pima Savings discussions were always contemplated as part of the agreement and referred to page 7, which states that they can make application for an acquisition and/ or branches for purposes of diversification; not for purposes of changing head offices. . . ."[35] After all, the odds were good that Dochow hadn't actually *seen* the letter to Barclay.

[4]

What Dochow had not realized was that acceptance of Wall's instructions to find a friendly resolution of the Keating matter had compelled him to deny the accuracy of the 1986 examination. Appointing Steve Scott of the Seattle Bank as examiner-in-charge for an examination to begin July 11, 1988, he ordered that the examiners should not look at the 1986 report but should start from scratch. As his deputy Alvin Smuzynski put it in a memo to the file, "Much of [the correspondence] was written in a way which may not present an objective view of Lincoln."[36] Eventually it was agreed that the new examiners would have a chance to look at the working papers of the people who had done the job in 1986. Dochow apparently conveyed to Scott (who has not testified or given interviews about his role in the Lincoln examination) his opinion that the examination was going to come out all right.

Keating might have done some unconventional things, but he had to be excused some technical rule violations because he was a great deals maker. In his testimony to the House Banking Committee, Dochow admitted that until the examiners turned up the illicit tax-sharing agreement, "I had believed that the insiders were not illegally using Lincoln for personal benefit."[37]

Within the system, though examiners volunteered from nine districts, there was an undercurrent of fear that Dochow wanted a whitewash. David Riley of the Atlanta district reported to the House Banking Committee that upon greeting the examiners, Scott told them they would not have access to ACC officers or employees and would not be given original documents. All requests for information were to be made through Tim Kruckeberg, a Lincoln vice-president, who would supply copies of documents. "Steve Scott further said that any examiner who harbored any prejudicial attitudes toward Lincoln should go home." Riley said that as the examiners found problems, Scott "continually expressed upbeat and optimistic opinions about Lincoln, the ability of its managers, and the quality of its assets."[38] Someone had decided not to do an appraisal of the value of the hotels, but to accept Lincoln's own valuations.

Sometime in August, word of the tax-sharing problem arrived in Washington, and Dochow sent a tax expert from the Bank Board to Phoenix. At that point he ordered an examination of the holding company, too, and sent in Alex Barabolak from Chicago to be examiner-in-charge on that project. He alo summoned a special meeting of the board of directors of ACC and informed them that no further tax-sharing payments were to be made from Lincoln to ACC and the $90 million or so already received was to be returned. Relations between the examiners and management now disintegrated. Attempts to examine loan files relating to Wolfswinkel and Garcia were greeted with complaints that this violated the Memorandum of Understanding and "rehashed" the discredited 1986 examination. Keating complained that no examination of the holding company was permitted by the MOU and demanded that the holding company examiners also report to Scott, who "was more reasonable."[39] Keating's rather splendid childishness reemerged. After an argument with Barabolak's people, he insisted they would be sorry for what they were doing and went storming into the hall calling loudly, "Get Alan Greenspan on the line!"[40]

By now there was a wild card in play. The California Department of Savings & Loan was the chartering authority for Lincoln and conducted the examination jointly with the Bank Board. Its examiner-in-charge, Eugene Seltzer, was not bound by any MOU. He was the one who found the tax-sharing agreement. In early September, his assistant, Richard Newsom, hunched shoulders, head down, working class, a "Columbo" character, to quote one description, joined the team of examiners in Phoenix. One of the first things he looked at was the unsecured loan to the Hotel Ponchartrain partners, which he described in his testimony to the Banking Committee as "probably a loss, obviously unsafe and unsound, and involved flagrant conflict of interest contrary to Federal Regulation." He had the file Xeroxed and indexed for future use in enforcement. Soon thereafter he met Steve Scott, who "advised me that his estimation of the total loan loss classifications for all of Lincoln's loans aggregated less than $10 million" after two months' work. "I responded to the effect, 'What about the Hotel Ponchartrain? It's a $20 million loss all by itself.' Mr. Scott answered that he considered it only doubtful."[41]

Newsom reported to his superiors and received authorization to alert the SEC directly about what he had learned on the Ponchartrain loan and about some oddities in ACC's stock purchases from the family. Keating then personally visited the examiners' area and asked why anyone was even looking at anything but the S&L. "My response to him," Newsom testified, "was something to the effect that one of our concerns was the proceeds of the ACC sub-debt sales to the public were being used to purchase treasury stock in order to support ACC's stock price."[42] Keating thereupon launched inquiries in Washington about the chance that he could shift Lincoln to a federal charter. Sometime later, after Newsom had put the Ponchartrain story in writing—he wanted everything in writing; he once said he liked an audit trail on which you could drive a truck—Scott decided that maybe this loan was a loss, after all.

Soon thereafter, Newsom ran into some loans to RA Homes,

$30 million unsecured to Senator De Concini's campaign finance chairman and others in his family. In his letter to Scott about this loan, Newsom wrote that it "gives the phrase unsafe and unsound a new dimension." The federal examiners had classified it as "substandard." And this one wasn't changed, though ultimately the loan was declared unrecoverable. Newsom then inquired into relations with Southmark and found $129 million outstanding in loans and junk bonds ($40 million over Lincoln's maximum permissible loans to one borrower)—to a company teetering on the brink of Chapter 11 bankruptcy (into which, presently, it plunged). The Southmark loans and junk bond holdings had not been classified at all. . . . Meanwhile, Seltzer in Irvine had found the fake sales of Hidden Valley property: "Since $74.3 million in profits had been recognized on these sales, this was of great significance."[43] Steve Scott's people had not found this and were not interested when Seltzer found it.

The worst blow of all to the Bank Board people was Arthur Young's resignation from the ACC account on October 13, 1988. Even more than the senators, Wall had relied on Arthur Young's certification of Keating's statements and approval of his procedures. An undated and unsigned memo in the Bank Board files presents the horror of the "termination" meeting between Dochow's people and Arthur Young on November 2. The immediate matter at hand had been an effort by ACC to book $80 million of profit from its Goldsmith ventures in a deal where Lincoln was putting up the cash for the purchase. (Indeed, part of the restructuring committed Lincoln to put up another $25 million if Goldsmith needed it.) This was to let ACC show a third-quarter profit. With Atchison gone to work for Keating, his former colleagues at Arthur Young refused. Keating demanded a hearing from a review committee, and when the committee backed the local examiners, he demanded an audience with the managing partner of Arthur Young in New York. When this meeting, too, produced a rejection of ACC's claim, Keating called the head of the Phoenix office and said, "You've cost your firm a client," to which she replied, "We've already resigned the account." Keating had told Dochow that the resignation occurred because of personal incompatibilities and that Arthur Young had agreed to leave the determination of the Goldsmith bookkeeping to its successor. Now it developed that Young had in fact refused to go along with Keating's claim of a profit on a sale.

The meeting with the Young representatives produced Young's statement of concern "about a pattern of parallel transactions between Lincoln and Centrust, Drexel, Saudi European Bank and Southmark." Also, the revelation that Young had accepted ACC's pricing of Goldsmith's stock at $8.25 per share when that price was in Canadian dollars, which meant the U.S. price was $6.80. Worst of all was the discovery that on issue after issue ACC had told the Bank Board that they need have no problem accepting some practice because it was okay with Young, while they told Young that it was fine to go along with that practice because it had been adopted "at the request of 'the regulators.' Who those 'regulators' are," the Bank Board memo notes sourly, "was left unclear." Yet another blow was the discovery that when Atchison had left Arthur Young to go work for Keating, the accounting firm had seriously considered redoing its audit.[44]

On November 7 state and federal regulators met with Lincoln personnel, and Scott presented his preliminary findings. Kind as they were, they displeased Keating. He warned the assembled examiners that if the FSLIC seized Lincoln, it would cost the insurance fund $2 billion. The federal and state regulators reacted to this statement in very different ways: Dochow and Wall felt that if the problem was that bad, only Keating himself could rescue them; State Commissioner William Crawford, by contrast, directed the preparation of a cease-and-desist letter to put Lincoln under state control, sent off a packet of new documents directly to the SEC, and met with representatives of the California Department of Corporations to stop the sale of ACC's subordinated debt out of the office of Lincoln S&L. This meeting had to be held in the Los Angeles offices of the Department of Corporations because all matters related to ACC had been moved there at the request of Franklin Tom, former commissioner of the department, who had approved the sale of these "lobby notes" and who now represented Keating. His senior partner in the firm of Parker, Milliken, Karl Samuelian, had been a fund-raiser for Governor George Deukmejian, to whom the Keatings had given $40,000.

The current commissioner, Christine Bender, had been an associate in the firm before assuming her present job. She saw no reason to stop the sale.

Now the jig was more or less up, though Ms. Stewart at the Bank Board was advising, as late as December 12, that a cease-and-desist order would violate the terms of the Agreement. Nevertheless, on December 20, Dochow initiated a "supervisory letter" that presented the results of the new examination and in intent, froze Lincoln's loans and investments until further notice. Keating now played his last card: His board "agreed" to sell the S&L to "an investor group." Dochow, on the twenty-seventh, told his assistant, Smuzynski, "Please make sure the ACC Supervisory letter has a tone of 'will work with ACC but need to ensure no undue leverage until Lincoln is sold' tone. Don't make it so harsh that they have only the option of fighting. Thanks."[45]

California State commissioner William Crawford has given the best descriptions of the three deals Keating came up with between December 20 and April 3. "Each buyer," he said to the House Banking Committee, "had the best legal advice that money could buy, yet they were unable to supply one completed application and none provided for the controlling stockholders to have more than $100,000 invested in the voting stock of Lincoln." No serious investor would be interested in an S&L that was, by its proprietor's admission to the examiners, $2 billion in the hole. But the level of ingenuity was high.

The deal would be that ACC would buy from Lincoln (for notes, of course) the hotels and the Goldsmith investment, at the appraisal values set by the California State Department. This would show enough of a loss to give Lincoln $500 million of "goodwill," restoring its capital to the levels the Bank Board required. The chairman of the independent Lincoln would be someone identified by Pat Forte of the Association of Thrift Holding Companies as "very traditional S&L folks," and some money would be provided by a "Trump Group" nobody could identify. Forte said that Touche Ross—who had bought into the ACC trouble after Arthur Young quit, and will pay for it—had designed the deal. The board would continue to be ACC insiders, headed by Jack Atchison. The beauty of this, from Keating's point of view, would be that the new Lincoln, supposedly on an "arm's-length" basis, could continue to fund all his deals.

In support of this new "concession" to the regulators, Keating called up his political troops. Through the next three months, Senators Cranston and DeConcini (but not, be it noted, Senators Glenn, McCain, and Riegle, the last of whom had already returned Keating's contribution) would be on the horn repeatedly to the Bank Board to urge "prompt resolution" of the applications and amended applications to transfer control of Lincoln to some new group of alleged buyers. At a press conference, Keating addressed the issue of the legitimacy of such help from legislators and made his most widely publicized contribution to American political theory. "One question, among the many raised in recent weeks," he said, "has to do with whether my financial support in any way influenced several political figures to take up my cause. I want to say in the most forceful way I can: I certainly hope so."

On January 5, Keating called Danny Wall for an appointment, leaving the message "culmination of my life—maybe my fortune." Wall saw him January 17 and was still sympathetic. Rosemary Stewart, who attended the meeting, recalled that Wall assured Keating that Kevin O'Connell, whom Keating considered "biased," was being taken off the team supervising Lincoln.[46] Even so, Wall had to tell Keating there was no deal.

On February 22, Dochow talked with Keating for forty-five minutes. The most recent supervisory letter had demanded that Keating stop selling his unsecured notes and sign an agreement to merge Lincoln into another institution if the Bank Board could find one. He said to Dochow, "I'm effectively shut down, no cash, people will leave, if I sign the document, I'm out of business. I can't survive a week with bond sales turned down. . . . Aren't there any concessions, if we work together, we can get out of this?"

Dochow replied: "We want to avoid catastrophe, too."

Keating said: "I can't get opinion [i.e., the auditor wouldn't certify his books] based on the pressures on Touche. I don't know how to handle that."

Dochow: "Every other institution signs consent-to-merge agreements. Regulators help put together [the deals] and approve."

Keating: "By then we'll be gone. . . ."

Dochow: "We are willing to work with you but need something acceptable policy-wise and regulatory-wise; we need a third-party buyer."

Keating: "Can't I sit with Steve Scott in Seattle or wherever for twenty-four hours and work out a deal?"

Dochow: "That's an affiliated-party transaction."

Keating: "If done concurrent with a sale of Lincoln to a third party. Possibly if we had a third party compatible with me . . ."

Dochow: "Sign the document."

Keating: "It takes away every right we have. . . . I guess I have to give you the institution. . . . I can't operate under these conditions."

Dochow: "The assets of Lincoln are causing the problems, not the directives or agreements."

Keating: "I was dreading the day it would come to this. This has plenty of valuable assets. . . . I guess I have to either go broke or to jail; I prefer to go broke. . . . Work out a deal this week or I will quit so I don't go to jail. . . ."[47]

But despair was not long with Keating. Presently he found another "buyer": John Rousselot, former congressman, who signed on as president of Lincoln and agreed to buy it. Peter Fishbein of Kaye Scholer was still representing ACC; Margery Waxman of Chicago's Sidley & Austin was representing Lincoln; the giant Washington firm of Hogan & Hartson was representing the "Lincoln Acquisition Group." Rousselot, who had recently been dismissed as president of the National Council of Savings Institutions, would have all of $8,000 of his own money in it; the whole group would have a million dollars; the book value of Lincoln was $5 billion. The board would be Rousselot, four ACC insiders, and four people acceptable to Dochow.

So Dochow, Smuzynski, and O'Connell met in Phoenix with Keating and his son, Atchison, Rousselot, and others on March 6. "Ready to close." Another offer: willing to transfer supervision back to San Francisco . . . sell all the land and the junk bonds (but to whom?), rely on mortgages for a living. Dochow's notes say, "No transactions contemplated with ACC." Touche Ross, Keating said, had promised to approve the crazy "purchase accounting" that would give Lincoln a $600 million asset in the form of "goodwill." None of the other losses found in the examination would be booked at all; in effect, the Bank Board would nullify the findings of its examiners. On March 7, Dochow was back in Washington, where one of the ACC lawyers wanted to set up a meeting "to discuss regulatory philosophy." But it was an exercise in futility: There was no possibility that the Bank Board could issue a federal charter, and Keating had never conned Crawford.

On April 5, 1989, a grim Bank Board held another "closed meeting" on "Possible Resolution of Lincoln Savings." The San Francisco Bank people participated by telephone. Dochow noted dolefully that he was not sure that the Trump Group in the proposed transaction was not in fact being funded by ACC.[48] And the documents by which assets were being bought by ACC (with notes) had been drawn up in ways that gave ACC everything and Lincoln nothing. There was just no way the deal could be approved, especially as a bill about to arrive on the governor's desk would give the California S&L people the power to take over Lincoln on the basis of the most recent examination, and California planned to do just that: "They see no benefits to this transaction as currently structured."[49]

"I would make the observation as well, for purposes of the record, I guess," said Danny Wall, " . . . there was no way that we had the level of information available on which to base an action last year other than the action such as we took. There has been, obviously, a good deal of passage of time, more information is available and a much better analysis of the institution by virtue of the examination, and so on. So we are dealing with a situation of what did you know and when did you know it. And we didn't know enough and we only recently have known more. So we find ourselves at this crossroads."[50]

There was another interpretation. L. William Seidman, chairman of the FDIC, told the House Banking Committee six months later that he had "asked our professional examination staff to review the 1986 Report of Examination of Lincoln and to indicate how we might have reacted to the findings if it had been an institution under our supervision. They told me that the . . . Re-

port ... depicted an institution that warranted immediate enforcement action. ... We would have sought an immediate cease-
and-desist order to stop the hazardous operations."[51] Even after
it was all over, Wall still wanted to believe Keating had been dealing
in good faith. When the Bank Board gave up and turned Lincoln
over to the FDIC for "resolution," in April 1989, Wall told Seidman's deputy, William Roelle, that he wanted John Rousselot to
remain as president of Lincoln Savings. Not until the FDIC said
it would decline to put Lincoln into conservatorship unless Rousselot left did Wall back away.[52] Eventually, Wall learned. When
House Banking Committee Chairman Henry Gonzalez commented that Keating had hoped to avoid going to jail by not
serving as an officer or director of the S&L he controlled, Wall
muttered in the background, "We'll see if that works."[53]

[5]

Yet more goofing off was possible. Though the Bank Board
was now trying to supervise Lincoln closely, the wire room was
still unsecured. The day after the April 5 vote, $40 million was
moved out of the accounts of Lincoln subsidiaries, through the
facilities of Bankers Trust, to recipients who have never been
identified. O'Connell sent Alvin Smuzynski a covering memo:
"You ought to be aware of this. ... Even our lawyers are *finally*
getting the message. Under every document is another scam, and
they seem to finally understand what type of thieves we are dealing
with and why we need to get them out."[54]

Under the system set up by President Bush shortly after he
took office, the conservatorship of busted S&Ls was given to the
FDIC. When the Bank Board notified the FDIC that Lincoln was
a goner, someone there made a phone call to a large law firm that
could supply forty to forty-five people over the next weekend to
close down a large S&L "in Irvine and Phoenix." The law firm
was Sidley & Austin.[55] The FDIC's contact at the other end
coughed gently and noted that the FDIC probably didn't know
the firm represented Mr. Keating and ACC. ... That night, John
Meek, the holding-company examiner from Chicago, noted "ex-

tensive movements of furniture between the Lincoln and ACC offices in Phoenix. We also observed a truck with a sign on it that said it was from the 'Document Destruction Center.' "[56] Asked at the House Banking Committee hearings about the paper-shredding the two nights before ACC declared bankruptcy and the government seized Lincoln, Leonard Bickwit, a lawyer representing ACC, said the paper being shredded had been donated "to a charitable organization that sells it for recycling. They shredded it simply because it contained financial information about their creditors and depositors."[57]

Nor was this the end of it. The FDIC, moving in, neglected to secure the wire room, and the Bank Board people who were being displaced believe that additional tens of millions of dollars moved out through Bankers Trust.[58] And F. Roger Clark, the man the FDIC put in to be CEO of Lincoln in conservatorship and then receivership, at a salary of $300,000 a year, seems not to have been the right choice. Less than three months after the agency took over, its man on the scene, Mark C. Randall, wrote to his regional director complaining of Clark's "inaction, questionable judgment and lack of contribution."[59]

One last effort to save appearances was made by Wall's friend, Karl Hoyle, a public policy expert and director of congressional relations and communications. There should be some way, he suggested, to retain control over the inevitable study of Lincoln's history: "Know you feel strongly that we ought to turn Lincoln over to the FDIC. Here's a concern with that move depending. . . . In the midst of the legislative process digging into the midden could turn up relics that could be used to float whatever hypothesis anyone chose. . . . At least if we did our own digging we would be in a position to lay out our own facts."[60] Keating could have helped with that; it was his specialty.

CHAPTER 9

Mr. Wright and Mr. Wall Haunt the Texas Wreck

WHAT was the most prominent on the Bank Board's mind as 1987 began was not the fight over Henkel or the question of what to do with Charlie Keating but the disaster in Texas and its ramifications in Washington. The damnedest people owned S&Ls in Texas, which until 1984 never had a change-of-control law. To get a charter for a new S&L in Texas, you had to show you weren't in jail and didn't have a number of convictions on charges of bank fraud (though there actually was a case where the wife of someone who had been convicted for bank fraud got a charter); but anyone could buy an existing S&L the same way he could buy a shoe store. In theory, application had to be made to the district Home Loan Bank for transfer of FSLIC insurance, but in Texas such applications went through the system like a dose of salts. In fact, Spencer Blain did not apply for such a transfer for more than a year after acquiring Empire of Mesquite, and nobody said boo.

The result was a cadre of scoundrels unique in the history of banking, native scoundrels and imported scoundrels (like the Louisiana "insurance magnate" Herman Beebe, who may have been involved with as many as a hundred failed S&Ls and who is one of the few people in the story to have gone to jail for his swindles). As an officer of the Federal Reserve Bank of Dallas put it, "The Texas S&Ls were notorious for their fraud and ebullience." Craig Stirnweis, former deputy director for regulatory affairs at the

Federal Home Loan Bank of Dallas, described the problems he found when he came in 1986: "massive fraud, widespread self-dealing, abusive conflicts of interest.... [C]riminal referrals ... totaled over 500 in 1986 and over 1,100 in 1987."[1] Imaginative use was made of wholly owned subsidiary service corporations to which S&Ls could lend depositors' money—"veritable pyramids of corruption," said Texas S&L commissioner Lin Bowman, "... where an examination force of hundreds could not possibly get to the bottom of these things because of the nature of the very transactions themselves."[2]

By honest accounting standards, which were all but unknown in Texas, half the S&Ls were broke by the end of 1985. The ADC loans of the immediate post–Garn-St Germain period had included a two-year "interest reserve" of money that was part of the loan but would be taken as income by the S&L as the payments came due. Many of those reserves were now exhausted, and the fact that the borrowers didn't pay was weighing on the income statements. And in 1986 the Texas economy suffered a triple whammy: West Texas Intermediate Crude, which had sold for thirty dollars or more per barrel at the start of the eighties, dropped briefly below ten dollars a barrel; drought hit the grain crop; and beef prices went through the floor. The financial consultant firm of Ferguson & Company reported that Texas thrifts as a group saw a drop in their gross operating income from 11.56 percent of assets for all of 1985 to 7.81 percent for the fourth quarter of 1986, as borrowers stopped paying interest.[3]

"Georgia and Massachusetts have a *problem*," said Thomas J. Wageman, a Chicago banker who in 1987 took over the carcass of Fast Eddie McBirney's Sunbelt Savings and seven other similarly decaying thrifts. "Texas had a *depression*." But the depression was caused mostly by the sometimes crooked, sometimes ridiculous, always-unsafe-and-unsound lending practices of Texas banks and S&Ls. In the four years after the passage of Garn-St Germain, Texas S&Ls grew from $36.3 billion in assets to $97.3 billion, and less than half that growth was in the single-family home mortgages they understood.[4] If the oil prices had stayed up, the merry-go-round might have run another year or so, but then the depression would just have been deeper, because as the real estate bubble neared bursting, the banks came blowing in. "The banks," says a Dallas builder, "were worse than the S&Ls. Republic Bank pissed away a billion dollars of real capital in real estate loans, and that's probably more equity than you had in the whole S&L industry down here."

Gray had hoped initially that the disaster at Empire of Mesquite was an isolated situation, but as 1984 became 1985, all the data showed that scores of Texas S&Ls were still doubling their assets every year. It became increasingly obvious that others had found the keys to the money machine. Within a month of the Empire collapse, Gray had sent Jack W. Pullen from the Federal Home Loan Bank of San Francisco and Lou Roy from Washington to take charge of supervision in Dallas. "What Pullen and Roy saw," wrote Allen Pusey of the *Dallas Morning News*, "was an entire regional thrift system growing wildly, swollen with brokered deposits and crippled with bad loans, mainly for real estate. Worse yet, many of those loans—particularly those for property in Dallas and Fort Worth—had been sold outside the region and threatened to cripple thrifts in other parts of the United States."[5] When the plan to put the examiners on the budgets of the Home Loan Banks matured, special attention was paid to staffing Texas. That staff would also need a special leader, and Gray found him in H. Joe Selby, a Texan long departed, who had been at the comptroller's office for 32 years and had reached his ceiling there during the months he was acting comptroller. Arriving in Dallas early in 1986, Selby found a disorganized shop in which examiners wrote their reports in pencil on pads, in a district where scores of S&Ls, many of them fast growers, had not been examined for two or three years.

Selby pulled together a crash program of examinations, staffed by volunteers from ten of the other eleven Federal Home Loan Bank districts. They took with them the new tool of asset classification: power to categorize a loan as a loss, doubtful, or substandard. Being told that their loans were no good or not much good was a disconcerting experience for operators who had grown accustomed to simply rolling over their bad loans and booking additional profits from the money they lent to the borrowers to pay the fees associated with the rollovers. As early as August 1986, congressmen began to hear complaints from constituents about "Gestapo tactics" in Texas. It was in August that Larry Taggart wrote his letter to Don Regan, warning that continuation of these exams would cost the Republican party money and support. On September 15, Gray met with a group of Texas congressmen from both parties to hear complaints from anonymous constituents. (They were afraid to identify themselves, they said, because the Bank Board might seek revenge.) What triggered the trouble between Congress and the Bank Board, however, was not a Texas S&L but a Texas builder in debt to, among others, a California S&L that had gone bust and was in conservatorship by the FSLIC.

The builder was Craig Hall, who had properties pretty much all over the southern part of the United States—65,000 apartments, four million square feet of office space—financed by loans approaching a billion dollars, almost all from S&Ls. The modus operandi was the limited partnership made popular by the tax bill of 1981, which authorized investors to deduct "passive losses" on their real estate investments. Assume a $10 million project financed with a $9 million bank loan. Each of ten investors puts up $100,000. For this he receives not only a 5 percent interest in the partnership (the general partner, who doesn't put anything up front, gets half, and the other half is divided among the limited partners) but also a deduction from his other taxable income based on the partnership's expenses for interest, taxes, fees, development costs, and depreciation. Under the 1981 tax law, the partnership could take as depreciation as much as 10 percent of the value *of the entire building*, including the 90 percent financed by the bank. This depreciation allowance could then be deducted from other income for tax purposes. (This is what Keating was doing with the Hotel Ponchartrain.) The development the investor helps to finance need not make economic sense for him to come out way ahead, but if something happens and the project does not get completed and sold, he loses not only his investment but the total of his tax deductions. As the Southwest economy turned to decline in 1986, Hall and his 325 partnerships badly needed a restructuring of their debts.

Not surprisingly, a number of the S&Ls that held Hall's loans were insolvent and had been placed under supervision by conservators sent by the Bank Board. The rules of the Bank Board retained each of these institutions as an independent entity, with decisions made by its conservator reporting to his own board of directors, not to the regulators in Washington. All but one of the S&Ls to which Hall owed money had agreed to give him long-term concessions. The exception was Westwood Savings & Loan of Los Angeles, which had written as much as $200 million of Hall's loans and then sold "participations" in the loans to other S&Ls. These others were even angrier at Westwood than they were at Hall, and the only deal Hall could make with them was one that forced Westwood to bear a disproportionate share of the loss. Advised by counsel, the Westwood conservator decided his institution would do better in a bankruptcy court than it had done in these negotiations, and instituted foreclosure proceedings. Hall now looked to his congressman, Jim Wright of Fort Worth, majority leader and soon to become Speaker of the House. Wright met with Hall in Fort Worth over Labor Day weekend, 1986.

It was a time of maximum leverage for Wright. In May 1986 the administration had introduced an FSLIC "recap" bill that would add $15 billion to the insurance fund over five years, with bonds for that purpose to be serviced through the premiums that S&Ls would pay for deposit insurance. The industry, interestingly, did not initially oppose the project. Leaders of many established S&Ls felt that higher insurance premiums were a reasonable trade-off for ridding themselves of competition from zombie thrifts that would pay anything for money because their owners had nothing of their own to lose. The bill moved through the Financial Institutions Subcommittee of the House Banking Committee on a voice vote on July 19, then sat on the full committee's docket into mid-September, when Gray reminded chairman St Germain that it was there and was badly needed: the FSLIC's funds were down to $2.5 billion for more than $800 billion of insured deposits, of which $48 billion were in insolvent S&Ls. Rep. Henry Gonzalez (D-Tex.) put some housing benefits into the bill, and it passed the committee on a vote of 47–1. The urgency of the matter was heightened by the fact that this was an election year and Congress would be leaving town for sure by mid-October. The "recap" was scheduled for a vote in the House on September 29, under a suspension of the rules, which meant that no amendments could be offered. Such suspensions create a requirement for a two-thirds vote to pass a bill, but that was not a problem because this was noncontroversial. Then the bill disappeared from the suspension calendar, and there seems no serious doubt that Wright ordered its removal.

The rights and wrongs of Hall's case are hard to sort out. There is not much to be said in favor of a policy that allows an insolvent S&L to continue to operate independently without control by the insurer who runs the risks. (Indeed, there is not much to be said for a policy that permits an insolvent S&L to keep operating on any terms.) We have already had occasion to note the problems of the FADA in dealing with properties where conservators for several insolvent S&Ls were suing each other for pieces of what was all the FSLIC's pie. To the extent that all the S&Ls that did business with Hall were going to go down—and the great majority of them did—there was no public interest in whether the loss to the FSLIC from the Hall loans fell on Westwood or on the others.

Correct policy probably would have called for letting Hall fail, because his rescue enabled these limited-partnership and syndication deals to go on for another couple of years. It wasn't until the investors were caught by the bad news in the 1986 tax bill, which put a stop to deductions on "passive investments" and greatly reduced the "depreciation" that could be taken as a loss on commercial property, that such partnerships lost their appeal. ("You washed out twenty, twenty-five percent of the value of real estate investment," said Donald Hovde, who was on the Bank Board while the new tax law was being debated, "and nothing was grandfathered.") Hall's troubles, of course, had nothing to do with the tax act; he had gone bust before it was passed. The Bank Board staff had known about and consented to Westwood's original decision, but the decision had not been theirs. Gray and Ann Fairbanks wrestled with their consciences and finally removed Westwood from the aegis of its San Francisco supervisor, replacing him with Angelo Vigna, who came from the New York Home Loan Bank, which was used to doing what politicians wanted.

On October 3, with Hall's problem behind them, Gray and Wright met again in Wright's office for half an hour at Gray's request. Wright listened to Gray's tale of FSLIC woe, but made no commitments. The bill went back on the suspension calendar for October 7 and passed on a voice vote. In the Senate, however, the bill was stalled, for reasons that came to light only in spring 1990, when Joe Selby at hearings of the House Banking Committee produced a letter Sen. David Pryor (D-Ark.) wrote to Gray on October 3, 1986. "S&L officials in my state," the letter begins, "have called to my attention what appears to be a deliberate system of harassment against many institutions in the 9th Federal Home Loan Bank Board District. . . . By forcing examiners to revisit 'clean' institutions until they find something to write up, the Bank Board is wasting resources. . . . By keeping those examiners at an institution longer than they need to be, the Bank Board forces the institutions to pay tens of thousands of dollars in costs. . . . *Before the Bank Board receives any recapitalization authority from the Congress, you need to assure us that your supervisory resources are being used effectively and fairly.* . . . [Emphasis added.] I have put a 'hold' on the Senate recapitalization bill and am anxious to receive assurances from you that you will correct the abuses which have been taking place in Arkansas and other states. I was pleased to learn that you have been discussing this problem with the House Majority Leader. . . ." Four years later, Senator Pryor served on the Ethics Committee that judged the Keating Five.

Finally, on the last day of the congressional term, the Senate returned the House bill to its owners with the housing provisions stripped out, a few goodies added for banks, and an amendment that reduced the new FSLIC money to $3 billion for one year. The bill also added an "exit fee" that the FSLIC could charge to S&Ls that converted to a bank charter and sought FDIC insurance. All this was too much for the corporal's guard still at the House awaiting adjournment that evening, and the bill died.

On October 21, back home again, Wright went to a lunch for 150 people involved in Texas S&Ls and real estate, given at the

Ridglea Country Club in Fort Worth. Its host was George Mallick, a local businessman with whom Wright had joint ventures and other dealings. (His wife was on Mallick's payroll.) At the lunch, according to Wright's assistant Marshall Lynam, about fifteen people spoke. They "recounted horror story after horror story about the capricious and arbitrary manner that the Bank Board was treating savings and loans in the Southwest."[6] As the lunch ended, Wright publicly asked Mallick, who knew nothing about the S&L business except as a borrower, to do a report for him. Mallick said he would.

Among those from whom Wright was hearing was an odd character named Tom Gaubert, an overweight, aggressive but plodding forty-five-year-old homebuilder, an immigrant to Texas from Minnesota, who as early as 1982 had bought an S&L to help him fund his operations. He had no more notion than a donkey engine on a building site of the fiduciary obligations accepted by the proprietor of a depository that invests other people's money. His first idea to stimulate growth for what he called Independent American Savings was to package the deserted I-30 condos left behind by Empire of Mesquite, not for the purpose of finishing or selling them to householders but as a tax dodge for investors.[7] He saw nothing wrong with making loans to entities in which he had an interest, even a controlling interest. There were essentially no books and records of the usual kind at Gaubert's S&L, just a rudimentary ledger and a bunch of IOUs. Nevertheless, Gaubert's S&L grew from $40 million in 1982 to more than $1.9 billion three years later. As a result, there was a trail of misdated and, in a couple of instances, forged documents of the kind banks are supposed to keep.

There was also a busted S&L in Mount Pleasant, Iowa, that had lent $65 million to Gaubert and Gaubert-controlled enterprises. The loans had financed sales of land from Gaubert to ventures Gaubert controlled, at grossly inflated prices (Gaubert's appraiser valued the land for the lender at eighteen times what Gaubert had paid three months before); and they were all delinquent.[8] Gaubert had pocketed the cash and let the separately incorporated entities die. All this came to light in 1984, and in

December of that year, while the details were being sorted out, the Dallas Home Loan Bank asked Gaubert to step down as CEO of his S&L. He did, retaining his majority ownership and his $240,000-a-year salary but putting his brother in as boss. Because the S&L kept growing with the sort of loans that generate big self-financed fees, Independent American kept looking profitable. The meeting to discuss the results of the investigation of the Iowa situation was attended by Rosemary Stewart from the Bank Board, who found Gaubert and his behavior disgusting and said so.

Gaubert now signed an agreement separating himself permanently from the management of Independent American. He sold some of his stock at a very good price (like Charlie Keating after him) to an ESOP. Then, as all the markets deteriorated in 1986 and Independent American lost all its alleged capital and then some, the regulators demanded professional management and offered to supply it. The Gauberts consented, and the executives of the Home Loan Bank who were put in the top jobs hired J. E. Roberts to do an evaluation of the portfolio. Roberts found "a large number of complex, unorthodox and 'screwy' deals . . . to create fictitious profits,"[9] as well as a bunch of dead-horse-for-dead-cow deals with other insolvent Texas S&Ls. After the new regulation-oriented management digested and acted on the Roberts information, Independent American claimed $600 million less in assets and showed losses of more than $750 million. Gaubert and his brother, who still controlled the stock, staged a raid on the place, deposing the Bank Board's management team and placing br'er Jack back in office. Texas commissioner Lin Bowman was having none of that and seized Independent American in the name of the state that same afternoon.

Later, Gaubert would sue to get his S&L back with the argument that the regulators had run it into the ground; and while he had no case whatsoever—Independent American was brain-dead long before the regulators took it over—the odds are that the institution deteriorated even further after conservators were put in charge. Third parties in Texas, none of whom would like to be quoted, are less than impressed with the management supplied by regulators after they step in. "First they kick out all the officers of the bank because they're crooks, including the ones who aren't crooks," says a borrower who claims he got away with repaying less of his loan to the government than he would have paid if the S&L had remained in private hands. "Then they waste months looking for the toys. The first question is always the Rolls-Royce and the corporate jets, the fancy homes and the expense accounts. Meanwhile, there are a lot of shaky loans to be policed, some of which could be rescued. I knew a case of a loan to a motel in Mobile which had missed three payments. There wasn't anybody left in the place who knew about that loan, and of course there weren't any documents, so they sent one of the secretaries out. She came back, said, 'Looks like a motel to me. They said they were very sorry, and they'll try to make some payments when they get some money.' "

Like the MCP, the conservatorships were a disaster, because the conservators had no mission. These places should have been closed down, the assets sold as fast as possible for what they would bring, and the deposits paid off or transferred to some other institution that wanted the money and would reduce the FSLIC's costs by paying the insurer a sort of commission for bringing the deposits. Such straightforward disposition was an impossibility, because the FSLIC didn't have the money to reimburse either the depositors or the other institution that took over the deposit liability. So the conservators were engaged in a holding action, trying to keep their S&Ls going at minimal losses, which meant they kept writing new business. They were, after all, treated as stand-alone enterprises. Any profits from new business presumably would diminish the ultimate cost of this insolvency to the insurance fund. But in reality, the conservators kept escalating the losses: Nobody who had good business brought it to a busted S&L operating under government conservancy, and the money brokers held them up for fees and high interest rates. The recap bill Congress would finally pass in August 1987 made the situation much worse by mandating "forbearance" for insolvent S&Ls in economically depressed areas; and Danny Wall, the new chairman of the Bank Board, perhaps by prearrangement, announced, "By definition, we don't shut down Texas institutions."[10]

It was Gaubert whom Wright wanted Gray to help in November 1986. Gaubert was one of the great goldfish in the aquarium of givers that Rep. Tony Coelho of California had stocked for the Democratic Congressional Campaign Committee (DCCC); in fact, he was finance chairman of that committee, which had raised $9 million for Democratic candidates in the election just concluded. So Wright called Gray and asked him to see Gaubert. Gray was so deep in the well of his own problems that he didn't know Gaubert was the finance chairman of the DCCC, and he insisted that for him to have private conversations with someone whose case might come before the Bank Board would violate the rules of the game. (He had not, however, held these rules entirely inviolate in the past: He had met with Charles Knapp on FCA problems while Knapp was still CEO, and he was in weekly or even more frequent contact with Knapp's successor William Popejoy.) For the sake of the recap, Gray yielded, after telling Wright that meeting Gaubert would mean he would thereafter have to disqualify himself from any Bank Board decision involving Gaubert's case. Nothing of this nature had ever been done before by a congressman seeking help for a contributor. One notes that in his astonishing whitewash of Jim Wright, John M. Barry deals with the Gaubert matter in half a paragraph:

"[Republican Congressman Newt Gingrich] sent out a 'Dear Colleague'—members of the press and Common Cause also got the letter—including copies of stories from *The New York Times* and *The Wall Street Journal* about the indictment of Thomas Gaubert. Gaubert, the former finance chairman for the DCCC, had co-chaired Wright's November fund-raising dinner and was one of the men for whom Wright had spoken to savings and loan regulators. The indictment dealt with unrelated charges, and Gaubert was later acquitted."[11]

Gaubert's claim turned out to be that he had been lured by the Dallas Bank into expanding by the acquisition of an insolvent S&L (Investex Savings of Tyler, Texas), and when that had gone sour, they had maliciously seized his enterprise and run it into the ground. This was significantly crazy, but Gray listened for two hours and finally agreed to the appointment of an "independent counsel" to investigate Gaubert's charges. This investigator was in fact chosen by the Bank Board's counsel from a list of candidates for such duties submitted by Gaubert's lawyer (something Gray did not know for several years). The independent counsel found Dallas to blame in having permitted Gaubert to expand at all (which Wright of course took as justification for his fund-raiser) but absolutely correct in taking away the honey pot. While Gray was trying to soothe Wright on the Gaubert matter, the incoming Speaker of the House called again, this time at Tony Coelho's request, to ask Gray to give Don Dixon of Vernon S&L time to find an investor who would put new capital into his utterly insolvent thrift (which was already under the supervision of the Texas S&L commissioner, a fact Wright apparently did not know).

The viciousness and arrogance of Wright and his friends now made themselves visible in other ways. They spread rumors that Joe Selby, the scourge of the Texas crooks, was a homosexual and was favoring "a ring of homosexual lawyers."[12] Texas S&L commissioner Lin Bowman (who had, to the disgust of Wright's friends and his own friends, moved against Gaubert and Dixon), was denounced for still having a partnership (in all of four condominium units) with a builder he had financed while running a little S&L in the early eighties. At about this time also, newspaper stories appeared accusing Gray of abusing his expense account and of taking too many trips at the expense of the U.S. League, various Home Loan Banks, and assorted conventions. There was, of course, something to it: With his wife in a separate establishment in California and two daughters in college, Gray lived like a pauper in Washington and enjoyed the swank of traveling as chairman of the Bank Board. Once, when he was in Indianapolis and his mother called to tell him his father was dying, he accepted a ride in a jet chartered for the purpose by the Federal Home Loan Bank of Indianapolis. In the end, there was $28,000-odd to be refunded; he borrowed the money and did so, vowing to serve his term. Nancy Reagan had always liked him, and he served his term.

Jim Wright was as disappointed as Charles Keating and Don Regan that Gray had decided to stick it out. At Wright's request,[13]

Rep. Doug Barnard at a January 1987 hearing on the recap bill told Gray, "[T]here have been some questions that individual home loan banks have been overly rigorous and arbitrary in their supervisory actions, including the closing of certain savings and loans. In Texas, people are especially concerned over situations like Vernon Savings & Loan and Independent American Savings and Loan."[14] On March 17, 1987, Wright told a meeting of the Democratic caucus on the House Banking Committee that they should understand what was really going on in Texas. The economy was passing through a hard time, but there wasn't, at bottom, anything wrong with the S&Ls. The problem was Gray and Roy Green of the Federal Home Loan Bank of Dallas, a nest of Republican regulators who were trying to kill off good Democrats, big contributors to the Democratic party. It was the duty of the Democrats on the committee to exert themselves and put a stop to that, first of all by holding down the FSLIC recap bill to $5 billion at the very most.

Henry Gonzalez from San Antonio was at the meeting and recalled it when he held hearings in San Francisco a few days after assuming the chair of the Banking Committee. He had been told, he said, that the Bank Board people were "saving the Republicans and damning the Democrats. . . . My request was, give me the documentation. And when the documentation was not forthcoming, I did not act and I did not speak up."[15] Another congressman who was at the meeting told me in early 1989, when commentators still believed the ethics investigation of Wright would fail to produce any action, that if the Speaker got into any real danger, and it began to seem unlikely that he could retaliate, the Democrats on the Banking Committee would abandon him. There are, after all, very few ways a man can lose his seat in the House, and one of them is going to bat for the likes of Don Dixon and Tom Gaubert. Wright had asked members to do that, and they would not forgive him for it.

Though the Special Counsel had recommended it, there was no way the Ethics Committee would find Wright in violation of House rules for his interventions with the Bank Board. One of the members of the Ethics Committee was Chip Pashayan (R-Cal.), who had taken contributions from the Keating crowd ($23,000 in 1986[16]) and had intervened with both federal and state authorities in efforts to help the most egregious of all the S&L crooks, dentist Dwayne Christensen. Christensen was the proprietor of North America S&L (which had, amusingly, led George Benston's list of thrifts that were prospering through direct investment). Among his devices to make his thrift look solid were forged bank Certificates of Deposit, which he would book as assets while spending the customers' insured deposits he supposedly had used to buy them.

Not even a congressman could save Christensen, who presently drove his Porsche into the pier of an overpass and died, leaving a $10 million life insurance policy for his girlfriend, who was convicted in early 1990 on twenty-two counts of racketeering and bank fraud.[17] Though Pashayan voted to proceed against Wright on the S&L charges, the vote was cast in what was clearly a losing cause, two other Republicans having defected to the Speaker's side on this issue. No congressional ethics committee that included someone who had spoken up for a constituent like Dwayne Christensen was going to condemn Wright for his assistance to constituents Don Dixon and Tom Gaubert. But it was clear that, if only as self-protection for the House, the Speaker had to go. When push came to shove late that spring, starting with the members of the Banking Committee, the Democrats did abandon Jim Wright.

The point of the recap bill was to close down Texas thrifts that were insolvent and losing depositors' money the FSLIC would eventually have to replace. The Texas S&Ls were fighting for their lives. Texas attorney general Jim Mattox, a former congressman who knew Wright and who had received a $200,000 gift from a land flip by Danny Faulkner of Empire of Mesquite,[18] now threatened to sue "to stop use of federal regulatory procedures that discriminate against the state's savings and loan associations."[19] (Mattox made the not unreasonable point that "we don't understand why the New York banks are given so much leeway, particularly in the bad foreign loans they've made, but on Texas loans we can't get the same forbearance and understanding.") Wright became an opponent of what less than a year before had been noncontroversial legislation. Coelho, now advanced from chairman of the campaign committee to Democratic whip, had found such opposition popular among contributors. That fall, he went to a meeting of U.S. League executives, where "a guy said, 'Don't give Gray his $15 billion to keep harassing us and helping his friends.' I said, 'I'm not for giving Gray any more money to run amok.' The place went wild, it went absolutely wild."[20] What emerged from the Banking Committee was a $5 billion recap, accompanied by mandated "forbearance," a requirement that if any accounting procedure could show an S&L with any net worth in an economically troubled state, the regulators would not close it down.

In March 1987 the GAO estimated that the FSLIC was insolvent by at least $4.2 billion. This was much disliked at the U.S. League. Kevin Yates of the Federal Reserve Bank of Dallas, who was then a young economist at the GAO, remembers that William O'Connell, the executive director of the League, came around to the GAO office and said, "You're entirely wrong. When you're going to issue these things, send them over to us, and we'll correct them." But in reality the amount was rising rapidly as the dollar collapsed on world markets, interest rates headed for the sky, and inventories of mortgage-backed securities lost market value. In California, Bill Popejoy was trying to earn back what Charles Knapp had lost by playing the bond market with insured deposits, growing fast and losing more and more money. By early fall, American Savings' portfolio of mortgage-backed securities would be $1.8 billion in the red. Washington had this tiger by the tail; all Popejoy's activities were cleared in advance by Ed Gray's office at the Bank Board.

At the Treasury, Under Secretary George Gould, out of the Wall Street house of Donaldson Lufkin Jenrette, became increasingly upset about congressional refusal to deal realistically with what could become catastrophic losses. Treasury Secretary Jim Baker went to his fellow Texan Jim Wright and promised that Gray's successor would be Danny Wall, who was entirely acceptable to the U.S. League and who would promise not to shut down

Texas. Meanwhile, Vernon Savings & Loan, for which Wright had intervened at Coelho's request, had collapsed in a tangle of delicious publicity about tours of Europe at the S&L's expense ("Gastronomique Fantastique," the owner's wife had written of one of them), an airline of private jets, pleasure palaces on the Pacific, and 96 percent of the loans in default. Vernon did, of course, boast a clean statement from Arthur Young. Nothing wrong here, said Sandra Johnigan, who supervised the Arthur Young Dallas office and chaired the S&L committee of the American Institute of Certified Public Accountants.

"The day of the House vote on the FSLIC recap," Gould remembers from his new life as an investment strategist for the money management firm of Klingenstein and Fields, "we sat around Treasury watching the proceedings on TV. I asked Baker to call Wright and see if we couldn't get the $15 billion we needed. Baker told me Wright had agreed to help. We saw the Speaker go to the well and deliver an impassioned speech. But our people on the Hill told us it was hopeless: While Wright was speaking, his whip Coelho had people all over the floor telling congressmen not to pay attention, the Speaker didn't mean it. And sure enough, the House repudiated its Speaker by a record margin. The hypocrisy was incredible."

The bill that came out of the House, then, provided only $5 billion of borrowing authority for the FSLIC. ("They wanted $2 billion," Coelho told Brooks Jackson of the *Wall Street Journal*. "The $5 billion was a compromise, if you can believe that.")[21] A Senate version called for $7.5 billion, lacked the forbearance provisions, and included some goodies for commercial banks. The conference dragged on beyond Gray's departure date, which was June 30, 1987. Gould let it be known that President Reagan would veto $7.5 billion as inadequate, and any thought of compromising down on the numbers should be abandoned. In the end, the conference okayed a fund of $10.8 billion, one-third of which would be available in the current and each of the two succeeding years. The money would be raised from sales of thirty-year bonds by a newly chartered "Financing Corporation" (FICO). Repayment was to be made by the community of S&Ls, whose insurance premium would increase to twenty-one basis points (.21 of 1 percent, $21 for every $10,000 of deposits); the bonds would not carry the full faith and credit of the United States.

The Bank Board and the investment banks that tried to place this paper with their customers insisted that FICO bonds were entirely safe, because Congress would never let an agency of the government fail to meet its obligations. Danny Wall and Austin Dowling, a New York banker recruited to run the FICO operation, traveled to the Far East to sell the bonds there. (Dowling, in Washington, handed out calling cards that had Korean as well as Japanese on the reverse.) But the "implicit guarantee" was the only reason to believe in this paper. The assumptions in the argument that the FSLIC could repay it were ludicrous: There would be no more S&L failures, the deposit base on which premiums were calculated would increase 8 percent a year, and the interest rates FICO would have to pay would average something like 7 percent. I wrote an article in the *Wall Street Journal* suggesting that Colombian government bonds backed by receipts from the cocaine trade would be a more conservative investment. The first FICO bonds sold at interest rates roughly one percentage point higher than those the Treasury had to pay, but then Salomon Brothers found ingenious ways to "strip" them—divide them into sections, one of which would simply repay principal when the bond matured in thirty years, while others would collect only interest payments. Such tricks might have kept FICO paper salable even after the passage of the Bush bailout bill (which made no mention of FICOs), but as the deposit base of the S&Ls shrank in 1990, Dowling decided not to sell the last $2 billion. Almost $9 billion of FICO bonds survive, the only part of the S&L refinancing package not guaranteed by the government and still a pretty dubious investment.

[1]

For Danny Wall, Ed Gray was the enemy. Gray came to his swearing-in ceremony, and Wall snubbed him. In his thirty months as chairman of the Bank Board (and executive director of its successor agency the Office of Thrift Supervision), Wall never once called Gray to discuss any of the matters that were, after all, Gray's legacy. Toward the end of his term, Gray had set in motion some substantial changes. The new direct investment rule, passed with Henkel's abstention, was strengthened in June by Gray and White (Henkel had not yet been replaced) to ban loans that put up more than 80 percent of the money for commercial projects. The criterion for determining the limits on direct investment became "tangible assets"—no goodwill, no Net Worth Certificates, no service contracts, no real estate donations at values including capitalized interest. Future capital standards were set at 6 percent of assets—that is, at least 6 percent of the money used to buy assets for an S&L would have to be the owners' money rather than depositors' or lenders' money. To get there, thrifts would be required to retain, rather than pay to their stockholders or use for expansion, an average of 75 percent of their annual profits. On the enforcement front, Gray permitted the staff to begin proceedings to bar Arthur Young from accounting jobs for FSLIC-insured thrifts, and he sent out for discussion a proposal to allow the district staffs to seek cease-and-desist orders without going through Washington. Rosemary Stewart of the Office of Enforcement saw this as a direct criticism of her work (which it was) and managed to stall its final consideration.

When Wall arrived, he put a hold on much of this—a hold that in some instances remained in place to the end. A born bureaucrat, Wall was scandalized by the Bank Board's organization chart, a nonsystem that left just about everything on Gray's (or, rather, Ann Fairbanks's) desk. There was no hierarchy of administration within the organization. Examiners were in the districts, on the district payrolls, reporting to supervisors in the districts. The supervisors in the districts reported to the principal supervisory agent, who was the president of the district Home Loan Bank. He reported on supervisory matters directly to the Bank Board, not to the supervisory staff in Washington. But no action that might produce a lawsuit could be initiated except in Washington. Meanwhile, there was very little communication across bureau lines at the Bank Board. "There were more than a dozen people reporting directly to Gray," Wall says disapprovingly. But the upshot of it all was that Wall had direct contact with only a handful of Bank Board employees, most of whom owed him their jobs. And he had virtually no contact with his fellow board members, because he was a preternaturally secretive man. Roger Martin, a veteran of the mortgage insurance business, who had joined the board in August, suggested a weekly Wednesday breakfast at which he and White could try to figure out what was on Wall's mind.

Wall was determined to be an optimist; his congressional and press representative Karl Hoyle said he ate four optimism pills every day. He declared himself most interested "in the eighty or ninety percent of all thrifts that are successful." He thought Gray by crying havoc had made the industry sick, as the risks the Bank Board chairman described ratcheted up the interest rates all thrifts had to pay for money. "You know," he said a few days after his resignation, sitting at the not-very-large conference table in the chairman's not-very-large office across from the Executive Office Building, "Ed Gray sat at this table with Charles Bowsher [the Comptroller General, boss of the GAO], and they had a bidding war about how big the losses were at the FSLIC. *And Gray's numbers were bigger than Bowsher's.*" To the visitor, that made sense: Gray knew more about it than Bowsher. To Wall, it was the essence of disloyalty. As late as the summer of 1987, he was insisting to Bowsher that "you only have a $2 billion problem here."[22]

Rebel Cole, a young University of North Carolina economics Ph.D. who came to the Bank Board in 1987, remembers that when Wall was going to Congress to testify, "we presented him with a menu of five options, from $2 billion insolvent to $50 billion insolvent. You could justify the $2 billion by saying, we did fifty shops last year, we'll do fifty this year—and then you pick the right fifty. Guess what Wall went to Congress with." This was the second Reagan administration, a time when regulators were not supposed to bother the private sector. It wasn't just Wall and the Bank Board. "During meetings with FDIC staff just after Mr. [L. William] Seidman took over the chairmanship of the FDIC in 1985," the House Committee on Government Operations reported, "he routinely made the following statements: 'bankers are our friends'; 'the FDIC should be a friend of the industry'; and it should be like a 'trade association' for the industry. To FDIC staff, the message was clear: 'Go easy on this industry.' "[23]

Wall's new director of regulation, Darrel Dochow, was also an optimist. In the fall of 1987, he held a retreat for senior personnel at Airlie House near Washington and at one point called for a show of hands on opinions about how big "the hole" was. "Some people dropped out at ten billion," Tom Bloom, then chief accountant, recalls. "More at twenty. Most at thirty. Darrel went to forty, then fifty. Mine was the only hand in the air. He went to sixty, and my hand was still up. He gave us a pep talk, said it was only ten or twelve, it would be manageable."

Dochow has a defense. He had come to the Bank Board in Washington from the chief supervisor's post in Seattle, which he had held since July 1985, when he had been the first recruit from the Comptroller's office to a top job in a district Bank after Gray moved the supervisors onto the new payrolls. "I knew what the problems were in Seattle," he says. "I thought the other districts knew, too. FSLIC, not my office, collected the information on how big the hole was. We were making judgments on 1985, 1986 examinations, and those examinations had not been geared to finding the source of the problems. They just looked for technical violations. When we went into the other districts, we found out how little we knew." Another man who worked with him says that Wall looked like a trapped animal when he was confronted with a column of figures; he was almost totally innumerate. Larry White, the economics professor on the Bank Board, said in the waning days of the institution that he felt he had let Wall down. If he'd paid attention to the numbers Wall was using, perhaps he could have kept him from feeding such malarkey to Congress.

Quality of supervision was in fact vastly improved in the Wall years. In August 1986, Gray had created within the Federal Home Loan Bank system, as a creature of all twelve district Banks, the ORPOS to coordinate the work of the supervisors in the field. To run it, he brought in William Robertson from the Comptroller's office. But the structure was hopeless. The examiners still turned over their work product to supervisors within the district Banks, who could, and not infrequently did, ignore the reports. Dallas was particularly prone to this abuse, and Selby had not by any means eliminated it. The examiners did a good job of appraising property, which became an increasingly important function as the decade proceeded, and they were sharp at catching technical violations of the regulations. "But," Dochow says, probably overstating their weakness and overestimating the willingness of the supervisors to hear bad news from the field, "they never put it into context, never asked what all this had to do with the condition of the institution." Dochow says that sometimes the people on the lending side of a Home Loan Bank, presumably rigorously separated from the supervisory side, would find out what the supervisors were thinking—and would tell the member S&Ls how to avoid what the supervisors were planning. All supervisory actions went through the president of the local Home Loan Bank—and he did not necessarily report to Robertson.

"There was a general sense in the districts," Dochow says drily, "that not enough guidance was coming from Washington." A group of district directors of supervision was formed, and Dochow became its first chairman. This informal group began circulating policy proposals to each other, and, says Dochow, "it began to come together despite Washington." So there was reason for Wall to call Dochow to Washington and place him in a position above Robertson's, beyond the fact that Robertson had called for action against Keating and Wall didn't want to do that. To ease the pain, Dochow named his operation the Office of Regulatory Administration (ORA) and kept Robertson on as his deputy. Dochow established peer-review procedures by which the district Banks rated each other's work and set in motion the creation of a series of handbooks to tell examiners what to do. Basically he adopted the procedures that had been building at the Comptroller's office since the mid-1970s—don't waste so much time counting the cash in the till, "take a top-down approach, look at the problems and how to prevent them, evaluate the management." On the evidence of the Texas banking collapse, it is less than clear that the Comptroller's examiners have performed this task effectively, but that's what it says in their book.

With the all-but-unlimited budget available from the Home Loan Banks (who found it convenient to bury other expenses in the regulatory account, too), Dochow expanded the fields of expertise in his office. A director of compliance came from the Federal Reserve, as did a capital markets man to examine the junk bonds, the futures, the options, and the complex securities the Wall Street houses were plastering onto the S&L portfolios. In 1989 the capital markets division hired a SWAT team to go into the districts and help local examiners look at fancy goods. Another division looked at the "service corporations" that did things with S&L assets that the S&Ls would not be allowed to do themselves.

The Achilles heel in all this was that once the supervisors decided that an S&L was insolvent by one cent, the examiners went away. They had performed their function, and now the FSLIC as receiver was to do all the work. The FSLIC was on the federal payroll, the number of its people and their salaries controlled by the OMB. There were ways to get around OMB control—an article by Stephen Pizzo in *National Thrift News* in late 1988 revealed that there were 986 people essentially working for the FSLIC in eighty-eight receiverships but being paid (probably illegally) out of the seized S&Ls themselves. These were not highly skilled people (their average salary was only $25,000 a year), and their jobs were deep in the swamp of asset liquidation. The work of ascertaining how bad the losses were and who was responsible was sloughed off to "outside fee counsel." These hired law firms did not monitor what was happening in this institution, which was now under the control of a receiver who had lots to do other than auditing chores. Indeed, the fee counsel were so concentrated on the question of what sort of lawsuit could be brought against former officers and directors that they rarely referred discoveries of criminal activity to the U.S. Attorney or the FBI. When the cops did find out that a crime had been committed here, it was not unusual for fee counsel to refuse to cooperate on the grounds that a criminal prosecution would slow down their civil case.

One must also say that the FSLIC, most of the time (the place was a revolving door), had not been very strongly led. A director of the FSLIC once testified before Congress, to the horror of the Bank Board staff in the audience, that things were going to be all right because the future stream of premium payments from the insured S&Ls added up to more money than the current estimate of existing losses. "He really didn't understand," said one of the economists, still awed by the experience, "that a dollar today is worth more than a dollar next year." In November 1987, Stuart D. Root, a New York lawyer from the socially prominent firm of Cadwallader, Wickersham & Taft (which had included among its fiefdoms the Bowery Savings Bank), became director of the FSLIC and brought to it several rigid attitudes. A small, highly confident man in his fifties, with thinning red hair and rosy cheeks, Root was convinced that the Texas market had bottomed and that it would be foolish for the FSLIC to sell at that point the properties it had accumulated from previous receiverships. (He also thought the FADA and Ros Payne were bad ideas.) He was sure that the drop in interest rates following the market crash would continue for several years, bringing back the value of many S&L portfolios. And he thought the GAO had "behaved very badly" in publicizing the insolvency of his agency.

Partly at Root's urging, partly because the members badly wanted answers, the Bank Board sent Bud Gravette, who had been associated with Root at Bowery, to look around Texas and form some opinion of the possibility of handling the crisis by merging insolvent thrifts into big institutions that would enjoy economies of scale. Among those who were all for it was Washington lawyer and Democratic bigwig Bob Strauss's friend Laurence Kosberg, whose First Gibraltar was by now deep in the tank. Kosberg had a project to take over half a dozen other busted S&Ls, write down their losses, and in the process credit First Gibraltar with $600 million in goodwill that could be booked as capital. With all that fake capital and all those brokered deposits—60 percent of *all* the money in the Texas S&Ls as 1987 became 1988 was brokered deposits—First Gibraltar could write well over $10 billion in loans and fund friends who would buy up quite a lot of the state. Strauss's son Rick cultivated board member Roger Martin, believing his father and Kosberg had Wall in their pocket. But there was no fresh money in the deal. The proposal, when analyzed, indicated that the Kosberg crowd was even going to pocket the tax breaks rather than invest them in the S&L. And it was Martin who pronounced at the private meeting before the deal was to be put before the Bank Board that he thought Kosberg and Strauss had been "too greedy"—which killed it.

Meanwhile, Gravette returned from three months in Texas with the good word that if the multitude of dying S&Ls could be blended into a few survivors, the whole of Texas could be resolved for $10–$12 billion. Those were the words Danny Wall wanted to hear. For 1987–89, the FSLIC would have $10.8 billion from the bond sales Congress had authorized, plus more than $6 billion from premium income. Might be enough. "The board," member Larry White recalls, "said, 'Let's do something coherent.' " Hence the "Southwest Plan," which in the end committed the American taxpayer to something like $40 billion of payments (plus $8 billion of tax benefits) to depositors and investors in Texas thrifts. The deal Kosberg had proposed eventually fell (modified to make it even sweeter for the acquirer) into the eager hands of Ron Perelman of Revlon.

[2]

The logic of the Southwest Plan, which took at least half the time of the senior people at the Bank Board in 1988, was that making giant S&Ls out of moderate-sized and little ones would yield economies of scale as branch offices were closed and separate lending, operating, and executive staffs were eliminated. More money would be saved as more competent managers got more responsibility and less competent managers got canned. These new aggregated S&Ls, some of which would have more than $10 billion in assets, would appeal to investors who liked the idea of controlling $30–$40 of investment funds for every dollar of their own money, even though the investments that could be made were now more limited than they had been. The FSLIC would guarantee the return of the principal of enough loans (or the sales prices of enough property) to eliminate the minus signs on the thrift's book value after the write-down of bad assets. The investors would not have to use their capital to make up any past losses.

And a big chunk of future profit would be guaranteed, too, because the FSLIC promised to pay any interest borrowers didn't pay on what might be as much as half the loan portfolio.

Given that the FSLIC had no money, the use of such guarantees was inescapable. In 1988 the Bank Board "resolved" 220 S&Ls (88 of them in Texas), with total deposits of $78 billion. The assets of these S&Ls were obviously worth a lot less than their liabilities. Even with "due diligence" examinations of a thoroughness the FSLIC never did, any statement as to how much less would be guesswork—but on the most optimistic assumptions, the number was higher than the $7.5 billion raised in the first two years of the recap bill Congress had passed. So the FSLIC could not possibly buy out for cash the bad assets on the books of the S&Ls it had for sale. The investor would have to trust the FSLIC to make good on the difference at some future time. On the other hand, the money these investors were putting into these deals wasn't really their own. Until the last day of 1988, when some provisions of the 1986 act sliced them away, there were very special tax benefits available to purchasers of S&Ls. The "new capital" they were supposed to be bringing to the industry was really the taxes they didn't have to pay on other earnings.

Under the 1981 tax law, which still governed until the end of 1988, payments from FSLIC guarantees were not taxable income to the S&Ls—but the losses the FSLIC payments made up could still (you may not believe this, but it's true) be used as deductions from the purchaser's other income.[24] The government made up the loss and then paid a second time in the form of reduced tax receipts. Not the least of what's wrong with this arrangement is that the lower the price for which an S&L sells a loan or a piece of property, the more money its owner gets, for the FSLIC payment to make up the loss is never taxable and the now nonexistent loss remains deductible from the owner's other income, for tax purposes. In the days of purchase accounting, S&L buyers had been eager to write down drastically the assets they had bought, because each dollar of loss claimed on the assets added a dollar to the goodwill they could consider capital. Now purchasers of S&Ls became eager to sell assets at a loss, because each dollar of loss generated both a payment from the FSLIC and a tax deduction. Unbelievably, this expensive lunacy has had defenders in Congress. "[A]s I understand the so-called special provision," Rep. Steve Bartlett (R.-Tex.) said at a House hearing, " . . . you would not have to pay income taxes on the assistance that you got from the Government because it would be the Government basically taxing itself. It does not seem to me . . . bad for the Government to say that it should not have to tax itself. But I may be missing something."[25] Yes, indeed.

The Garn-St Germain Act in 1982 had ordered bank and thrift regulators to dispose of insolvent depositories in the way that imposed the least cost on their insurance funds. Obviously, the government did not gain if tax payments by acquirers dropped by more than the money the acquisition saved the FSLIC, and there was some argument at the Bank Board as to whether deals should be done when the Treasury's loss of tax revenues exceeded the savings the FSLIC could claim from selling rather than closing the thrift. White especially insisted that before he would sign off on a deal, somebody would have to do an analysis showing that the taxpayer was not a loser. When it was all over, White claimed that in only four of the eighty-eight Texas deals did the tax loss to the Treasury exceed the gain to the FSLIC. Maybe.

Stuart Root made the defense of the Texas deals at the San Antonio hearings of the House Banking Committee in March 1989. They were, he said, "an alternative to widespread liquidations" that would "eliminate savings facilities to serve the public and jobs in an irredeemable way." Liquidations involved "income reduction for all employees, . . . loss of revenues for businesses from institutions as ongoing customers; and reverse multiplier effect of the foregoing." Liquidations would even "reduce the flow of insurance premium income . . . and hence *increase* the taxpayer/Treasury cost." By contrast, keeping these thrifts in being, as part of larger institutions, would "help create a healthy, productive system of financial services; . . . provide for increased franchise values of thrifts; . . . wring out the overcapacity in a measured way, but avoid throwing the baby out with the bath; [and] attract private capital and management accountable to such capital to help insulate the deposit insurance fund while franchise values were being recreated and/or enhanced." Meanwhile, the cost of funds to Texas thrifts would be reduced, partly because some of the gamblers who paid sky-high rates for money would no longer be running their S&Ls, partly because the public would feel confidence in the new capital and new management.[26] While bathing in this hogwash, the Bank Board also launched projects with no purpose other than reducing the cost of funds for bad S&Ls (including one in which well-regarded S&Ls were commissioned by the Bank Board to sell CDs in their own name and pass the proceeds on to insolvent thrifts).

The worst problem with all this was the overwhelmingly strong bargaining position enjoyed by potential acquirers doing business with a FSLIC that couldn't liquidate. Purchasers forced the FSLIC to promise to make good on vast quantities of assets and to guarantee income on as much as half the portfolio. And everybody was in a hurry, because the tax breaks were expiring. "When we approved a transaction," Roger Martin remembered (and he was the man who made most of the deals), "we didn't know who was involved. All we had time to concentrate on was the numbers." This may be a bit self-serving, because all these negotiations were conducted in deep secrecy, and some bidders feel that the race was not to the swift; but it's plausible.

FSLIC notes were written to cover three categories of commitment:

1. For the properties the FSLIC took out of the portfolio and held in its own name (like the Palm Springs windmills and Rick Strauss's Stonebridge in chapter 1).

2. To bring the yield on loans in the portfolio up to the standard set in the contract with the purchaser. Some deals promised as much as 2.75 percentage points above the average Texas cost of funds to S&Ls. If the borrower didn't make his interest payments and the average cost of funds was 9 percent, the FSLIC promised to pay the purchasers of this S&L 11.75 percent interest on the amount of the nonperforming loan or the unsold property.

3. For the difference between the face value of the loan

and what the S&L received from the borrower when the loan came due.

In early 1989 the present value of these guarantees was estimated by the Bush administration at $26 billion, and the total cost of paying off the notes (including interest) was estimated at $40 billion.

What these notes were really worth, however, was by no means a settled question in 1988. I described them in several articles in *American Banker* as a form of counterfeiting by a government agency. The GAO, in a letter to Rep. Toby Roth (R-Wis.) in October 1988, did accept them as full faith and credit obligations of the United States. The rather strained argument was that the National Housing Act of 1934 had empowered the FSLIC "to issue notes, bonds, debentures, or other such obligations upon such terms and conditions as [the FHLBB] may determine." In 1958, ruling on insurance contracts issued by the Secretary of Commerce in connection with the Merchant Marine Act, the attorney general had held that "in the absence of congressional action disclaiming the liability of the United States," an agency of government can commit some future Congress to appropriate funds to cover the debts the agency incurs. Under these circumstances, the GAO thought the FSLIC notes were indeed a legitimate pledge of the credit of the U.S. government.

There were two problems with this ruling, the more obvious being the constitutional insistence that "no money shall be drawn from the treasury, but in consequence of appropriations made by law,"[27] an insistence enforced in American polity by the separation of authorization and appropriation in congressional procedure. Worse, because the Constitution can always be fudged, there was an awkward line in the House Banking Committee report on the National Housing Act to the effect that FSLIC issues " 'are not insured or guaranteed by the United States.' In our opinion," the GAO letter reported, "this remark should not be viewed as controlling. . . . [W]e find nothing in the language of the Act . . . that makes manifest an intent to disclaim liability."[28] So it was okay with the GAO if the holders of these notes took them to their

Federal Home Loan Bank and used them as collateral for cash borrowings, and a number of holders tried to do so. But only the Dallas Bank was prepared to accept the notes as good collateral —and its auditor (Deloitte, Haskins & Sells) would not give the Bank a clean statement as long as it included such notes among its assets. In 1987, one of the last $2 billion had to be cleaned out of the FSLIC reserve to pay off those notes, to avoid the embarrassment of a qualified annual statement for a Federal Home Loan Bank. In 1988, perhaps fortunately, the accounting profession eliminated the old "qualified" statement, substituting an ambiguous "third paragraph," which the Dallas Bank received.

Nobody ever defended the first of the Southwest Plan deals, which took a bunch of S&Ls, combined them under the name Southwest Savings, and gave them to Carolyn Hunt of the Hunt family in return for her agreement to convert to equity some $25 million of their debt instruments, which she already owned. Gerald Levy of Milwaukee's Guaranty Savings described this arrangement before the Senate Banking Committee as "a continuation of allowing institutions to remain on the street that are operating without capital, putting the entire system at risk."[29] Larry White, who as a member of the Bank Board had to approve all these deals, notes special discomfort with this one and recalls that Root himself described it as a "loss leader." In 1990, having run up a negative net worth of more than $350 million, Southwest was taken once again to its government's bosom. Other deals, supposedly, were less subject to criticism.

The most publicized of the Bank Board's deals was not a Texas deal at all but the sale of American Savings of Stockton (now back up to $38 billion) to Robert M. Bass, of the big-money Bass family in Texas. This deal involved a cash infusion of $550 million but gave Bass the right to use $1.5 billion of American Savings' deposits as a merchant bank that could play takeover and leveraged buyout games. California commissioner William Crawford, who would have to give his okay (American Savings was state chartered), would not agree to do this, and in the end the deal was restructured to let Bass put in only about $350 million, without merchant banking powers. American was split into two thrifts.

The surviving American would have about $16 billion in good assets, plus the branches and the retail deposits. A new "bad bank" would have about $22 billion of assets Bass didn't want, funded partly by an $8 billion note from the new American Savings, partly by the thrift's highest-cost brokered deposits, and partly by the FSLIC itself. The loss to the FSLIC was originally estimated at some number between $2 billion and $3 billion. This may have been reduced in the fall of 1989, when interest rates dipped briefly, allowing William Popejoy, whom Bass had kept on to be head of the bad bank, to sell off the portfolio of mortgage-backed securities that Knapp and he had been playing with for almost ten years, at a net loss of "only" $800 million.

One should note that this deal reported itself the next year as a considerable success. Mario Antoci, whom Bass stole from Home Savings to be CEO of American Savings, expanded American's origination of adjustable mortgages, sloughed branches, and cut general and administrative costs from 2.2 percent to 1.7 percent of assets. For 1989, American reported profits of $214 million (all tax sheltered by earlier losses). But it should be kept in mind that at least $160 million of those profits were, in fact, returns on the loan to the bad bank, guaranteed by the FSLIC, and that it's much easier to make money when absolutely all the nonperforming loans have been cleansed out of the bank. It is not clear that running American Savings as a standard one- to four-family housing lender will satisfy the Bass interests, however; American Savings will probably become a player, for better or worse, in the asset-management and asset-disposition business that will grow out of the government's efforts to clean up the larger S&L mess. (This is what Gray's former assistant, Ann Fairbanks, is working on for Bass.) Meanwhile, in the summer of 1989, which turned out to be exactly the wrong time, American Savings took a flier in the junk bond market Congress was about to ban as a locus for thrift investments and dropped something more than $50 million, very quickly.

Other out-of-Texas deals exploiting the tax benefits available until the last day of 1988 included one that gave Ford Motor Company's First Nationwide Savings control of the two largest

S&Ls in Colorado and one of the three largest in Ohio. There was a complex deal that sold Mera Bank to that state's power and light company, which soon exhausted the FSLIC guarantees and was driven to the brink of insolvency by unexpected losses in its thrift. But Texas had most of the dogs and Texas got most of the biscuits.

Many of the acquirers were pretty unsuitable: For example, an operator of country clubs and resorts that "didn't rule out lending to some of its residential real estate developments" from the thrifts it was acquiring.[30] The archetype was the purchase of a group that included what had been Vernon Savings and First Gibraltar. The buyer was Ronald Perelman, proprietor of Revlon and protégé of Michael Milken. Perelman got $12.2 billion list price in assets supported by a $5 billion FSLIC assistance package. It said in the paper that he put $315 million of his own money into the deal, but later we learned that he had borrowed all but $65 million of it. In return, he got tax deductions valued at $897.3 million. For calendar 1989, Perelman's new First Gibraltar reported payments from the government of $461 million and net profits to Perelman (all tax-free) of $129 million. Wow!

In fact, the Southwest Plan was a terrible mess. It did accomplish some of what its designers had hoped. Some 88 Texas S&Ls were consolidated into 17 larger shops, which closed 238 of their 836 branches. The cost of funds was reduced somewhat, which was no doubt good in itself, cutting the monthly loss of the industry in Texas from about $350 million to about $250 million—but most of the reduction was done by gimmicks, like the substitution of Home Loan Bank advances for brokered deposits. In fairness, the Bank Board probably could not have shrunk the industry much more even if it had wished to do so. (Which Wall didn't: It was understood in the administration that he was not going to have a Gray-like war with the Texas congressional delegation.) Sizable cutbacks would have required selling a lot of assets, and the FSLIC simply didn't have the money to pay the difference between the book value of the portfolios and the prices this garbage would command in the market. As the buyers became familiar with what they had bought, moreover, the losses that would have to be taken on the portfolios got worse and worse; the FSLIC's "flexible" guarantees were bottomless pits.

"The notes," Comptroller General Charles Bowsher told the House Banking Committee at the same San Antonio hearing where Root testified, "will have to be considerably larger than what [the Bank Board] originally agreed to."[31] A month later, a GAO report on the deals projected that "during the first five years of operations, FSLIC assistance will make up more than half of the projected gross income of seven of the eight thrifts we reviewed in detail. . . . These income projections are based on optimistic business assumptions."[32]

Just in case Congress refused to appropriate money to pay off the FSLIC notes, the Bank Board gave all the acquirers in the Southwest Plan "pocket charters," licenses to open new S&Ls whenever the acquirers wished to do so. If for any reason the FSLIC assistance was not forthcoming, the purchasers could launch a new S&L that would absorb as much of their deposit liabilities as was necessary to support the book value of the bad paper. This new S&L would immediately go broke, and the FSLIC would pick up the deposits, getting the Southwest Plan purchaser off the hook. The tax consequences were an atrocity. Robert Adelizzi, president of Home Federal of San Diego, bitter about the costs imposed on his well-managed S&L by the thieves, clowns, and politicians who had made policy for his industry, added up the totals: "To attract $3 billion in capital, the FSLIC handed out $8 billion worth of tax breaks."[33]

Root's assumption in early 1988 that the Texas real estate market was about to turn had been wildly in error: Prices were lower in most of Texas a year later and were no better than their 1988 levels in 1990, despite a good deal of hype about forward progress. (And between 1988 and 1990, interest, upkeep, and taxes had cost the S&Ls and the FSLIC at least 30 percent of their value in carrying costs.) Oilman "Bum" Bright, owner of the Dallas Cowboys, was on Root's side of the debate. His Bright Banc, eventually a $4.7 billion monster, bought up lots of little S&Ls in 1987, foreclosed on their bad real estate loans, and held the resulting properties in eager anticipation of the upturn. An examiner from another district who worked on the examination of this operation remembers how flattered his local colleagues were that they could actually meet Bum Bright—and how unconcerned they were that some of the defaulted assets were being purchased by a Bright family fund in what might or might not be arm's-length transactions. In February 1989, Bright Banc, admittedly $242 million in the hole, was seized by the federales. When Bright Banc was sold to Banc One of Ohio a year later, the cost to the taxpayer was estimated at $1.7 billion.

Even if its execution had been more savvy, the Southwest Plan was wrong in principle, like the mergers by which the FDIC kept Texas banks alive. The spirit of capitalism demands that winners in fair competition gain the fruits of their victory and that losers go off to try other things. With their competition kept in operation by the government, stronger thrifts and banks had to pay higher interest rates for their funds—the famous "Texas premium." "This process," Genie Short and Jeffrey W. Gunther of the Federal Reserve Bank of Dallas wrote, "not only weakens the financial condition of the solvent banks and thrifts in Texas, it also penalizes the stronger institutions *because of* the problems of the most troubled institutions. Thus, the efforts of the FHLBB to assist insolvent institutions to continue operations have a negative impact on the current operations of the unassisted institutions in the state. . . . [T]he funding programs implemented by the FHLB-Dallas encourage depositors to move their funds into the more troubled institutions. The Southwest Plan has this result as a *stated objective*."[34]

Admittedly, the denunciation of what the Bank Board did in 1988 is a lot easier than the construction of an alternative. But the losses in the industry would have been much less if the Bank Board had truly and sincerely abandoned the foolish hope that its wards might somehow be able to grow out of their problems. Much better than the Southwest Plan would have been vigorous promulgation and enforcement of cease-and-desist orders to force the Texas S&Ls to stop making loans and soliciting deposits. These zombies should have been made to use repayment of principal on home mortgages to shrink their deposit base. They certainly should not have been allowed to hit up Wall Street for more loans to buy more bad paper. The sweetheart deals the Bank Board made in the last week of 1988 haunt not only the budget but the reputation of the people who signed off on them.

Information on the worst of these deals surfaced only in July 1990, when an article by Jeff Gerth in *The New York Times* described the aggregation of fifteen Texas S&Ls into one $3.5 billion thrift and its "sale" to James M. Fail of Phoenix with a FSLIC contribution of $1.85 billion. Fail had been indicted for securities fraud in Alabama, and had pleaded guilty on behalf of the company he then controlled. He had only $1,000 of his own money in the deal, he had been outbid by a rival without this sort of record, and the staff at the Dallas Home Loan Bank had recommended against him. But he was represented by Robert J. Thompson, a former Bush aide; Seidman's FDIC had let him buy a bank in Oklahoma the year before; and Dallas HLB president George Barclay, who had done what Wall wanted in the Keating matter, overruled his staff. In 1989, Fail's S&L made $40 million on $60 million in equity—after a gift of $250 million from FSLIC.[35]

When the House Banking Committee met to hear testimony from the Bank Board before C-Span cameras on January 6, 1989, the worst deal appeared to be First Gibraltar.

Rep. Charles Schumer (D-N.Y.) brought out all the nice things the Bank Board had done for Ron Perelman. The next questioner was Walter Fauntroy from the District of Columbia.

"Did I understand you to say," said Representative Fauntroy, "that Mr. Perelman, in return for $315 million cash, received tax benefits of $897 million?"

"It might not work out that way," said Danny Wall.

"But it might?"

Very reluctantly: "Yes, it might."

Fauntroy leaned forward. "I have just one question for you, Mr. Wall," he said.

"Yes?"

"Why is it only white folks who get that kind of deal?"

CHAPTER 10

Can This Industry Be Salvaged?

I believe that specialized financial institutions—including, but not limited to, thrifts and community banks—have served us well and that we should therefore not be so single-minded in the name of reform as to produce a total homogenization of the financial system.

—E. Gerald Corrigan, then president, Federal Reserve Bank of Minneapolis (1982)

MONG the issues on which the presidential candidates agreed in 1988 were two touching upon our subject: (1) The most pressing piece of domestic business for the incoming administration would be the need to stanch the bleeding at the S&Ls, and (2) there was nothing to be gained by making the decay of the S&Ls a matter of contention in the campaign. It was, to be sure, a technical subject, the kind of thing voters really don't want to hear about—not a patch on crime or abortion or patriotism or clean air. The S&L outrage did have a lot to do with taxes, but only the handful of people who understand the workings of government finance would know why that was true. (The FICO borrowings that funded the Southwest Plan actually appeared as revenue in the unified federal budget, apparently reducing the deficit!) In late September, as his campaign was being dragged down by alligators, Governor Michael Dukakis did suggest (exactly once) that there might be something worth noticing in the S&L situation; and Vice-President George Bush, well prepared, sneered that this was yet another example of the Democrats' desire to raise your taxes.

What should be done with the S&Ls was in truth an extraordinarily difficult question. But there were different ways to go. The failure of the political process to pay attention in 1988 meant not only that the taxpaying public was shocked to find a $50 billion invoice in the mail three months later but also that alternative disaster-reduction proposals and philosophies were never considered. The Financial Institutions Reform, Recovery, and Enforcement Act of 1989 (FIRREA) was intelligently amended in Congress (especially in the House), but the draft legislation that came out of the White House in February was pretty much the law that Congress enacted in August. The financial centerpiece was still $50 billion to finance an RTC that would act as receiver for busted S&Ls and make certain that insured depositors got their money back. Another $40 billion would be needed to make good on the FSLIC notes issued in the Southwest Plan. Some of this was to be financed by raiding the kitty at the twelve Federal Home Loan Banks. Most was to come from selling bonds on which the taxpayer would pay the interest; the total was supposed to be $159 billion in ten years.

The Bank Board was dissolved and replaced by an Office of Thrift Supervision under the guidance of the Treasury, like the Office of the Comptroller of the Currency, which charters and supervises national banks. S&Ls would have to boost their capital and eschew some of the accounting atrocities and devote a higher share of their investments to residential housing. The FSLIC would also go and be replaced by a Savings Association Insurance Fund that would be operated as part of the FDIC. The enlarged FDIC would have power to examine all state-chartered S&Ls and to deny insurance to S&Ls that sought to exercise powers the federal agency believed might endanger the insurance fund—even if the state that chartered the S&L approved them.

The bill could have been quite a lot worse than it was. The hero who kept it from becoming so was Rep. Jim Leach (R-Iowa), who steamrollered through the House Banking Committee an omnibus amendment that struck all the special-interest baubles that members had hung on the tree through the write-up process. (An aborted attempt to do the same on the Senate side produced a truly grand disaster. Richard Carnell, senior counsel of the Senate Banking Committee, was asked to produce a list of the things in the bill that might be considered special favors, and somehow this list got into the hands of the press.) But the law doesn't, won't, and can't work. The organization is faulty, the financial analysis is egregiously optimistic, the incentives are perverse, and the politics are disabling. Robert Litan of the Brookings Institution said, when the proposal was first made public, that he was surprised by it. He had expected the new administration to come up with something that would look good for at least five years, until after the next elections, but FIRREA was sure to explode in three or less.

Three people were primarily responsible for the Bush proposal: Robert Glauber, a young Harvard Business School finance professor who had worked as Treasury Secretary Nicholas Brady's chief of staff on Brady's study of the stock market crash of October 1987; Richard Breeden, an even younger Wall Street lawyer, still under forty, who had been George Bush's staff director for a study the vice-president made on the deregulation of financial services toward the end of Ronald Reagan's first term; and L. William Seidman, almost as old as the other two put together, chairman of the FDIC, an accountant and lawyer from Michigan who had been Gerald Ford's economic adviser and dean of the business school at Arizona State University. Except for shared vanities and thin skins, the three men could scarcely have been more different, and they didn't get on with each other.

Glauber was the model of the new generation of business professors, making more money as a consultant to corporations around the country than he made from Harvard, generating slogans and ideas rather than any substantial body of work. Reputedly able—but nowhere near so able as he thought—he was well regarded as a man who built and enjoyed working with first-class staffs, which is not as common an attribute as you might think. In the Brady Report, the result was excellent investigation and nitty-gritty analysis of what had happened on the day of the worst market collapse ever. But there was another result, a major fallacy, an analytically crippling statement that the stock, futures, and options markets had become "one market." (The fallacy here was obvious to people who knew that the century-old wheat futures market and the cash market for hard winter wheat are still far from being "one market"; but not many people do know that.) Glauber knew relatively little about S&Ls and less about the relationship between these rather strange institutions and their customers. Like most academics, he thought the growth of alternative sources for housing finance had made the industry obsolete.

Glauber was apparently the source of a proposal leaked the first week in January that the S&L bailout should be funded by taxing deposits, on the grounds that it was depositors who benefited from the insurance. He did not realize that depositors were already paying, through their acceptance of interest rates normally a percentage point below what they could make on money market mutual funds, and he did not understand that the political fallout from such idiocy could be lethal.

Breeden, also able but even more egotistical than Glauber, had learned about S&Ls by serving on the Federal Savings & Loan Advisory Council. He understood the need to close down a good fraction of the industry very quickly so that confidence in the rest of it could be reestablished. But it was his idea that the first step toward establishing trust should be a dramatic seizure of 220-odd insolvent S&Ls by the FDIC, which had a much better reputation than the FSLIC. Instead, the much-advertised arrival of the feds to take over the busted S&Ls (in each city, the local television news people were notified from Washington before the cops moved in) provoked a certain amount of panicky withdrawal and great reluctance by the neighbors to make new deposits. If the aim had been to shrink these institutions, the tactic might have made sense, but in fact there was no way in the first seven months of 1989 to do anything but sustain them. Thus the local deposits lost by publicity had to be replaced through the money brokers on Wall Street, who gleefully increased their commissions for the service.

Seidman is a man of unusual appearance and individual speech mannerisms—roundheaded and entirely bald, with large ears laid back and a tic of shaking his head and clearing his throat before delivering his proposals in a nasal voice. He is good company, and as Washington goes, he is passing honest. His abilities have been focused on the Beltway game, which he likes and plays superbly, cultivating Democratic congressmen and newspeople while playing ball with the banking industry and state Republican leaders. The agency he headed was the smallest of the bank regulatory potatoes until the 1980s. Nationally chartered banks were examined by the Comptroller of the Currency; state-chartered banks that were members of the Federal Reserve System were examined by the Fed; and the FDIC had direct relations only with the many, but small, state-chartered banks that were not members of the Federal Reserve. "When Frank Wille was chairman of the FDIC," said Federal Reserve Board Governor Martha Seger in some wonderment, referring to Gerald Ford's FDIC chairman, "nobody in this town knew who he was."

William Isaac had been a more visible FDIC chairman, because banks began failing in greater numbers and more noisily. The looting of the Butcher chain of banks in Tennessee and Kentucky, the lunatic oil-patch lending at Penn Square, Continental Illinois's purchase of a billion dollars of Penn Square's garbage—all these came on Isaac's watch. But Seidman had gone many steps beyond: He was everywhere, on all the television news shows and both radio and television talk shows, making four, five speeches a week around the country, reveling in his own prominence and that of his agency.

There can be no doubt that Seidman had an agenda quite separate from Glauber's or Breeden's. Through 1988, to the intense fury of Danny Wall, he had been making noises about how awful the situation was in the thrift industry and how big the losses were going to be. He would protect the banks' insurance fund, the FDIC, from being tapped to help pay for the losses at the S&Ls—but if the White House and Congress absolutely insisted, he personally would bear this cross, too, for his country. So the first thing that happened as the new administration reached to drain the thrift swamp was that the Bank Board appointed the FDIC rather than the FSLIC to be the conservator and eventual receiver for distressed S&Ls. This triggered, I think (I can't prove it), the second phase of Seidman's agenda.

In speeches and statements, Seidman's thesis since 1986 had been that in the banking world as it is, most larger banks are "too big to fail." (The preferred FDIC formulation was "too important to pay off."[1]) And if big banks can't be closed, it's not fair to close little ones. Whenever a bank becomes insolvent, some federal agency will have to prop it up, reorganize it, and put up enough subsidy so that somebody will wish to buy it and keep it going. But most of the biggest banks are not funded with the insured deposits of American little folk. Banks like Morgan Guaranty and Bankers Trust carry insured domestic deposits for as little as 10 percent of the money they use. If the FDIC is going to stand behind *the banks*, insuring all their liabilities, then of course it will have to examine and supervise all the nation's banks, regardless of whether they are state- or nationally chartered or members of the Federal Reserve. The day when nobody in Washington knows the name of the FDIC chairman will be gone forever: He will be some important fella.

Since 1913, the "lender of last resort" to American banks has been the Federal Reserve. The Fed's policy has always been to lend only on good security to banks that have a problem putting their hands on ready cash to pay back depositors or other creditors, *not* to banks that are insolvent and can't repay what they borrow. It's the government's money the Fed lends; if a borrower welches on the Fed, the Fed's annual payment from its profits to the Treasury ($18 billion and up) will be lower, increasing the budget deficit. And the Fed can control fallout from the failure of an insolvent bank by supplying a lot of money to the market, enabling solvent banks to handle any run on the system. In fact, *only* the Federal Reserve can be the lender of last resort, because only the Fed can create money at will, purchasing U.S. Treasury bills and notes in the market to "monetize" the government debt.

The FDIC is not so well placed, because it cannot create money; its resources are limited to the insurance fund created by bank premium payments, plus a $5 billion line of credit at the Treasury.

To serve its new grand function, then, the FDIC would need an unlimited line of credit from the Fed. The study Seidman commissioned from his staff, *Deposit Insurance in the Nineties*, is quite specific on the subject: "It is recommended that the deposit insurer be given explicit authority to borrow from either the Treasury or the Federal Reserve System. To minimize delays, the amount and term, within specified limits, of such borrowings should be at the sole discretion of the FDIC."[2] The first steps in this direction had already been taken: In the Continental Illinois rescue and the First Republic of Texas matter, the FDIC had assumed liability for advances the Fed had made to these institutions, *but did not repay the Fed* when the deals were completed. "I guess they could foreclose on us and take us over if they want," Seidman told Rep. John LaFalce in his most jocular manner at a House Banking Committee hearing in the summer of 1988.[3]

Glauber and Breeden were obsessed by the continuing losses at the S&Ls, and a significant source of these losses was the high rates the insolvent thrifts had to pay to gain or hold deposits. Seidman—again, I can't prove it—offered them a prospect of funding the S&Ls by borrowing cheap from the Fed. Just before the three-day "President's weekend" in February 1989, Seidman informed Manuel Johnson, vice-chairman of the Fed, that there might be a disastrous run on the seized S&Ls over the long weekend and he had better have cash available to pay off the depositors.

The plan was for 45 percent of the money to come from the Fed, 45 percent from the Home Loan Banks, and 10 percent from the FSLIC's $750 million line of credit at the Treasury. Chairman Greenspan was holed up in a hotel, writing his annual report to Congress on employment and money, and didn't want to touch this one with a pole, anyway. Johnson arranged a telephone meeting of the presidents of the twelve district Federal Reserve Banks for the Friday morning before the three-day weekend. These district Reserve Banks are the actual sources of the Fed's money. If you look at the currency in your pocket, you will see a rosette printed with a letter indicating which of the Banks it was printed for. Johnson told the presidents that in this emergency it was necessary for them to appoint him as their lending officer de facto and to make advances from their coffers, regardless of security, to whatever S&Ls might need money in these desperate times.

Three of the presidents resisted, saying they had to talk to their boards before they could yield such control over their activities, and the story got out from those boards to Representative LaFalce, who at the next week's hearings asked Greenspan about this extraordinary break with the Fed's traditions. He got a choked response that the matter was too sensitive to talk about. As a result, Seidman was informed that he was not to come to the Fed so long as his S&Ls could get money from the Wall Street brokers, regardless of the terms.

Meanwhile, William McKenna at the Federal Home Loan Bank of San Francisco had refused to go along with the plan to make loans without good collateral. Danny Wall thereupon deposed him as chairman of the Bank, but he remained on the board, and very influential. San Francisco was the system's largest bank. Bank Board member Roger Martin flew to Los Angeles to inform McKenna that if his Bank continued obdurate, Breeden would kill the Home Loan Bank system in the new bill. San Francisco signed on. But Glauber and his sidekick David Mullins at Treasury continued reluctant, and the Seidman juggernaut stalled. In the end only one large loan was made—to Charlie Keating's Lincoln Savings, which turned out not to have the collateral the regulators thought it had. Greenspan, who never wanted to hear Keating's name again, was sufficiently angry that presently the Fed *did* call the FDIC's borrowings on Continental and First Republic and put Seidman on a cash basis.

Glauber and Breeden, however, Seidman eventually overwhelmed. The best explanation, probably, is in the *Weltanschauung* he gave to *Who's Who* for its forty-third edition: "Be prepared: Luck is where opportunity meets preparation. Be people oriented: Treat others the way you would have others treat you. Be confident: Remember the opposition puts their pants on one leg at a time, too. Be innovative: Good planning consists of innovating around a general sense of direction. Be your enthusiastic self: You can't be anybody else, successfully."[4] If you have enough brass in Washington, you don't need much gold. And, in general, people *like* Bill Seidman; and they don't much like either Glauber or Breeden.

So the failed S&Ls were turned over to the FDIC to operate even before there was a new law, and the bailout bill made the chairman of the FDIC the chairman and CEO of the new RTC, which was to dispose of the busted thrifts and their assets by 1996. Seidman's victory was a little too complete: Representative Gonzalez, especially, got nervous about the concentration of so much power to reward friends and punish enemies in the hands of someone with no commitment to housing finance. Meanwhile, John Robson, formerly vice-chairman of Searle, the pharmaceuticals company, and dean of the business school at Emory University, had arrived at the Treasury as under secretary and had been told to take over the Seidman problem from Glauber. A little man with thin sandy hair, a quick study, knowledgeable about the Washington scene, and hard as nails, Robson counterattacked and won congressional approval for an RTC "oversight board" consisting of the secretaries of the Treasury and of HUD, the chairman of the Federal Reserve Board, and two members of the public to be chosen by the president. (These slots were filled some eight months after the passage of the Act, with politically oriented bankers, a bad mistake.) The oversight board, of which Robson became acting president, would make policy for the RTC and control its fund-raising.

This oversight board would prove to be a bone in Seidman's throat, but on balance he had every reason to be content. As of the spring of 1990, the chairman of the FDIC was no longer the obscure head of a minor bureaucracy that cleaned one part of the government's garbage. He was the titular head of organizations that would have almost ten thousand employees and an annual budget approaching $3 billion. He was in the headlines at least once a week. Mostly, Seidman had done it by straightforward arguments about turf, which everybody in Washington understands, rather than about substantive issues, which few people in

Washington understand. But just as the likable Dick Pratt was the prime mover in the hugely expensive tragedy of the S&Ls, the likable Bill Seidman will be more responsible than anyone else for the RTC disaster that lies ahead.

[1]

The root problems are what they have always been: the unbelievable enormity of what the veterans call "the hole": $50 billion doesn't touch it. The numbers are so awful not so much because more S&Ls than expected are insolvent (though in fact the casualty ratio is bad) but because the loss per failed institution is way over what anyone had imagined. "I had a thin staff, only about ten people," says former Deputy Treasury Secretary George Gould, explaining the $15 billion figure for the FSLIC recap request in 1986, "and we got our estimates from the GAO and the Bank Board. They said that when the FSLIC took over an S&L, the losses on the book value of the assets were usually about 20 percent. We figured about $125 billion in the insolvent thrifts, which meant a payout of $25 billion. About $10 billion would be available through premiums, and that left the fifteen. But when we got into the Vernons, it blew those numbers to the sky." And, of course, nothing of substance was done for more than three years after Gould made his initial estimate. Now most observers place the *average* loss on the thrifts taken over by the RTC at about 40 percent of book value, and some see losses approaching 60 percent. This industry was not well run.

The failed S&Ls were placed in the hands of bureaucrats who did not understand (and were never told) that their established procedures were vastly inadequate for the management of this horror. A friend asked a senior official at the FDIC how they were going to blend in the staff moving over from the old FSLIC to the new SAIF and was told, "They'll just have to learn to do it our way." A surviving old FSLIC (now yet another division of the FDIC) remains custodian for about $12 billion of properties taken before January 1, 1989; a knowledgeable observer says he expects that "they'll just sit on these assets until all the value evaporates."

(The FSLIC's glossily printed view-book of commercial property for sale in the summer of 1989 gives possible purchasers a non-working phone number to call.)[5] With no function other than the management and disposition of those assets, the FSLIC is retreating from the front. A Washington lawyer with clients who want to buy one set of apartment houses from the old FSLIC and another set from the RTC finds that he can't do business with either but that the difference in their attitudes is striking. "It's like the scene in *War and Peace*," he says, "where the carts with the wounded are moving out from Borodino while the cavalry comes down the road singing their way to the battle."

Lamar Kelly, who came over from the FDIC to be the supervisor of asset disposition for the RTC, is a large, thoughtful man with a mustache and a deep southern accent. He knew he had an impossible job ("a real challenge") but soldiered on, anyway. His first task was to make a catalog of 36,000 "parcels of REO [real estate owned]" by the 220 thrifts seized early in the game and put a list price on each parcel, and he did that. This was not a proposed price or an upset price for an auction—it was a list price. Somebody who wanted to buy a shopping center or apartment house or office building was supposed to pay the RTC what it said in the book. Even if a purchaser offered the list price, however, he had to wait quite a while before gaining possession. "We have asset approval committees in each area," Kelly said as 1989 became 1990. "They meet with the managing agents who have replaced the boards of directors of the institutions. The asset-decision-making process starts locally, and it might come all the way up here. I'm a great believer in decentralization, but there is a certain level of complex issues.... We reserve certain authority to ourselves. We have an RFP [request for proposal] out for an MIS [management information system] for services in the area of market studies of major markets...."

Kelly was clearly an able man and a hard worker; none of this was his fault. But the FDIC has never been skilled at selling assets. The flow chart for the FDIC-Acquired Loan Liquidation Process shows no fewer than thirty-five separate boxes.[6] The efficiency of the operation does seem to have improved under Isaac and Seidman, but as of September 1988, it still took an average of twelve years for the FDIC to sell the last assets acquired in a bank failure, and what's coming out of the S&Ls is at least fifteen times as much as the FDIC has ever handled. Shocked by its experiences in Texas (which cost the fund its first losing years) and having failed to forecast the blows it was about to suffer in New England, the FDIC entered into its new responsibilities in a seriously weakened condition. It had not examined some of the state banks for which it was responsible in three or four (in one documented case, five) years. "In 1987," the House Government Operations Committee reports, "it lost 33% of its most experienced mid- to senior-level staff, primarily because of wholly inadequate compensation."[7] The agency has always been supercautious. Other sellers typically "warrant" the accuracy of their description of what they are selling, but the FDIC never gives a warranty on anything. And it is pathologically secretive about claims it may or may not wish to introduce in legal proceedings.

The fact is, to quote a Dallas real estate broker, "these people are not dedicated sellers." In his book about the Penn Square disaster, Philip Zweig quoted a borrower named Dan King: "Talking to the FDIC is like visiting a very expensive Disneyland. It's like talking to Huey, Louie and Dewey. You can't get them to make a decision."[8] This is not necessarily anybody's fault. Despite a major effort by Bill Isaac to persuade staff of the time value of money, the perception at any government agency is inevitably that holding assets doesn't impose a cost on the agency, and Congress may raise hell if something is sold for less than its price on the books. Both the FDIC and the Comptroller, moreover, value REO at "fair market value," without reference to carrying costs. If an appraiser says it will sell for a million dollars in five years, that's the list price on the books.* But it can't be sold today for what the appraiser calls fair market value, or for anything like that.

---

*The equivalent at the S&Ls is the much more honest "net realizable value," which counts the cost of carrying the asset to sale date. When Michael Patriarca, whom we have met at the Federal Home Loan Bank of San Francisco, was Deputy Comptroller of the Currency, he put through a memo ordering national banks to value real estate according to the more rigorous procedure. Shortly after Robert Clarke became Comptroller, he restored the status quo.

Better delay; inflation will float all the boats. At the RTC, these normal tendencies were strongly reinforced by a foolish provision in FIRREA forbidding the sale of property in distressed areas for less than 95 percent of appraised value.

Seidman's preference at the FDIC had been "whole bank" deals, in which the insurer put in enough money or guarantees to bring the failed bank back to zero net worth and a purchaser then capitalized the institution to start all over again. This kept the assets in private hands and saved the FDIC from the traumas of liquidation. As in the Bank Board's Southwest Plan, the "new capital" the purchaser invested usually came from the government itself, via tax benefits, which meant the cost was imposed on the taxpayer. Because the FDIC does not pay the tax benefits the buyer receives, it does not take tax consequences into account in its analysis of whether liquidation or subsidy to an acquirer is the "least cost" resolution. And the question of what will happen to the other banks in the region is not even asked.

Whenever a substantial fraction of the banks in an area fail, reason argues (or should argue) that the area has too many banks. The deals the FDIC and the Bank Board made in Texas lead to a situation where the ultimate survivors will be those that went broke first, and worst, and thus got the lion's share of government assistance. Because the purchaser in these schemes was paid to recognize *all* the losses in the bank, he started off with a much cleaner portfolio than his competitors who had not been reorganized by the government and who were carrying at historic cost much paper that they knew would eventually generate a loss. FDIC insistence that even the most insolvent larger banks must be kept going created the domino collapse of the Texas banks—and the fearful losses suffered in Texas by Chemical Bank of New York and First Interstate of Los Angeles, both of which bought into Texas at precisely the wrong time and could not get the benefits of their deep pockets because the FDIC put its even deeper pockets at the disposal of their failed competitors. But both the Bank Board and the FDIC considered their efforts in Texas to have been triumphant, because most of the fellows they put back in business and continue to prop up are making money.

And it should be noted that the Federal Reserve Bank of New York in a quiet way is playing much the same games with our superfluity of money-center banks.

Instinctively, then, the FDIC as proprietor of the RTC wanted to keep at least the larger thrifts intact, selling them off as a whole. A mistake in the banking context, where overcapacity is still latent, this procedure was catastrophic when applied to the grossly over-served thrift market. As Robert Adelizzi of San Diego's Home Fed put it: "A central truth about insolvent financial institutions is that their so-called assets—nonearning loans and investments—have become so devalued that they have actually turned into liabilities, in the real-world sense of the term. Meanwhile, retail deposits—liabilities in the balance-sheet sense—have become the only assets of any real value to a would-be acquirer. . . . Inaction and delay only weakens this value. . . . Regulators must proceed on the understanding that their proper objective is to remove excess capacity, not perpetuate it. . . . The best way to resolve these cases, then, is to split the institutions apart and dispose of assets and liabilities separately. The alternative—an insistence on selling insolvent institutions whole—will only preserve overcapacity. It is certain to delay the resolution process (thereby simultaneously boosting costs and diminishing remaining values) and may in the end force regulators to again resort to the costly improvisations —interest-rate guarantees and tax breaks—that marred the Southwest Plan."[9]

Seidman believed that keeping the institution together preserves the "franchise value" of the S&L's name and community status and thus reduced the cost to the insurer. But, as John Oros of the Wall Street house Goldman, Sachs likes to put it, "Deposits have franchise value; assets have only market value." For an institution like California's Gibraltar Savings—almost $13 billion when seized in April 1989—the branch structure that gathered deposits had great value for a bank or S&L looking to enter the enormous Southern California market. But nobody wanted the thankless job of caring for and selling the pile of junk gathered as Gibraltar reached for ways to compensate for its accumulated losses. If an acquirer must take the assets, too, he will demand government subsidy to guarantee him against loss of income or principal on these loans and properties—plus payment for his trouble.

Seidman worried properly about the decay of assets in government custody. "You need people to manage these properties," said Kelly. "We can't hire the expertise, can't pay the salaries. We have to contract with firms that don't have conflicts of interest." But retaining Gibraltar as an entity with its inherited assets means that Gibraltar willy-nilly becomes the manager of property it has already demonstrated it can't manage, like the hotel it wound up owning in Shreveport, Louisiana. Managers working for either the RTC or busted thrifts have very little incentive to do a bang-up job. To minimize the cost to the taxpayer, these properties have to get into the hands of new owners very, very fast.

Guided by John Robson, the RTC oversight board adopted policies that led toward Adelizzi's objective. Seidman was given orders to sell as much as he could as quickly as he could. Ten days after the passage of the act, there were newspaper stories about seven S&Ls that had been put on the block for quick sale, and there were lots of bidders; the first of them was sold five months later. Mind you, the deals Robson permitted Seidman to offer were not in the same ballpark as the deals both he and Wall made in 1988. The law dictated that buyers of thrifts would have to meet capital standards from the beginning (i.e., at least 1.5 percent of the money the reorganized S&L would have at its disposal would have to come from its new owners, and another 1.5 percent from sources other than the depositors).

Robson insisted that the RTC could not guarantee the assets in the portfolio or subsidize their yield to purchasers of the S&L for more than six months. At the end of the six months, the acquirers would have the option of turning assets back to the RTC or keeping them, but they couldn't let the game drag on, with continuing costs to the government. Robson saw the need to avoid the situation structured by the Bank Board in Texas, where lots of assets in the thrifts the FSLIC reorganized are not for sale at all, because management knows it can't make as much interest on a safe loan as the FSLIC pays in its guaranteed-yield agreement.

The oversight board insisted that assets kept by the RTC should be sold as soon as possible for whatever the market would pay. Buyers of property would be expected to put up at least 25 percent of the purchase price in cash. Seidman accepted the guidelines (letting it be known in the press that he considered them unrealistic), made a great show of getting organized, and moved some paperwork—but no property. He was, obviously, girding his loins to battle for the right of the FDIC to create the RTC in its own image and to operate the new agency in its usual manner.

The fights over the RTC's capacity to issue notes and raise working capital became the crucial determinants of the ultimate cost of the bailout. The first occurred in the House-Senate conference committee that wrote the final version of FIRREA in the summer of 1989, and it produced a compromise: The RTC was given authority to issue notes collateralized by the value of the assets it held, up to a maximum of $50 billion. Thus, some of the funds expended to acquire assets could be used again to subsidize buyers of thrifts or of property. This relatively innocent leverage was still undesirable, because its implementation would mean that the RTC could hide costs the way the Bank Board did, but the damage would be limited. The oversight board then further reduced the harm that could be done, forbidding the RTC to issue yield guarantees—pledges to make up any shortfalls of income from the failure of assets to generate revenues—for periods longer than six months. So Seidman came back in January 1990 with a demand for "working capital," the right to borrow more on the security of the United States, to hold assets on the books of the RTC. The oversight board was reluctant to go along, but because the RTC had sold only $4 billion of the $105 billion book value in institutions it had controlled for almost a year, there was a real danger that the operation would run out of funds, so Robson finally consented to a limited borrowing.

With the approval of working-capital borrowing by the RTC and the accompanying political decision to accept Seidman's claim that it was the oversight board that was slowing the process, the risks of the bailout rose exponentially. Even before winning his battle in Congress, Seidman called for permission to use the RTC funds for "open-bank assistance" (the FDIC version of Bank Board forbearance), to thrifts that might make it if the regulators let them hang on. As Robert Trigaux of *American Banker* wrote, "Six months into the thrift industry cleanup, regulator L. William Seidman is beginning to sound like M. Danny Wall."[10]

There was another way—probably several other ways. One developed by John Oros of Goldman, Sachs, who was highly confident he could raise the financing, would have treated all the assets of all the thrifts for which the RTC was receiver as a single estate. That estate would then be broken up into giant parcels of assets that related to each other: hotels, office buildings, shopping centers, theaters, apartment houses, single-family homes, raw land. In half-billion to billion-dollar pieces, large enough to draw the attention of major players, these could be put on the auction block with an upset price. The winning bidder would have to put up a deposit of, say, 20 percent to pay for any shortfall in receipts. (This is the money Oros would raise.) He would then have five years to sell off the parcel. Nearly all proceeds of early sales would go to the RTC, but as the totals neared the price of the winning bid, the acquirer would retain a higher proportion and would get to keep perhaps as much as half of what he received over and above the bid price. Meanwhile, the "core deposits" of the thrifts would be transferred (for a commission) to other banks and thrifts that would be happy to pay for secure sources of funding. In the end, the RTC would still be holding some tens of billions of dollars of loans in some way disputed, undocumented, or otherwise uncollectible. Smart fellows in the carrion trade would make hundreds of millions of dollars. But the taxpayer would pay many billions less.

The first president of the RTC Oversight Board was Daniel Kearney, a New England real estate man who had served ten years in Salomon's real estate financing arm. He made his peace with Seidman, which meant that Robson sat on him, "micromanaging" his office, until he quit. His departure raised wails of anguish from the congressional figures and reporters Seidman had cultivated. Robson a few days later noted it with Mark Twain's comment on Wagner's music: "It sounds worse than it is." William

Taylor, a large and forceful Federal Reserve officer from that organization's supervisory side, was brought in as acting president. It was Taylor who found a loophole in the FIRREA requirement that required the RTC to set property prices at no less than 95 percent of appraised value. At a much publicized meeting in early May 1990, the RTC board announced a policy of marking property prices down by 15 percent after six months and another 5 percent six months after that.

Meanwhile, the Oversight Board consented to several changes in its original rules. Purchasers of whole thrifts would be given two years rather than merely six months to kick the tires and decide which assets they wished to keep and which they wished to return to the RTC (at list price). In addition, there would be some yield maintenance guarantees, à la Southwest Plan. Purchasers of assets would have to put up only 15 percent, not 25 percent, of the price. And the committees would be told to speed up their deliberations.

Seidman told Congress and the press the obvious truth that the final price tag was going to be much larger than originally estimated, and now the White House took an interest—it is probably not too much to say that the White House panicked. This was not supposed to hit the fan until after election day, 1992; and now there was a real chance that it would blow into the faces of political candidates before election day, 1990. The Treasury was already concerned about disturbances in the money markets from the sale of government paper to supply RTC with Seidman's "working capital." John Sununu, the president's chief of staff, let the press know that a replacement was going to be found for Seidman, who then let the press know that by statute his job ran until summer 1991 and he would decide when he wished to leave. Peace was declared when both sides agreed that Taylor would be an excellent replacement someday. (Taylor's great advantage from the White House point of view was that his training at the Fed had emphasized the importance of keeping your mouth shut except when you can say what your superiors have told you to say.) Bowing now to the policy Robson had been advocating from the start, Seidman proclaimed that the RTC would sell 140 thrifts before June 30, 1990, come hell or high water, and would unload the mortgage-backed securities from the vaults of the defaulted thrifts without waiting for some fairy godmother to come and buy the S&L complete with its assets. The more assets the RTC sold, after all, the fewer Treasury bills the government would have to sell for the purpose of carrying what it had seized from insolvent thrifts.

Unfortunately, the bailout is still institutionally flawed. If the RTC is to be a masterful sales operation, it can't be cloned from the FDIC, which has never been much good at selling. Selling the defunct S&Ls individually was never a viable strategy. The FDIC cannot operate a $200 billion financial-services institution and cannot effectively sell that quantity of assets. These are situations where the seller has to do the due diligence, understand what he's selling, and warrant it: Warranties of the merchandise are much less costly than guarantees of yield or price. Every instinct in the FDIC bureaucracy works to impede this process. The first step away from the brink of costs exceeding half a trillion dollars is the separation of the RTC from the FDIC.

"Government-sponsored enterprises" that permit their proprietors to make money with government help have proliferated dangerously in recent years, and it goes against the grain to recommend yet another one. But for this purpose, that's what's needed: an RTC largely private in its direction, with high-paid executives, a defined mission, and an assured sunset provision to put it out of business in less than a decade. When Michael Milken was indicted in the spring of 1989, I wrote in the Los Angeles *Times* that if he should be convicted his sentence should include ten years' community service working out the S&Ls. When Milken copped his plea a year later, Charles Keating said more or less the same thing to the *Wall Street Journal*. And we can't both be wrong. Milken of course is an impossibility; but there are guys just as bad and almost as smart who are still walking around and could be recruited.

What can't possibly work is the other policy Seidman announced in early 1990, to subsidize sick thrifts again and keep them out of government hands until a buyer can be found for their "franchise value."

Surviving S&Ls can keep surviving only if the dead are allowed to die. The final vice of governmental activity in this industry—from the regulatory accounting lies to the phoenixes to the Management Consignment Program to forbearance to the Southwest Plan to Seidman's working capital for open-bank assistance—was that they encouraged continuing overcapacity. For all of the decade of the eighties, it was unquestionably, unarguably true that the United States had more S&Ls than it needed. Among the informed, the real question was whether the United States needed S&Ls at all.

[2]

Housing finance is a special study, because the loan to the householder runs so much longer than the borrowings of the intermediary who supplies the funds. A percentage-point rise in interest on a $100,000 loan to a retailer to carry stock that turns over four times a year adds only $250 to the cost of the merchandise; on a thirty-year self-amortizing $100,000 mortgage, the added cost of a percentage-point rise in rates is about $17,000. From the lender's point of view, if that one-point rise becomes permanent, he winds up short $17,000 of the money he needs to pay his depositors, his loans are worth less than they were when they were written, and he can't make it up on the other part of the cycle the way he can with a long-term fixed-rate commercial loan or a corporate bond. Bonds continue to yield the same interest until they are paid back, which means that if rates go down, loans the banker made and bonds he bought some time ago are worth more. Mortgages, by contrast, can always be refinanced by the householder. When the rate goes down any distance below what the householder is paying, his high-yield mortgage vanishes from the S&L's portfolio. As Jonathan Gray wrote in his FDIC paper about S&Ls, "The fixed-rate mortgage is long when the lender would like it to be short, and short when the lender would like it to be long."[11] Historically, then, commercial lending was done by banks, which were businesses. Until the McFadden Act in 1927, nationally chartered banks weren't even permitted to write home mortgages. Home-mortgage lending was done by some sort of cooperative association. And mortgage lending by cooperatives wasn't really a business.

California in the years after World War II proved that with government insurance of deposits and control on interest rates and an all but unimaginable demand for single-family homes on tiny plots of land, investor-owned mortgage lenders could indeed strike it rich. But even in California, the system aborted when first Richard Nixon and then Jimmy Carter lost control of the federal budget, the money supply, and the foreign exchange value of the dollar. When the Housing Commission met in 1981, one of our worries was the onrushing insolvency of the big California S&Ls. Meanwhile, the mutual thrifts that still dominated the industry were demonstrating that self-contained and self-perpetuating boards of directors do not always choose resourceful management and rarely police what management does. At mutuals as well as at stockholder-owned thrifts, one found grand two-story indoor waterfalls outside the CEO's office, yachts in the basins, and Learjets in the hangars. But the malaise at the mutuals had a more penetrating quality: Mutuality and cooperatives were fuddy-duddy in the American 1980s. There was money to be made for the Wall Street investment houses, the big lawyers, and the accounting firms in the conversion of mutuals to joint-stock companies—and those were the people who were calling the shots. So conversions to stockholder ownership proceeded apace through the decade, even as experience with such conversions worsened.

It is fair to say that FIRREA changed all the rules. After years of expanding the asset powers of thrifts, Congress in 1989 substantially diminished them. Starting in 1991, an S&L will be required to keep 70 percent of its assets in housing-related investments if it wishes to pass the Qualified Thrift Lender test. Doing so gives added value to the thrift charter in the form of tax deductions for loan loss reserves and inexpensive advances from its Federal Home Loan Bank. Failing the 70 percent test will trigger automatic conversion to a bank charter, loss of branching powers, and repayment of Home Loan Bank advances.

Under FIRREA, no more junk bonds may be bought with

insured deposits, and the junk bonds already held must be out of portfolio by 1994. Soon after the bill had passed, the accountants ruled—necessarily, though the U.S. League of Savings Institutions complained bitterly—that such investments had to be carried on the books at market value (if you can find out what market value is in the junk bond market) rather than at cost price, because an S&L can no longer claim that it plans to hold the bond to maturity. Several of the larger players were bust even before FIRREA—Keating's Lincoln, Albuquerque's Sandia, Western of Dallas, and Western of Phoenix were already in receivership; San Jacinto of Houston, Centrust of Miami, and Imperial of San Diego were under water. The decline of the junk bond market in October 1989, followed by a collapse in January 1990, took down the others. Among the drowned was Columbia of Beverly Hills, which had lived cheek by jowl with Drexel, paid its CEO Drexel-size salaries ($9 million in one year), and maintained a pleasure dome in Jackson Hole for the use of Drexel's Michael Milken (no charge). It was a problem that fed on itself: The disappearance of Milken from Drexel had taken away the master of the market, and the disappearance of the S&Ls now took away at least 15 percent of the buying power Drexel had controlled. The S&Ls had to sell into a falling market, which made the market fall further.

Under the terms of the new law, loans made by S&Ls to one borrower, like loans made by banks to one borrower, may not exceed 15 percent of the institution's capital. This broke up many sweetheart relationships between large builders and relatively small thrifts that were accustomed to lending 100 percent of capital (and even more, if the Bank Board wasn't looking) to finance real estate development by friends, neighbors, and partners. When President Bush spoke to the home builders in January 1990, they demanded that this provision be changed. To his credit, the president made no promises.

Furthermore, the law requires that land-development ventures beyond the limits set by Garn-St Germain must be spun off to a subsidiary that may not borrow from the parent. And "loans" for acquisition, development, and construction must be accounted for as investments, which means that fees may not be recognized and interest from the "reserve fund" provided by the thrift as part of the loan may not be credited until the loan is paid back.

Capital standards for S&Ls were mandated equal to those for banks. S&Ls that booked goodwill as part of their Bank Board–encouraged acquisition of other S&Ls are allowed to count that goodwill for one-half this equity requirement, but only until 1995, when it must all phase out. The other half had to be tangible assets from the beginning. Thrifts with no capital other than goodwill are of course a menace to the insurer, because every penny they lose is a charge to the taxpayer. Nevertheless, this provision in the bailout bill produced the biggest fight in the House, where lobbyists for the U.S. League insisted that the government was bound forever by its agreements with S&Ls that took over failed thrifts under Bank Board sponsorship. Those agreements had let the acquirers count as "core capital" the difference between the book and market values of the portfolios they had bought. Rep. Henry Hyde (R-Ill.) appeared on the floor of the House wearing a big button, "A Deal Is a Deal." It did not occur to Hyde or his supporters who donned similar buttons that the outside world regarded this slogan as a statement that contributions to a Congressman's political campaign will indeed buy you his professional assistance. The effort to preserve "supervisory goodwill" was the closest vote on the floor, but to everyone's surprise the spokesmen for the taxpayer proved more persuasive than the spokesmen for the League.

Finally, the law deep-sixed the tax breaks that made the Southwest Plan so lucrative for the buyers.

FIRREA has, in short, many good things—assuming that the regulators will enforce the rules, which seems entirely possible. They're scared and will be for a while. If the deposit insurance funds need more money after 1995 (and they will), the FDIC can raise the premium as high as 32.5 cents. Insurance premiums will remain higher for S&Ls than for banks until 1998. S&Ls, except for one in Sen. James Sasser's native Tennessee (there was nobody in the Senate to do the yeoman service Leach did in the House), cannot shift from SAIF to the banks' insurance system for several years and thereafter will have to pay a high exit fee from the one and entrance fee to the other. Banks that buy distressed S&Ls, however, will be able to transfer those deposits to the lower-cost insurer without penalty if the FDIC agrees—and of course it will, partly because banks given this privilege will sweeten the deal a little, partly because the FDIC thinks banks are better than S&Ls, anyway.

Leaders of the thrift industry are painfully conscious that banks acquired nearly all the deposits from the S&Ls that Seidman's RTC sold in its first nine months of activity. This was in part deliberate: James Montgomery, CEO of Great Western in California, the nation's second-largest thrift, said over lunch about a month after FIRREA passed that prices would be lower in the second year, and the strong S&Ls were in an excellent position to wait. But it may also be the miner's canary dying as the gas accumulates in the mine. Academics, certainly, think the separate S&L industry is a terminal case and that the country will be better off when it dies. The academic argument is that the giant federal mortgage packagers, Freddie Mac and Fannie Mae, will support housing construction and sales with marketable paper. These government-sponsored enterprises, which have retained all of their support in Congress, have insuperable advantages over S&Ls. Their paper has an implicit government guarantee recognized by the ratings services, for which they pay not a penny. The market allows them to operate on capital of perhaps one-half of one percent, and nobody questions lots of questionable accounting at Fannie Mae. Banks have reason to hold collateralized mortgage obligations, because under the international capital adequacy standards that become fully effective in 1992, mortgages require only half as much backing as commercial loans (and government-insured mortgage paper like GNMA requires only a fifth as much capital). Thrifts shrank in 1989–90, making a hash of the administration's RTC financing scheme, which had assumed 7 percent deposit growth every year. But banks picked up their mortgage paper—and also, for the first time, originated more mortgages than S&Ls.

FNMA, FHLMC, and GNMA paper can also be tailored to be

attractive to pension funds, insurance companies, finance companies, mutual funds, and the Japanese. Mortgage bankers, academics in and out of government argue, will originate the paper inexpensively from upstairs offices. Everybody wins in this best of all possible worlds: Homebuyers pay a little less for their mortgages, and pension funds get a little more for their money; the better S&Ls become banks, and the others don't count. To the extent that the public successfully fights off the hated ARM, the holders will hedge their risks effectively in the futures, options, and forwards markets.

But the argument is not entirely convincing. Every industrialized capitalist country has specialized housing finance institutions. They serve to protect homebuilding and households that have most of their wealth tied up in homes from the extremities of the interest-rate cycle. With few exceptions (in France, for example, a key source of housing finance is a tax on industrial enterprise), these institutions mobilize household savings in the service of housing. Close links between household savings and housing finance are correct in both practice and theory. The Housing Commission was correct in stressing that a greater share of housing finance should now come from "contract thrifts" like pension funds, life insurance companies, and mutual funds, because greater shares of household savings have migrated to these chassis. But this does not mean that housing finance should be integrated into a system that blends all sources and uses of funds into a unified worldwide market for commoditized money. And that, in effect, is what the government-sponsored enterprises do.

The belief here is that our parents and grandparents built better than they knew, or than we have realized. Quite apart from the cost and fragility of the apparatus that now moves more than a trillion dollars a day through the banking system to pay for securities and foreign-exchange trading, institutional barriers that block the free flow of money to different purposes will be over time the most socially efficient and quite possibly the most economically efficient way to mobilize and employ savings. It is not an accident, as the Marxists used to say, that a decline in American savings has accompanied, step by step, the deregulation of the financial markets. If one can appear to accomplish without saving the objectives saving seeks, why accept the discomfort of postponed gratification? The most spectacular example of such fakery is governmental: the alleged Social Security trust fund, in which about 90 percent of the supposed $4 trillion surplus in the year 2010 will consist of accumulated compound interest on the government bonds the fund has bought to make the federal deficit look smaller. But all our national income accounts are littered with devices to make borrowings look like savings.

This water has gone over the dam: We could not and if we could we should not reconstitute the S&L industry that existed a generation ago. Profits from housing finance in the years ahead will derive more from origination, servicing, and securitizing fees than from holding the paper until the householder pays it off. Most of the money to be made from converting mortgages to marketable securities will be expropriated by Fannie Mae and Freddie Mac—but they will give a decent tip to the messenger who brings the paper. Servicing fees are subject to major economies of scale: It costs a Citicorp or a GMAC much less per piece to handle people's mortgage payments than it would cost an ordinary or even a large S&L. But there will be some pennies from selling the rights to these fees. (Indeed, the FDIC allows projected revenue from sales of such servicing fees to be counted as part of a bank's or thrift's capital.) And the origination fees belong to the originator.

Local builders need financing, and the local S&L will know the local market—especially what is on other people's drawing boards, for this is a clubby world—better than some national operation with a local loan production office. And the fact that the local S&L is part of the local network—it's here now and will be here tomorrow—means that it can charge slightly higher rates. Better-than-average credit judgment will yield better-than-average returns. The lending agent who works on commission is much more easily controlled if the people who employ him live in the neighborhood. When he goes off drinking with the real estate appraiser, the people at the S&L will hear about it, but Citicorp won't. The fellows who wrote the original law that restricted S&Ls to lending within a fifty-mile radius of their office may have been old-fashioned and may have put more trust in homespun virtue than they should have, but they weren't stupid. Assuming ethical standards can be enforced, which may be a large assumption, in this business local is better.

Even if only limited rewards can be expected from the 70 percent of their assets that must be held in housing-related investments, S&Ls can benefit from other relations with the customers whose mortgages they write. Some endowment of low-rate deposits remains almost everywhere; with the help of data processing services to distribute and concentrate the checks and post the accounts, checking accounts can pay their way. People need credit cards, traveler's checks, safe deposit boxes. The institution that writes the mortgage has an edge in getting the rest of the business. This does not make a small-town S&L vastly different from a small-town bank, but because of its housing commitments the S&L does not have the option of selling its depositors' money upstream to great national and international banks. The government has reason to structure the nation's financial system so that some of the nation's household savings *must* go to housing. Such structures will inevitably fail if inflation again runs riot for more than the briefest periods, but that's merely another of many reasons to exorcise inflation, as the Germans and Japanese have done.

Keith Russell, fortyish, tall, and athletic, came out of Security Pacific to be president of Glenfed in a Los Angeles suburb. "There's an old Chinese proverb," he said: " 'Choice creates confusion.' We recently converted from mutual status, in 1983. The man who hired me, Gordon Klett, felt that when we went public we would lose our commitment to housing, and he didn't want that. The mutual philosophy was that community service came first." You don't, of course, get rich that way. But you weren't supposed to get rich in the S&L business. If this industry dies, it will be because in the heady, early Reagan days—and I was there, Charlie, I remember—too many people in government and in the industry forgot that you were never supposed to get rich in the S&L business.

You weren't supposed to go bust, either.

CHAPTER 11

Can This Country
Be Saved?

O N APRIL 12, 1989, deeply insolvent, American Continental Corporation of Phoenix—Charles Keating's holding company—filed for bankruptcy for itself and all its subsidiaries except Lincoln Savings & Loan, which under law could not claim the protection of a bankruptcy court. But corporate subsidiaries of Lincoln could do so and did. One of them was Lincoln Financial, or Linfin. Among Linfin's liabilities was $350 million in corporate notes sold in London on the Euromarket. These notes were secured by U.S. government-guaranteed mortgage obligations, but they were not U.S.-registered securities and could not legally be held by American nationals. The trustee for the notes, keeping custody of the mortgage paper, was Bankers Trust of New York, one of the nation's six largest banks. Bankers Trust had many dealings with Keating; it was, among other things, the trustee for ACC's ESOP, paying Keating cash money for worthless stock. And it was the conduit for Lincoln's wire transfers of funds, which accelerated dramatically in the two days between ACC's bankruptcy filing and the federal seizure of Lincoln.

On Friday, April 21, Moody's, the ratings service, put the Linfin Euronotes on its "credit watch" list.[1] Merrill Lynch, which had been an underwriter for the paper in London, declared that the bankruptcy filing had been an act of default that triggered immediate repayment of the notes. Merrill went to Bankers, which four days later sold the collateral and passed on the money to repay the noteholders. The *International Financing Review* carried an article in which a Merrill spokesman acclaimed the incident as a tribute to "the liquidity of the Euromarket."[2]

But the bankruptcy law applies an "automatic stay" to the sale of any assets of a company applying for protection from its creditors. Bankers Trust, in releasing the Euronote collateral for sale, could have been held in contempt of court. There was never any question that the holders of the Euronotes would get their money—they were fully secured—but if the bank had played by the rules, they might have had to wait as much as thirty days. And if the court had been nasty, it could have required the note holders to identify themselves as claimants, which some of them probably did not wish to do (maybe because they were Americans for whom this paper was not a legal investment or perhaps because they were Colombians washing some money in London).

Bankers Trust hears, sees, and speaks no evil in this situation, but the four-day delay argues that its lawyers were upset. Their first approach seems to have been that the bankruptcy filing for Linfin was defective, which meant that there was no stay. But the fact that the Chapter 11 filing might be voidable did not mean it was void from the start. On the day when Moody's put the Linfin notes on credit watch, Linfin was in bankruptcy and subject to the automatic stay.

There was, however, another way out. As part of its effort to hold down the cost of funds to shattered S&Ls, the Bank Board as proprietor of the FSLIC had agreed that collateral pledged by S&Ls to loans from Wall Street houses would not be considered assets available to help the insurance fund pay off depositors. The Wall Street houses would have prior claim. It was through comfort letters of this sort that Ed Gray had kept Financial Corporation of America afloat through 1986 and 1987. (Wall's Bank Board went a step further, inserting into the Federal Register a formal notice pledging that if American had to be taken into receivership, the FSLIC would live up to all its "obligations under Repos" and the Bank Board would "use their best efforts" to force Freddie Mac and the district Banks to make purchases or loans "to enable the Receiver to perform the obligations.")

The collateral for these Euronotes had been pledged by Linfin, not Lincoln, and the Offering Circular said specifically that the notes "will not be obligations of, or guaranteed by, Lincoln Savings."[3] But the mortgage notes underlying the collateral had never been endorsed over to Linfin, and the title had never been formally transferred. From the beginnings of the secondary market for mortgage-backed securities, the participants had saved money by neglecting the legal formalities that transfer ownership of paper associated with real estate. Eager to promote the growth of the market, the banking regulators had okayed the trading of paper in very dubious legal form. The Housing Commission in 1982 had called for changes in the law that would have given the buyers of collateralized mortgage obligations a perfect title to the underlying mortgages, but Congress had never done anything about it.[4]

Now, to protect "the liquidity of the Euromarkets" and the identity of (Colombian?) purchasers, Bankers Trust at a stroke destroyed the legal status of a $750 billion market. The bank was not subject to the automatic stay, its attorneys concluded, and its actions in selling the Linfin collateral did not constitute contempt of court, because Linfin had never owned the paper, anyway. Lincoln Savings had owned the paper, and the FSLIC had agreed that paper pledged by Lincoln Savings could be sold to satisfy financial-market creditors without interference by the government.[5]

So deep did the corruption and the irresponsibility go. With luck, no one would notice that Bankers Trust had just demolished the legal status of an investment held by pension funds, insurance companies, banks, and S&Ls all across the country. And Bankers and Merrill Lynch would get off the hook. The stink of Charlie Keating and Lincoln Savings would attach to senators and regulators but not to them. They could mingle with the crowd at the execution, excoriating the scoundrels who had wasted hundreds of billions of dollars of public money in the S&L outrage.

About a year after this episode, the RTC was confronted with an analogous problem. Centrust, Lincoln's partner in its Goldsmith fiddle, had issued $1.2 billion of secured zero-coupon Eurobonds due 2010. The trustee was IBJ Schroder in New York.

(That's Industrial Bank of Japan.) Shortly *before* the RTC took over Centrust, IBJ Schroder sold the collateral and bought zero-coupon U.S. Treasuries to a maturity value of $1.2 billion. The RTC decided that it was not obliged to make the American tax-payer continue paying Centrust's lavish 1985 interest rate for an-other twenty years and notified the trustee that the bondholders were entitled only to the accreted value of the bonds as of the day Centrust went under. "The row," the *Financial Times* reported censoriously, "threatens to compromise [RTC]'s reputation with international investors and casts fresh doubt on investor protec-tion clauses used in other S&L issues."[6] The worm will turn.

[1]

Among the discouraging aspects of the S&L story has been the reluctance of juries to convict executives and directors who very obviously—often, indeed, admittedly—abused their position and their institutions. The defense almost invariably has been that while these deals may look raw to the layman, that's the way you do business in America. A generation brought up on *Dallas* and similar trash seems to feel there is something to this argument. Reporter Steve Klinkerman writes that the fraud team of 160 lawyers assembled in Dallas by Atty. Gen. Richard Thornburgh "has virtually given up trying to prosecute the most sophisticated transactions that could have caused the greatest losses in Texas. 'The juries have difficulty understanding complex transactions, and we have difficulty understanding them,' said [Marvin] Collins, [U.S. Attorney for the Northern District of Texas]."[7] Before its dissolution, the Bank Board had made five thousand criminal referrals, but it seems unlikely that more than a few hundred will lead to punishment. Even the Empire of Mesquite case produced only eleven jurors for conviction on any of eighty-eight charges at the first trial. The Justice Department's Texas team had gained forty-seven convictions by January 1990, but most were for what they called "personal offenses," taking kickbacks, forging records, paying company money for prostitutes.

The FSLIC has done a little better in civil suits, especially against law firms, five of which as of early 1990 had ponied up something more than $50 million in pretrial settlements. The profession as a whole has not been a loser, of course: In 1988 alone, the FSLIC paid $100 million in legal fees, and the S&Ls on the other side of these cases probably paid even more. (After all, they were paying with insured deposits.) Another two dozen suits against accounting firms have generated much smaller returns to date. (The government originally decided not to sue some big accounting firms because it needs them to work on aspects of the bailout, but by mid-1990 mutual need created a compromise under which only individuals or local offices would be barred from new contracts because they were being sued.) Even some big Wall Street houses have been sued: In the spring of 1989, the Bank Board sought money damages from Kidder Peabody, Shearson Lehman, Prudential-Bache, and the Chicago commodities house of Gelderman for luring assorted unsophisticated S&L managements into the abuse of futures-and-options markets.[8]

One of the best things in FIRREA is a set of provisions that transfers to administrative law judges the assessment of penalties against people and firms that defraud S&Ls. Three levels of liability are created—$5,000 a day for each day the violation continues if the offense is just negligence; $25,000 a day for "reckless" violations; and $1 million a day for violations that "knowingly or recklessly cause a substantial loss to a financial institution." These penalties can be assessed by the regulators themselves, after the usual internal hearings, and appeals go to the Circuit Court of Appeals. There is no trial by jury.

A certain amount of handwringing has accompanied the enactment of these provisions: Men of substance will no longer be willing to serve as directors of S&Ls; accounting firms won't audit S&L books; lawyers will be unwilling to represent thrift institutions, etc. "The greater exposure," John Deal of Columbus, Ohio, told the American Bar Association *Journal*, "may dissuade some law firms from counseling a troubled financial institution."[9] But perhaps it will merely make a law firm more careful about suggesting to its client that he can probably break the rules with impunity, because nobody will catch him or do anything to him if he's caught.

Economists speak of the "moral hazard" when the owners of

an S&L no longer have their own money in the institution and are working entirely with public deposits. Lawyers who have nothing at risk when they conspire with their clients have a moral hazard, too. The firm of Kaye Scholer proceeded to help Keating create the 1988 registration statement for the unsecured debentures sold in the retirement colonies *after* its own senior attorney had written a sixty-one-page memo excoriating ACC's self-dealing, "suspicious" behavior, and "ridiculous" claims of profit.[10] A Lincoln house counsel wrote the California Department of Corporations in connection with Lincoln's first such issues that "every step in the process of structuring the sales program was reviewed by Kaye Scholer and [by] Jones, Day, Reavis & Pogue," which is the second-largest law firm in the United States.[11] This may not be true—at every turn Keating says that somebody else, lawyers or Bankers Trust or Arthur Young or even the San Francisco Home Loan Bank and its examiners, made him do some awful thing in the awful way he did it. But pending trial of the bondholders' suit, in which Kaye Scholer and Jones, Day are defendants, it hasn't been denied.

Franklin Tom of the Los Angeles firm of Parker Milliken, who had been California Commissioner of Corporations, signed on as Keating's lawyer to shepherd this note issue through the state authorities and got them to transfer the file from Sacramento, where some people in the department were looking at it somewhat cross-eyed, to Los Angeles. As noted in chapter 1, the list of law firms that collaborated with or conspired with Keating at one time or another is very long and very distinguished. We are not talking here of a man who is charged with a crime and can't find a lawyer to defend him. These firms took money from someone California Department of Savings & Loan commissioner William Crawford called a con man to help him create and defend what Rep. Toby Roth called a quasi-criminal enterprise. Sophisticated, knowledgeable people run these firms.

"Everything was referred to the law firms," Crawford recalled from his years of trying to rein in Lincoln. "And the law firms would send you the nastiest damned letters, quoting Supreme Court decisions, saying you're stupid. They knock you flat, I can tell you, they overwhelm you." Lin Bowman of Texas, who says he is being sued for about $2 billion all told for his not-always-arduous efforts to regulate the Texas thrifts, comments sourly that "my father and grandfather were judges, and when I went into this job I thought lawyers walked on water. What lawyers have done here has just shocked me. When you go in to catch one of these sharks, you find you're facing the best lawyers. They take you to court and you're the criminal." Lawyers get business by reputation, and it is by no means unfair that repeated, long-term identification with the legal affairs of a crook should harm a firm's reputation. When a corporation looks for a law firm, its chairman *should* say, "Gee, I don't want to have the world think I'm represented by the same people who were willing to do those things for Charlie Keating." Surely the partners in such firms should not be held up by their bar associations as models for the young or spokesmen to the public.

Some significant law firms have indeed been made to pay up and have suffered losses of reputation: Jenkens & Gilchrist in Dallas; Blank, Rome, Comisky & McCauley in Philadelphia; Ramsay, Cox, Bridgforth, Gilbert, Harrelson & Starling of Pine Bluff, Arkansas. But the great majority of the firms that counseled S&Ls to stretch the law are still regarded as leaders of their profession. Robert S. Draper of O'Melveny & Myers, as counsel to Parker Milliken, said of their involvement with Keating's worthless notes that they were doing "exactly what a lawyer is supposed to do."[12] Among the antiseptics we need if the corruption of the S&L industry is not to spread still further is a redefinition of "what a lawyer is supposed to do." On March 27, 1990, in return for being dropped from the suit, Parker Milliken agreed to pay the California old folks $4.3 million (its insurance coverage), plus another $10 million if necessary to make up any shortfall in damages won from the other defendants.[13] A little more of that might go a long way. In June, Kaye Scholer signed up for $20 million.

The accountants are the same, or worse. "The Wall Street houses came out here," Lin Bowman recalls, "and they'd say, 'We can recapitalize your shortfall right down to your bottom line.' They'd bring out a Big Eight accounting firm with them. I'd say,

'*Surely*, that can't be okay in GAAP. They'd say, 'Oh, yes, it is.' '"
What was then Ernst and Ernst not only certified the crooked
accounts of the Butcher banks but tried to bully the bank examiners who questioned the assets. Arthur Andersen endorsed Charlie Knapp's accounting at Financial Corporation of America and
later cooperated on file stuffing for Charlie Keating. Deloitte,
Haskins & Sells okayed David Paul's books at Centrust in Florida,
where the boss used insured deposits to buy yachts, old masters
that he hung in his home, and hotel suites in New York. After
all, he used these when entertaining customers. Touche Ross gave
a clean bill of health to Beverly Hills S&L, which congressional
hearings revealed as a clearly criminal enterprise. Arthur Young
went to bat for Keating, put its seal of approval on Vernon Savings
when 96 percent of its loans were bad, and helped Western of
Dallas grow after it was insolvent. "The practice," a young accountant who worked on Sunbelt in Texas said cautiously, "wasn't
contradicted by the literature."

Every one of these institutions when seized complained bitterly
that all the profits it had claimed over the years had been approved
by a major accounting firm. How dare these pipsqueaks in Washington say they were fake? But they were fake. The GAO, a branch
of Congress, studied the eleven largest thrift failures in 1987 and
found seven of them audited with so little regard for honest practice that it referred the firms involved to the AICPA for disci-
plinary action. In spring 1990, no action had been taken. ("We've
begun an intensive educational effort," said an AICPA spokesman helpfully.) A draft of a new AICPA guide for auditing
S&Ls emerged in 1989, but many of the scams still pass the
AICPA's audit test. "The Institute's committee," says a member
of the Financial Accounting Standards Board, "is composed of
the partners of the firms that do the most work. They are both
the most knowledgeable and the least independent. They say to
us, 'You don't understand the practice.' When the Guide says,
'Lower of cost or market,' they ignore it. They tell us, 'We can't
follow that—it would be disruptive.' Reputations were made in
these firms by the huge fees that were paid for this work."

Never again, one hopes. Joseph Mauriello of Peat Marwick,

the new chairman of the S&L committee for the AICPA, says that for publicly held thrifts it was never as bad as it looked, because publicly held thrifts were reported to their stockholders on a GAAP basis with only unaudited footnotes to reflect the deferred losses and appraised equity capital the regulators' rules permitted. It's the bankers, he insists, not the accountants, who misled themselves. "They say that an ADC loan becomes nonperforming when the interest reserve runs out, but we say it's when the value runs out. What we're trying to say in the Guide is 'Please tell the examiner how do we get paid back.' If the borrower doesn't have any of his own money in it, you probably don't have a loan." The resistance to this commonsense view remains strong—when the Comptroller tried to impose it on the New England banks in spring 1990, Senator Ted and Rep. Joe Kennedy plus Governor Michael Dukakis raised hell, demonstrating once more that supervision can never replace regulation because the politicians will beat up the supervisors at the behest of their contributors. But Mauriello says further changes are coming in the accounting rules, whether the bankers like them or not. "Historic cost just doesn't work anymore, because it counts on your holding the paper to term, and you don't do that anymore. So you have Wall Street redesigning product to get around the accounting model, and that has to stop."

Public policy has said, Stop. Next time, the regulators will have a congressionally mandated woodshed where these fellows can be spanked. But regulation cannot be enough. Great law firms, great accounting firms have reputations that awe the people who work for regulatory agencies. Those reputations are part of what clients buy when they retain lawyers to represent and lobby for them, accountants to certify their statements. In 1982, two accountants working for Laventhal & Horwath ran into improper deductions for tax purposes at a Houston oil-drilling tax-shelter client that was paying $150,000 a year for accounting services, and asked their managing partner in New York whether he believed Laventhol's reputation was "enhanced by our association with this type of sham." The answer came from Laventhol managing partner Leonard Douglas: "Every person is entitled to be represented by as competent a professional as he can get. Even in criminal law, there is a guaranteed right under the Constitution."[14] The end result of this one was that the IRS disallowed the deductions and imposed penalties on the investors, and a jury awarded them $72 million (settled for $13.5 million) in their suit against Laventhol. Such denouements, unfortunately, have been rare.

The Laventhol partner, of course, misunderstood the Constitution: Even in criminal law, a lawyer can be disbarred for introducing testimony he has reason to believe is false. But regardless of the rules, companies should not wish to be represented by firms that will extend the mantle of their reputation over anyone. "The law is not yet a common carrier," Emory Buckner wrote in one of his last lessons for the young associates of Root, Clark, Buckner & Howland, "and everybody is not entitled to a ride on a lawyer's back by paying his nickel."[15] In an America of corroded ethics, only assiduous attention by the press can make lawyers and accountants accept the responsibilities of reputation. If the names of their lawyers and accountants and bankers are prominently and repeatedly linked to the doings of the malefactors they counseled and certified, professional behavior will improve. And an investor looking at a corporation's annual report certified by one of these accounting firms will know enough to pause a moment and think, Aren't these the guys who gave a clean statement to Centrust, or Vernon, or FCA? Why should I trust them this time?

Unfortunately, FIRREA neglects to provide for punishment of what were equally culpable Wall Street broker/dealer firms. One has not heard from the financial markets the complaints one would hope to hear, that the law will discourage investment houses from doing business with S&Ls. Nothing could discourage them, if only that business would come back. "Lost, and by the wind grieved . . ." There will long abide on Wall Street the memory of the money made from these fellows when the corn was green. Jonathan Gray of Sanford Bernstein believes that the malaise of the Wall Street firms in 1988–89 (when trading volume was mostly not bad by historic standards and the deals business was great) resulted from the loss of the S&L trade, which had accounted for as much as one-third of the total revenues of Wall Street in the

1983–87 period. I believe it. I sat one night at a dinner where he was the host with the man in charge of S&L relations for one of the half-dozen largest Wall Street firms. The other guests included four CEOs of large California S&Ls. We drank an exquisite Chardonnay, as our host in effect brokered into his guests' institution the funds they would then use to buy his paper. At the end of the dinner, I said to him, "I don't think this is an honest business." "Fine," he said. "Change the law."

Merrill Lynch was advertising "a tradition of trust" in its television commercials while its London office was solidifying the reputation of the Euromarkets by selling Linfin's collateral to pay off the big boys. Meanwhile, in California, 23,000 small investors, some of them no doubt Merrill's customers, were learning that the money they had put into the notes of Linfin's ultimate parent was gone forever. In fairness, Merrill had got out of supplying funds to Keating some months earlier (and had nothing to do with the unsecured debentures), but there were continuing relationships. Pru-Bache and Dean Witter were taking two or three times as much in commission from Keating as their customers were receiving in premium interest rates for putting their money in Keating's thrift. Salomon was screwing thrifts all over the country and leaving them with financial AIDS. So was Kidder Peabody, not to mention Drexel. And far from discouraging such behavior, the Federal Home Loan Bank Board was scurrying about to structure deals that would insure the loans these houses made to S&Ls on a basis that put their repayment ahead of the depositors.

We can contrast the code Larry Connell enforced when he was National Credit Union administrator in the 1970s and found a case where a medium-sized credit union had lost all its members' funds playing the options market under the tutelage of one of Wall Street's household names. (Connell won't say which.) "It was a $36 million credit union," Connell remembers, "and it owed $360 million, and the Wall Street house was urging it to borrow more. I called them and gave them the choice of making restitution or seeing their names the next day in the *Wall Street Journal*." The house canceled the sucker's marker rather than suffer the publicity.

No one need idealize the Wall Street of the years before 1980. Outsiders were never treated nearly as well as insiders. But this was an agency business, with clients rather than customers and a code of conduct the SEC expected to see enforced by "self-regulatory organizations." The looting of insured deposits by what World Savings' Herb Sandler called "the tin men," like the abusive trading Michael Lewis described in *Liar's Poker*, is the sort of thing that even in the 1920s was done by bucket shops, not great names. In the 1980s everybody did it, in part because government was willing to blink at anything that might someday, somehow bring the S&Ls back.

In a book about a teachers' strike written in 1968, I argued that "the root problem of politics in a modern society [is] the control of professional performance."[16] That statement was already true then, and it is more true now. What makes the S&L outrage so important a piece of American history is not the hundreds of billions of dollars but the demonstration of how low our standards for professional performance have fallen in law, accounting, appraising, banking, and politics—all of them. We are farther along than anyone thought on our road to a Hobbesian society: These days you can't trust anybody. Americans really don't want to live this way. But they have forgotten that there are other ways.

[2]

In the realm of economics, the touchstone of what we have learned from this massive failure will be the future of deposit insurance. As a practical matter, reforms to take the dangers out of deposit insurance are relatively simple. But deposit insurance is also a symbolic matter, indicative of the demand for risk aversion in our supposedly capitalist society. Deposit insurance has been an entering wedge for the socialization of losses, for establishing governmental safety nets not only under those who cannot take care of their own interests but also under active and consenting adults who demand to be rescued from the consequences of their own mistakes.

Coupled with interest-rate controls and limited to relatively small accounts, deposit insurance does no harm. As the historian and consultant Carter Golembe has pointed out, it is really a program of government guarantee, not "insurance"—the competence of bankers is not an insurable risk. But as long as governments charter depository institutions and thereby take some responsibility for their administration, governments can be asked to stand behind the safekeeping function performed by such institutions. Indeed, to the extent that governments enforce "bank secrecy," so that depositors can't find out what their money is being used for, they have some obligation to make the depositor whole for any losses he may suffer.

Once interest rates are decontrolled and larger accounts are insured, however, deposit insurance inevitably generates overcapacity—too many dollars to lend chasing too few good loans. Despite much mumbling about supervision replacing regulation, the fact is that without preexisting written rules government insurers cannot effectively police what insured depositories do with these dollars. Indeed, witnessing the deterioration of the spreads between what the depositories have to pay for their money and what they can earn when they lend it, the government insurers tend to encourage banks and S&Ls to reach for yield, to make riskier investments, and to earn their way out of their dilemmas. Thus, the Bank Board in 1981–82 demands that Congress permit more direct investment by S&Ls; the FDIC in 1987 (at exactly the worst time) permits the nation's state-chartered banks to start making direct investments in real estate; the Federal Reserve in 1990 advocates "universal banking," virtually unlimited investment powers for banks, as a way to make American banks "competitive."

"Moral hazard," the temptation to take excessive risks with money that isn't yours, is inherent in deposit insurance with no rate controls. Whatever is lost today can be replaced tomorrow. The cushion of capital comes to be regarded as supernumerary by the players. As he accelerated his lending to the less developed countries, an act that future historians will see as a classic of moral hazard, Walter Wriston of Citicorp and his then colleague George

Vojta published a pamphlet arguing that in the modern world banks didn't need to have any capital ever, because a giant bank can always borrow whatever funds it needs in the marketplace. If the regulators demand capital and losses eat it up, there's enough time between exams to buy more deposits and make more bets, until eventually one of them pays off. In the process, the banks and S&Ls inflate the property, stock, and bond markets; encourage aggressive takeovers and leveraged buyouts; and discourage real capital formation by creating apparent increases in wealth without savings.

Eventually, deposit insurance itself becomes perverted to form a safety net—not under depositors but under the banks themselves. Some, then many, banks are "too big to fail." Uninsured lenders to these banks are protected as though they were insured depositors, either by "open-bank assistance" from the insurer or by deals the insurer subsidizes to sell off "the whole bank," requiring the purchaser to assume the uninsured liabilities. These actions maintain and subsidize overcapacity, with the results that are so visible in Texas, where virtually every depository that has *not* gone through a government-sponsored reorganization has hemorrhaged money, while the successor organizations to those that failed first, washed clean of their sins by their loving government, show highly profitable activities.

From the regulators themselves come suggestions for deposit insurance "reform" that would raise premiums for banks that engage in riskier activities. But none of the regulators has suggested a penalty premium rate greater than 25 basis points (0.25 percent) over the 1991 uniform rate of 15 basis points for banks, 23 basis points for thrifts. In early 1988 the average interest rate Texas thrifts had to pay to lure depositors was 143 basis points higher than the average rate in the rest of the country—and they were paying brokerage commissions on top of that. Charlie Keating paid Prudential-Bache a *398-basis-point* commission on top of 150–200 basis points extra to Pru-Bache's customers. What reason is there to believe that a 25-basis-point or even a 100-basis-point penalty on the insurance premium discourages thieves and gamblers from running depositories into the ground?

Meanwhile, the regulators would need either an army of examiners to form opinions on how risky depositories' investments were, or an immense taxonomy of activities and the risk weights assigned to them. One could not rely on the sort of limited categorization approved by the members of the Bank for International Settlements as a technique for assessing bank "capital adequacy," because these categories impose no special weighting for so many investments that are very risky indeed (for example, residual or equity "strips" that claim only the very last payments on a large portfolio of mortgages or junk bonds). While doubtless better than today's flat-rate deposit insurance premium, the risk-adjusted premium is an essentially frivolous approach to a serious difficulty. It simply increases the cost of funds at institutions that already tend to run recklessly. Joel R. Wells, Jr., chairman of Florida's SunTrust, wrote in 1985, in a letter of comment on one of Bill Isaac's last efforts to make sure large depositors would be put at risk, "We fundamentally believe that asset risk follows deposit risk, and that high paying institutions are almost always riskier."[17] As an educational device, risk-based premiums seek to teach the relationship between risk and reward to bankers, who presumably already know it or they shouldn't be bankers.

The Cato Institute and others on the libertarian right have argued that deposit insurance should be privatized, but the risks here, as noted (and as the S&L crisis demonstrates), are not insurable. No doubt people would start companies to insure deposits as they have started companies to guarantee the payment of mortgages, municipal bonds, and even junk bonds, but unless the insurer is truly selective, these are bunco-steerage games that rely on a normal distribution of events in a world where the insurance is bought to take care of improbabilities—when the insurer fails. Even in the mortgage context, which is the safest, we have seen spectacular billion-dollar failures of TICOR, EPIC, and others. Anyway, people insist on a government guarantee; the runs on the Ohio and Maryland S&Ls should be proof of that. Worse, the people of Ohio and Maryland were right. So long as government permits bank secrecy, federal insurance is obligatory.

Banking Committee Chairman Henry Gonzalez has already

told the bank regulators that unless the deposit insurance fund is entirely insulated from such risks, Congress will not give back to the commercial banks the power to sell securities taken from them in the New Deal. So the American Bankers Association (ABA) has adopted a proposal that originated with Bill Isaac, calling for an automatic 10 percent "haircut" on all deposits of more than $100,000 in any bank that requires government assistance. The ABA would also specifically repudiate the "too big to fail" doctrine. Even L. William Seidman, whose doctrine it is, has felt the wind blowing from such quarters and has said that perhaps "too big to fail" has had its day. The Isaac proposal would also permit only one $100,000 account per customer, anywhere in the country, and would regard the money broker rather than his client as the customer, putting an end to that business.

The Shadow Financial Regulatory Committee, a self-appointed group of seven or eight academics and lawyers, has dealt with deposit insurance from the other end, demanding that the owners of insured institutions shield the insurance fund by putting up much more capital. Losses are not assessed against the insurer until the owners' capital is used up. The shadow regulators would set up a sliding scale. Thrifts and banks operating with more than 10 percent capital would be free to do virtually anything they wanted. Institutions with more than 6 percent but less than 10 percent capital would be subject to regulation roughly equivalent to what they receive today. If capital levels fell below 6 percent, the thrift or bank would be prohibited from paying dividends to its owners and forbidden to grow except through local "core" deposits by its immediate customers. Fall under 3 percent and the regulators would in essence take you over and sell you off or liquidate you. A key part of this proposal is the adoption of accounting rules that present much more truthful pictures of a bank's or thrift's condition than anything investors or depositors are offered today.

The real solution—and it could come soon if there is a will to do the job—is the end of bank secrecy. As the banks securitize more and more of their portfolios—convert loans to marketable paper—there is less and less reason for depositors to be kept ignorant of the uses to which their money has been put. Once the portfolio is known, ratings services can pronounce judgment on the safety of uninsured deposits. This information would be so easily computerized and so widely desired that it could be provided at low cost to each consumer. People should not be asked to bone up on ratings and the reasons for them before they put ten or twenty thousand dollars in the bank, but at some point on the cost-benefit continuum, it becomes reasonable to say to depositors, "Look. That's a hundred thousand dollars you're giving to these guys. You should be willing to spend a few bucks to find out whether they're running a safe ship." Once bank portfolios are public knowledge, in their broad composition and in some detail, a strong case can be made for cutting back insurance to $50,000 and telling the world that on everything over that quota the depositor is at risk. And not just for a measly 10 percent of the deposit. At risk. Period.

William Isaac, as his parting shot on leaving the FDIC, urged that examination reports be made public. With some help from the SEC, which believed stockholders in bank holding companies should know the extent that their banks were exposed to Third World debt, he shamed the other agencies into requiring banks to publish their not-very-informative "call reports," the self-descriptions they are required to file with regulators every quarter. Much more is needed, but securitization is proceeding at a $150-billion-a-year clip. A good deal of this packaging of loans for sale to the public is happening for the wrong reasons as banks try to get out from under credit risks they should not have assumed. But it's happening. By the mid-nineties, the case for restricting deposit insurance to small depositors should be overwhelming.

Between now and then, there is a simple cure for the worst diseases risked by the use of deposit insurance: a link between the rate of interest paid and the proportion of the deposit that is insured. Each week, a team of maybe three statisticians with a modem and a PC would sample the nation's depositories and establish the average rate being paid for money market accounts and CDs of different durations. That rate at each duration would establish a benchmark for the deposit insurance that banks and

thrifts could offer new depositors this week. Full insurance would
be given to accounts and CDs paying up to, say, fifty basis points
(one-half of 1 percent) more than the benchmark rate. If a bank
or S&L wished to pay more than half a percentage point over the
national average, the account or CD would receive only 90 percent
insurance; more than a full percentage point over, only 75 percent
insurance; more than one and one-half percentage point over,
only 50 percent insurance. The rate paid for purposes of both
the benchmark survey and the insurance decision would be from
the institution's point of view. Commissions to money brokers
would be considered part of the interest rate. A failing institution
could no longer grow, because fifty basis points split between
customer and broker would be nowhere near enough inducement
to depositors to move any great amount of money, and the partial
loss of insurance coverage at higher rates would be a strong dis-
couragement. The system would cost almost nothing to administer
and would perform a major educational function, teaching the
American public that there is normally a relationship between risk
and reward.

[3]

One of the lessons of the 1980s is that the linkage between the
money system and the real economy is more complicated than we
thought. Sometimes money matters a lot: The Fed, through monetary means, killed off inflation early in the decade by promoting
a vast growth of imports at competitive prices and by shrinking
real industrial activity. Sometimes money doesn't matter much: A
22 percent one-day drop in stock prices, devastating the nation's
reported wealth, caused only a burp in the demand for goods and
services. Growing money supply need not create either inflation
or growth in real product if people slow down the speed with
which they spend it: By the end of the decade, few economists
spent a great deal of time with the crystal ball of the "monetary
aggregates." We learned that real interest rates at much higher
than normal levels do not promote savings and do not necessarily
impede investment. We discovered that government deficits can

be financed for long periods of time by foreigners spending the proceeds of the trade surplus, which is their side of the equation that holds down American prices by supplying competitive imports.

But below this stability the pressures are building on the plates. I have used in my chapter headings the metaphors of an automobile accident because it's fun. But the real metaphor is geologic. The S&L disaster is an earthquake of large but not quite catastrophic dimensions that temporarily relieves some of the pressures in the system, allowing real estate prices to sink toward more realistic values. It is in itself a ponderable cause of national discomfort.

Counting the interest on the paper the government must sell to pay off depositors and to continue carrying the assets the government cannot or does not wish to sell, the cost of the bailout in the 1990s will probably fall somewhere between $300 and $400 billion, eating up the "peace dividend" from the decline of defense expenditures in the decade. And despite a certain amount of academic comment to the contrary, this is a real cost. When the government borrows to pay out the difference between the value of the assets in a bank and the value of its insured deposits, the result is an addition to the national debt. That borrowing displaces borrowing that could have supported, say, increased salaries for teachers or nurses or soldiers. The exact analogy to the bailout costs is an increase in the interest rate the government has to pay on its outstanding debt. There is no estimating what the country loses from the misallocation of its resources that results from such follies.

The aspect of this story that casts the longest and most frightening shadow is the decline in standards of professional performance. On a lower time horizon, the terror is in the stupidity. As late as 1986, paying for the mistakes honestly and not unintelligently made in 1981 and 1982 might have cost something under $20 billion. By 1989 the price was probably just under $200 billion. The decision that year to structure the bailout along bureaucratic lines and to put it in the hands of the veteran bureaucrats doubled the ultimate loss. If the bank regulatory agencies have not learned from this experience, and there is evidence that they haven't, we can easily impose another doubling of these costs by failures in an overstimulated and overextended banking system.

The disconnection of the real and monetary economy can be stretched only so far. Eventually, the loss of capitalist discipline damages the pricing system that is the central source of information for participants in a market economy. There's a limit to how foolish you can be and remain competitive.

What the S&L fiasco tells us is that we are testing that limit.

AFTERWORD
(1990)

———◆◆◆———

As the Toll Mounts . . .

———◆◆◆———

There will not be much good news from the scene of this disaster, though contrivances will doubtless be found to cheer up the voting public when political strategy calls for giving the crowd some candy.

Heading into summer 1990 and the first anniversary of the passage of the bailout bill, good soldiers dominated the leadership of the agencies created by the legislation. T. Timothy Ryan, a political lawyer active in the Bush campaign, was director of the Office of Thrift Supervision; Peter H. Monroe, a former Florida real estate developer and a friend of Housing and Urban Development Secretary Jack Kemp, headed the Resolution Trust Oversight Board; and William Taylor, who was associated with the Rouse Corporation's urban retail reconstruction operations before he went to the Federal Reserve Board, was scheduled to replace L. William Seidman as chairman of the FDIC and Resolution Trust itself as soon as Seidman felt like leaving. Recruiting good people to work in any of these operations was proving extremely difficult: "These places," said a former Treasury Department senior bureaucrat, "are all death ships. You know that if they're on your employment record, you'll be barred forever."

In summer 1990, both congressional committees and White House operatives were stressing vigorous prosecution to jail the thieving bastards from the S&Ls who had done this to the American people. Both were in essence maneuvering to redirect the anger of a public increasingly convinced that politicians could find the real villains of this horror story simply by looking in the mirror. But behind the scenes, favors were still being done.

From August 1989 to April 1990, David Dahl of the *St. Petersburg Times* reported, "at least 25 members of Congress or their aides . . . called S&L and bank regulators to pressure them or to enquire about enforcement actions."[1]

Buried in FIRREA was a provision that denied bank and S&L examiners the whistle-blower protection given almost all other federal employees. A dismissed S&L examiner named Trish Cosgrove, a staid, bespectacled young lady who looked like central casting's idea of a librarian, couldn't find anyone in the House or Senate Banking Committee willing to sponsor repeal of that provision—though all other reforms will be stymied if examiners can be punished because they are "aggressive" by supervisors acting at the behest of administrators who may be acting for political reasons.

Even as the world condemned the old Bank Board for permitting S&L operators to pay themselves giant dividends while their thrifts were really losing money, the new Office of Thrift Supervision relaxed the rule against dividend payments by undercapitalized S&Ls that Ed Gray had instituted at the end of his term.

The Resolution Trust Oversight Board apparently agreed to finance 85 percent and maybe more of the purchase price of the assets it had for sale—including (or so Columbia Savings & Loan said) the junk bond portfolios that historically had always been sold and bought for cash.

The Internal Revenue Service promulgated Revenue Ruling 90–27, which retrospectively validated prior uses of an S&L tax dodge Congress had prohibited in FIRREA.[2]

A little thing like $500 billion will not stop Washington from doing business as usual, especially if the business is technical enough not to interest the producers of the nightly news.

During the second quarter of 1990, the RTC accepted many of the arguments proposed in chapter 10, abandoned Seidman's original plan to sell "whole thrifts," and sold off 155 S&Ls on a basis whereby the purchaser bought only the branch offices and the immediately salable assets, while RTC kept everything else. We now pause briefly for an example to refresh our understanding of what these words really mean. Insolvent Ladro S&L has $1 billion in deposits backed by assets with a book value of $1 billion, but a real value very much less. Onesto S&L acquires Ladro from the RTC, keeps $300 million worth of Ladro's headquarters and branch office property, cash, government paper, and easily marketable mortgage-backed securities from Ladro's portfolio. The RTC keeps the other $700 million of book value (really worth much less—the difference between the real value and the book value is the ultimate cost to the taxpayer). RTC pays Onesto the full $700 million, which Onesto needs to balance the $1 billion Onesto now owes the old Ladro depositors. For these services, Onesto leaves RTC a tip, which may run anywhere from one-half of 1 percent to 6 percent of the deposits (depending on whether they are stable "core" deposits or flighty brokered deposits). This tip is reported as the "purchase price" Onesto paid the RTC for Ladro. Onesto's total cost is, say, $30 million (3 percent of the deposits); total cost to the taxpayers will be more than ten times that.

Moving busted thrifts' bad assets out of the hands of S&L managers was probably desirable in itself, permitting them to be sensibly categorized by kind—raw land, shopping center, single-family residence, hotel, junk bond—rather than randomly pigeonholed according to the irrelevant criterion of which institution had been dumb enough to buy them originally. Moreover, once the government has a grip on what these assets *are*, it should be possible for a wide community to be involved in deciding what to do with them: RTC assets, unlike the contents of an S&L portfolio, are not shielded by bank secrecy laws.

Unfortunately, this activity, like the original seizure of 212 S&Ls by the FDIC in early 1989, was essentially a political response to political pressure, and—with all respect for people who worked very hard—it was not well executed. Great Western of California, for example, had agreed to buy Centrust's Florida branches from their owner for $150 million in March; RTC canceled the deal when it seized Centrust, then made the same sale to the same buyer in June for about half as much. Worse, there seems to have been no thought given to the future of the industry. By keeping all these deposit-taking operations in business in towns that have too many banks and S&Ls, the RTC set up the dominoes for the sort of crash we saw in Texas, where the rescue of each bank led to the failure of several others. A man with a bank or thrift cleansed of its bad assets by its loving government can beat the whey out of competitors who don't have government help and whose books are still laden with nonperforming loans.

And RTC bought the assets of these 155 thrifts without a policy—let alone a strategy—for disposing of them. One can argue that the asset managers whose services RTC will hire are likely to be more professional than the S&L operators who owned this stuff before, or the over-the-hill and overpaid gang the FDIC had put in charge of the S&Ls the government seized. But the asset-management contracts are political plums of great value, and many of the people who get them will be the same fellows who bled the S&Ls—by summer 1990, for example, Lewis Ranieri from Salomon Brothers had already become one of the largest thrift proprietors in the country, and had a virtual lock on consulting work for the RTC related to mortgage-backed securities.

Eventually, there will be heavy costs and great scandal arising from continuing RTC ownership and financing of assets that should have been sold into the private sector very soon after the agency took possession of them. But this blade of the scissors was not sharpened, partly because Seidman hoped for too long that the S&Ls his agency had seized could be sold as going concerns (relieving the RTC of the need to manage and sell the assets), partly because the job is intrinsically damned hard, and partly because the bureaucracy assigned to do it lacks the habits, instincts, or incentives to do it right. The heavily publicized televised auctions with pickups from London, Frankfurt, and Tokyo are a gimmick, not a procedure.

In late June, the Texas Housing Commission went public with a complaint that they could not use $140 million the Texas legislature had appropriated for affordable housing to buy any of RTC's huge inventory of residences. There were already almost seven hundred RTC employees in Texas (one wag of a Texas builder said Dallas commercial real estate was going to get well through the demand for space by RTC and the lawyers, brokers, appraisers, and accountants under contract to RTC), but nobody could be detailed to show homes to representatives of the Texas Housing Commission. The work of analyzing (rather than merely listing) properties has scarcely begun, and some of the delays are startling. Aficionados of these matters found quiet fun in chapter 10 with Lamar Kelly's statement that to help it dispose of assets properly RTC had put out an RFP (Request for Proposal: six months to prepare, six months to find a winner) for an MIS (Management Information System: a year to write the software, another year to find it doesn't work) that would track the condition of fifty-seven major real estate markets. In early summer 1990 it was announced that Kelly had withdrawn his original RFP and issued a new one, because only thirty firms (!) had been invited to submit proposals the first time and as many as one hundred forty might wish to do so.

The economic effects of all this bungling remain uncertain. Many prominent economists have argued that really nothing much has happened, because the money is simply going to the depositors. Others, less prominent, have made newspaper headlines and the TV news shows by claiming that the S&L bailout creates a "wealth transfer" from most of the country to the handful of states with the worst records of thrift failure—Texas, Arizona, New Mexico, Arkansas, Oklahoma, Colorado, and Florida. (California is not a winner on this analysis, because its proportion of the nation's economy is even larger than its proportion of the dead S&Ls.)

Both these statements are nonsense. Depositors are not the beneficiaries of RTC's largesse. Their situation has not changed at all: They always thought they had the money, and in practice they always did. What is happening is that the RTC is buying bad assets from the estates of insolvent S&Ls. Some of that money is indeed being used to repay the highest-rate brokered deposits (which had come from Wall Street—the flow of cash into mutual funds and stocks in spring 1990 was an almost automatic result of RTC's labors, because brokers whose customers' money was returned by the cancellation of high-rate term CDs naturally got themselves another commission by purchasing something for the customer). Some of the money simply feeds back into the system, to acquire the mortgage-backed securities the RTC is selling, or the Treasury bills being sold to fund the RTC. But a lot of it is a loose cannon of new liquidity in the banking system, and because this is something new under the sun, the Fed must watch it very carefully.

Nor can it be said that RTC is transferring wealth to the states with the busted S&Ls. The acquirers of the dead thrifts do not purchase local assets with the money RTC gives them. And RTC will eventually sell for bargain prices the assets the agency has kept from these transactions. All the states with many busted S&Ls have seen a major collapse of real estate values, which is certainly not remedied (though probably not worsened, either) by RTC sales into the depressed market. Because the preponderance of the wealth in virtually every American community is in the form of homes and other real estate, and the prices of property are way down in most states where many S&Ls have died, the "wealth effect" of the S&L collapse has obviously been a reduction of wealth in the states with the worst record. To the extent there has been a wealth transfer, the wealth has gone to the Perelmans, Basses, Ranieris, and Wall Street professionals and consultants whose money pours directly down the pipelines from the regulators.

Perhaps the most important development in spring 1990 was the decision by the Treasury Department to propose legislation that would increase the capital requirements of Fannie Mae and Freddie Mac. These profit-seeking government-sponsored enterprises issue mortgage-backed obligations that carry implied government guarantees, and they have hundreds of billions of dollars of paper in the market. They pay no premium whatever for their guarantee, and they are, to quote Treasury Under Secretary Robert Glauber's statement to the House Committee on Oversight, "among the most thinly capitalized of U.S. financial entities." The way to protect the taxpayer, Glauber suggested, was to require these agencies to earn a triple-A from the private rating services on the assumption that there was no government guarantee.[3]

The agencies bought ads in all the major newspapers and big magazines about how they make it possible for Americans to buy houses (when *The Economist* printed a favorable report on the Glauber testimony, FNMA pulled its ad schedule), sent big-time lobbyists like Harry McPherson and James Smith to sit at the hearings and glare at the Congressmen who had taken their money, and trotted out the grand auctioneers, especially New York's Senator Alphonse D'Amato and California's Cranston, to denounce any interference with these splended benefactors of the American people. But the protagonists of legislation include several of the agencies' former allies (among them Office of Management and Budget director Richard Darman and Rep. Charles Schumer, who have been meeting secretly to discuss ways of reducing the government's exposure in this area), and the subject is a natural adjunct to deposit insurance reform. If in fact a bridle can be put on Fannie Mae and Freddie Mac, the prospects for the survival of an S&L industry will be greatly brightened.

The big threat to the taxpayer in the 1991–92 Congress will be the pressure to "deregulate" banking by repealing most of the Glass-Steagall Act of 1933. Some of our older banking legislation (including deposit insurance, which is part of Glass-Steagall) has no doubt been outmoded in an age of electronic communications and institutional dominance over the capital markets. But the changes sought and the arguments in their support are almost identical to what we heard in the time of Garn-St Germain (the same people are making the arguments, too: the academic point man for the banks is the George Benston who on commission from Charlie Keating praised the crooked S&Ls that made the direct investments). Once again, the government proposes to remedy a problem of overcapacity by encouraging growth through "diversification" into lines of work others already perform at least as efficiently as depositories can. The Wall Street firms that once fought against increased "powers" for banks have changed sides: With the S&Ls eliminated from their market, they need new suckers to buy what Michael Lewis called the "toxic waste" from their more exotic products.

Bankers, bank regulators, and their acolytes in Congress and the press all proclaim that American banks cannot be internationally "competitive" unless they are let loose to underwrite and trade all sorts of securities, write insurance policies, take major equity positions in nonfinancial corporations, etc. Yet the evidence is that Big Bang, which released the British "clearing banks" from their government's shackles, wound up weakening the international position of British banking, and that the Canadian banks have been losers by their government's decision to demolish the "four pillars" of Canadian finance and make the banks dominant players in all sectors.

American financial institutions find it hard to compete internationally because American domestic savings are inadequate and because debtors have to pay more for money than creditors do. If they wish to try, anyway, the lesson of the S&L disaster is that they should do so with their own money and the money they can raise by selling their paper in the market, and not with ours.

If that lesson has not been learned, nothing has been learned. Exit laughing: Wouldn't that be a joke?

EPILOGUE
(1992)

——— ◆•◆ ———

Eighteen Months Later

——— ◆•◆ ———

[1]

Early in 1991, one of the participants recalls, former President Gerald Ford held a reunion party at his home in Palm Springs for people who had worked in the Ford White House. It was a convivial gathering, with people telling what they were doing a dozen years after their days of glory with the President. Among those in attendance, the story goes, was L. William Seidman, chairman of the Federal Deposit Insurance Corporation and the Resolution Trust Corporation. He said he'd been doing exciting, fascinating, and important work, and it was beginning to come out right despite what some people had considered a slow start.

Another celebrant then got to his feet and begged to disagree. He thought Seidman's RTC still had bureaucratic problems. He had been trying to buy from the RTC a Ramada Inn in Palm Springs, which had fallen into government hands because the S&L that foreclosed on it had gone broke. The RTC had advertised the property at $26 million, and he had gone to the agency to say he wanted to buy it for $26 million, all cash. That had been about ten months before, and he still hadn't been able to close the deal. He took a check out of his breast pocket. This, he said, was the check for $26 million that he'd offered the RTC and they wouldn't take. Seidman, so the story goes, ran across the room, grabbed the check, put it in his pocket, and said he would take care of it. I told this tale to Senator Donald Riegle and the Senate Banking Committee, and suggested that they might look into whether Seidman had been able to cut through his own agency's red tape.

The eighteen months after this book was completed were a series of nightmares come true. Real estate values collapsed, the administration and the regulators abandoned the S&Ls to an increasingly perilous fate, and the Treasury Department did as predicted by bringing in a banking reform bill that would, if adopted, visit the abuses and costs of Garn-St Germain on the banking industry and then on the taxpayer.

Seidman, a ubiquitous presence on television and in the newspapers, failed to give coherent direction to either the FDIC or the RTC, and hung on month after month, remaining in office until the expiration of his term in fall 1991. (At one point it appeared he would stay even longer: he paid $50,000 of taxpayer money for a legal opinion from a prominent Washington law firm that by the language of FIRREA his term of office, which everyone thought would end in October 1991, had been automatically extended to 1993.) Seidman's insistence that he and his pipsqueak Federal Deposit Insurance Corporation could handle the immense problems of asset evaluation and disposition in the S&L and banking industries won him as a personal matter deference from journalists who repeatedly referred to him as "the nation's top bank regulator" (a strange encomium for the head of an agency that regulates only the state-chartered banks that are not members of the Federal Reserve, which means that no bank with more than a billion dollars in assets is subject to FDIC jurisdiction unless and until it goes broke).

But the decision in early 1989 to put the dead S&Ls and their assets temporarily under FDIC control, to be administered and sold according to the FDIC rule-book, had prevented rational planning to clean up the detritus of a decade of perverse policies. A man who worked on the committee that was supposed to plan the oncoming RTC while Congress was debating the law reports that Seidman insisted nothing could be committed to paper, because once there was a piece of paper in circulation somebody could use it to squeeze you off turf you wanted to seize or keep. Interviewed after he announced that he would not seek to have his term extended, Seidman exquisitely said that the one big mistake in his time as FDIC chairman had been to join the RTC to the FDIC, which wasn't equipped to handle it, but that was what the administration and the Congress had wanted, and he had acquiesced.

Bungling by the jerry-built Reconstruction Trust Corporation in the management and disposition of assets from failed S&Ls has added at least $50 billion (with interest, about $150 billion) to the cost of this disaster, and has devastated the near-term prospects for economic health in the construction or banking industries. The Treasury kept coming to the Congress for $30 billion here, $50 billion there of new "loss" authority for the RTC, plus well over $100 billion of additional "borrowing" authority to permit the agency to acquire property from failed S&Ls and hold it and hold it and hold it (for the RTC is not much good at selling) with the expectation that eventually its sale to the private sector will repay this part of the money Congress provided. On the projections of the Office of Management and Budget, the federal deficit is supposed to go down in future years because the RTC will become profitable. Meanwhile, the General Accounting Office noted in August 1991, more than six months after Seidman told the Ford party that everything was under control, that the RTC lacks adequate systems to monitor asset disposal, and that at the Denver office of the FDIC (and perhaps others) "Basic controls were not in place to insure that the manual and automated records were properly updated . . . and FDIC itself was often unaware of the actual condition of the loans."

In fact, having been through a bruising struggle to get more money from Congress in fall 1990, RTC improved its attitudes and selling procedures in 1991. Nonstandard mortgages were finally packaged for sale at what looked to the newspapers like good prices (though in fact they were so overcollateralized—for every $100 face value of RTC notes, about $120 face value of performing mortgages was pledged—that it's hard to believe RTC got better prices from direct sale than it would have received from sale to an intermediary). Properties were lumped together in cognate groups of hotels, or shopping centers, or office buildings, as suggested in these pages many months before, to put them under expert rather than opportunistic management. (Many packages, however, still combined very disparate properties, and there is reason to suspect that some of them were designed to give favored buyers a selection of crown jewels for the price of costume jewelry.) Even the "affordable housing" component, which the administration for some reason hated, began to generate cut-price homes for the lower middle class. But it was all late, and grudging—not, after all, the way FDIC did things—and subject to blockage by any of a number of committees.

By fall 1991, there was all but universal agreement—the departing Seidman as cheerleader—that RTC had to be reorganized. Albert V. Casey, formerly CEO of American Airlines (who had briefly and disastrously tried to salvage First Republic Bank in Texas on a previous assignment from the banking regulators, who had created that monster themselves), was installed as the new operating boss of the RTC in an effort to persuade Congress that the administration knew what it was doing.

Meanwhile, the S&L industry, which in the original Bush legislation was to grow at a rate of 7 percent a year out to the horizon (one of the ways the taxpayer was to get off the hook was by the growing deposit insurance premium revenues to be paid by an expanding S&L industry), shrank in two years by more than one-third, with the bottom nowhere near in sight. An accelerating collapse in the California commercial real estate market, coupled with unwise investments in Southeastern or Arizona projects, destroyed or endangered such former pillars of the S&L industry as HomeFed (Bob Adelizzi was unceremoniously removed from his job), GlenFed (Keith Russell was gone), and Great American (Gordon Luce was evicted, and then his S&L was taken into receivership). Of the dozen people I saw for this book on a swing through southern California in spring 1989, all but two were gone by summer 1991—and one of those two was a lawyer in the U.S. Attorney's office. ... The grand design of the Federal Reserve System, to save the banking system by widening the spread between the big banks' cost of funds and what they could charge for their loans, had made the banks look good in the first half of 1991, but had not done much for the thrifts. To the extent that there was a grand design for them, it required the absorption of the thrift industry by the larger banks, who would find those resources helpful as they ventured to grow out of their problems. And I find I can't exit laughing: it is not a joke.

Richard Breeden, who had moved from the Bush White House to be chairman of the Securities and Exchange Commission, began a crusade in mid-1990 to reform accounting practice in banks. "Bank regulators," he said, "are inducted into an order of secrecy soon after their employment. We've had eleven hundred bank and thrift failures. I wanted to know how much investors lost in those failures. None of the bank regulators had those records. I asked our economists to go out and look at the situation, and in twenty institutions they found investor losses of more than eight billion dollars—and climbing." The Financial Accounting Standards Board, which advises the SEC, proposed early in 1991 definitions that would force banks to disclose (if not necessarily to *recognize*, a term of art meaning to acknowledge) decreases in the market value of their assets. The Federal Savings & Loan Insurance Corporation had recently incurred liabilities for deposits that exceeded its resources by at least $225 billion, mostly because government-approved but dishonest accounting had permitted thrift institutions to keep "selling" insured deposits to the public long after they were hopelessly insolvent and quite certain to lose the money being entrusted to them. Nevertheless, the Treasury Department and all the federal banking regulators united in opposing Breeden's and FASB's proposals—and because the White House was terrified of a "credit crunch" in 1991, the SEC pulled in its horns. Breeden says he'll be back, and I believe him; but much of the momentum has been lost.

Writing a new definition for *chutzpah*, the Treasury then proposed a "reform" that relied upon regulators' evaluation of banks' capital (which is, in banking analysis, nothing more than the difference between a bank's reported assets and its reported short-term liabilities) as the "trigger" that would force government intervention to protect the taxpayer against losses from deposit insurance. Mergers (perhaps like those of First Texas and Gibraltar or California's State Savings and American Savings in the S&Ls) would enable banks to reduce their costs, while their income would rise through new powers to play the securities markets. And the holding companies that would own banks could make direct investments in whatever businesses looked appealing. To bring in new capital to an industry that already had severe overcapacity, the Treasury would let non-financial corporations own banks—on a basis by which the corporation could simply walk away from any losing investment in this area, compelling the taxpayer to pick up the pieces.

"Experience," Oscar Wilde once noted, "is the name we give to our past mistakes." Federal Reserve Governor Henry Wallich back in the 1950s when he was still a professor at Yale uttered a corollary: "And policy is the name we give to our future mistakes." Why don't our policies benefit from our experiences? The reason, I think, is that governments—Republican as well as Democratic —really in their hearts don't trust markets. Politicians and bureaucrats alike want to control the results of their policies. They will sometimes change the policies originally adopted by the opposing party, but only very rarely will they abandon their own. When the results of their policies go awry, they feel the reason must be their lack of control, not the defects of the policy. Obvious examples are numerical targets for affirmative action, housing and zoning regulations, and the use of arbitrary standards rather than economic incentives for fuel efficiency control in automobiles and emissions control in electric power generation. Where government policies directly affect the profitability of private enterprise, those who make money out of some aspect of a policy seek (usually successfully) to divert public attention from any alteration of what benefits them.

The crisis in the S&Ls and the banks was created by institutional and technological change (the shift of savings from depositories to "contract thrifts" like pension funds and mutual funds, and the easily accessed data-retrieval systems that made the information-gathering facilities of banks all but redundant in dealing with large borrowers). Without government intervention, these changes would have made it increasingly difficult for banks and S&Ls to raise the money that is the raw material of their production process. But the government, by chartering these institutions and insuring their liabilities, frustrated the normal action of the markets. Senior research officer John Boyd and Stanley L. Graham of the Federal Reserve Bank of Minneapolis see a world where "the market [is] slowly eliminating large banks while the government systematically resuscitates some of them." If the government had chartered and insured blacksmiths and buggy whip manufacturers the way it charters and insures banks, the arrival of the automobile would have been very expensive for the taxpayers.

Both in the 1980 Depository Institutions and Monetary Control Act and in the Garn-St Germain Act of 1982, Congress and two Administrations (for the first of these was a Carter Administration product) deliberately altered deposit insurance from a protection for depositors to an engine of growth for banks and S&Ls. In 1987, in the ludicrously named Competitive Equality Banking Act written essentially by and for the friends of House Speaker Jim Wright, the deposit insurance agencies were told to exercise "forbearance" and not close down busted S&Ls if they could possibly avoid it. Thus at the very time that the market would have shrunk our banks and S&Ls, the government gave them an unwarranted and unwise capacity to grow.

Predictably, the banks outgrew the need for their services. It then became necessary, by the perverse logic of public policy, to find new services they could perform, presumably at a profit. To make the banks and S&Ls compete with the existing providers of these services without the benefit of the government guarantees that reduce their cost of funds would, however, deny certain "synergies" supposedly generated by the combination of different kinds of financial services. Therefore, "firewalls" to protect the taxpayer from liability for failure in part of the new financial services conglomerate would have to be designed and installed . . . by the bank regulators whose dedication to the growth of the industry they supervised was a prime cause of the crisis. President Bush, after all, will not be eligible to run for re-election in 1996, and the Treasury's "reform" proposals were not likely to self-destruct until well after the elections of 1992—and neither the 41st President nor the 102nd Congress had much vision beyond that date.

[2]

The word *robbery* in the title of this book has occasioned comment. Some like it, believing that most of the $200 billion extracted from the taxpayers' pockets was indeed the fruit of crime. An observer whose name is lost in the mists of time once noted that "the best way to rob a bank is to own one." Others consider *robbery* an irresponsible word, encouraging readers to believe that what made the trouble in the S&Ls was an irruption of criminals into the business, when the real horror story was the seduction of mostly decent businessmen to fraudulent behavior by the government's perversion of law, regulation, and accounting rules. Both sides of the argument are right.

Robbery is a crime, defined by law, requiring *mens rea*, or a consciousness of wrongdoing. By that standard, only a small fraction of what happened in the industry was robbery. Opening hearings into some S&L matters at a time when the political pundits were saying that the 1990 Congressional elections would be heavily impacted by this scandal, Rep. Frank Annunzio caused to be hung at the front of the House Banking Committee's hearing room a banner with the strange device JAIL THE S&L CROOKS. (Very suitably, the banner hid the portrait of the immediate past chairman of the committee, Fernand St Germain.) And no doubt there are people who should go to jail but won't, because it's no great trick to raise "reasonable doubt" in the minds of jurors who are asked to label as criminal some business practices that to them are simply incomprehensible. And many of those the outside world would like to put in jail never in fact did anything criminal, like Neil Bush, who surely had no *mens rea* when he approved loans to men who had business dealings not only with him but with the other leading members of the board of Silverado Savings, the very people who had put this unqualified young man on that board.

There was, however, a great deal of fraud in the S&L scandal, if you will accept a definition of fraud that includes arguing cases before regulatory agencies with information one knows to be false, or certifying what are known to be false balance sheets and P&L statements. Such activities are probably not criminal, but they are—to use old-fashioned lawyers' language—"tortious." Those who conduct them are "tort-feasors." And people can be sued for torts by anyone who believes he has lost money because of them —and the anyone includes the deposit insurance corporations as the receivers of the dead bank or S&L.

Here one must praise the L. William Seidman who has been roughly handled elsewhere in these pages, because it was Seidman, himself a lawyer and an accountant, who insisted on going after his brethren who had been partners in tort, if not crime. He had strong support from Harris Weinstein, who left a flourishing private practice to become general counsel of the Office of Thrift Supervision, but if Seidman had not been offended by the behavior of his two professions, neither the lawyers nor the accountants would have even begun the self-examination that may yet generate a benefit from the orgiastic greed this book describes. Seidman is entitled to still further credit for the lawsuits against the boards of directors of several of the banks and thrifts, composed of leading citizens who accepted legal responsibility for the conduct of these institutions and then failed to exercise that responsibility. And in summer 1991, after saying for several years that such actions would be counterproductive, Seidman began using the leverage FIRREA and some throwaway clauses in the old Southwest Plan contracts gave the government to force the acquirers of December 1988 to renegotiate their overly profitable deals—even though they were all, like Seidman himself, good Republicans.

[3]

One hopes historians will give more than a footnote to the S&L disaster of the 1980s, for it is a story rich with evocation of what went wrong in this country as the sun began sinking on the American Century. No analysis of our society, economy, polity in that decade can be truly convincing that does not explain how such things could happen, and persist.

For me, there is a clue to the answer in the origins of this book. I had lived with this story and written about aspects of it since

1981–82, when I served on the National Commission on Housing. In summer 1988, I went to the half-dozen publishing houses that had published previous books of mine, all but one of which had made money by doing so, and proposed to them a book about the S&Ls. None was interested. The subject was complicated and technical, the editors said, narrow in its significance, unlikely to appeal to a general audience. By fall 1990, which was about the earliest one could hope to have the book in the stores, nobody would have any interest in it. It was only because I had a chance lunch with Ned Chase of Scribners, who had been involved at other houses for which I wrote *The Fate of the Dollar* and *The Money Bazaars*, that this book came to be written—and Ned in effect said he was prepared to risk Macmillan's (and thus Robert Maxwell's) money on it because he trusted my judgment.

Publishers didn't want books about the S&Ls; magazines didn't want articles; TV news shows didn't want segments; newspapers didn't want stories. The "gatekeepers" through whose sensibilities information flows to the American public were unanimously of the view that you couldn't "sell" this one. And it was simply not in their heads in the 1980s that they had an educative function.

When the quiz show scandals broke in the late 1950s, Frank Stanton of CBS, by far the most reputable head of a network and his industry's most convincing spokesman, was put in the uncomfortable position of telling Congress he had always believed that "the public interest" was whatever interested the public. That was not a respectable position in 1959; by 1990 it had become one of those obvious truths that, as the French put it, go without saying. Thomas Jefferson once wrote, before he became President, that "Were it left to me to decide whether we should have a government without newspapers or newspapers without a government, I should not hesitate to prefer the latter." Editors use this aphorism as directed, in annual conventions and appearances before legislatures considering taxes on publications. But for Jefferson's somewhat sententious observation to have any force at all, the editors must fight against what Walter Lippmann called "preference for the curious trivial as against the dull important."

In the end, the S&L outrage happened *and continued to happen* because not enough people knew what was going on, and not enough people knew what was going on because their normal sources of information thought they wouldn't care to know. It is not clear that this lifeboat, having capsized, can right itself. But perhaps the drop in audience for the television networks and the loss of advertiser interest in the more popular magazines in 1991 may lead some of our gatekeepers—as well as our bankers and lawyers and accountants and appraisers—to seek less of their job satisfaction from money and more from the performance of their higher functions. As Bernard Shaw wrote, looking into the twentieth century from the last decade of the nineteenth, You never can tell.

APPENDIX A

"The Thrifts and the Unthinkable"

The neat thing about an S&L is that it very nearly can't go broke unless there is a panicky run on the bank.

Even if the S&L doesn't write any new mortgages at higher interest rates, the average yield on its portfolio rises steadily in inflationary times, because the mortgages paid off most rapidly are the oldest ones, with the lowest rates. Self-amortization implies that most of the householder's money in the early years of the loan goes to the payment of interest, while most of the monthly check as maturity date nears goes to the repayment of principal.

Moreover, while sales of existing houses have slowed down and an unconscionable share of what sales there are involve assumed or wrap-around mortgages, lump-sum repayments still run better than $50 billion a year, much of it to the S&Ls.

Cash flow is guaranteed to be positive, because more than 1% of the portfolio gets repaid every month, while even the most terrifying bursts of disintermediation don't take that big a share of the deposits out of the bank.

Thus the Federal Home Loan Bank Board can keep S&Ls going at no cost to the public, just by changing definitions—so long as the accountants go along.

Two quite spectacular gambits have already been opened in this game.

In one of them, S&Ls are permitted to sell their decayed mort-

Originally published in *Financier*, December 1981, pp. 12–15.

gages at a loss without reflecting that loss on their books at the time of sale. Eventually the loss will have to be taken, but it can be amortized over the life of the loan.

An 8% mortgage with ten years to go, for example, now carried on the books at $100, can be sold for $65 with only $3.50 of the loss to show up in the P&L or the balance sheet for this dreadful year. Then the 65% can be invested at top yields which will net out to a lot more than the return on the old mortgages—without any sacrifice of safety, because it includes interest on the present value of the $35 loss.

This is presented to the public as a way to keep the S&Ls liquid, to get them cash to repay depositors—which is balderdash. The S&Ls have plenty of cash. What it does is turn reported losses to reported profits, Presto-Chango, Now-You-See-It-Now-You-Don't.

In the other approved piece of magic for bookkeeping, two unprofitable S&Ls can be merged to form one apparently profitable institution, because the acquiring association is permitted to write up as Good Will the difference between the book value and the market value of the portfolio it has bought.

Thus an S&L with a $100 million portfolio of mortgages worth $65 million can sell off its loans, reinvest the proceeds at current rates, and show enough earnings on that portfolio to indicate profitability as it slowly writes off the acquired Good Will.

I have proposed an only slightly different scam, based on the practice of the Danish Mortgage Associations. These estimable institutions package mortgages as bonds and sell them on the Bourse.

Government limits the interest rates they can charge borrowers, so to get the market to pay the money the borrower needs, the Association writes up the value of the loan to a sum well above that actually lent. If the Government limit on mortgages is 10% and the market rate is 16%, the Association might write a mortgage for $150,000 while giving the borrower only $100,000.

In Denmark, this is a wash for the Association, which doesn't hold the mortgage. But for an American S&L, there would be a chance to show a $50,000 "profit" on that mortgage the day it was booked, which could very quickly bring the color back to the cheeks of the most moribund.

The vice with all these ideas is that they are ways to lie with numbers.

The virtue is that they also express a truth: that the S&L, though it is losing its surplus—and its shirt—right now, really will come back in time as a viable if not vibrant institution, and ought not to be put out of business. Especially since it will, after all, stay afloat unless a regulator does put it under.

Unfortunately, none of this works for the Mutual Savings Banks, especially those in New York City. Their problem appears to be well understood. Because they are located in the most sophisticated money market in the world, they have suffered worse from the disintermediation—loss of deposits to money market funds and the like—that afflicts all the thrifts. And because of state usury ceilings, plus the greater stability of homeownership in the Northeast, they are stuck with a worse bundle of low-yield mortgages.

Interestingly, neither part of this commonplace understanding is true. In 1980, the MSBs still had 34.5% of their liabilities in the form of passbook savings accounts, and 57.5% of their liabilities in some combination of passbook accounts and term deposits subject to Reg Q ceilings. Meanwhile, those out-in-the-boondocks S&Ls had been hit so hard by the money market funds that their total passbook savings ledger accounted for only 19.1% of their liabilities, and their total passbook-plus-time-deposit ledger was only 42.2% of their liabilities.

The conventional wisdom looks correct on the asset side—79% of NYC MSB mortgages at the end of 1979 were yielding less than 9%, while the national average for S&Ls was only 37% at or below that level. But the reason for that discrepancy is less the fact that New York State was stupid about usury ceilings or that the pace of house sales was slower in the Northeast, and more the fact that the New York MSBs have made very few mortgage loans anywhere.

Instead, they ran up the proportion of their portfolio held in coupon bonds, locking in those great long-term yields that were available in the late '70s. The average yield on their mortgage portfolio is so bad because the MSBs never looked for opportunities to average it up—opportunities that were available through the dark days of the usury ceiling, because loans could be made outside the state—and indeed *were* made outside the state.

This was a mistake in lots of ways. Its immediate impact is on cash flow, because the bonds don't yield a steady return of principal. Thus the NYC MSBs are in somewhat worse shape than the S&Ls in terms of their losses, are more greatly imperiled by possible deposit outflows because they have more of their liabilities in passbook accounts that will not stay where they are, and lack the cash flow to pay depositors if (when?) these withdrawals occur.

A further aspect of their troubles is that the FDIC has decided to put much of the cost of rescuing any bank that needs its services onto the survivors rather than on the insurance reserves. The deal that kept Greenwich Savings Bank from insolvency will cost the NYC MSBs about $17 million in the loss of insurance premium refunds in the first half of 1982, with more to come. (It will also, incidentally, cost Chase Manhattan about $7 million; there's good news for everybody.)

The NYC MSBs, too, are probably viable over time, as their average earnings on portfolio increases and their average cost of funds drops from the crisis rates of mid-1981. But getting them over the hump may be quite expensive, and it is by no means clear who is going to foot the bill.

Bank of America is the candidate most frequently mentioned for a bailout of a big New York savings bank, if the laws can be changed to permit out-of-state commercial-bank acquisitions.

That's a good-sized "if" in itself—and B of A, which back in the days of radical agitation used to boast that it was really just the biggest S&L in the country, is not exactly barreling ahead in profits these days.

At a hearing before the thrift industry task force of the President's Housing Commission, Stuart Davis of California's Great Western S&L said that if his association had enjoyed in 1977 the asset powers it is now receiving, it would be making money today.

This got amended in discussion with the admission that the

profits would probably have come from the writing up of mortgages that were undergoing "negative amortization," but it does represent a well-considered and intelligent approach to the long-term problems of the industry.

Increasing their opportunity to invent mortgage instruments and to acquire investments that turn over more rapidly than mortgages—consumer loans, commercial loans and the like—will, over time, give the S&Ls some protection against abrupt increases in the cost of money.

By the same token, however, the S&Ls will be losing their protection against competition from banks. Perhaps more important, they will be sitting ducks for competition from newly chartered S&Ls, which will be able to go after both their depositors and their borrowers. The newcomers will not be burdened by the need to carry that staggering weight of unprofitable old mortgages, and will be able to offer rates that reflect only current costs.

Barring help from regulators who hold off applicants for new charters—an action that would be mightily frowned upon by both the Treasury and the White House—it is not entirely clear how many of today's S&Ls can make it under their own steam, with existing management surviving at the helm, into President Ronald Reagan's promised land.

This is a business where well-wishers often do more harm than good. With 6-month Treasuries at 11.8% in mid-November, that bundle of 12.4% one-year All Savers Certificates sold in October now looks like a bummer rather than a bonanza—especially after you add up the costs of advertising it, the commissions paid to brokerage houses for the sale of the certificates (honest: the Depository Institutions Deregulation Committee okayed a 2% commission rate), and the fifth or so of the sales that represent money formerly in passbooks.

The adjustable rate mortgages the progressive S&Ls have been putting on their books the last couple of years are likely to be a mixed blessing in 1982, when declining interest rates will trigger a quick reduction in yields from investments as well as a drop in the cost of funds.

There is no disposition here to quarrel with the idea that S&Ls

should have expanded asset powers, but in the back of my mind there keeps rising the nasty thought that the MSBs *had* greater power than the S&Ls, and got themselves into worse trouble. And the social purpose of these institutions, after all, is to help *housing*.

The reason for expanding their asset powers is to keep them functioning so that they can continue to supply money for housing, even if not quite so much as they poured out in years past. This is a reasonable approach, and, really, there isn't much choice. In the structure of financial intermediation, the wing that used to be occupied by the traditional S&L has been gutted, and will not be habitable again.

The important point to keep in mind is that real losses have been incurred here. The depositors bear them in their role as consumers of housing; borrowers bear them in the context of purchases and sales lost and homes unbuilt.

But there is no practical way to make either depositors or borrowers bear them *directly*, or to avoid some division of loss between the institutions and the government, which did, after all, dig their grave.

In the long run, one has to expect that contract thrifts (pension funds and perhaps, again, insurance companies) will be the carriers of most mortgage loans, and that the S&Ls will merely initiate and service them.

The task of Government will be to develop appropriate incentives for contract thrifts to invest in mortgages (or perhaps appropriate disincentives for them to invest in some other things).

How to do that—and how to get there from here once you've figured out what you want—will require a deep understanding of how all the games play, both in Washington and in the markets.

In the meantime, one way or another—on the cheap, please —we have to shore up what we have.

APPENDIX B

"Earn 100% at Mountebanks"

We all know now why the old Prudential National Trust company changed its name to Crazy Louie Bank N.A., because by now everybody's heard the commercials:

"Shop the banks! Shop the savings banks! Shop the money market funds! Then take your money to Crazy Louie's. He'll beat them all! Crazy Louie's Maniacal Money Account will *always* pay the highest interest rates in town! And that interest is *guaranteed*, because Crazy Louie is a member of the FDIC, an agency of the Federal Government, which insures your deposits—not only the principal, but the interest, too."

There was resistance at Prudential when the name change was proposed, but now all the directors are delighted. The bank's assets have almost doubled. Of course, there's been a little trouble finding investments that pay enough to give Louie's Bank a profit on the new accounts, but as Louie himself says, even if you lose a little on every piece you can make it up with volume. Besides, the bank is establishing "customer relations" that will be invaluable later.

As the Government set up these accounts, a customer has no reason *not* to move his money to whatever shlock bank or S&L offers the highest rate. Crazy Louie's commercial is straight truth-in-advertising: the FDIC or FSLIC insures not only the principal in an account (up to $100,000) but all the interest.

Originally published in the *New York Times*, December 17, 1982.

That's better than a money market fund, all right. A money market fund not only can't offer Federal insurance on either principal or interest, it can't (by law) pay out more than it earns by investing the shareholders' money. But the commercial and savings banks can offer to pay interest rates far beyond what they can earn with the money—and the Government will see to it that the depositor gets paid.

This is undesirable as well as ludicrous. An Administration enamored of market forces has made it possible for banks to escape market judgments entirely. No matter how badly the business has been run, no matter how much public policy would prefer to see depositors' money in other institutions that lend more productively and prudently, these accounts will permit failing banks to go on for some time, even grow, by paying higher interest than well-run banks will pay.

"The thing that troubles me," says Stuart Davis, chairman of the executive committee at California's Great Western Savings, "is that the weakest institutions will offer the highest rates." You bet. There's been worry recently about the liquidity of some savings associations and some banks, but we'll never have to worry about that again. Any bank or S&L that's short on cash need only raise interest rates on the new deposits and it can have all the money it wants.

"I never thought I'd live to see the day when the Government was providing a marketing tool for banks," said Charles Lord, until recently Acting Comptroller of the Currency. The FDIC and FSLIC know the Government has done something nutty and have suggested that maybe banks should be charged different insurance premiums according to how foolish they are in the interest they pay. But that's still just a suggestion, and it wouldn't stop Crazy Louie.

At the least, and soon, we need a change in the law so that deposit insurance would be restricted to the principal, letting people worry a little about whether their accounts really will pay off at those super-high rates.

There is another shoe to drop. The account the Government authorized for December limits the depositor to six withdrawals

a month. In January, we get Son of Maniacal: a checking account
with unlimited interest and unlimited checks. But soon after—
are you ready?—we will see the end of free checking. Authorities
disagree about how much it costs a bank to process a check, but
the lowest figure you can find is about 35 cents, and it costs several
dollars every month to maintain an account. If the banks are going
to have to pay market rates for their funds, then they are going
to have to charge market prices for their services. How the banks
handle the inevitable imposition of fees for once-free services will
be a stiff test for their advertising and public-relations departments.

Some of the confusion ahead is the fault of the bank regulators,
but most of the blame lies on Congress, which responded to the
banks' need for a "product" to compete with the money market
funds by ordering the regulators to approve something like the
Maniacal account. Because Congress deals with one issue at a time,
it never looked at the insurance problem once interest rates were
deregulated, or at the systemic implications of an interest-bearing
checking account that forces the end of free checking. Everyone
who is pushing to have Congress give orders to the Fed about
managing the money supply might look at the mess it made of
this relatively simple change, and think again.

APPENDIX C

Greenspan Letter

Alan Greenspan
120 Wall Street
New York, NY 10005

February 13, 1985

Mr. Thomas F. Sharkey
Principal Supervisory Agent
Federal Home Loan Bank
600 California Street
San Francisco, California 91420

> Re: Application of Lincoln Savings and
> Loan Association for Permission to
> Exceed Ten Percent Limitation on
> "Direct Investments"

Dear Mr. Sharkey,

I am writing on behalf of Lincoln Savings and Loan Association and in support of its application for an exemption from the 10 percent limitation on direct investments that will be imposed by the new direct investment rule, 12 C.F.R. 563.9–6, announced by the Federal Home Loan Bank Board on January 31, 1985.

I have reviewed and commented on the direct investment rule in its earlier forms, and I have reviewed the rule in the form announced on January 31. I note that it contains a provision expressly allowing an association to apply for an exemption raising the limit on the percentage of its assets which it may place in direct investments. I note, too, that the Board states in its notice of the rule (at p. 4) that the prior proposed rule added a "presumption" in favor of approval of applications and that the January 31 rule preserves that presumption (at p. 43). The rule requires that a Principal Supervisory Agent "shall approve an application" unless he makes one of four specific findings.

The Board's notice states (at p. 8) that "direct investments can be prudent and desirable" when they are "supported by adequate capitalization, a sound business plan, managerial expertise and proper diversification." On the basis of my review of Lincoln's application and of its audited financial statements and the criteria established in the new rule, I believe that Lincoln Savings and Loan has demonstrated that it has the adequate capitalization, sound business plans, managerial expertise and proper diversification to which the Board refers.

I have reviewed the application Lincoln has submitted to your office, and it is my opinion that Lincoln clearly merits the exemption it seeks. Its application establishes the critical and dispositive facts:

1. Lincoln's new management, and that of its parent, American Continental Corporation, is seasoned and expert in selecting and making direct investments;

2. the new management has a long and continuous track record of outstanding success in making sound and profitable direct investments;

3. the new management succeeded in a relatively short period of time in reviving an association that had become badly burdened by a large portfolio of long-term, fixed-rate mortgages and unfavorably structured adjustable rate mortgages whose relatively low yields had been forcing large losses on the association and pushing it nearer the point of insolvency;

4. the new management effectively restored the association to a vibrant and healthy state, with a strong net worth position, largely through the expert selection of sound and profitable direct investments;

5. the new management is devoting a large proportion of its assets to the financing, servicing and construction of residential housing; and

6. the new management has developed a series of carefully planned, highly promising, and widely diversified projects—a high percentage of which involve the development and construction of residential housing—requiring sizeable amounts of direct investments.

Given these facts, Lincoln in my judgment meets the requirements that the new direct investment rule establishes for granting a waiver of the 10 percent limit.

Finally, I believe that denial of the permission Lincoln seeks would work a serious and unfair hardship on an association that has, through its skill and expertise, transformed itself into a financially strong institution that presents no foreseeable risk to the Federal Savings and Loan Corporation. Consequently, Lincoln should be allowed to pursue new and promising direct investments as and when they become available, in accordance with the plans and proposals outlined in its application.

It is my opinion that Lincoln's record and its application satisfy the requirements for an exemption that the new direct investment rule establishes. I strongly support Lincoln's application and urge that it be granted.

In closing, let me thank you for giving my letter your attention.

Very truly yours,
ALAN GREENSPAN

ACKNOWLEDGMENTS

A book that presents things taught and things learned over two decades owes more debts than an author can remember, let alone repay. The late Tom Waage and George Mitchell educated me in banking; Roger Starr and Lou Winnick, in housing; and John Heimann, in both. I had help from Preston Martin when he was chairman of the Federal Home Loan Bank Board, when he ran his own mortgage-insurance operation, when he was a fellow commissioner on President Reagan's Housing Commission, when he was vice-chairman of the Federal Reserve Board, and when he was Bill Simon's sidekick in S&L investments. Maurice Mann, Bill McKenna, Ken Thygerson, Richard Helmbrecht, Bernie Carl, and Ann Fairbanks were significant others on the Housing Commission, and I learned then and later from staff members Tom Stanton, Kevin Villani, John Tuccillo, Andrew Carron, John Weicher, Charles Field, and, of course, Kent Colton.

All three chairmen of the Bank Board in the 1980s were helpful: Richard Pratt, Edwin Gray, and M. Danny Wall. So were both chairmen of the FDIC, though William Isaac will be happier with what's here than L. William Seidman will be. Larry White, Donald Hovde, and Roger Martin helped fill me in on what was happening at the Bank Board during their terms as members. Don Crocker was informative on matters relating to Lincoln Savings & Loan and asset disposition. Ros Payne helped with more than just FADA. Karl Bemesderfer and Philip Jennings improved my understanding of what happens in workouts. James Cirona, Michael Patriarca, and William Black of the Federal Home Loan Bank of San Francisco were generous with time and information. So were Bob Showfety, Paul Hill, and Maria Rich of the Federal Home Loan Bank of Atlanta. Also Genie Short, Kevin Yeats, and Rebel Cole at the Federal Reserve Bank of Dallas. And nobody has done more for my education in recent years than Walker Todd of the

Federal Reserve Bank of Cleveland. I have long-standing debts to Sen. William Proxmire and his staff chief, Ken McLean. Reps. Charles Schumer and John LaFalce were notably helpful. Gillian Garcia and Bart Dzivi of the Senate Banking Committee staff and Gary Bowser of the House Banking Committee staff contributed hugely to both my stock of information and my understanding. Allen Pusey of the Dallas *Morning News* contributed his file of outstanding reports. Jeff Gerth of the *New York Times* shared with me the results of his investigations relating to Silverado, Columbia of Beverly Hills, and the Lincoln Savings–Bankers Trust relationship.

Among those who freely supplied the fruits of their labor were William C. Ferguson in Texas, Carter Golembe, John Kriz, Bert Ely, Don Brumbaugh, James Barth, Ed Kane, Ned Eichler, and Ken Rosen. My sister-in-law Professor Mary Moers Wenig of the Bridgeport University Law School supplied much material on legal involvements. Salomon Brothers had me on its mailing list for two immensely informative years. Chairmen Donald Kirk and Paul Kolton of the Financial Accounting Standards Board helped teach me where the practitioners went wrong. Joe Mauriello, chairman of the S&L committee of the American Institute of Certified Public Accountants, defended what was defensible. Henry Hill of Shelter Island and his friend Walter Schuetze of Peat Marwick were most helpful, as was Tom Bloom, formerly chief accountant of the Bank Board. Bill Zimmerman of *American Banker*, by commissioning a twice-a-month column from me, gave me reason to remain in close touch with these matters while I was writing about other things. Among S&L executives, I'm most grateful to Bob Adelizzi, Gordon Luce, Stuart Davis and James Montgomery, Robert Dockson and Jerry St. Dennis, Larry Connell, Herbert and Marian Sandler, Thomas Wageman, and Steve McLin.

Among my nearest and dearest, Karin Lissakers and Thomas Moers Mayer read the manuscript with a critical eye, as did Maury Mann, Walker Todd, Larry White, Bill Black, Sol Linowitz, Charles Ramond, Paul Volcker, and Ned Eichler. James Moers Mayer helpfully read proof. Edward T. Chase of Scribners saw the importance of this subject and the potential of this book when other editors thought interest in the S&L outrage would rapidly disappear. He also vigorously, and I hope successfully, labored to keep me from loading the reader with technical material beyond what was necessary to make sense of the story, just because I knew it. All these people made this a better book; what continues to be wrong with it, of course, is my fault entirely.

NOTES

CHAPTER 1   The Dimensions of the Disaster

1. Ann Devroy, " 'Selective Enforcement' Issue Raised by NAACP," *Washington Post,* January 23, 1990, p. A8.

2. Jonathan E. Gray, *Financial Deregulation and the Savings and Loan Crisis,* prepared for the Federal Deposit Insurance Corporation, Office of Research and Strategic Planning, 1989, p. 3.

3. "Problems in the California Thrift Industry," Hearings before the Subcommittee on Commerce, Consumer and Monetary Affairs, Committee on Government Operations, San Francisco, June 13, 1987, p. 138. Typescript.

4. Replies by Larry Taggart to questions from Rep. Jim Leach, printed in *Investigation of Lincoln Savings & Loan,* House Banking Committee, Serial No. 101–59 (Washington, D.C.: U.S. Government Printing Office, 1990), part 5, p. 1012.

5. Exhibit 8, Testimony of Edwin J. Gray to the House Banking Committee, November 7, 1989, p. 1. Typescript of a letter.

6. Ibid., p. 125.

7. "Vernon Savings' Chief Executive Officer Woody Lemons Gets 30 Years in Prison," *Wall Street Journal,* April 6, 1990, section B, p. 8.

8. Paul Zane Pilzer with Robert Dietz, *Other People's Money* (New York: Simon & Schuster, 1989), p. 89.

9. "Texas Thrift Merger Cleared by Bank Board," *Wall Street Journal,* June 6, 1984, p. 7.

10. "A House of Mortgages Comes Tumbling Down," *Business Week,* September 26, 1988, p. 98.

11. Robert M. Garsson, "Hearings into Silverado May Help Even the Political Score," *American Banker,* May 21, 1990, p. 6.

12. Edward J. Kane, *The Gathering Crisis in Federal Deposit Insurance* (Cambridge, Mass.: MIT Press, 1985).

13. P. J. O'Rourke, "Piggy Banks," *Rolling Stone,* August 24, 1989, p. 43 @ p. 134.

14. Emory Buckner, "The Trial of Cases," speech delivered January 31, 1929, p. 8. In Martin Mayer, *Emory Buckner* (New York: Harper & Row, 1968), p. 9.

15. The numbers are from Andrew S. Carron, *The Plight of the Thrift Institutions* (Washington, D.C.: Brookings Institution, 1981), Table 1–2, p. 15.

16. *The Report of the President's Commission on Housing* (Washington, D.C.: U.S. Government Printing Office, 1982), p. 131.

17. Martin Mayer, "The Thrifts and the Unthinkable," *Financier,* December 1981, p. 12 @ p. 13.

CHAPTER 2   An Accident Waiting to Happen

1. *The Report of the FDIC Mutual Savings Bank Project Team* (Washington, D.C.: FDIC, 1981), part 1, p. 7.

2. Governor's Task Force on the Savings and Loan Industry, Report to the Honorable William P. Clements, Jr., Governor of the State of Texas, Austin, January 25, 1988, p. 45.

3. Norman Strunk and Fred Case, *Where Deregulation Went Wrong: A Look at the Causes Behind Savings and Loan Failures in the 1980s* (Washington, D.C.: U.S. League of Savings Institutions, 1988), p. 97. Emphasis added.

4. Ibid., p. 164; from Conference Report No. 210 of the House of Representatives, June 8, 1933.

5. R. Dan Brumbaugh, Jr., *Thrifts Under Siege: Restoring Order to American Banking* (Cambridge, Mass.: Ballinger Publishing Co., 1988), p. 25.

6. Thomas Marvell, *The Federal Home Loan Bank Board* (New York: Praeger Publishers, 1969), p. 225.

7. In House Banking Committee San Francisco hearings, November 13, 1989, p. 8. Typescript.

8. Martin Mayer, *Money Bazaars* (New York: E. P. Dutton, 1984), p. 266.

9. Senate Banking Committee Hearings Re: Thrift Industry, Washington, D.C., August 2, 1988, Federal News Service transcript, p. 19–1.

10. If a thrift has a billion dollars in assets and earns an 0.84 percent return, it shows profits of $8,400,000. Assuming that it's stockholder owned and the stockholders have $50 million of their own money in it, the return on equity is about 17 percent, which is quite satisfactory. Note now that if the regulator changes the rules and allows you to operate with only 3 percent capitalization or $30 million of your own money to back a billion dollars in assets—which happened in 1982—your return on equity goes up to 28 percent, which is sensationsl.

11. *Change in the Savings and Loan Industry*, Proceedings of the Second Annual Conference of the Federal Home Loan Bank of San Francisco, 1977, pp. 246–47.

12. *Bernstein Research: The State of the U.S. Thrift Industry, July 1988* (New York: Sanford Bernstein, p. 15.

13. Strunk and Case, p. 58.

14. Pilzer, p. 56.

15. Statement of Thomas H. Stanton to the Committee on Banking, Housing and Urban Affairs, U.S. Senate, on "Oversight of Government Sponsored Enterprises," October 31, 1989, p. 6.

16. *The Report of the President's Commission on Housing* (Washington, D.C.: U.S. Government Printing Office, 1982), p. 121.

17. John S. Reed, "Competitive Relationships Now Top Policy Agenda," *Financier*, September 1989, p. 15 @ p. 18.

18. Michael Lewis, *Liar's Poker* (New York: W. W. Norton & Co., 1989), p. 35.

19. *Wrongdoing, Fraud Main Factor in Thrift Industry Crisis*, Washington, D.C., GAO/T-AFMD-89-4, March 22, 1989, pp. 16–17.

20. Allen Pusey and Christi Harlan, "Land-Flip Deals Netted Millions for Select Group," *Dallas Morning News*, January 28, 1986.

21. Paul S. Nadler, "Stock S&Ls Hurt Northeast Real Estate," *American Banker*, September 18, 1989, pp. 4, 6.

22. Pilzer, p. 142.

CHAPTER 3   Mr. Pratt Puts the Pedal to the Metal

1. *Expanded Competitive Markets and the Thrift Industry*, Proceedings of the Thirteenth Annual Conference, Federal Home Loan Bank of San Francisco, 1988, p. 143.

2. Eichler, p. 81.

3. Ibid., pp. 80–81.

4. Thirteenth Annual Conference, SF Bank, p. 201.

5. James R. Barth and Michael G. Bradley, "Thrift Deregulation and Federal Deposit Insurance," in *1988 Conference: Perspectives on Banking Regulation* (Cleveland, Ohio: Federal Reserve Bank of Cleveland), p. 6. The numbers on unprofitability and insolvency are taken from this paper as well as the quote.

6. Eichler, p. 80.

7. House Banking Committee hearings, January 13, 1989, pp. 175–76, 175.

8. *Wrongdoing, Fraud Main Factor in Thrift Industry Crisis*, GAO T-AFMD-89-4, March 22, 1989, pp. 13, 14. This was Vernon S&L, noted *supra*.

9. Practising Law Institute Course Handbook #406, *The Depository Institutions Act of 1982* (New York: Practising Law Institute, 1983), p. 20.

10. House Banking Committee Hearings, January 13, 1989, p. 174.

11. Steve Klinkerman, "Court Permits S&L Deduction on Swap Losses," *American Banker*, November 13, 1989, p. 1 @ p. 6.

12. Nina Andrews, "U.S. Sues Ernst & Young on Savings Unit Audits," *New York Times*, March 3, 1990, p. 35.

13. Michael Lewis, p. 114.

14. Martha Brannigan and Alexandra Peers, "S&L's Art Collection, Ordered to Be Sold, Faces Skeptical Market," *Wall Street Journal*, October 18, 1989, p. 1 @ p. A6.

15. Floyd Norris, "GAAP over RAP," *Barron's*, March 7, 1983, p. 70.

16. Federal Home Loan Bank Board, *Agenda for Reform* (Washington, D.C.: U.S. Government Printing Office, 1983), p. 18.

17. Eichler, p. 84.

18. Gray, p. 11.

19. Edward J. Kane, *The S&L Insurance Mess: How Did It Happen?*, preliminary draft (February 9, 1989), pp. 2–11.

20. Christi Harlan, "Ruling Favoring Ex-Thrift Head Cheers Accused S&L Executives," *Wall Street Journal*, February 27, 1989, p. B5.

21. PLI Course Handbook, p. 25.

22. Figures from Carron, p. 12. The numbers in 1980 were 14 basis points of profit for the S&Ls, −12 basis points of loss for the MSBs.

23. Figures from Kane, *The S&L Insurance Mess*, Table 1–3. The 1981 and 1982 figures showed losses of −73 and −65 basis points for S&Ls, −94 and −80 basis points for MSBs.

24. Letter from FFIEC to Senator Daniel Patrick Moynihan, May 6, 1980.

25. "Savings Banks in a Hostile Environment: An FDIC Assessment," an address by William M. Isaac. FDIC news release PR-41-82, with speech attached, pp. 2, 5.

26. "FDIC Chief," *Wall Street Journal*, July 26, 1982.

27. Testimony by Bert Ely to the Resolution Trust Corporation Task Force of the Subcommittee on Financial Institutions, etc., House of Representatives, October 19, 1989. (Alexandria, Va.: Ely & Company), p. 12.

28. Edward Boyer, "A Giant Thrift Sprouts in Buffalo," *Fortune*, February 21, 1983, p. 114 @ p. 118.

CHAPTER 4   Congress Disconnects the Brakes

1. Martin Mayer, *The Bankers* (New York: Weybright & Talley, 1975), p. 4.

2. Thomas P. Vartanian, *The Depository Institutions Act of 1982* (New York: Practising Law Institute, 1983), p. 25.

3. Michael Binstein, "Up Against Danny Wall," *Regardie's*, December 1989, p. 62 @ p. 65.

4. Senate Conference Report No. 641, 97th Congress, 2nd session, p. 87.

5. Transcript, Senate hearings, August 28, 1988, p. 37–1.

6. Ibid., p. 25–2.

7. Edward J. Kane, "Dangers of Capital Forbearance: The Case of the FSLIC and 'Zombie' S&Ls," *Contemporary Policy Issues*, Vol. 5 (January 1987), p. 77. The study itself is still unpublished. The quote is Kane's paraphrase.

8. William B. O'Connell, "A History of Defying Public Policy," and Donald J. Kirk, "The Costs of Accounting Legerdemain," *New York Times*, September 6, 1987.

9. *The Savings and Loan Crisis*, Field Hearings before the House Committee on Banking, San Francisco, California, January 12 and 13, 1989 (Washington, D.C.: U.S. Government Printing Office, 1989), pp. 197, 205.

10. Statement of CEO Charles Knapp in Financial Corporation of America annual report (Los Angeles, Cal.: 1981), pp. 4–5.

11. Ibid., p. 12.

12. Jaye Scholl, "Why FCA Failed," *Barron's*, September 26, 1988, p. 15.

13. Quoted from "Supervisory Chronology of American Savings," a document submitted by James Cirona, president of the Federal Home Loan Bank of San Francisco, in connection with his appearance at the House Banking Committee hearings in San Francisco, January 13, 1989.

14. Jerry E. Pohlman, *Managing Risk at Financial Corporation of America* (Los Angeles, Cal.: Financial Corporation of America, 1984), pp. 1, 2, 7.

15. Martin Mayer, "FCA Is a 'Financial Zombie' That Can't Live on Its Own," *Los Angeles Times*, February 7, 1988, sec. 4, p. 3.

CHAPTER 5   Mr. Gray Throws Himself Beneath the Wheels . . .

1. Jim McTague, "An Introspective Gray is Bloodied but Unbowed," *American Banker*, June 27, 1987.

2. Ibid.

3. David Maraniss and Rick Atkinson, "In Texas, Thrifts Went on a Binge of Growth," *Washington Post*, June 11, 1989, p. 1 @ p. 16.

4. "Washington's Matador," *Newsweek*, March 5, 1984, p. 76.

5. Addendum 1, Opening Statement of Edwin J. Gray to Committee on Banking, Finance and Urban Affairs, House of Representatives, January 13, 1989, p. 17. It may be that Gray's speeches are especially impressive because he has circulated them in excerpt form. But recollection reinforces the selected documents.

6. SEC Docket 1149, vol. 17, no. 16 (July 17, 1979); note at p. 1151 "made untrue statements of material facts and omitted to state material facts, in filings with the Commission"; at p. 1152, "absence of documentation concerning the large numbers of 'out of area' loans"; at p. 1153, "loans on preferential terms" [to] "Lindner associates and friends."

7. Oliver Wendell Holmes, Jr., "An Address Delivered at the Dedication of the New Hall of the Boston University School of Law, on January 8, 1897"; in Max Lerner, *The Mind and Faith of Justice Holmes* (Boston: Little, Brown, 1945), p. 71 @ p. 74.

8. *Troubled Thrifts. Use of Supervisory Enforcement Actions*. Briefing Report to the Chairman, Committee on Banking, Finance and Urban Affairs, House of Representatives. (Washington, D.C.: GAO/GGD-89-105BR, July 19, 1989), p. 4.

9. Barnard and Garn references are all from a 202-page photocopied document of his own and others' statements on money brokerage circulated by Edwin Gray. The page references are 89 and 164.

10. Tim Carrington, "Agency Chief Pressed Thrifts, Senator Charges," *Wall Street Journal*, March 22, 1984, p. 6.

11. Quotes from soundtrack: some also reported in Rick Atkinson and David Maraniss, "Turning Light Into Heat on Thrifts," *Washington Post*, June 13, 1989, p. 1 @ p. 16.

12. Christi Harlan and Allen Pusey, "Condo Firms Under Probe Offered Investor Bonuses," *Dallas Morning News*, November 29, 1983, p. 1-A.

13. Ibid., p. 6-A.

14. Allen Pusey and Christi Harlan, "Sen. Lyon Profited from Condo Ties," *Dallas Morning News*, November 29, 1983, p. 7-A.

15. House Committee on Government Operations, *Federal Home Loan Bank Board Supervision and Failure of Empire Savings and Loan Association of Mesquite, Tex.* (Washington, D.C.: U.S. Government Printing Office, August 6, 1984), p. 38.

16. Ibid., p. 28.

17. *Proposed Audit and Accounting Guide: Audits of Savings and Loan Institutions*, AICPA File Reference #4310, draft, August 23, 1989, p. 9-8.

18. Tom Leander, "Ex-Football Team Owner Found Guilty of Bilking S&L," in *American Banker*, February 2, 1990, p. 4.

19. Strunk and Case, p. 134.

20. Letter from George Benston to FHLBB, January 15, 1985, in *Federal Regulation of Direct Investments by Savings and Loans and Banks; And Condition of the Federal Deposit Insurance Funds*, Hearings before a Subcommittee of the Committee on Government Operations, February 27 and 28, 1985 (Washington, D.C.: U.S. Government Printing Office, 1985), p. 945.

21. Ibid., pp. 896–97, 948.

22. Martin Mayer and Cornell Capa, *New Breed on Wall Street* (New York: Macmillan, 1969), p. 82.

23. AICPA, pp. 9-2 to 9-4.

24. *Investigation of Lincoln Savings & Loan Association*, Hearings before the House Banking Committee (Washington, D.C.: U.S. Government Printing Office, October 31, November 7, 1989), p. 112. Mr. Gray amended his comment to read: "To be honest with you, they didn't want the regulation at all."

25. Gray documents, p. 27; testimony at March 27, 1985 hearings of the Financial Institutions Subcommittee of the House Banking Committee.

CHAPTER 6 ... Which Roll over Him

1. Paul Marcotte, "Lawyer S&L Malpractice," *ABA Journal*, vol. 55 (November 1989), p. 24.

2. National Housing Act, Sec. 407(f) (l), 12 USC 1730. See discussion in *Federal Home Loan Bank Board Supervision and Failure of Empire Savings and Loan Association of Mesquite, Tex.*, House Committee on Government Operations (Washington, D.C.: U.S. Government Printing Office, 1984), pp. 51–52.

3. John M. Berry, "Boom to Bust in Arkansas," *Washington Post*, August 30, 1987.

4. "Workout Solutions: The FADA Approach," speech by Roslyn B. Payne, U.S. League, November 10, 1987, p. 1.

5. Paulette Thomas, "S&L Sale: First Wave Hits Market," *Wall Street Journal*, January 2, 1990, p. B1 @ B6.

6. Strunk and Case, p. 70.

7. Ibid., p. 88.

8. Brumbaugh, p. 102.

9. David Lagesse and Nina Easton, "Bank Board's Hovde: FSLIC Not in Peril," *American Banker*, November 1, 1985, p. 1.

10. *Wall Street Journal*, June 17, 1985.

11. *Mesquite* report of the Government Operations Committee, p. 52.

CHAPTER 7 Lincoln Savings Kills the Women and Children . . .

1. Testimony of Patricia S. McJoynt, senior vice-president of the Federal Home Loan Bank of Seattle, October 31, 1989, before the House Banking Committee, in *Investigation of Lincoln Savings & Loan Association* (hereafter, *Lincoln Hearings*) (Washington, D.C.: U.S. Government Printing Office, 1989), part 3, p. 260.

2. "A Thrift for Our Time," *Grant's Interest Rate Observer*, New York, May 13, 1988, p. 1.

3. See memo to Kevin O'Connell from Darrel Dochow, August 22, 1988: "we do not want them off the hook per the Agreement to sell debt and that subordinated debt protects the FSLIC." Document in "Known Calls and Meetings Between Bank Board Officials and Keating and Associates," prepared by House Banking Committee.

4. Michael Donovan and Edward Seglias, "S&L Regulators' Silent Conspiracy Protects Banks First, Investors Last," *Connecticut Law Tribune*, February 5, 1990, p. 14.

5. George Williamson, "Ex-Lincoln Workers Say Tellers Got Bonuses for Pushing Bonds," *San Francisco Chronicle*, November 17, 1989, p. 1.

6. SEC Docket vol. 17, no. 16 (July 17, 1979), p. 1149 et seq. Also *SEC v. American Financial Corp., et al.*, U.S. District Court for the District of Columbia, Civil Action No. 79-1701, pp. 1–3.

7. Stephen P. Pizzo and Mary Fricker, "The Making of America's S&L Scandal," *Arizona Republic*, Perspective section, p. C6.

8. Memorandum for Enforcement Review Committee from Darrel Dochow, February 16, 1988, ORPOS, p. 2.

9. Report of Conference Call Meeting Between Federal Home Loan Bank Board Staff and Staff of the Federal Home Loan Bank of San Francisco, February 16, 1988, p. 20, *Lincoln Hearings*, part 2, p. 971.

10. Memorandum, July 5, 1988, from R. A. Sanchez to C. A. Deardorf, Federal Home Loan Bank of San Francisco, Docket #3805, detailing meeting of Charles Keating, Jack Atchison, Robert Kielty, and others from ACC/Lincoln with Jordan Luke, Darrel Dochow, George Barclay, Rosemary Stewart, and others from the Federal Home Loan Bank Board: "Mr. Keating indicated he would go to the grave with a Bible in one hand, but he knew Lincoln Savings was in desperate trouble. . . . Discussion refocused on former management of the institution. Mr. Kielty indicated that when documents were filed with the SEC there was no intent to change management. Mr. Keating then advised the committee members that [former] management was a total disaster. Mr. Keating made reference to a conversation about the impossible situation wherein Don Crocker asked Keating to change personnel." *Lincoln Hearings*, part 2, p. 929.

11. "California Thrift Regulation May Be Changed in Wake of Lincoln Scandal," *BNA Banking Report*, Bureau of National Affairs, Washington, December 4, 1989, vol. 53, p. 838 @ p. 840.

12. Minutes of the April 5, 1989, Special Bank Board Meeting: "Possible Resolution of Lincoln Savings," p. 28.

13. *Lincoln Hearings*, part 6, pp. 781, 796.

14. Letter from Darrel Dochow, in *Lincoln Hearings*, part 6, p. 494.

15. "Recommendation and Statement of Supervisory Concerns," report from R. A. Sanchez, supervisory agent, Federal Home Loan Bank of San Francisco, to A. W. Smuzynski, Assistant Director for Regional Operations, Federal Home Loan Bank Board, May 1, 1987, p. 171.

16. Description taken from Federal Home Loan Bank Board Memo from Norman H. Raiden to the members of the Board on the Petition of Lincoln Savings and Loan to Reconsider PSA Action in its direct investment application, undated, in *Lincoln Hearings*, part 2, pp. 371–72.

17. Report of On-Site Supplemental Examination of American Continental Corporation, Fall 1987, by Alex Barabolak, Examiner in Charge, *Lincoln Hearings*, part 6, pp. 786–88. The examiner's conclusion is "ACC has realized substantial gains which should have been realized by Lincoln." Every penny that went to ACC rather than Lincoln, of course, was a penny taxpayers had to put up when Lincoln failed.

18. Paulette Thomas, "Keating, Son Testify in Suit over Lincoln," *Wall Street Journal*, January 5, 1990, p. A8.

19. "Recommendation and Statement of Supervisory Concerns" to A. W. Smuzynski, assistant director for Regional Operations, from R. A. Sanchez, supervisory agent. Subject: Lincoln S&L, May 1, 1987. *Lincoln Hearings*, part 6, pp. 125–26.

20. James Ring Adams, *The Big Fix* (New York: John Wiley & Sons, Inc., 1990), p. 224.

21. M.D.C. consent decree, 34/27208, 44 SEC Docket 912 @ p. 917.

22. *Resolution Trust Corporation as Conservator for Lincoln Savings and Loan Association, F.A., Plaintiff, v. Charles H. Keating, Jr., et al.*, U.S. District Court, District of Arizona. Complaint with Jury Trial Demand, pp. 69–70.

23. May 1, 1987, Recommendation and Statement of Supervisory Concern, *Lincoln Hearings*, part 6, p. 171.

24. 1988 examination, *Lincoln Hearings*, part 6, p. 534.

25. Jerry Kammer and Andy Hall, "Public Likely Stuck with Tab in Keating's Detroit Hotel Deal," *Arizona Republic*, August 20, 1989, p. 1 @ p. 15.

26. Lincoln Savings and Loan Association Examination as of July 11, 1988, *Lincoln Hearings*, part 6, pp. 525–36.

27. *Lincoln Hearings*, part 6, p. 308.

28. ORA letter, December 20, 1988, paginated 1881.

29. Jim McTague, " 'See No Evil' Lincoln Sale Is Described," *American Banker*, January 3, 1990, p. 2.

30. Paulette Thomas, "Keating Defends Thrift's Accounting But Admits Obscure Records in One Deal," *Wall Street Journal*, January 8, 1990, p. 14.

31. Testimony of John J. Meek, senior examiner, Office of Thrift Supervision, Chicago, Illinois, October 31, 1989, *Lincoln Hearings*, part 3, p. 533.

32. ORA letter, December 20, 1988, paginated 1886.

33. 1988 examination, in *Lincoln Hearings*, part 6, pp. 657–58.

34. *Lincoln Hearings*, part 6, 866-67; also part 3, p. 47.

CHAPTER 8 ... And Some Bureaucrats and Five Senators

1. James Bates, "Taggart Testimony in Doubt Amid New Revelations," *Los Angeles Times*, November 11, 1989.

2. "Statement of Chairman Edwin J. Gray," September 19, 1986, p. 2.

3. Written Testimony of Michael Patriarca, October 26, 1989, *Lincoln Hearings*, part 2, p. 156.

4. *Lincoln Hearings*, part 6, p. 274.

5. Sanchez Recommendation and Statement, *Lincoln Hearings*, part 6, p. 153.

6. Letter to five senators, March 13, 1987, on Arthur Young stationery, *Lincoln Hearings*, part 3, p. 869.

7. *Resolution Trust Co. v. Keating et al.*, Complaint, p. 50.

8. Andrew Mollison and Bill Roberts, "Atlantan's Stance on Banking Board Stirs Questions of Ethics," *Atlanta Journal and Constitution*, December 28, 1986, p. 1.

9. Kathleen Day, "Bank Board Appointee Faces Conflict Charge," *Washington Post*, January 7, 1987, Business Section, p. 1.

10. Michael Binstein, "In the Belly of the Beast: Renegade v. Regulator," *Regardie's*, July 1987, p. 46 @ p. 50.

11. Jim McTague, "Riegle Visited Keating in 1987, Toured Lincoln S&L Projects," *American Banker*, November 14, 1989, p. 1.

12. Memorandum from Laurie A. Sedlmayr to Senator De Concini re: American Continental, March 19, 1987, Exhibit 13, House Banking Committee, in *Lincoln Hearings*, part 3, p. 694.

13. Pizzo, Fricker, and Muolo, pp. 392–404.

14. David Dahl, "Smith Asked Regulator to Help Thrift Where He Was a Director," *St. Petersburg Times*, April 22, 1990, p. 2A.

15. David Dahl, "Lawmakers Still Pressure Bank Regulators," *St. Petersburg Times*, April 22, 1990, p. 1.

16. Glenn R. Simpson, "Did Carroll Hubbard Go Too Far to Help an S&L?", *Roll Call*, April 16, 1990, p. 1.

17. *Lincoln Hearings*, part 3, pp. 117–19.

18. Cranston letter to Gray, June 7, 1989.

19. Numbers and comment from Barabolak report, *Lincoln Hearings*, part 6, p. 829 et seq.

20. See *RTC v. Keating et al.*, Complaint, pp. 58–63.

21. *Lincoln Hearings*, part 5, p. 931.

22. Statement of L. William Seidman, chairman of the FDIC, October 17, 1989, *Lincoln Hearings*, part 1, p. 81.

23. July 23, 1987, Memo for Bank Board Members from William L. Robertson . . . Actions for Lincoln Savings, p. 9.

24. "Minutes of the April 5, 1989, Special Bank Board Meeting," p. 28.

25. Memo from Monica J. Gawet, San Francisco Home Loan Bank, to Lincoln correspondence files, February 10, 1988.

26. Wall testimony, *Lincoln Hearings*, part 5, p. 425.

27. Special Meeting, May 5, 1988, minutes, *Lincoln Hearings*, part 5, p. 803.

28. Letter to Enforcement Review Committee from James R. Faulstich, Federal Home Loan Bank of Seattle, March 11, 1988, *Lincoln Hearings*, part 5, p. 961.

29. May 5 minutes, *Lincoln Hearings*, part 5, p. 793.

30. Statement on Lincoln Savings by Darrel W. Dochow, November 21, 1989, *Lincoln Hearings*, part 6, p. 405 et seq.

31. May 5 meeting, *Lincoln Hearings*, part 5, pp. 810, 812.

32. Carol Sowers, Andy Hall, Jerry Kammer, and Lisa Morell, "Riches to Ruin: The Meteoric Life of Charles Keating," *Arizona Republic*, December 3, 1989, p. 1.

33. Interoffice Memorandum, May 24, 1988, Kevin O'Connell to File, *Lincoln Hearings*, part 5, pp. 676–77.

34. Letter from Charles H. Keating, Jr., to George Barclay, June 20, 1988, *Lincoln Hearings*, part 5, p. 536.

35. Memo to File—Lincoln S&L, from Darrel W. Dochow, subject: Telephone call with Mr. Keating, July 13, 1988, *Lincoln Hearings*, part 5, p. 538.

36. Memo from Alvin Smuzynski to File, July 6, 1988.

37. Dochow testimony, *Lincoln Hearings*, part 5, p. 234.

38. Statement of David W. Riley, October 31, 1989, *Lincoln Hearings*, part 3, p. 515.

39. Testimony of Richard E. Newsom, October 31, 1989, *Lincoln Hearings*, part 3, p. 273.

40. Testimony of Kevin T. O'Connell, November 21, 1989, *Lincoln Hearings*, part 5, p. 956.

41. Newsom testimony, October 31, 1989, *Lincoln Hearings*, part 3, p. 269.

42. Ibid., p. 271.

43. Eugene Seltzer testimony, October 31, 1989, *Lincoln Hearings*, part 3, p. 463.

44. "Material Findings from the Termination Meeting with Arthur Young (AY)," *Lincoln Hearings*, part 5, p. 843 et seq.

45. Memo from Monica C. Chisholm to Alvin Smuzynski, subject, ACC Supervisory Letter, December 27, 1988, *Lincoln Hearings*, part 5, p. 684.

46. *Plaintiffs v. Federal Home Loan Bank Board*, U.S. District Court of Arizona, No. CIV 89-0691 Phx-Clh. Deposition of Rosemary Stewart, Washington, D.C., January 23, 1990, vol. II, pp. 282–83.

47. From Dochow's handwritten notes on conversations with Keating, *Lincoln Hearings*, part 5, p. 567 et seq.

48. April 5 minutes, *Lincoln Hearings*, part 5, p. 880.

49. Ibid., p. 896.

50. Ibid., p. 904.

51. *Lincoln Hearings*, part 1, p. 21.

52. Ibid, p. 29.

53. *Lincoln Hearings*, part 5, p. 141.

54. Defendant's exhibit 188 in *American Continental Corp. v. Office of Thrift Supervision and Resolution Trust Corporation*, Washington, D.C.

55. *Lincoln Hearings*, part 5, p. 67.

56. Meek testimony, *Lincoln Hearings*, part 3, p. 533.

57. Brooks Jackson, "Thrift Examiners Say They Saw Signs of Criminal Wrongdoing at Lincoln," *Wall Street Journal*, November 1, 1989, sec. C, p. 20.

58. *Lincoln Hearings*, part 3, p. 108.

59. Gregory A. Robb, "U.S. Memos Are Cited By Keating," *New York Times*, April 12, 1990, section D, p. 7.

60. Interoffice memo, Hoyle to UFFDA, August 4, 1989, *Lincoln Hearings*, part 5, p. 924.

CHAPTER 9 Mr. Wright and Mr. Wall Haunt the Texas Wreck

1. Statement of Craig Stirnweis, in *Financial Condition of the Federal Savings and Loan Corporation and the Federal Deposit Insurance Corporation at Year-End 1988*, Field Hearings before the House Banking Committee, San Antonio, Texas, March 10–11, 1989, p. 67.

2. Statement of L. Linton Bowman, San Antonio hearings, p. 70.

3. William Ferguson, *Texas Thrifts: Impact of a Depressed Economy* (Irving, Texas: Ferguson & Co., 1987), p. 3.

4. Ibid., p. 6.

5. Allen Pusey, "S&Ls: How They Self-Destructed," *Dallas Morning News*, November 8, 1987, p. 1.

6. *Report of the Special Counsel in the Matter of Speaker James C. Wright, Jr.*, Committee on Standards of Official Conduct, House of Representatives, February 21, 1989, p. 214. Later, *Phelan Report*.

7. Pilzer, p. 95.

8. Quoted from the study of the Iowa S&L deal by independent counsel, in Brooks Jackson, *Honest Graft* (New York: Alfred A. Knopf, 1988), p. 268.

9. *Business Week*, July 13, 1987, p. 96.

10. Jim McTague, "Analyst Lists S&L Candidates for Liquidation," *American Banker*, July 5, 1988, p. 6 @ p. 7.

11. John M. Barry, *The Ambition and the Power* (New York: Viking Press, 1989), p. 605.

12. *Phelan Report*, pp. 256–57.

13. *Phelan Report*, pp. 251–52.

14. *FSLIC Recapitalization Act, Hearings before the House Banking Committee*, January 27, 1987, p. 430.

15. Banking Committee hearings, November 13, 1989, typescript, p. 127.

16. Glenn R. Simpson, "Contributions from Keating, His Family, and His Employees

Went to 19 Members and Ex-Members in Addition to 5 Senators," *Roll Call,* January 11, 1990, p. 2 @ p. 10.

17. David Greenwald, "S&L Insider Guilty of Theft, Fraud," *Orange County Register,* March 30, 1990, p. 1.

18. Allen Pusey, "Mattox Receives $200,000 from Developer Faulkner," *Dallas Morning News,* January 26, 1986, p. 1.

19. "Federal Regulators Accused of Intimidating Thrift Operators," *El Paso Herald-Post,* January 29, 1987, p. 1.

20. Brooks Jackson, *Honest Graft,* p. 282.

21. Ibid.

22. San Antonio hearings, p. 161.

23. *Combating Fraud, Abuse and Misconduct in the Nation's Financial Institutions: Current Federal Efforts Are Inadequate.* Seventy-second Report by the Committee on Government Operations, House of Representatives, October 13, 1988, p. 83.

24. *Current Tax Rules Relating to Financially Troubled Savings and Loan Associations,* prepared by the Staff of the Joint Committee on Taxation for hearings before the House Committee on Ways and Means, February 22 and March 9, 1990, pp. 24–25.

25. San Antonio hearings, p. 172.

26. Stuart D. Root, prepared testimony, San Antonio hearings March 11, 1989, pp. 775–76.

27. Constitution of the United States, Article I, Section 9.

28. Letter to Toby Roth, October 11, 1988, GAO document B-233063, p. 5.

29. Senate Banking Committee hearings, August 8, 1988, p. 16.

30. Robert E. Taylor and Michael Totty, "Thrift Rescues So Far Cost U.S. Over $20 Billion," *Wall Street Journal,* October 3, 1988, p. A11.

31. Steve Klinkerman, "Texas S&L Needs Another Rescue 10 Months Later," *American Banker,* March 15, 1989, p. 1.

32. *Failed Thrifts: Bank Board's 1988 Texas Resolutions,* Report to the Chairman, House Banking Committee, March 1989, General Accounting Office, p. 4.

33. Robert F. Adelizzi, *Deregulation, the S&L Crisis and S&L Reform* (San Diego: Home Fed Corp., November 1989), p. 11.

34. Genie D. Short and Jeffrey W. Gunther, *The Texas Thrift Situation: Implications for the Texas Financial Industry* (Dallas: Federal Reserve Bank of Dallas, September 1988), p. 8.

35. Jeff Gerth, "Misuse of Savings Bailout Reported in Texas Purchase," *New York Times,* July 8, 1990, p. 1.

CHAPTER 10   Can This Industry Be Salvaged?

1. *Deposit Insurance for the Nineties: Meeting the Challenge,* A Staff Study for FDIC; Draft Edition (Washington, D.C.: FDIC, 1989), January 4, 1989, p. 264.

2. Ibid., p. 277. One should note that no suggestion is offered as to what the "specified limits" should be.

3. House Banking Committee hearings, August 3, 1988, transcript, HBA 216000, p. 65.

4. *Who's Who in America,* 43d ed. (Chicago: Marquis Who's Who, Inc., 1984), p. 2945.

5. Maggie Mahar, "The $100 Billion Fiasco," *Barron's,* September 11, 1989, p. 8.

6. *Failed Banks: FDIC's Asset Liquidation Operations* (Washington, D.C.: General Accounting Office, 1988), pp. 60–61.

7. *Combating Fraud, Abuse and Misconduct,* House Committee on Government Operations, October 13, 1988 (Washington, D.C.: U.S. Government Printing Office, 1988), p. 14.

8. Philip Zweig, *Belly Up* (New York: Crown Publishers, 1985), p. 395.

9. Adelizzi, pp. 9, 18.

10. Robert Trigaux, "Seidman's Rx for RTC Strikes Familiar Chord," *American Banker*, February 7, 1990, p. 1.

11. Gray, p. 52.

CHAPTER 11   Can This Country Be Saved?

1. Federal Home Loan Bank Board No. 88-1491, Power of Receiver and Conduct of Receiverships; Repurchase Agreements. *Federal Register*, vol. 53, no. 47, p. 7800 @ p. 7801.

2. "FRNs Crisis—What Crisis?" *International Financing Review*, issue 722, April 22, 1989.

3. Lincoln Offering circular.

4. Housing Commission report, p. 147.

5. Jeff Gerth, "Some Lincoln Investors Escape Loss in Collapse," *New York Times*, January 1, 1990, pp. 31, 36.

6. Andrew Freeman, "S&L Dispute Casts Doubt on Investor Protection," *Financial Times*, April 26, 1990, p. 24.

7. Steve Klinkerman, "Thrift Villains: Easy to Spot, Hard to Nail," *American Banker*, January 18, 1990, p. 1 @ p. 11.

8. Jim McTague, "FSLIC Sues Kidder, California Firm Over S&L Failure," *American Banker*, May 11, 1989, p. 1.

9. "Lawyer S&L Malpractice," *ABA Journal*, November 1989, p. 24.

10. Rita Henley Jensen, "Walking a Tightrope in Lincoln Imbroglio," *National Law Journal*, January 29, 1990, p. 8.

11. Rita Henley Jensen, "Reverberations from a Failure," *National Law Journal*, November 13, 1989, p. 1.

12. Ibid.

13. Andy Hall and Jerry Kammer, "Keating Paid SEC official," *Arizona Republic*, March 27, 1990, p. 1.

14. Lee Berton, "Laventhol & Horwath, Beset by Litigation, Runs into Hard Times," *Wall Street Journal*, May 17, 1990, p. 1.

15. Emory Buckner, 21 *Bull.* 44, February 3, 1940. In Mayer, *Emory Buckner*, p. 9.

16. Martin Mayer, *The Teachers Strike* (New York: Harper & Row, 1969), p. 118.

17. Letter from Joel R. Wells to Hoyle L. Robinson of the FDIC, May 22, 1985, p. 2.

AFTERWORD   As the Toll Mounts . . .

1. David Dahl, "Lawmakers Still Pressure Bank Regulators," *St. Petersburg Times*, July 22, 1990, p. 1.

2. Lee A. Sheppard, "Bailing Out the Thrifts Through the Back Door," *Tax* Notes, April 16, 1990, p. 264 @ p. 258.

3. Statement of the Hon. Robert R. Glauber, Under Secretary of the Treasury for Finance, Before the Subcommittee on Oversight of the House Committee on Ways and Means, May 14, 1990, Treasury Department, Washington, D.C., p. 3, p. 5.

INDEX